Stopping Wars

STOPPING WARS
Defining the Obstacles to Cease-fire

James D.D. Smith

Westview Press
BOULDER • SAN FRANCISCO • OXFORD

Copyright © 1995 by Westview Press, Inc.

Published in 1995 in the United States of America by Westview Press, Inc., 5500 Central Avenue, Boulder, Colorado 80301-2877, and in the United Kingdom by Westview Press, 12 Hid's Copse Road, Cumnor Hill, Oxford OX2 9JJ

Library of Congress Cataloging-in-Publication Data
Smith, James D.D.
   Stopping wars : defining the obstacles to cease-fire / by James D.D. Smith.
      p.   cm.
   Includes bibliographical references and index.
   ISBN 0-8133-2467-X
   1. Armistices.   2. War (International law)
JX5173.S65   1995
341.6—dc20   94-47232
                                                                    CIP

Printed and bound in the United States of America

 The paper used in this publication meets the requirements of the American National Standard for Permanence of Paper for Printed Library Materials Z39.48-1984.

10   9   8   7   6   5   4   3   2   1

For my family, and for Clare

Contents

Figures

Acknowledgments

For better or worse, this book began as a PhD dissertation, and although many changes have been made to the original work, those who supported and helped me through that time deserve as much gratitude now as then. Thanks first of all go to my supervisor Efraim Karsh, whose thorough scholarship and attention to detail ensured a greater understanding of the wars I have studied than might otherwise have been possible. Though we may have differed on any number of issues, these differences only served to strengthen the work in the end. Moreover, there was never any question about his willingness to help.

Some people have read the manuscript, or parts of it, and supplied helpful criticism at a number of crucial junctures. Of these, I am most grateful to Barrie Paskins at the University of London and Trudy Govier at the University of Calgary; both found the time to read various incomplete drafts despite the imposition on their time. I have also benefitted greatly from comments and support from Hugh Miall, Andrew Acland, Adam Curle, Sydney Bailey, Greta Brooks, and Jane Saunders. Finally, a great debt is owed to James Gow for his advice on many portions of the manuscript that deal with Yugoslavia. Needless to say, what follows is my responsibility alone and should not necessarily be taken to be representative of any of their opinions.

Finally, I would like to thank the Association of Commonwealth Universities, who funded a great part of the original research, and the British Council, who judiciously administered those funds.

Some of the material in Chapter 8 appeared previously in the *Journal for Peace Research* and is reprinted here with their kind permission.

J.D.D.S.
Bradford, England

PART ONE

Introduction

1

The Long and Winding
Road to Peace

The road from war to peace is a puzzling and uncertain one. To those who fight and die on it, it is seldom clear just when the journey will end; those responsible for finding the path are rarely more perceptive. Of the few signposts that exist, perhaps the most visible is the cease-fire:[1] no war ends without one. To reach that point on the road, however, a number of obstacles must be overcome. Many of these will be conflict-specific; that is, they are more or less unique to the violent conflict in question, and are either unlikely to be encountered a second time, or are too specific to place into broad theoretical constructs. It seems likely that at least some of the difficulties encountered, however, will be common to virtually *all* cease-fire negotiations, whether between or among non-state or extra-state actors, nations and nation-states. These difficulties, strewn like rubble across the path to peace, come up time and time again, and if attempts at stopping wars are to be consistently successful, they need to be identified and addressed. This book, then, is an attempt to understand what stops wars from ending. More specifically, since there must be a cease-fire before any war can end, and since the cease-fire is the most obvious sign that the war may be ending, the book is an attempt to catalogue the most common barriers to successful cease-fires in international and civil wars.

At first glance, there is a single, uncomplicated explanation to this problem, one that many of us have been hearing all our lives. As a child, I can remember watching footage of the Second World War and other conflicts, and thinking, *"Why can't they just stop fighting?"* I could not accept the possibility that all those people really hated each other so much and that there was no more sensible way to resolve their differences. When I asked adults the answer to my question, they invariably replied, *"Because they don't want to stop."* (In academic terms, the political will was absent: the leadership, whoever they may have been, believed that more could be gained by fighting than by not fighting.) Today, the violence of the former

3

Yugoslavia, of Somalia, and of Rwanda and elswhere, leads me to ask the same question I did when I was younger, and people still give me the same reply now as they did then. One of the points of writing this book is to propose that their answer, sincere and guileless though it may be, is simply not good enough.

Admittedly, the most obvious obstacle to stopping a war is in fact a lack of political will. Unless it is present, and excepting those cases where a cease-fire is imposed, no cease-fire will occur. Yet even where there is some will to cease fire, what researchers have failed to recognize is that a number of factors sometimes affect its translation into *effective* and *sufficient* political will which actually brings the fighting to an end. This study therefore qualifies and deepens the more traditional theories of war termination which suggest that where both sides *want* an end to their war, the war *will* end.[2]

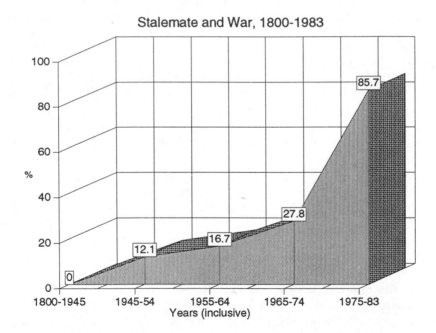

FIGURE 1.1: Stalemate and War, 1800-1983. Percentages refer to wars where military stalemate was considered to be the decisive factor in belligerents' decisions to try to end the war. Raw data can be found in Dunnigan and Martel, 1987, pp. 207-262. It is noteworthy that their own (valid) conclusion was that only 11% of wars since 1800 have ended in stalemate (p. 270).

Thus, by the end of this book it should be clear that there are identifiable obstacles to cease-fire which are common enough that they may exist in every international and civil war. As with any obstacle blocking a path, they may come in different combinations and be more or less difficult to surmount -- but they will arise. Moreover, and more worrying, these obstacles interact; the existence of one obstacle often increases the likelihood that other obstacles will arise. These latter barriers may then affect and strengthen the original one, and the cycle may continue. (See Appendix 2 for an illustration.) The existence of any obstacle decreases the likelihood of a cease-fire, and while their removal does not automatically end the fighting, it will make this more likely.

For anyone with a humanitarian interest in ending war, the importance of understanding the process of cease-fire should be obvious: if we can work out how to remove these barriers, actively encouraging possibilities for cease-fire, the chances of being able to stop the violence must increase dramatically. On the practical level, too, an understanding of the process is a sensible step. It is of course possible to argue that when there is a straightforward winner/loser relationship between belligerents[3] at war's end, making cease-fires successful is both less of a problem and less interesting; although terms for cease-fire must still be accepted, the victor can often dictate those terms with relative impunity -- *"Do what I say, or else."* However, where the "winner" is less clear, or where no winner is present -- such as in the case of a stalemated war[4] -- stopping the fighting tends to be much more laborious and intricate. The power relationship between belligerents is more equal, but the belligerents themselves may not see it that way, and may make conflicting demands justified on the basis of how much power they *think* they have. It is thus that an understanding of the process of cease-fires is important in a practical sense, for whereas wars in the past have tended to end on clear victor-vanquished terms, this appears now to be much less often the case.

In the past, many studies have looked at war statistically in order to discover trends of one sort or another.[5] Two more recent works -- Paul Pillar's *Negotiating Peace* (1983) and Dunnigan and Martel's *How to Stop a War* (1987) - indicate (inadvertently) that there is a strong trend in modern times towards war ending in something other than clear winner/loser belligerent relationships. Pillar's data, for example, tells us that most modern wars (64%) end either through negotiation, or with the withdrawal of all parties to the conflict.[6] Dunnigan and Martel's data included 389 wars of varying types from 1800 to 1987.[7] Assuming the data is reliable, and specifically from the point of view of the relevance of stalemate, the picture is even more remarkable. Figure 1.1, compiled here and based on their raw data, provides a dramatic visual illustration of the growing importance of stalemate as a factor in ending war.

"Victory," then, is becoming increasingly elusive in modern warfare. The quick and decisive victories of both the Falklands War and the Gulf War of 1991 are exceptions to a rule -- the numbing stalemate of the Iran-Iraq war is more representative. It is precisely because a negotiated settlement on relatively equal terms will be the eventual result in most cases that it may be no more than an act of *pragmatism* to understand the best way of initiating the move toward settlement. In other words, because it will make sense to seek (as a minimum) a cease-fire at some point, it makes all that much more sense to understand from the start exactly what may act as a barrier to that objective.

The realization that all wars must end at some point, that a cease-fire is a necessary part of that process, and that it might be a good idea to understand as much about that process as possible, seems to be lost on political leaders generally and on war theorists in particular. In 1970, William T.R. Fox noted that "[w]hat makes wars end ... and what keeps wars from ending, has been much less studied than what makes wars start ... or what keeps them from starting."[8] One explanation for this, of course, is that if war can be prevented, there is no need to study how to stop it[9] (thus the concentration on the causes and prevention of war[10]). It may also be felt that to study how a war ends may be tantamount to conceding that it *cannot* be prevented -- something many (this author among them) would be loath to admit.

Whatever the explanation, Fox's observation still holds true. Even today, there are still very few major works on war termination.[11] As for cease-fires, they seem to be of even less concern. Where it is mentioned at all, the cease-fire is considered only as a mere stage in the larger process of war termination -- and not necessarily its most integral stage.[12] The obvious value of what does exist is granted, but even the most recent works did not have the opportunity to consider some of the more interesting conflicts from the point of view of war termination and cease-fires: the Iran-Iraq war (one of the most devastating conflicts of the twentieth century), the Gulf War (a war conducted in the "new" international environment), and the Yugoslav conflict (a failed attempt at an imposed cease-fire), to name just three.

The point, in the end, is this: while research into war termination and cease-fires may be on the rise, and while that research may be relevant, as far as cease-fires go, a great many questions have to this point been left unanswered or inadequately answered. What exactly is a cease-fire, and how does it differ from related terms such as truce or armistice? What obstacles exist in trying to effect a cease-fire (humanitarian or otherwise)? What problems exist in negotiating a cease-fire agreement? What problems exist in actually implementing agreements once they have been negotiated? Are there common obstacles and problems? Are there common solutions?

This book is by no means an attempt to answer all of these questions, but it will attempt to answer at least some of them.

This does not mean that specific solutions will be provided to *all* the problems raised. Solutions are of obvious importance, but no solution will be forthcoming before a complete understanding of the problem; this book is about understanding the problems. Having said that, by the end of the book some general ideas about dealing with these difficulties will become clear, and some ideas will be put forward as the problems are discussed. The book closes with some recommendations, but these are certainly not intended to be the final answers. They are merely to be used as points of discussion, or as jumping off points to find the best answers. So, in sum, this is not a "how-to" book on stopping wars; it asks a different question: "What makes stopping wars so hard?"

In order to answer that question, we will look at relevant war termination literature, as well go through a number of case studies. The latter consisted of selected international and intrastate wars[13] which have occurred since 1945,[14] the year when, with the end of the Second World War and the creation of the United Nations, the modern international environment came into being. Wars chosen for analysis within that period were selected for a variety of reasons. Some were chosen for the reason that the war was perceived by belligerents as being a "fight to the death"; the Algerian War of Independence is a good example. Others were chosen primarily because of the significant number of casualties which resulted, such as the Nigerian Civil War (over 2 million dead). Finally, the war may have been a primarily stalemated war, or had an international component which highlighted the degree to which the global community held it to be important (the Iran-Iraq war, for example).[15]

Some of the criteria may seem callous, but the intention was to take those cases where it was assumed that the obstacles to cease-fire would be strongest, where both sides would be the most committed, and where the efforts of third parties to end the conflict would be at their most intense (yet generally ineffective). They are in that sense "worst-case" studies, and were chosen on that basis. If the obstacles to cease-fire can be understood in these cases, it may be easier to understand what it takes to surmount such obstacles in future, less "serious" cases (or to understand that they cannot be surmounted).

It is important to understand that this book does *not* assume cease-fires are always a good idea. It is readily admitted that cease-fires do not automatically resolve any of the underlying political issues in any given conflict. Furthermore, cease-fires "may simply fix the conditions under which the fighting will be resumed, at a later date, and with a new intensity,"[16] an assertion which highlights the importance of resolving the underlying conflicts. Sydney Bailey has pointed out that if "one party is more responsible than the other for the outbreak of hostilities, an immediate cease-fire may place it in an unduly advantageous position."[17] Pillar has argued that peace negotiations in general can be used "an extension of combat, a nonviolent way of bringing about some of the results of combat."[18] In all these cases, the humanitarian intentions often implicit in cease-fire effectuation would appear to be inadequately served, and all these difficulties need to be addressed.[19]

The cease-fire is, however, a means to an end: whether or not it was the original intention of the belligerents or concerned third parties, the cease-fire will (by definition) create an atmosphere relatively -- if not completely -- free of violence, an atmosphere in which, given time, a more permanent peace can be concluded. As one cease-fire mediator has put it, "if people stop shooting at each other for one day, they have broken the habit. Perhaps they might find that it feels pretty good."[20] Moreover, it should be obvious that a cease-fire is a necessary condition of both ending the war, and of resolving the conflict. Finally, a successful cease-fire always has a humanitarian component; the saving of lives is an inevitable and undeniable advantage to any cease-fire. The crucial point, however, is this: while a cease-fire may be impractical or undesirable at certain points within the time span of a given conflict, it is always desirable *at some point* in the conflict, and we therefore need to understand what may stand in its way.

Given all of this, it remains only to briefly outline the contents of the chapters to follow, if for no other reason than to impart a sense of the direction of the study. Here, at least, we can provide a relatively clear path.

The journey begins with an examination of the most obvious necessary condition for cease-fire: a willingness to consider cease-fire in the first place. It will become clear that in most cases, the major factor inhibiting the evolution of sufficient political will to cease fire is a disagreement between belligerents over their relative bargaining power (the ability to achieve their objectives) and the likelihood of that bargaining power growing or diminishing with the passage of time. That is, and at a minimum, political will to cease fire requires both belligerents to perceive either that the war is stalemated and likely to remain so, or that one has decisively more power than the other. Having perceived this, belligerents must both believe that this power balance is unlikely to shift either in their favour through military action or against them under a cease-fire.

Each successive chapter then details one general obstacle to cease-fire, most of which can exert additional influences, both positive and negative, on the strength of political will. The third chapter, for example, deals with belligerent concerns about avoiding the appearance of weakness, and seeking the appearance of strength. The behaviour has both psychological and practical origins, and while not necessarily a problem in itself, can nevertheless prevent a cease-fire, as the desire to avoid looking weak may inhibit sufficient political will to cease fire. The obstacle is especially difficult to overcome, as strategies chosen by belligerents to avoid appearing weak -- or which make them appear strong -- are often strategies which run directly counter to those needed to achieve a cease-fire.

The fourth chapter concerns the tendency of belligerent leaders in wartime to make strong, uncompromising, and aggressive public statements. They do so for a number of reasons, but being public statements, they also have multiple audiences, and the statements convey different messages to each of those audiences. Like the avoidance of appearing weak, the making of strong public statements is explicable, and is not necessarily a problem in itself. Where this becomes a problem is when initial aims change or the war begins to go badly, and the belligerent leadership needs to back away from the stated opening position. Retreating from an initially stated position (and certainly reversing it) will often be precluded even where the military situation makes this the rational course. The making of strong and aggressive public statements, for whatever reason, leads directly to psychological and political entrapment with few means of escape.

Chapter 5 assumes the case where a belligerent leader is unwilling to cease fire, but at least some of his immediate underlings recognize the necessity to halt the fighting. In such cases, the structure of the belligerent's "inner circle" has a strong relationship to the possibilities for cease-fire. Three basic belligerent inner circle structures will be identified and discussed, each structure based on two variables: the inner circle's willingness to criticize, and the amount of power they wield. The probability of cease-fire rises most dramatically in those cases where the critical inner circle is both willing to vocalize its criticism, and has a strong power base.

The sixth chapter examines those cases where belligerents see themselves as unable to cease fire even though they may want to. There may be unbridgeable gaps between what one side may want and what the other side feels it can give, and the result may be that there appears to be no option but to continue to fight. Alternatively, a belligerent may lack effective control over its military forces, and despite some will to cease fire may be unable to exercise the authority necessary to bring that about.

Chapter 7 assumes the case where the decision to seek a cease-fire has been made, but the belligerent proposing cease-fire (by means of an offer or a demand) is unable to come up with a proposal that the other belligerent will accept. There may be a lack of communication, an unwillingness to accept the political legitimacy of the opponent, or a concentration on one's own interests. The end result is the same: belligerents fail to realize that it is their enemy who will eventually decide on whether or not there will be a cease-fire -- often even in the case where that enemy has been decisively defeated. The failure to come up with an acceptable cease-fire proposal will tend to preclude a cease-fire in all but the most one-sided conflicts.

Finally, and even where proposals are accepted and agreements made, their success or failure -- even given the best of intentions -- may hinge upon whether the agreement is specific enough.

The final two chapters move the focus away from the belligerents and on to third parties, and the obstacles that third parties may face in attempting to effect a cease-fire. Chapter 8 deals with the importance of the objectivity of the proposed mediator. While this chapter may appear to go against many mediation theorists who contend that mediator impartiality is *not* a requirement for successful mediation, this is not at all the case. It will become clear that there is more than one style of mediation. Mediator impartiality may indeed be unimportant to powered, coercive mediation (the type of mediation conceived by those who argue against impartiality), but in a non-coercive, private, and voluntary mediation, impartiality is crucial. In any case where mediators either fail to act impartially, or are perceived to be acting partially, they will generally be rejected by at least one of the belligerents. The most common reason that mediators fail to be seen as impartial has to do with the fact that the proposed mediators generally play more than one role in the conflict. Any individual or organisation involved in mediation efforts must therefore avoid this "two-hat" dilemma as far as possible.

The ninth and final substantive chapter deals with the option of the "forced" cease-fire. In the absence of political will, or the presence of seemingly insurmountable obstacles, third parties may attempt to impose a cease-fire. The chapter makes it clear that although this is possible, any attempt to force belligerents to agree to cease fire must be accompanied by third party guarantees to ensure implementation. Any third party undertaking the task of imposing a cease-fire must be willing to guarantee that cease-fire. The failure to do so will, if the cease-fire breaks down, usually result in general increase in distrust and any later cease-fire attempts will be less likely to succeed.

The road from war to peace is, indeed, a long one.

Notes

1. See Appendix 1 for a full discussion of the definition of "cease-fire."
2. Geoffrey Blainey, for example, concludes his study of the causes of war by asserting that "wars usually cease when the fighting nations agree on their relative strength" and that when expectations concerning the duration and outcome of the war cease to be contradictory, "war is almost certain to end" (Geoffrey Blainey, *The Causes of War* [New York: Free Press, 1973], pp. 246-47). See also Clark Claus Abt, "The Termination of General War" (MIT Ph.D. thesis, 1965; William Kaufmann, supervisor). Abt outlines four stages of war termination (p. 234), which assume that once the military, internal political and internal domestic conflicts are resolved,

termination follows on virtually automatically. See Janice Stein, "War Termination and Conflict Reduction or, How Wars Should End," *Jerusalem Journal of International Relations* 1(1) (1975), pp. 1-27, and Michael Handel, "The Study of War Termination," *Journal of Strategic Studies* (May 1978), pp. 51-75, for more on this point.

3. For the purposes of this book, "belligerent" essentially refers to either to "a party at war," or to "those persons in charge of making decisions for the party at war."

4. For a definition, see Robert F. Randle, *The Origins of Peace: A Study of Peacemaking and the Structure of Peace Settlements* (New York: Free Press, 1973), p. 7.

5. See, for example, J. David Singer and Melvin Small, *The Wages of War, 1816-1965* (New York: John Wiley and Sons, 1972), and Lewis F. Richardson, *Statistics of Deadly Quarrels* (Pittsburgh: Boxwood Press, 1960).

6. The figure was 54% for all wars between 1800 and 1980. See Paul R. Pillar, *Negotiating Peace: War Termination as a Bargaining Process* (New Jersey: Princeton University Press, 1983), pp. 16-17.

7. James F. Dunnigan and William Martel, *How to Stop a War: The Lessons of Two Hundred Years of War and Peace* (London: Doubleday, 1987), p. 12.

8. William T. R. Fox, "The Causes of Peace and Conditions of War," in William T.R. Fox (ed.), *How Wars End -- Annals of the American Academy of Political and Social Science*, Vol. 392 (Philadelphia: Academy of Political and Social Science, 1970), p. 1.

9. Stuart Albert and Edward C. Luck (eds.), *On the Endings of Wars* (London: Kennikat Press, 1980), p. 3.

10. See, for example, Michael Howard, *The Causes of Wars* (London: Temple Smith, 1983), Robert I. Rotberg and T.K. Rabb (eds.), *The Origin and Prevention of Major Wars* (Cambridge: Cambridge University Press, 1983), Harry B. Hollins, Averill L. Powers, and Mark Sommer, *The Conquest of War* (Boulder: Westview Press, 1989), and Blainey, *The Causes of War*.

11. Five notable exceptions include Sydney D. Bailey, *How Wars End: The United Nations and the Termination of Armed Conflict, 1946-1964* (2 vols.) (Oxford: Clarendon Press, 1982); Fred Charles Iklé, *Every War Must End* (London: Columbia University Press, 1971); R.F. Randle, *The Origins of Peace: A Study of Peacemaking and the Structure of Peace Settlements* (New York: Free Press, 1973); Paul L. Pillar, *Negotiating Peace: War Termination as a Bargaining Process* (New Jersey: Princeton University Press, 1983); and Nissan Oren (ed.), *Termination of Wars* (Jerusalem: Magnes Press, 1982).

12. Only one major work on cease-fires currently exists -- Bertrand de Montluc's unpublished thesis, "Le Cessez-le-feu" (1971). The study is primarily useful in terms of looking at the cease-fire from a legalistic point of view (see Bertrand de Montluc, "Le Cessez-le-feu," doctoral thesis, Université de Droit et d'Economie et de Sciences Sociales de Paris (president of thesis examining committee Madame Paul Bastid [see *q.v.*, note 3 in Appendix 1]), 1971 (photocopy available from British Library Lending Service, Ref. No. fF6 8526). One other work of note is by Robin Hay at the Canadian Institute for International Peace and Security. Hay puts forward humanitarian cease-fires as a tactic which can be undertaken by third parties to help end a given war (see Robin Hay, "Humanitarian Cease-fires: an Examination

of Their Potential Contribution to the Resolution of Conflict" [Ottawa: Canadian Institute for International Peace and Security, 1990]).

13. Singer and Small's definitions of war will be used, *viz.* interstate war -- 1,000 or more battle deaths with one member of the state system on each side; extrasystemic (or what is generally here called intrastate or civil) war -- 1,000 or more battle deaths, with only one member of the interstate system involved (see Singer and Small, pp. 381-82). Readers should also note that we generally assume a basic two-party war.

14. The single exception to this rule will be the mention of relevant examples taken from Leon V. Sigal's study of war termination processes at the end of the second World War. Sigal's study (*Fighting to a Finish: The Politics of War Termination in the United States and Japan, 1945* [London: Cornell University Press, 1988]) is a recent and well-researched work which illustrates many of the problems which occurred in conflicts subsequent to the Second World War; it was decided that such a detailed study of war termination could not go unrecognized.

15. Readers may note that the case studies have been confined to international and civil wars, and the conclusions of this work must therefore be similarly limited. No assumptions should be necessarily made that the obstacles to international and civil wars will be the same for low-intensity intrastate and/or guerrilla conflicts, or in other types of violent conflicts. Reference made to smaller scale violent conflicts, such as that in Northern Ireland, may be of use as illustrations, but it will not be assumed that they automatically validate findings arising out of the examination of international and civil wars.

16. Michael Walzer, in Sydney D. Bailey, *How Wars End*, Vol. I, p. 3.

17. Bailey, *How Wars End*, Vol. I, p. 352.

18. Pillar, *Negotiating Peace*, p. 52.

19. See Bailey, *How Wars End*, Vol. I, pp. 2,3,342 for comment on this.

20. Richard Reid, in Hay, "Humanitarian Cease-fires", p. 29.

PART TWO

Belligerents During War

2

Power and the Willingness to Settle: *"Why stop now?"*

If there is one requisite condition for stopping a war, it is that the people in charge must have some willingness to try and end it. Unless someone can force the warring parties to stop -- a difficult task, rarely attempted -- there will be no cease-fire until the belligerents themselves see it as a viable option. This is an obvious point. What is less obvious is what factors prevent consideration of the alternative in the first place. What this chapter intends to show is that in most cases, the major factor inhibiting a willingness to cease fire is a disagreement between belligerents over their relative bargaining power -- their ability to achieve their objectives -- and the likelihood of that bargaining power growing or diminishing with the passage of time. As we shall see, there are a number of things which reflect this tendency: belligerent concerns with the gains the enemy might make under a cease-fire, actual or expected victory, and actual or expected intervention, can all decrease interest in a cease-fire. In the final analysis, a willingness to cease fire requires both belligerents to agree on their respective bargaining positions, and those positions must be either very different (there is a clear winner) or relatively equal (there is a stalemate). Further to this, each belligerent must perceive that although its opponent *might* gain something by continuing the fight, its own power will not be increased, and that goals can now be achieved without violence. Finally, there must be a perception that the cease-fire will not decrease their own power in any major way. Provided that belligerents are not under pressures which lead them to believe that they either must or can not cease-fire, it is only under these conditions that belligerents will even consider ending the fighting.

Gaining the Upper Hand

War is a situation in which the resort to violence has been taken on the expectation that it will result in fresh bargaining power deemed necessary to achieve an objective. Generally, both sides expect their powers to be increased through force, and they will in all cases attempt to maximize their bargaining power in the course of the war. The problem is that events tend to be valued differently by belligerents, and until a power balance has been established, agreed, and until it is seen as unlikely to change, a cease-fire is unlikely to be seen as a useful option.

That belligerents consciously consider their bargaining positions is reflected most obviously in their concern with the gains that their enemies might make under any proposed cease-fire.[1] Difficulties in effecting cease-fires frequently arise in cases where belligerents believe that if there were to be a cease-fire, their enemies would gain something they do not want them to gain. They may also believe that they will be denied something under a cease-fire, or that they would get less than their opponent would. After having talks with both the Arab League and David Ben-Gurion in the Palestine conflict of 1948, the UN mediator, Count Folke Bernadotte, could not help but note "how eager they both were to point out that a truce would be of advantage simply and solely to their opponents." Later in that same conflict, Azzam Pasha, Secretary of the Arab League, wanted to know if Bernadotte could guarantee that the Arabs "in the event that they accepted a truce, would not find themselves in a worse military position after the expiry of the truce than they were at present."[2] At a closed Security Council meeting during the Gulf War (1991) the UK representative, Sir David Hannay, castigated Iraq for spurning a number of peace initiatives and for its verbal attacks on the Secretary-General, and concluded that

> [i]n these circumstances, the idea of an unconditional pause of any kind makes no sense at all. It would only give Iraq time to regroup its forces and to repair the damage to its military installations, thus ensuring that any renewed hostilities were larger and more costly in human lives that [sic] would otherwise be the case.[3]

During the Bosnian phase of the conflict in the former Yugoslavia, a UN plan for cease-fire was rejected when all sides felt that their opponents would gain something under the plan. Muslims and Croats (now allies) believed that a four month "truce" was too long, as it would allow Serbs to consolidate their gains. Serbs, on the other hand, wanted a long cease-fire on the basis that a shorter truce would allow Muslims and Croats to regroup their forces and attack.[4]

The concern, then, is that belligerents will either be unable to achieve their objectives under a cease-fire (they can still be better achieved through war), or their opponents will achieve more objectives than they will, or if the fighting resumes the cease-fire will have put them in a worse position than they had been before the cease-fire.

The concerns are valid. Belligerents do take whatever advantage they can under a cease-fire, a problem evident, for example, in all of Bailey's case studies,[5] and other examples exist. In Algeria, when French leader General Charles de Gaulle ceased fire unilaterally in the Spring of 1961, the Algerian Front de Libération Nationale (FLN) not only failed to follow suit, but used the opportunity to regroup its forces.[6] Later in the summer, a French unilateral cease-fire was "virtually ended" partly because, according to a military spokesman in Algiers, FLN activities had almost doubled since its declaration.[7] Adam Curle, a Quaker mediator in the Nigerian Civil War (among others), has published transcripts of his attempts to mediate between various wartime leaders.[8] One of those conversations dealt specifically with the question of the activity allowed under a cease-fire. The leader in this case had initially suggested to Curle that the enemy should cease fire first, and that they would follow suit. Curle pointed out that such a proposal "would be as unacceptable to them as it would be to you," primarily for the reason that there would be a fear that the enemy would make gains while the other side had ceased fire. The belligerent leader admitted that this was indeed the case, but even the idea of a simultaneous cease-fire had no appeal. When asked for his reasons, the leader simply asked, "How would I know that they would not use the opportunity to consolidate their positions and bring forward more troops and supplies?"[9]

In international relations generally, and more specifically in international law, there are two schools of thought on this matter. The first of these contends that belligerents may do *anything* not expressly prohibited by the agreement -- what is not forbidden is allowed. Oppenheim, an authority on international law, has insisted that

> [e]verybody agrees that belligerents during an armistice may, *outside the line where the forces face each other*, do everything and anything they like regarding defence and preparation of offence; for instance, they may manufacture and import munitions and guns, drill recruits, build fortresses, concentrate or withdraw troops.[10]

The argument is that belligerents are entitled to continue the war on other than strictly military fronts -- even under a cease-fire -- and it probably arises out of the fact that wars are *legally* ended only by formal peace treaties.[11] Thus, because they are still in a legal state of war, two or more nations under a cease-fire, presumably with the intention of arranging more favorable or permanent political solutions, are not prevented from engaging in what could be called "non-violent acts of hostility" (economic "warfare," for example). It is "a continuation of war by other means"[12] which could easily prevent the implementation of a cease-fire, or could lead to its break-down where such implementation is successful.

Conversely, a second (probably larger) school of thought argues that belligerents are allowed to take only those actions which they could have taken absent the cease-fire, *i.e.* they are not allowed to take advantage of the cease-fire to gain militarily or politically. To be more precise about this, the argument is that so far as it is possible, belligerents' bargaining powers should be affected neither positively nor negatively by the cease-fire or by its violation. (The evacuation of wounded, for example, would generally not count as increasing anybody's bargaining position.) Some authorities insist that that it is this second position which has the weight of authority behind it,[13] and practice seems to lend further weight to the argument. In its resolution of 19 August 1948 (during the Palestine conflict), the United Nations Security Council specifically ordered that "no party is entitled to gain military or political advantage through violation of the truce," and Ralph Bunche, the UN mediator (after Bernadotte's assassination), later called this "the *fundamental principle* under which the truce [had] been applied" (emphasis added), and this despite the fact that several other provisions had been included in the resolution.[14] Earlier, it was made explicit to Bernadotte that the intent of the UN Resolution of 29 May 1948 was "that no military advantage shall accrue to either side as a result of the application of the truce."[15] Parenthetically, while there is technically a difference between "gaining advantage under a cease-fire" and "gaining advantage through violation of the cease-fire," it can be argued that the two positions are not dissimilar. In either case, the idea is to prevent any increase in the power of the belligerents. Increases in power are to be avoided both *under* the cease-fire, and also to be avoided should the cease-fire be *violated*.

As a final example, one of the reasons the armistice negotiations took so long in Korea was the United Nations concern for ensuring the maintenance of the *status quo* under the cease-fire. US Vice-Admiral C. Turner Joy, the first chief UN negotiator, noted the concern in his diary:

> (21 Aug. 1951) Stated necessity for maintaining present even balance of military effectiveness in order to present [prevent] one side from gaining strength and other losing strength thereby encouraging violation of armistice;

> (28 Nov. 1951): [United Nations Command] again defined arm[istice] as a cessation of hostilities under mutually agreed conditions and stated that a cessation of hostilities as a prelude to a settlement of the Korean problem was possible only under an armistice which would prevent either side building up a decisive mil[itary] advantage for its duration ...[16]

The general consensus, then, would appear to be that the cease-fire, once implemented, should give neither military nor political advantage to either belligerent. Their bargaining power should remain stable as far as that is practicable.

What *should* happen, however, is very different from what *does* happen, or what is perceived to happen. In practice, not only will belligerents almost inevitably insist that the advantage during the cease-fire has been given to their enemies, but will argue that virtually any action which they themselves wish to take, apart from those directly excluded by the agreement, is permissible under the cease-fire.[17] Until consensus over what is and is not permissible under a cease-fire can be enshrined in international law, including what counts as "advantage," this will continue to be the case. It does not augur well for bringing about successful cease-fires; where any potential agreement is seen by the belligerents as decreasing their own bargaining power, or increasing that of their enemy, either under the cease-fire or through its violation, belligerents will be unlikely to agree to it, or indeed to express any desire to cease fire.

Effects of Victory

Achieving military victories is one obvious way belligerents see of enhancing their bargaining power. The assumption is that *any* battlefield victory automatically translates into bargaining power either during or after the war, and this may prevent interest in a cease-fire. The assumption is probably a valid one to make. The difficulty, however, is that there is always the question of *how much* bargaining power is gained by any particular victory or set of victories, and it is this relative assessment of power which figures so prominently in the decision to cease fire. Battlefield victories do change belligerents' demands and expectations: the winning side may decide to ask for more because it is winning, the losing side to give more because it is losing. The trouble, however, is that the extra amount the winning party demands may be more than the extra amount the losing party is willing to give.[18]

Part of the difficulty is that (primarily for maintaining an optimistic outlook and the "will to win") belligerents will weight their victories differently. Almost inevitably, a victory by either side will tend to be valued more highly by the winner than by the loser. Conversely, "failure is seldom self-evident,"[19] and the way belligerents perceive battlefield actions generally is therefore heavily weighted toward the side of victory. Both these tendencies create a trend away from stopping the war. Victories (however small), appear to be more easily perceived than defeats, and it is therefore more likely that a small victory will decrease the possibility of cease-fire than it is that a similar defeat will increase the likelihood of cease-fire. In sum, battlefield victories are weighted more heavily by the winner than by the loser, and they tend also to be noticed more than defeat; in war, change for the better tends to be noticed more than change for the worse.

If both belligerents agree that a victory which drastically changes the course of the war has been won, the chances of a cease-fire sometimes increase. This is because, and as one student of war termination has phrased it, "finite change in relative military position is an inadequate basis for war termination; battlefield results must be gross if they are to serve as a politically decisive mechanism."[20] In other words, something drastic has to happen if a war is to end. There are two things to be said about this. First, the "grossness" of battlefield results can be interpreted in more than one way. While a victory weighted equally by both sides is a "gross" result, battlefield results could be considered "gross" if it is obvious to both belligerents that *no* drastic battlefield victories have been won, and that none are likely to come for a long time. That is, *no* change is as important a battlefield result as change. If, for example, "finite change in relative military position" is all that occurs in a war, and it is all that occurs for long enough, belligerents will perceive the stalemate and attempt to end the war by other means.

Second, and more importantly, there is the difficulty that change (like change for the better) is always more noticeable than lack of change, and belligerents appear to concentrate more on victories than on a lack of movement in the war, and when they do, this has a profound effect on their estimation of their ability to win overall. This was the case, for example, in both the Vietnam and Korean wars where, in Fox's words, tactical successes "snatched unlimited stalemate from the jaws of limited victory."[21] Thus, and while there have been those who have asserted that

> when the formerly excluded [*i.e.* weaker] party is able to show some increase in its power, although it may thus find to continue the struggle until the tables are completely turned, it is more likely to be satisfied by the recognition of its improved position signalled by the other party's agreement to begin negotiations[22]

this latter situation would appear *not* to be more likely. In fact, belligerent thinking runs entirely counter to this, generally being: "If one victory yields X amount of bargaining power, then several victories will yield even more, and if one can be achieved, so can others, so there is no point in ceasing fire until we have maximized our power through military force." Expected victory simply inhibits a belligerent's desire for a cease-fire; anticipated military gains tend to outweigh all other considerations.[23] Expected or actual battlefield victories preclude a cease-fire because belligerents gain an "appetite" for victory *i.e.* "peace, yes, but not just yet."[24]

The Nigerian Civil War can provide a brief illustration. By the end of the summer of 1968, the war had been raging for just over a year. On 3 August, major peace talks had been convened in Addis Ababa under the auspices of Ethiopian leader Haile Selassie. The talks were failing miserably,[25] but despite this, by 14 August Adam Curle was in possession of a new Biafran[26] proposal which had been put to him privately by the chief Biafran negotiator (Eni Njoku). The proposal appeared to be highly promising, and Curle quickly relayed its contents to Yakubu Gowon, the federal Nigerian leader. Gowon said he would consider the proposals, but by this point it appeared that he had simply lost interest in a cease-fire. Gowon was quite convinced that the federal forces were winning in any case, and that even guerrilla activity which might take place after the main battle had been won could not last long. The proposals did cause fierce discussion in Lagos (the federal capital), but in the end the hawks prevailed. It seemed likely, in fact, that the decision to continue the war in any case had already been made even before the Addis Ababa conference.[27] Senior federal field commanders had been making victory noises since July ("as far as I'm concerned, the war is over"; "in fifteen days time there will be no more Biafra"),[28] and John Volkmar, another Quaker mediator, was informed personally by federal authorities on 16 August that the war would be pursued. Finally, on 24 August, Gowon publicly announced the "final push" -- he expected the war to end within four weeks.[29] The timing of Njoku's proposals in this case was unfortunate. They had come too late; Gowon had decided on a military solution. Despite the presence of a proposal to end the fighting, it was eclipsed by anticipated military gains.

The Iran-Iraq war, too, provides a clear example. After four unsuccessful efforts to end the war, Olaf Palme, the UN Secretary-General's personal representative during the conflict, concluded on 2 March 1982 that "there is no way to get any further as long as the political will to make peace is missing."[30] Palme had come to the conclusion that there was no political will to reach a settlement, and he was probably right, but that did not deter others from continuing to try and bring peace to Iran and Iraq. A new initiative was announced by the Islamic Conference Organisation on 8 March 1982,[31] but a number of statements by Iranian officials in the week following the announcement made it clear that the initiative would be unlikely to succeed. "I believe that we can achieve our rights through strength" stated the President of the Iranian Parliament, Ali Akbar Hashemi Rafsanjani; "our fighting forces on the fronts should compel Saddam Hussein through their victories to submit to truth." The Iranian spiritual leader, Ayatollah Ruhollah Khomeini put it this way: "Making peace with a criminal and reaching a compromise with him is like committing a crime against faithful people, and it is a crime against Islam."[32] The Iranian foreign minister, Ali Akbar Velayati commented on 8 April 1982 that Iran had "come to the conclusion that the Iraqis only understand the language of force."[33]

Recalling the argument concerning the effect of expected victory on cease-fire offers, it is particularly striking that Iran's insistence on its ability to settle the matter by force came at a time when it had been conducting a successful counteroffensive, having gained over 2000 km^2 of territory which Iraq had held since the war's beginning.[34] That counteroffensive (begun 21 March) had another effect, however: Iraq's conditions for peace suddenly became much less harsh. On 14 April 1982, Saddam Hussein offered a full withdrawal and a committee to establish war guilt if guarantees to end the war were available, and if Iran agreed that the war had ended.[35] There had been a "gross" battlefield result which led directly to an Iraqi attempt to end the war.

Even more interesting, this suddenly conciliatory tone was more pronounced by the summer. On 10 June, Iraq was ready to observe a cease-fire and accept arbitration,[36] and on 20 June 1982, Saddam Hussein announced that his troops were "withdrawing" from Iran. It is worth noting the reaction of Tehran to Saddam Hussein's announcement:

> [f]lushed with its newly-won successes, the revolutionary regime dismissed the Iraqi initiative as "too late" and escalated its war aims to include not only the overthrow of Saddam Hussein ... but also $US 150 bn in reparations and the repatriation of some 100,000 Shi'ites expelled from Iraq before the outbreak of war.[37]

In a final effort to halt Iranian advances, on 2 July Iraq called for a neutral peacekeeping force to patrol the border to monitor a cease-fire and a withdrawal, adding that the latter was really a moot point as its forces had already pulled back to international boundaries.[38] (Whether they pulled back or were pushed there is open to interpretation, of course.) Hussein also reiterated the fact that Iraq was still ready to accept a fact-finding committee to determine who started the war.[39] There was no response from Iran. Iranian battlefield success resulted in a continued adherence to stated conditions which would be seen as unreasonable by Iraq. Although Iraq offered more, Iran wanted still more -- and it could make its demands based on its battlefield success.

Battlefield victories, then, tend to be overvalued both in their own context, and in the overall context of the war; belligerents' ability to rationally assess their overall bargaining power is significantly diminished by small perceived increases in that power. Part of the reason this creates an overall trend away from the presence of political will to cease fire is because the focus is always on what can be achieved *next* as opposed to what has been achieved *to this point*. That is, instead of *current* relative bargaining positions being assessed, it is *future* relative bargaining positions which are assessed, and assessed (usually) incorrectly.[40] Belligerents in the course of war who believe that they are winning have little reason to seek a cease-fire: "*Why stop now?*" Thus, even where a drastic battlefield victory has been won, and the loser sues for peace, cease-fire is not guaranteed -- the winner may believe that better terms can be achieved by continuing to fight. On this last point, one need only examine some little known events of the Gulf War of 1991 to find a clear illustration.

The Gulf War of 1991

When allied forces attacked the military machine of Saddam Hussein in the winter of 1991, their main demand was that Iraq withdraw from Kuwait (or at least announce its intention to withdraw) before a cease-fire could be contemplated. True, UN Resolutions demanded much more than this, but the allies were fairly consistent in stating that the announcement of an Iraqi withdrawal, or an actual withdrawal, would result in a cease-fire.[41] The evidence indicates that withdrawal was actually begun on 25 February. The allied ground offensive (launched on 24 February) nevertheless continued for three more days. While many, if not all, other allied aims -- including the implementation of the remaining Security Council Resolutions -- could have been achieved by other means after the withdrawal had begun, the use of force appeared to provide the quickest and most visible means of securing those objectives. They therefore refused to cease fire until all their demands had been met, an event which did not occur until 28 February.

On 19 February 1991, just over a month after the allied air offensive against Iraqi forces had begun, Mikhail Gorbachov announced a last ditch Soviet effort designed to give Iraq a "dignified" future as soon as it withdrew from Kuwait. The plan was said to include a cease-fire which would follow Iraq's agreement to unconditional withdrawal. Iraq's borders were to be guaranteed, talks were to be held between Iraq and Kuwait, foreign forces would leave, a new security arrangement would be put into place, and an international conference would be held on the Palestinian issue.[42] Whatever its content, and despite Soviet protestations that it was in keeping with UN Resolution 660 (which called for negotiations between Iraq and Kuwait and demanded an Iraqi withdrawal), it was going nowhere. As far as George Bush was concerned, "The goals have been set. I'm not going to give."[43] If coalition positions had been hardened before, now they were adamantine. The Kuwaiti foreign minister even went so far as to state that his country "would not hold talks or negotiations after withdrawal, neither with the present nor with a new Iraqi leadership."[44]

It was important, of course, for the allies to maintain the illusion of an interest in peace. On 19 February, the allies announced that any Iraqi withdrawal, once begun, had to be completed within 14 days. Defence sources in London noted that a withdrawal could take up to twice that -- unless Iraqi forces left a great deal of their equipment behind.[45] The demand resulted in perhaps the only major public disagreement between Britain and the United States over strategy, Britain taking the view that demanding that Iraqis "walk home" stretched the UN resolutions.[46] It was entirely clear that the Americans were confident of a complete victory, and prepared to make demands on that basis.

On 22 February, the day before the Security Council was to continue deliberations in closed session, Saddam Hussein accepted an amended Soviet peace proposal.[47] It was hardly a surprising development. The American position had hardened, and Hussein now saw no point in dealing with them or the Security Council directly; to do so would have been to admit weakness (a point to which we will return in the next chapter). At the same time, however, he was subject to incredible military pressures. Karsh and Rautsi give a vivid account of the situation:

> allied aircraft rained devastation on Iraq, proceeding methodically from North to South, from Iraq to Kuwait. The feather in Saddam's cap, the cherished nuclear program, had been essentially reversed as the allies wiped out Iraq's four primary nuclear research reactors. His chemical and biological weapons factories had been badly damaged as well. The economic and strategic infrastructure of Iraq was being systematically destroyed: roads, bridges, power stations and oil installations. His armed forces were subjected to heavy bombardment, with them command and control systems and logistics lines severely disrupted. The Iraqi air force was virtually paralysed ... [48]

For Saddam, then, the situation was entirely out of control, and had he not been so concerned about appearing weak and unwilling to give in to threats, it seems likely that he would have withdrawn at that point. The Soviet proposal did not contain everything he wanted, but that was no longer the issue. His own survival (not to mention the survival of the remainder of his armed forces) now depended on getting out of Kuwait quickly, and as it was now, the best he could do was to accept the Soviet proposal and make in appear as a magnanimous gesture of peace, not as a scream for help: "Iraq wants peace and has seriously worked to support the Soviet initiative and facilitate its success, not out of fear of Bush's threats, or out of respect for him."[49]

The Security Council resumed its closed session on 23 February at 1030 am New York time. The Soviet representative immediately made it clear that Iraq was ready to withdraw unconditionally from Kuwait. The rest of the Soviet proposal was then outlined. It included: withdrawal to begin one day after cease-fire, completed within 21 days, completion of withdrawal from Kuwait city in four days, the abolition (after withdrawal) of other Security Council resolutions pertaining to the situation, the return of POWs 3 days after cease-fire, with the whole process monitored by UN peacekeeping forces.[50]

Both Britain and the United States outlined first of all why the abolition of other UN resolutions was impossible, particularly resolutions 661 (sanctions), 662 (regarding the invalidity of Iraq's annexation of Kuwait), 664 (relating to safe conduct of third party nationals) and 678 (which allowed the use of "all necessary means' to implement the Council resolutions). The arguments did make sense: there was a fundamental element of mistrust in this case, which should not be underemphasized -- even if Iraq withdrew, there could be no question of nullifying Security Council Resolutions which ensured that other means could be brought to bear in achieving secondary objectives. Apart from these specific objections, however, the Soviet proposal was still seen as unacceptable. The US representative laid down the American ultimatum, insisting on full compliance with all Security Council resolutions. A ground war would not be initiated if Iraq began withdrawal by noon on 23 February (a deadline which by this point in the debate could have been literally only minutes away). Iraq would have *one* week to withdraw (a comedown from the 14 day proposal initially discussed), and 48 hours to get out of Kuwait city and release all POWs.[51] Hussein called the ultimatum "shameful."[52] The deadline passed, and the ground war began eight hours later, at 0400 Baghdad time on 24 February.

The fifth closed session of the Security Council during the Gulf War came at 2300 hrs (New York time) on Monday, 25 February 1991. The press had little to say about it, other than that it had met, and decided that it had no useful role to play while hostilities continued.[53] The uninteresting coverage belied the drama which unfolded in Council chambers that evening, which began with an announcement by the Soviet representative. A message had been received by Gorbachov from Saddam Hussein. It read:

> The Iraqi leadership has decided in accordance with resolution 660 (1990) immediately to withdraw all its troops from Kuwait. The order to that effect has already been issued. I request you to make urgent efforts for the adoption of a resolution of the UN Security Council calling for a cease-fire. The time frame for the implementation of the withdrawal, which has already begun, will be very brief.[54]

The message contained no reference to the Soviet proposal, no demands that other resolutions be dropped, and contained no attached conditions. It was an *unconditional withdrawal* from Kuwait -- a demand the allies had been making since the outset of the conflict. Given the extent of damage caused by the ground war -- 14,000 prisoners had been taken by the allies in the first 24 hours, a total of 20,000 in the next[55] -- it was undoubtedly more an unconditional retreat, but that was hardly the point; Iraq had announced that it was leaving. Even more importantly, the Soviet representative made it clear that the announcement was accompanied by clear action: "I should like to stress that, as the Iraqis have declared, the troop withdrawal has already begun, and accordingly the Security Council can adopt the relevant decision." It was a clear call for a cease-fire by the Soviet Union. The United States reaction, given by US representative Thomas Pickering, was negative. It saw "no reason to change [its] approach," arguing that, and despite Soviet assurance, there was "no evidence of an Iraqi withdrawal." Pickering also added that the US had "no intention of attacking retreating forces. But such forces should certainly lay down their arms and leave. If they are moving as a combat unit with combat equipment, then in our view they are still subject to the rules of war."[56]

Iraq, in its turn at the meeting, attempted to clarify its position, requesting only that "the Council immediately adopt a resolution for a cease-fire in which it established the necessary machinery to guarantee respect for the cease-fire and the completion of the withdrawal of Iraqi troops as soon as possible." Once again, there were no demands and no conditions whatsoever. Then two nations, Yemen and Cuba, which had called for a cease-fire from the first day of the war, now once again put their case forward. To date, the vast proportion of the Yemeni and Cuban rhetoric attempted to do no more than score political propaganda points, a tactic which had yielded few results. Now, however, the tone was serious and reasoned. Yemen proposed a resolution which affirmed the validity of previous resolutions, but which called for a supervised cease-fire, and Cuba made a particularly eloquent speech, free from its usual criticisms of imperialism and Western values, and which underlined something critical to our discussions of cease-fires in the Gulf War:

> I heard neither the representative of the Soviet Union, nor the representative of Iraq say that in order to fully implement the resolution and thus withdraw Iraqi troops from Kuwait, anyone was demanding the nullification or modification, or anything else, of the Council's resolutions. It has been requested simply that the Council take the basic measures that have always been a part of any process of the withdrawal of military forces in any conflict situation. No one could seriously think that there can be a withdrawal of military forces under bombardment, under fire, under war conditions ... human beings on both sides are paying with their lives for our disquisitions and diplomatic manoeuvring. Those human beings on both sides deserve our respect and they oblige us here and now in the Security Council to adopt a resolution like the one our colleague from Yemen has proposed.[57]

Apart from the second half of the statement, about which no more need be said, the first half brings out a critical point which makes the United States' position absolutely clear: the use of force as a "necessary measure" was needed in the first instance *only* to get Iraq out of Kuwait, *not* to implement other Security Council resolutions. The Council had imposed sanctions and an embargo which would still hold, even under a cease-fire. With concomitant international will, they could have been maintained almost indefinitely. In time, it could be argued, Iraq's compliance with all other resolutions might have been gained without the use of force, and now that the withdrawal was taking place, a cease-fire could have been the first order of business for the United States. It was not. More likely, the coalition was concerned with the fact that alliance cohesion would be jeopardised in a drawn-out waiting game, that international will could not be sustained. Moreover, the coalition aim of ensuring the decapitation of Iraq's military potential[58] (which was beyond the UN mandate[59]) could not be achieved were there to be a cease-fire. Under the circumstances, therefore, military force was seen as the fastest and most reliable method of securing Iraq's compliance with all Security Council resolutions and allied objectives, and military force was the option which continued to be employed. The Security Council meeting ended at 0035 hrs, New York time, on 26 February.

On 27 February, President Bush declared that Saddam Hussein was not withdrawing, he was retreating: "He is not voluntarily giving up Kuwait."[60] The "withdrawal" would not be accepted until Iraq announced at the UN that it would comply with all twelve UN resolutions. Other conditions were added as well, including a demand that Iraq divulge the location of all booby traps and minefields. At the same time, the ground offensive was proving catastrophic for Saddam Hussein. Apart from the POWs which had been taken, 370 tanks had been destroyed, and up to 100,000 men had reported to headquarters that they were unable to fight:[61]

> Saddam watched with increasing dread the developments at the front. Not only had his hopes of giving the coalition a "bloody nose" been dashed, but "the mother of all battles" turned out to be a military catastrophe of the rarest stamp. Unless halted immediately, the allied offensive would culminate not only in a humiliating Iraqi withdrawal, but in the collapse of Saddam's own rule, as well.[62]

Tariq Aziz cabled the President of the Security Council twice on 27 February. The first cable informed the president that Iraqi forces had started to withdraw, and that the withdrawal would hopefully be completed "within the next few hours." It also informed the president that Iraq would comply with resolutions 662 (regarding the annexation of Kuwait) and 674 (which included a requirement to adhere to all previous resolutions) if other resolutions including 665 (naval blockade) and 670 (embargo) could be "nullified."[63] The second informed the president that the withdrawal from Kuwait had been completed at dawn, 27 February, but that Iraqi forces were still under attack.[64] Neither message brought a halt to the fighting.

By 28 February, the coalition land offensive had "rendered ineffective" 29 Iraqi divisions, destroyed three quarters of its tanks, two thirds of its artillery and 50,000 prisoners had been taken.[65] Saddam Hussein was left with no choice. The UN received a short message affirming that the "Government of Iraq agrees to comply fully with Security Council Resolution 660 (1990) and all the other Security Council Resolutions."[66] At this point, it was either comply, or have the coalition on his doorstep within hours. Better now, in Hussein's view, to deal with the potential rebellion of the Iraqi people than have the coalition simply remove him from power. It was only at this point that the US ceased fire. Iraq had done all that had been demanded of it, and the military action was halted at 0500 gmt, six weeks to the day from the moment it had begun.

In this case, perceptions of the relative bargaining positions of the belligerents were finally agreed, those perceptions being that the allies had a great deal of bargaining power, and Saddam Hussein had little or none. Military action had proved effective in securing an Iraqi withdrawal from Kuwait, and there was no reason to doubt that continued military action would fail to secure other allied demands. Bargaining positions were set, and if anything were likely to improve in the allies' favor. A cease-fire in this case was therefore highly desirable from the Iraqi point of view, but not at all from the allied perspective. For the allies, the relative positions dictated their actions; a cease-fire was seen as unnecessary -- even a hindrance -- to achieve allied objectives. Force was seen as an effective and easy means, and therefore the only means necessary, to achieve stated objectives. A cease-fire, had it taken place, would have been seen by the allies as inhibiting their powers, and increasing those of Iraq. Under those circumstances, the political will to cease-fire failed to arise on the allied side. Conversely, the clearer it became to the Iraqis that they would have a better chance under a cease-fire than by continuing the war, the more effort was put into accepting, little by little, every allied demand.

Now, before going on to discuss the effect of intervention and political recognition on belligerent willingness to cease-fire, it is worth examining one more case in detail -- the October War of 1973 -- in order to gain a fuller appreciation of the relationship between belligerent perceptions of power, victory, and cease-fire.

The October War

> "The main thing is to end the war and to end it in victory ... "[67]
> Golda Meir, 10 October 1973

Underlying more obvious and visible objectives, the war between Israel and its Arab neighbors in 1973 was a war about power. More precisely, it was a war in which the desire to increase political bargaining power was the root motivation behind the use of massive military force over a period of several weeks. That this is the case is particularly evident if attention is focused on two of the main combatants, Egypt and Israel.[68] For Egypt, the object of war was not to annihilate the state of Israel. It was to regain territory, and it would do this by using force to achieve bargaining power. When that power looked as if it might diminish rather than increase, Egypt attempted to end the war. By then, however, it was too late. Israel, forced into a war it did not want but in which it eventually gained the upper hand, now had the identical objective to Egypt at the war's outset -- to break the political stalemate -- and it would achieve this goal by using force to achieve bargaining power. The goal was attainable; an expected victory was imminent, and a complete military victory was only prevented by Israel's willingness to submit to superpower pressure for a cease-fire. In the end, however, and despite submitting to superpower wishes, Israel gained and retained a great deal of the power it sought and was able to consider cease-fire. In that sense, the October War was a war begun by Arabs, but ended by Israelis. Overall, however, it was only when *both* sides accepted their relative power and bargaining positions and realized that continued fighting would be unlikely to change them for the better that a cease-fire came into effect.

There is no doubt how the October War began, for actions were taken in full view of UN observers in the area.[69] At 1400 hrs on the afternoon of 6 October 1973, Egypt launched a surprisingly damaging air strike across the Suez Canal, closely followed by a land assault. About the same time, Syrian forces attacked across the Golan heights. It was a combined attack which had been planned, executed, and would be continued in order to break a diplomatic deadlock which had been in place for almost three years. Since March 1969, Egypt had been waging what eventually became known as the War of Attrition, which included heavy bombardments and occasional commando attacks on Israeli forces along the east bank of the Canal. In June 1970, an American plan for a 90-day cease-fire was put to Egypt, which accepted it on 22 July. (Israel accepted on 6 August.) Since then, there had been a political stalemate.[70] Given that, Egyptian President Anwar el-Sadat -- who came to power in September 1970 following the death of President Nasser -- concluded that the only way to recover the Sinai and reopen

the Suez Canal would be to force Israel to the negotiating table. In a
Newsweek interview on 9 April 1973, Sadat categorically stated that

> [t]here is only one conclusion -- if we don't take our own case in our own
> hands there will be no movement ... Every door I have opened has been
> slammed in my face by Israel -- with American blessings. The situation is
> hopeless and... highly explosive... The time has come for a shock. ... Diplomacy
> will continue as before, during and after the battle.

The interviewer then asked Sadat whether what he was saying was that
one has to fight in order to be able to talk. "At the very least" came the
reply.[71]

So Sadat went to war not to destroy Israel, but to achieve a political
settlement. From the Egyptian point of view, that would only happen if
Egypt could gain the bargaining power that would come with the Israeli
recognition that it was no longer an invincible military force.[72] Sadat himself
noted that the initial gains in the war, particularly the opening air strike
"restored the confidence of our armed forces, our people, and our Arab
nation. It also restored the world's confidence in us, and exploded forever
the myth of an invincible Israel."[73] As Kissinger recalls, "[r]are is the
statesman who at the beginning of a war has so clear a perception of its
political objective; rarer still is the war fought to lay the basis for moderation
in its aftermath." The shock of an Egyptian success -- even an incomplete
success -- "would enable *both* sides to show a flexibility that was impossible
while Israel considered itself militarily supreme and Egypt was paralysed
by humiliation."[74]

In theory, Sadat's strategy was a good one, but it would only be successful
if Egyptian forces could either inflict a painful blow on the Israelis or, at
the very least, fight them to a standstill. Events augured well from the
start. At the end of the first day of fighting, the Suez Canal had been crossed,
Israeli defences breached, and substantial gains had been made by the
Syrians on the Golan heights.[75] Moshe Dayan, the Israeli Defence Minister,
later commented that "the first day of fighting was hard. Our losses in
men were not light, and we also lost ground and positions of considerable
value."[76] Major-General Avraham Adan went so far as to say that "even
in our worst dreams, nobody could have anticipated such a situation."[77]

As far as both superpowers were concerned, Sadat had made his point
that day, and both approached the Egyptians with a view to a cease-fire.
With that in mind, Kissinger spoke to Mohamed Hassan el-Zayyat, the
Egyptian foreign minister, in Washington on the evening of 6 October.
Zayyat did not "readily embrace" Kissinger's suggestion of a return to pre-
war lines, and was "even less receptive" to the idea that Egypt would stand
to benefit from such an arrangement as Israel would be reversing the Arab

advance at any time. Zayyat called the ideas "very strange ... madness." Yet, perhaps surprisingly, he did agree in the end that the Arab point had been made, and that an end to the fighting was desirable.[78]

To the Soviets as well, the first day had proved decisive. The Soviet ambassador to Cairo, Vladimir Vinogradov, saw Sadat less than six hours after the war had begun to ask for Sadat's approval to work towards a cease-fire. He informed Sadat that the Syrians had requested on 4 October that the Soviet Union undertake this task no later than 48 hours after hostilities had begun. Sadat refused to believe that Syrian President Hafiz al-Asad "had really demanded a cease-fire before the war started." Sadat informed the ambassador that he would contact Asad to find out what was going on (Asad later denied the charges), and then added that "even if Syria did demand it, I won't have a cease-fire until all the main targets of my battle have been achieved."[79]

Sadat, then, despite having made a number of gains on the first day of fighting, clearly expected to make more. He assumed that his initial successes could be followed up, despite that fact that the Israelis were now well on the way to full mobilization, and despite the fact that to many outsiders, his initial strategy -- that of proving Israeli vulnerability -- would have been successful had he chosen to stop at that point. Once again, the effect of expected victory on desire for cease-fire is evident. Sadat now had bargaining power, but he could have even more if he continued and was successful -- *that* was the point of continuing military action after the first day. And so he did.

As for Israel, even if Sadat had been interested in cease-fire, it is likely that any proposal would have been rejected. As Abba Eban, the Israeli foreign minister, later commented, "[n]othing at that time seemed more disastrous for Israel ... than to cease fire with the Egyptians and Syrians well beyond their previous lines."[80] Late in the day on 6 October, he received a message from Meir that Israel would not agree to a cease-fire until the status quo had been restored.[81]

October 7 was a day for "diplomatic stocktaking," and superpower movement to convene the Security Council was consequently minimal.[82] Despite some reports that Sadat wanted a cease-fire, the terms he apparently offered -- an Israeli withdrawal from all occupied territories, followed by a peace conference -- seemed less than realistic.[83] Neither the Egyptians nor the Israelis seemed genuinely interested in cease-fire. In his memoirs, Sadat denied any interest in a cease-fire at that point, and indeed until 20 October. He notes that the Soviet ambassador returned that evening, blanching visibly when informed that Asad had denied asking for a cease-fire. As for any future cease-fire, Sadat was very clear: "Now listen ... this subject is closed; I don't want you to take it up any further with me. You know -- and I told you yesterday -- that I won't have a cease-fire until the objectives of the battle have been achieved." According to Sadat, the ambassador persisted every day of the conflict, urging him to cease fire.[84]

By 8 October, the Israeli counteroffensive had begun, and the CIA was predicting an Israeli victory within 48 hours. Yet Kissinger was puzzled: "If all this was true, why were the Arabs not grasping at a cease-fire? What did they know that we didn't?"[85] It turned out that the Israeli situation was worse than had been imagined. Nearly fifty aircraft and 500 tanks had been lost by 9 October, a "staggering" figure which required Kissinger to reassess the entire US strategy (which had to that point been based on awaiting an Israeli recovery and push back to the original lines, at which point the US could support a "cease-fire in place" in the Security Council[86]). Despite Israeli successes on the Syrian front,[87] things were so bad by 9 October that Meir reportedly authorized Dayan to "activate" Israel's nuclear arsenal (although the evidence for this particular event seems unclear).[88] Israel needed arms badly if it were to completely reverse Syrian and Egyptian advances, lest they end up in a bitter attrition war.[89]

For the US, the decision was made to guarantee the replacement of all Israeli losses, a decision which would allow Israel to use their badly needed reserves without fear that they would be permanently lost. In a letter to the Israeli ambassador, Kissinger went even further: "You have the additional assurance that if it should go very badly and there is an emergency, we will get the tanks in even if we have to do it with American planes."[90] That same day, probably in retaliation for Syrian missile attacks on Israeli settlements in the previous two days, Damascus was bombed killing about a hundred civilians.[91] Among the casualties was the Soviet cultural centre, where thirty were killed,[92] as well as a UN observer, his wife and daughter.[93] The attacks increased Soviet (and international) pressures for a cease-fire.

As for Egypt, by 9 October it was even less willing to cease fire than it had been before. Brezhnev had made his decision to begin an airlift to Egypt, and had informed Sadat on 8 October.[94] Vinogradov nevertheless informed Sadat of Syrian setbacks on the northern front, and after getting a clear understanding of Sadat's political objectives in the war, again pressed Sadat on the question of cease-fire. Sadat's replied that he wanted to exploit his country's "immense military success."[95]

On 11 October, an Israeli counteroffensive had been launched in the north,[96] and on 12 October, Israel had informed the US that it was willing to accept a cease-fire in place, but that it would prefer that the vote on such a resolution not be taken until the following afternoon.[97] Kissinger explored the possibility of having such a resolution tabled by the British, but given what we know of Israeli objectives in the war, and subsequent Israeli actions, the move seemed a strange one. According to Golda Meir, Israel had only one aim in the October War: a lasting settlement: "[t]his time, the Arabs were going to have to meet us, not only on battlefields but at the negotiating table, and together with us find a solution to a problem which had taken thousands of young lives -- theirs and ours -- over the past three decades."[98] Israel may have wanted peace, but as is so often the case, it would be peace on Israeli terms if the power to dictate those terms could be achieved. It is the desire for that power which explains the continued fighting after the 22 October cease-fire, the continued defiance of UN and US pressure, and the willingness to cease fire only after Sadat accepted the Israeli proposal for face-to-face talks. What it does not explain is why they would be willing to cease fire "in place" on 12 October, a point at which there was no indication that Sadat would meet them at the negotiating table. Eban provides the explanation: "The reasons were starkly realistic. There was no early prospect of expelling Egyptian forces in the South, while in the North, we had reached the peak of our success and might not be able to push the Syrians farther."[99] Thus, it would simply be incorrect to assert, as Stein does in her analysis of the war, that "one of the belligerents [Israel] was willing to end the war when victory and defeat were not clearly established."[100] *At that moment*, from Israel's point of view, the balance had been established. American aid had not yet begun to arrive in large enough quantities to enter into Israeli calculations of power balancing, and the equation at that point seemed decidedly in favor of Egypt, with little prospect of change. The power balance had been established, and seemed unlikely to be altered in the near future. The decision to seek a cease-fire had been the result.

By Sunday, 14 October, however, the US airlift had begun to flood into Israeli calculations, and the mood had changed dramatically. It was the turning point in the war. Messages from Jerusalem were now "buoyant and hopeful," and all desire for a cease-fire vanished. Israel now expected to ensure a complete reversal of their ill fortune, and interest in a cease-fire diminished proportionally. Eban comments that "[i]n these conditions, I decided to leave the cease-fire problem alone. It was evident that if our military situation continued to improve, an Arab interest in a cease-fire would soon emerge."[101] Thus came Meir's reaction to Kissinger's 18 October proposal of a cease-fire linked with Resolution 242. The resolution, she argued, grew out of the 1967 war and was irrelevant to the current war; "it was not a 'panacea'; there was 'no reason for undue haste'"[102] Like Egypt, Israel was in the business of gaining bargaining power through military success. The greater the success, the greater the power:

> [w]hen the day [13 October] dawned, Israel had no assurance of sufficient arms and was ready for a chastening cease-fire. By midnight the arms were flowing and our forces were moving from one triumph to another ... All talk of a cease-fire had now become obsolete.[103]

The turning point in the war came on 14 October for another reason: a failed Egyptian armored offensive in a battle involving over 2000 tanks -- one of the largest in history.[104] At least 250 Egyptian tanks were destroyed through a combination of Israeli armored, air, and anti-tank attacks, and it was here that Egyptian fortunes began to change. In this case, the failure did not go unnoticed by Egypt (no doubt because of the magnitude of the defeat), and Kissinger received a letter from Hafiz Ismail (Sadat's security advisor) on 15 October. Ismail denied any intention to humiliate Israel, expressed his appreciation for US efforts to achieve a cease-fire as a preliminary step towards political settlement, and invited Kissinger to Egypt "to discuss any subject, proposal or project, within the framework of two principles ... that Egypt cannot make any concessions of land or sovereignty."[105] Whether this message came originally from Sadat can never be known (as Sadat insisted that he never considered cease-fire until as late as 20 October), but it seems at least possible. If anything, Sadat probably agreed with Kissinger's assessment of the situation at that point, laid out in a letter to Ismail on 16 October:

> Egyptian forces have already accomplished much. The humiliation which Egyptians and, indeed, the Arab world felt after 1967 has been erased ... The Egyptian side therefore has an important decision to make. To insist on its maximum program means continuation of the war and the possible jeopardy of all that has been achieved. The outcome will then be decided by military measures. ... If diplomacy is to be given a full opportunity, a cease-fire must precede it.[106]

On the same day, Soviet Prime Minister Alexei Kosygin arrived in Cairo, to seek an assurance that Sadat was ready to cease fire, an assurance which he apparently failed to receive. On the seventeenth, Kosygin had also apparently shown Sadat satellite photographs of the west bank of the Suez Canal (where Israeli armor was massing) and, argues O'Ballance, "at last the seriousness [of the situation] dawned on the Egyptian high command." Still, Sadat and his inner circle were projecting the image that they were "anxious to continue the war unless it could be terminated by the withdrawal of all Israelis from the occupied territories."[107]

Sadat, then, did not yet officially ask for a cease-fire, and the question remains -- why? Did he still expect some kind of battlefield success? Did he expect to at least meet the Israelis in some kind of stalemate (the next best alternative)? The plausible answer to both questions seems to be "yes." When Israeli forces began crossing the canal through a narrow gap in Egyptian lines on 16 October -- the beginning of the end of the Egyptian Third Army -- Sadat explains in his memoirs that he had given orders to "deal with the infiltrating forces ... to stop the advance of the trickle of men that had already crossed and confine them to the narrow strip they had captured," a task he says could have been accomplished had his orders been promptly obeyed.[108] On 16 October, then, Sadat was apparently still of the opinion that he was in control of the battlefield, and that at the very least, he could beat the Israelis to a standstill. Chaim Herzog, an Israeli general and official military spokesman in the October war, argues that when Sadat spoke to his people on 16 October, he was simply unaware of how serious the Israeli crossing to the west bank really was.[109]

The seriousness of the situation was not brought home to Sadat until 19 or 20 October. The latter date is probably more accurate, as we shall see, but the evidence is conflicting. On some occasions, Sadat has claimed the "decision" to cease fire was not made until 19 October (note that the phrasing implies neither that Egypt made a demand nor a request to cease-fire); on others 20 October was the given date.[110] Given that Sadat claims that he told Kosygin on his departure (19 October) that he wouldn't have a cease-fire "until the final stage of my War Plan has been carried out,"[111] it would seem to make sense that the decision to cease-fire came on the night of 19/20 October, as Sadat claims in his memoirs.[112]

After reporting to the Operations room, and being told by General Ismail that "[t]he war is over. A catastrophe has occurred. We must withdraw from Sinai,"[113] at 0130 hrs (probably 20 October), Sadat made the decision. His stated reasons are straightforward:

> the United States was now taking part in the fighting by supplying Israel with weapons still being tested, with the Maverick bomb, and many other items -- to save Israel. I knew my capabilities. I did not intend to fight the entire United States of America ... I would not allow the Egyptian forces or Egypt's strategic targets to be destroyed once again.[114]

Whether or not Sadat believed his rhetoric about US involvement,[115] Egypt was now in a precarious military situation: Israeli forces had now manoeuvred well behind Egyptian lines and were driving towards Suez city in an attempt to encircle the Egyptian Third Army. It was at this point then, that Sadat "activated"[116] Kosygin to seek a cease-fire. The power balance had shifted, was unlikely to improve, and threatened all Egyptian gains to that point.

By 21 October, the Israelis, too, appeared to be making cease-fire noises. Kissinger states that Moshe Dayan, the Israeli defence minister, proposed a cease-fire based on one of two conditions: a return to pre-war lines, or retention of positions occupied at the time of cease-fire. (Either way, Israel would be in a good position, as it was preparing to encircle the Egyptian Third Army). That same day, a message reached Kissinger from Ismail. Sadat, too, was prepared to cease-fire, and for the first time willing to separate it from overall settlement.[117] In discussions with Brezhnev, Kissinger suggested a resolution calling for a cease-fire in place, a call to implement Resolution 242,[118] and the beginning of negotiations towards political settlement. To his amazement, the proposal was accepted, and this eventually became UN Resolution 338, which was passed in the early hours of 22 October.[119] Under extreme US pressure -- the full story of which shall be left until our ninth chapter -- Israel accepted the resolution later in the day.[120]

Despite this, one had to question the sincerity of the Israeli moves. It was entirely clear that given only a little more time, the Israeli army could have the Egyptian Third Army completely encircled -- thereby inflicting a very visible humiliation upon Sadat. As it turned out, this was in fact the Israeli desire. Meir complained of the "indecent" speed with which the resolution was passed:

> [w]e would have liked the call for a cease-fire to have been postponed for a few more days so that the defeat of the Egyptian and Syrian armies would be even more conclusive than it was, and on 21 October there was every reason to believe that, given just a little more time, this would have happened.[121]

It was true, but it was exactly what the US wanted to avoid. The Americans believed the best hope for long term settlement depended on avoiding an Arab humiliation by arranging a cease-fire after an Israeli recovery but before a decisive win.[122] Israel viewed the situation very differently, of course. The overall objective was still power, and the greater the military victory, the greater the bargaining power gained. Eban comments:

> Mrs. Meir hoped that in the course of our counter-offensives, we should be able to seize military positions across the canal and beyond the previous line in the Golan heights, with the aim of ensuring ourselves against new assaults of the enemy and of strengthening our position in the political negotiation. There was no controversy among ministers about the desirability of these two aims.[123]

Israel sought a "posture of attack" so that "there was more chance of our opponents' agreeing to an acceptable cease-fire."[124]

Thus, while US strategy was intent on having Arabs and Israelis approach the bargaining table as equals, Israeli and Egyptian strategy lay in gaining the upper hand. Dayan recalls that on 21 October he "urged" Lt. General Bar-Lev to gain territory which would "cut off and isolate the Egyptian Third Army and the city of Suez."[125] That objective remained incomplete by the time the cease-fire was to come into effect (at 1952 hrs on 22 October).

It is hardly surprising, therefore, that the cease-fire of 22 October failed to be implemented.[126] Ismail informed Kissinger that Israeli forces had broken the cease-fire and "were in the process of occupying new positions." Egypt was taking counter measures, and Ismail wanted to know what the superpowers were doing to ensure compliance. Israel, of course, blamed the Egyptians for breaking the cease-fire: "we are *not* liars. The allegations are *not* true."[127] While Meir admitted that her military commanders had pleaded for two or three extra days to complete the encirclement of the Egyptian Third Army, she stated that the cabinet had overruled them. When Egypt broke the cease-fire, however, she ordered the Israeli army to "continue fighting until the Egyptians stopped."[128] Herzog claims that Egyptian units attempted to join up with each other or to break out of the impending encirclement and that Israeli forces therefore "reacted."[129] A formal complaint about Israeli violations was made to the UN by Egypt, which demanded a Security Council meeting. Secretary-General Kurt Waldheim, in response, recommended an international peacekeeping force. The US was not averse to such a force, and Kissinger informed the Soviets of this fact.

Kissinger then contacted the Israelis, and was told via Ismail that Meir wished to tell Kissinger "personally, confidentially, and sincerely, that none of the actions taken on the Egyptian front were initiated by us." Kissinger was not impressed:

> [i]t was not plausible that the Egyptian Third Army should launch attacks after a cease-fire that had saved it from being overwhelmed; and that it should then immediately ask everyone within reach for yet another cease-fire, shooting all the time at passive Israelis who were only defending themselves while advancing.[130]

O'Ballance clearly blames the Israelis:

> [w]hile the Egyptians seemed determined to honor the cease-fire ... the Israelis, on the contrary, rushed troops across their three bridges throughout the night of the twenty-second/twenty-third. It seemed they had no intention of observing the cease-fire but were set upon exploiting their position on the west bank.[131]

As an apologist for Israeli actions, Herzog argues that the Third Army was cut off by noon of 22 October, *before* the first cease-fire had come into effect. If this were true, all claims that Israel took advantage of the violation of the cease-fire to complete the encirclement could be diluted, if not invalidated altogether. It is important to examine Herzog's evidence for this claim. "Captured records" of Egyptian communications included a message from the 19th Brigade commander to Third Army commander, who said that the cutting of the Suez-Cairo road "has cut off all supplies to you." As further evidence, Herzog cites a communication from the Third Army commander to Brigadier Kabil: "The Suez road is cut, Kabil. We have to open the Suez road. ... the army is *being* surrounded" (emphasis added).[132] The operative word in that communication is *being*: the encirclement had not been completed. True, the road had been cut, but at the time of the cease-fire it would seem that Israel had not fully completed and consolidated the encirclement action. Even Herzog later admits this fact, noting that consolidated encirclement did not occur until 24 October.[133] Major-General Avraham Adan, commanding the Northern sector of the Egyptian front, readily admitted that after 22 October he planned to "mop up" the captured areas, "hope that the enemy would violate the cease-fire, thus leading to an expansion of the fighting so we could complete our task of encircling the Egyptian Third Army."[134]

Whatever the truth, in the end, the Third Army was completely cut off. By noon on 23 October, Simcha Dinitz, Israeli Ambassador to the United States, informed Kissinger that Israeli forces would not withdraw from positions which they now occupied. About the same time, Nixon received a message from Brezhnev, urging united action by the superpowers to impose a cease-fire. In an attempt to placate the Soviet Union -- which felt that it had been double-crossed by Kissinger and that the Americans were encouraging Israel to complete its military operations[135] -- the United States decided to support a new call for a cease-fire which would require a return to the positions occupied when the first cease-fire had come into effect, a line which was and would be in dispute, and which would require negotiations between Israel and Egypt.[136]

Israel refused to discuss the matter. Meir informed Kissinger on the afternoon of 23 October that Israel would not comply with the proposed resolution. "Israel seemed determined to end the war with a humiliation for Egypt."[137] They apparently saw little point in giving up an indisputable advantage in exchange for some nebulous American promises about a workable formula for peace.[138] That same afternoon, a message arrived from Sadat (signed by him personally and therefore testifying to the gravity of the situation). Undoubtedly aware of the Soviet communications to the US earlier in the day, he proposed that the US intervene directly to guarantee the cease-fire, a proposal rejected by the US.[139] That evening, Dinitz informed Kissinger that Israel would now cease fire if Egypt did also. UN Resolution 339 was passed, which reaffirmed the first cease-fire, and "urged" that the parties return to the lines of the first cease-fire.[140] The parties agreed to observe the cease-fire by 0700 hrs local time, 24 October.

It is at this point that the political strategy of Israel came to dominate the events of the war. Golda Meir had set out the conditions under which there could be a cease-fire to the Knesset on 23 October. The cease-fire had to be binding on all regular an irregular forces of all belligerents, assure prevention of a blockade or interference with freedom of navigation, ensure the release of prisoners and, most importantly, ensure direct negotiation.[141] It was only when that final condition was met that the war finally ended.

If Egypt and Israel ceased fire on 24 October as they agreed, it was not for long. According to Dinitz, the Third Army attempted to break out of its encirclement, and the Israeli army attempted to repulse that breakout, defending itself and blocking Egyptian offensives. It seemed a repetition of the first cease-fire. Sadat again pleaded for the US to intervene militarily, and was again refused, although it was made clear that the US opposed further Israeli military action. Dinitz assured the US that if it could verify that Egypt was honoring the cease-fire, Israel too would stop shooting. Kissinger considered this to be a time-wasting device, as it would take "many hours of exchanges to establish another cease-fire and to get American military observers to the farthest part of the Sinai."[142] The message was nevertheless conveyed to Sadat.

Israel continued to insist that they were trying "to absorb fire without answer," that they had concrete evidence that Egypt was planning to continue fighting. Sadat was now calling for a joint US-Soviet force to intervene, a proposal which horrified Kissinger.[143] At a Security Council meeting which convened at 1800 hrs on 24 October, el-Zayyat called for joint superpower intervention on the basis that letters asking for such had been sent by Sadat to Brezhnev and Nixon:

> These two superpowers have forces in the Mediterranean. It think the reason they give to their taxpayers is that they are there to preserve the peace of the world. Well, the peace of the world is in danger and we are calling on them to make good their promise [that UN Resolutions would take effect].

The Americans responded that a joint superpower force would not be "helpful in creating conditions of peace," and that they were only prepared to support a UN force without superpower participation.[144] That view was made widely known and the US prepared to use its veto in the Council. As for the Soviet Union, they called the Egyptian request "undoubtedly justified" and that evening (24 October), Brezhnev threatened to act unilaterally if the US did not join the USSR in guaranteeing the cease-fire with superpower troops. Soviet airborne troops were put on alert for rapid deployment.[145] The move was even more shocking than the initial Soviet proposal, and infinitely more worrying for the United States. The American response to the Soviet ultimatum was to go to DefCon III, the highest state of American peacetime military readiness -- which included the alerting of strategic nuclear forces. The reason for the strong reaction was made clear in a press conference on 25 October:

[i]t is inconceivable that the forces of the great powers should be introduced
in the numbers that would be necessary to overpower both of the participants
... The United States is even more opposed to the unilateral introduction
by any great power, especially by any nuclear power, of military forces into
the Middle East ... The United States will support and give all assistance...
to a United Nations observer force ... It would be a disaster if the Middle
East, already so torn by local rivalries, would now become, as a result of
a UN decision, a legitimized theatre for the competition of the military forces
of the nuclear powers.[146]

Apart from authorizing the military alert, the United States had also
increased pressure on Israel, which responded with a proposal late in the
evening on 24 October. Dinitz proposed that Israel and Egypt withdraw
to 10 kilometres on either side of the Suez Canal, the area in between then
becoming a demilitarized zone. Kissinger considered the plan "impossible":
"Sadat would consider it an insult to be asked to vacate territory that not
even the Israelis challenged as Egyptian. Nor could he end the war by
withdrawing ten kilometres from where he had started it."[147] It would
have appeared as weakness, and as a humiliating defeat, and Kissinger
(probably rightly) believed that Sadat would never have accepted.

A few hours later Dinitz returned, urging on behalf of Meir that Israel
not be asked to pull back to the position it occupied at the time of the 22
October cease-fire. Kissinger replied that Israel would not be coerced in
response to a Soviet threat (to intervene militarily).[148] The next morning,
25 October, messages were received by Kissinger from Sadat who made
it clear that he was withdrawing support for a superpower force, and now
supporting an international force without superpower contingents (which
made Kissinger's job of defusing the situation with the USSR that much
easier).

According to Kissinger, by 2000 hrs on 24 October, all fighting in the
Middle East was over,[149] but this was obviously not the case, as UN
Resolution 340 was passed on 25 October, *demanding* a cease-fire and a
return to the original cease-fire lines of 22 October.[150] (Kissinger recalls
that the word "return" replaced the more emotive "withdraw" in the final
draft.[151]) The resolution also established a UN force composed of UN
members excluding the five permanent members of the Security Council.
As far as a return to the 22 October lines was concerned, Meir rejected
the resolution. (It is significant, however, that the fighting after 24 October
was only sporadic in nature, and in this sense, at least, Kissinger's claim
is accurate.) The Egyptian Third Army was still trapped at this point, slowly
being starved into submission. The reason, as we shall see, was to ensure
Egyptian acceptance of face-to-face negotiations.

Sadat complained to Nixon early Friday morning (26 October) that the
Israelis were attempting "to establish themselves astride the lines of

communication of the Third Egyptian Army in an attempt to isolate and oblige it to surrender," then threatening to break the cease-fire if the situation did not change. The US now backed even further away from its support of Israel. As far as the US was concerned, the destruction of the Egyptian Third Army was not in anyone's interest, so it began to put pressure on Israel to allow supplies to reach the Third Army. Too late, it seemed, for word came that the Third Army was now attempting to break out of its encirclement north of Suez city. Kissinger's response was to ask Israel to allow the UN observers to monitor the cease-fire and thereby allow supply of the Third Army, and to ask Sadat to "avoid taking any irrevocable actions" while all that was taking place.[152]

That afternoon, Dinitz put forward a "personal" idea: that anyone wishing to leave the Third Army could do so, provided that they left their equipment behind -- tantamount to a public humiliation for Egypt[153] (and a familiar demand to anyone acquainted with the Gulf War of 1991).[154] There would be no way that it could be accepted. Meir comments on that "personal" proposal in her memoirs:

> someone had to pay to bring about a relaxation of tension. The price demanded, needless to say from Israel, included our agreeing to permit supplies to reach the encircled Egyptian Third Army and accept a second cease-fire ... We would gladly have given them all this had the Egyptians been willing to lay down their arms and go home. But this was exactly what President Sadat wanted to avoid.[155]

In the meantime, fighting had resumed, Israeli forces launching air and ground attacks against the Third Army as it attempted to break out of the trap. Zayyat had informed Waldheim that the Third Army would never surrender, and would be forced to take "unilateral action."[156]

In the evening, Meir offered direct talks: "We believe we have something to offer them -- something which is neither surrender nor humiliation, but an honorable way out of the situation. All the Egyptians have to do is suggest the time, the place, and rank of their representative." Kissinger notes that "the reality was more complicated. The psychological difficulty for the Arabs in accepting direct talks was hardly likely to be eased by the deliberate humiliation of the Third Army." Nevertheless the message was transmitted, but Kissinger finally felt compelled to make the US position crystal clear:

> we cannot permit the destruction of the Egyptian army ... it is an option that does not exist ... [Nixon] would like from you no later than 8:00 A.M. tomorrow an answer to the questions of non-military supplies permitted to reach the army. If you cannot agree to that, we will have to support in the UN a resolution that will deal with the enforcement of [Resolutions]

338 and 339. ... your course is suicidal. You will not be permitted to destroy this army. You are destroying the possibility of negotiations.[157]

Notably, the message avoided any reference to an Israeli withdrawal to the cease-fire line of 22 October.

Finally, on 27 October, Sadat took up the Israeli offer of talks at the rank of Major-General "to discuss the military aspects of the implementation of Security Council Resolutions 338 and 339." The sole conditions would be a "complete" cease-fire before the meeting (scheduled for 1500 hrs Cairo time at Kilometre 101 on the Suez-Cairo road), and the passage of one non-military convoy to relieve the Third Army. The message passed to Israel and was accepted, and the final cease-fire of the October war came that same day. It was at that point -- and contrary to the assertion of one student of the war "at no point during the war did the three parties simultaneously conclude that it was in their interest to end the war"[158] - that the unspoken agreement by all parties to cease fire was made. However formidable the international pressures were, without such agreement, the war could not have ended.

According to Yitzhak Rabin, the October War was not fought by Egypt and Syria to threaten Israel's existence. It was, instead,

> an all-out use of their military force to achieve a limited political goal. What Sadat wanted by crossing the canal was to change the political reality and, thereby, to start a political process from a point more favorable to him than the one that existed.[159]

Thus, underlying more visible and tangible goals, the October War was a war over bargaining power, with military force used as a tool to attain that objective. The war was begun in order to gain power which Sadat believed could not be secured without resort to military force. Egypt fought the war to the point where it believed it had maximized its gains, after which it only saw a decrease in bargaining power as the likely outcome.[160] It considered and desired a cease-fire on that basis. Israel, too, fought the war for power. Once it had recovered from the initial attack, it had two objectives: humiliating Sadat and ensuring direct negotiations. But both those objectives depended on achieving military victory, and were designed primarily to increase Israeli bargaining power in the post-war settlement. When the first cease-fire broke down (by accident or by Israeli design), it was hardly surprising that Israel completed its encirclement of the Third Army: what power had been gained could now be increased. It was a way of ensuring that Israeli demands would be met in the end. It really was a question of *"Why stop now?"* If anything, the refusal of Israel to give in to international pressure to relieve the Third Army is yet another reflection of a desire to increase power. As long as Israel believed more could be gained by holding out than giving in, Israel would hold out.

Effects of Intervention

There is at least one other factor which impinges on belligerent assessments of their relative bargaining power: intervention by outside parties. Intervention can be defined in any number of ways but, in general, definitions focus on the coercive character of intervention. Hedley Bull, for example, sees intervention as "dictatorial or coercive interference by an outside party or parties, in the sphere of jurisdiction of a sovereign state."[161] With regard to cease-fires, for example, intervention could be defined as any action taken by third parties intended to force belligerents to cease fire. (This type of intervention will be the subject of chapter nine.) Here, however, we would like to address intervention which is of a non-coercive character. Intervention here, then, refers to any *supportive* action by third parties intended either to aid belligerents in winning the war, or to make them more willing to cease fire.[162] Thus, rather than *withdraw* support or interpose military forces between belligerents in order to make them more willing to cease-fire (coercive or *negative* intervention), the third party will *provide* support (non-coercive or *positive* intervention), either to make one or both belligerents more willing to end the war. Positive intervention, however, can have the opposite effect to that intended, making belligerents less rather than more willing to cease fire. This can be made clear by an examination of two types of positive intervention: the provision of material support, and the political recognition of an extra-state actor.[163]

In general, and as we have seen with the October War, third parties intervene in conflicts to prop up one or another belligerent as a way of ending the war more quickly. (There are obvious exceptions, such as the Iran-Iraq war, where intervention was undertaken as a means of ensuring stalemate.) Regarding political recognition, for example, third parties generally recognize belligerents whose political status is in doubt as a means of bringing the conflict to an end more quickly. The reasoning is that where political legitimacy is in doubt, recognition by nations not involved in the conflict will remove the doubts at least partially, if not entirely. The belligerent who had to that point challenged the legitimacy of its enemy now finds itself isolated internationally, and should therefore becomes more willing to settle. During the Yugoslav conflict, this was the European motivation for the recognition of a number of Yugoslav republics, for example.

In fact, positive intervention, including both political recognition and the provision of political and military support, may sometimes have exactly the opposite effect. The belligerent who is supported in some way suddenly has at least two new reasons to continue the struggle. First, further intervention, and therefore increased bargaining power, could be achieved through continued resistance, and second (perhaps less importantly), to quit *after* the intervention is seen as disappointing those who intervened, not to mention one's own domestic population. That is, positive intervention is seen not only as increasing one's bargaining power, but as an achievement which needs to be defended. Thus, despite a third party's intention to end the conflict through intervention, that intervention is often *perceived* as an encouragement to win the war -- not as an attempt to prop up the losing belligerent to the point where its enemy will see that continuing the war is pointless. Finally, and as we have seen in the October war, the provision of support at a critical moment can actually reverse the decision to seek a cease-fire. As for the belligerent who is the enemy of the newly-supported nation, it will not necessarily be any more willing to settle, and even if it is, there remains the difficulty that it will sometimes undervalue the intervention, whereas its opponent will sometimes overvalue it, and the dilemma is once again apparent: an action taken by a third party to increase the bargaining power of one belligerent is valued differently by both sides, and the differing valuation will not necessarily create the conditions necessary for the presence of political will to cease fire.

The adverse effects of positive intervention are well-illustrated by the Nigerian Civil War, where two types of intervention distinguished themselves as factors contributing to the war's length: political recognition of Biafra by foreign countries, and foreign arms shipments to Biafra at crucial moments.

The Nigerian Civil War

In the Spring of 1968, four African countries (Ivory Coast, Gabon, Tanzania, and Zambia) all recognized Biafra as a political entity, an action which had a profound effect on both federal Nigerian and Biafran leaders. Paradoxically, it appears that the political recognition of Biafra was *not* meant to imply support for secession. Raph Uwechue, the former Paris spokesman for Biafra and post-war critic of Chukwuemeka Ojukwu (the Biafran leader), explains:

> [Recognition] was not an approval of the political choice of Eastern Nigeria to secede. This was made clear by the fact that the first recognition did not take place until full ten months after secession. It was the magnitude of the war and enormity of the suffering it produced that made the leaders of these

countries revolt against the methods used by the Nigerian government to solve the problem ... [recognition], like secession itself, was more a *reaction against* than *a decision for.*[164]

This was certainly the case for Zambia,[165] as well as for the government of Gabon which, in a press release of 10 May 1968, deplored "the human tragedy which has befallen the Ibo people and denounces the bloody and fratricidal war" and "decided as a result to recognize Biafra as an independent state ... "[166] Tanzanian President Nyerere, too, publicly outlined his country's reasons for recognising Biafra:

> For 10 months we have accepted the Federal Government's legal right to our support in a "police action to defend the integrity of the State." On that basis we have watched a civil war result in the death of about 100,000 people ... It seemed to us that by refusing to recognize the existence of Biafra we were tacitly supporting a war against the people of Eastern Nigeria -- and a war conducted in the name of unity. We could not continue doing this any longer.[167]

So the idea of recognition had been solely to give the Biafrans something to bargain with, something with which to force Nigeria to the negotiating table.[168] The action backfired. Biafran hawks hardened into their positions, Ojukwu himself arguing that abandoning secession now would "be letting our African friends down."[169] In his address at Addis Ababa on 5 August 1968, Ojukwu deepened the misunderstanding:

> [w]hile these peace discussions go on, let us not forget that four leading African countries ... have carefully considered the issues involved and have accorded us diplomatic recognition. These countries have set out their reasons for considering our case just and our independence deserved.[170]

On the Nigerian side as well, positions hardened and their determination to win militarily now increased in order to counteract any gains Biafra might have scored diplomatically.[171]

As for arms shipments, these too had a decisive effect on when the war would eventually end. According to Ntieyong Akpan -- Chief Secretary to the Biafran Government and Head of the Civil Service of Eastern Nigeria (Biafra) before the war -- the war could have ended as early as September 1968 had it not been for these outside supplies. Ojukwu was convinced at that point that the war was lost, and told his council so. He suggested that the intelligentsia fly to other countries -- he would begin guerrilla warfare instead. But the countries which had recognized Biafra were consulted, supplies provided, and the advance of the North was checked, leading to the subsequent year long stalemate.[172]

In this and similar situations, third parties were admittedly in a dilemma. By refusing to supply arms, their ally would likely be defeated, but by supplying arms, they could prolong the war and the suffering beyond the necessity to save their clients. Where the decision is made to supply arms, the difficulty is that the intentions of that support may be misunderstood. Rather than accepting that arms may be provided by third parties to prevent defeat, the action may be seen as incitement to win the war: where a third party may want a stalemate or a return to the status quo, the belligerents desire victory.

At worst, no clear statement of intention may be forthcoming from the supportive third party, leading to a situation where the belligerent itself is left to decide what that support is intended to do. This appeared to be the case, for example, with regard to French arms supplies in the war. Suzanne Cronje, who has written a detailed diplomatic history of the war, has noted that French arms supplies arrived in such numbers as to "prevent the complete defeat of the Biafrans," but were nevertheless "not enough to allow them to make substantial gains." The on/off policy was probably not deliberate and may have been the result of divisions in Paris, where the Foreign Office was opposed to aid, while the Africa Department, under the supervision of de Gaulle, was in favor of preventing a Biafran defeat.[173] France's official position was that it was observing an arms embargo declared against both sides by Foreign Minister Michel Debré on 12 June 1968, and that only humanitarian and medical supplies were being sent to Biafra.[174] Despite this official position, however, the sympathies of many, including de Gaulle, lay with Biafra. The reasons for this were varied. Nigeria had vehemently condemned French nuclear tests in the Sahara, and had a large English speaking population which might come to dominate its French neighbors were the country stable and successful. Biafra, on the other hand, had oil and was on good terms with the neighboring (French) Ivory Coast.[175] Whatever the reasons, the divisions in Paris resulted in a failure to be clear about the intentions of French intervention.

However uncertain the flow of arms or the reasons for that flow, French support was "crucial"[176] if for no other reason than that they had a significant impact on Ojukwu's decision to continue the war. As mentioned earlier, and according to Adam Curle, in September 1968 many on the Biafran side were saying, "We can't go on," and Biafra was on the verge of being ready to settle. The infusion of arms from France and elsewhere, however, bolstered morale and gave Biafra the means to continue the struggle. "The French arms had enabled them to retake Owerre, which they had lost, and this protected the [strategically important] Uli airstrip ... "[177] The supplies, "belated and halfhearted"[178] though they may have been, were nevertheless "enough to change Ojukwu's mind."[179] Thus, by 25 September, with at least the guarantee of new arms supplies, Ojukwu made it clear that there was no possibility of the war ending. He told his Consultative Assembly that he refused to surrender, he called on the people to recommit themselves to the war and noted, significantly, that "[w]e are stronger today than we were two weeks ago ... and indications are that we shall continue to grow from strength to strength."[180]

Intervention, certainly in the form of arms shipments, has always been an accepted method of showing support for one or another belligerent. Its intent is relatively clear and, to the suppliers, free of ambiguity. The difficulty in this case was that both arms supplies and political recognition were misunderstood by Ojukwu. This was particularly the case as far as political recognition was concerned, as Ojukwu (understandably) believed that those African countries who took the step truly believed in Biafran independence as opposed to any other kind of negotiated solution. The lesson here, then, must be that if countries are to intervene, the intention of the intervention must be made clear. That the intention is mere support is not clear enough. Is it intervention to achieve the stated goals of one belligerent? Is it designed to show only moral support? Is it aimed only at propping up one side to give it the bargaining power it needs to achieve a reasonable negotiated solution? Lack of clarity about the purpose of intervention in the Nigerian Civil War may have contributed significantly to its prolongation.

Conclusions

Both military victories and positive intervention can have a negative effect on the ability of belligerents to be objective about the amount of bargaining power they wield. Victories may be more easily perceived than defeats, and overvalued in terms of the bargaining power they may impart. Moreover, belligerents' assessments of their ability to win the war tend to rise with each victory, no matter how small, and likely fail to diminish to the same degree with each defeat. Expected or actual positive intervention can create a trend away from the willingness to cease-fire for similar reasons. While not always the case, and whatever the form of intervention, be it political recognition, or the supply of material or political support, it can be over-valued by the supported belligerent, and undervalued by its enemy. Bargaining positions have changed, but each side values the amount of change differently, and unless the values match, political will to cease-fire will be absent.

It is because what is rational for one side may not be rational for the other at any given point in the war[181] that the willingness to consider cease-fire requires that belligerents *agree* about their respective bargaining powers -- expected or actual military victory and intervention will impinge on this assessment. Beyond that, a willingness to cease-fire generally requires three things: first, that the cease-fire be seen as not providing any additional bargaining power to the enemy; second, that the bargaining positions either be relatively equal, or immeasurably disparate and, third, that those positions are seen as fixed for the foreseeable future. That is, both belligerents must perceive either that the war is stalemated and likely to remain so, or that one has decisively more power than the other. Having perceived this, belligerents must both believe that this power balance is unlikely to shift in their favor through military action or against them under a cease-fire.

Notes

1. Michael I. Handel, "War Termination -- A Critical Survey" in Nissan Oren (ed.), *Termination of Wars* (Jerusalem: Magnes Press [The Hebrew University], 1982), p. 63.

2. Count Folke Bernadotte, *To Jerusalem* (translated by Joan Bulman) (London: Hodders and Stoughton, 1951), pp. 34,39, and also in Sydney D. Bailey, *How Wars End: The United Nations and the Termination of Armed Conflict, 1946-1964* (2 vols.) (Oxford: Clarendon Press, 1982), Vol. I, p. 110; Vol. II, p. 190; or see "Report of the UN Mediator on Palestine to the Security Council," UN doc. S/888 (12 July 1948).

3. United Nations Security Council Provisional Verbatim Record (SCPV), doc. S/PV.2977, p. 76 (14 February 1991).

4. Reported in *The Independent*, 7 June 1994. This had been a long-standing problem. Haris Silajdzic, the Bosnian Foreign Minister, in speaking of Serb attacks on Sarajevo in 1992, told one newspaper that "Judging from our previous experience, they have a cease-fire whenever there is an important meeting like [that with Lord Carrington]. Then they use the cease-fire to regroup, and to attack again -- worse than before." (*The Independent*, 26 June 1992).

5. Bailey, *How Wars End*, Vol. I, p. 112. The studies included Indonesia (1947-48), Kashmir (1947-49), Palestine (1947-49), Indonesia (1948-49), and Korea (1951-1953).

6. Martha Crenshaw Hutchinson, *Revolutionary Terrorism: The FLN in Algeria, 1954-1962* (Stanford: Hoover Institution Press, 1978), p. 16.

7. *The Guardian*, 12 August 1961.

8. These transcripts mention no leader, war, or place by name, reflecting Curle's concern with the confidentiality of the proceedings. Contextual clues, however, go to indicate that most of these transcripts came from the Nigerian Civil War.

9. Adam Curle, *Tools for Transformation: A Personal Study* (Stroud: Hawthorne, 1990), p. 79.

10. L. Oppenheim, in H. Lauterpacht (ed.), *Oppenheim's International Law, vol. 2: Disputes, War and Neutrality* (7th ed) (London: Longmans, Green & Co., 1952), p. 551.

11. Morris Greenspan, *The Modern Law of Land Warfare* (Los Angeles: University of California Press, 1959), p. 589; Colonel Howard S. Levie, "The Nature and Scope of the Armistice Agreement," *American Journal of International Law* 53 (1956), p. 885; Castel has remarked that both "armistice" and "simple cessation of hostilities" do end the state of war, while "cease-fire" does not; Castel, however, neither defines nor elaborates upon these terms (see J.G. Castel, *International Law (chiefly as interpreted and applied in Canada)* [Toronto: University of Toronto Press, 1965], p. 1153).

12. Paul Seabury, "Provisionality and Finality," in William T.R. Fox (ed.), *How Wars End -- Annals of the American Academy of Political and Social Science*, Vol. 392 (Philadelphia: Academy of Political and Social Science, 1970), p. 102.

13. See Levie, "The Nature and Scope of the Armistice Agreement," p. 886. De Montluc, for example, while not a recognized authority, has nevertheless done a thorough survey of international expert opinion (pp. 196*ff*) and concluded that the idea of the cease-fire "is always the same: immobilization, 'stasis,' that is to say pause and status quo." The function of the cease-fire, the thing which it is designed to do, is to solidify a situation. (See Bertrand de Montluc, "Le Cessez-le-feu," doctoral thesis, Université de Droit et d'Economie et de Sciences Sociales de Paris, 1971.) Madame Paul Bastid, having evaluated de Montluc's work, further supports this view: "a cease-fire does not imply the restoration of the *status quo ante bellum*; what it does is to paralyse military operations and leave them as they are at the time of its entry into force" (Madame Paul Bastid, "Le Cessez-le-feu," *Societé Internationale de Droit pénal militaire et de droit de la guerre [Actes du]*, 6ᵉ Congrès internationale, La Haye, 22-25 May 1973 [1974], p. 38).

14. See Security Council Resolution 56 (S/983), 19 August 1948, reprinted in Bailey, *How Wars End*, Vol. II, pp. 271-272; Ralph Bunche, in Bailey, Ibid., Vol. I, p. 132.

15. "Telegram to Bernadotte from the President of the Security Council," in Count Folke Bernadotte, *To Jerusalem* (translated by Joan Bulman) (London: Hodders and Stoughton, 1951), p. 55. Bernadotte went to great lengths to attempt to ensure this (see Bernadotte, pp. 65-67, 72, 86, and "Report of the UN Mediator on Palestine to the Security Council," UN doc. S/888 [12 July 1948]).

16. Vice Admiral C. Turner Joy, *Negotiating While Fighting: The Diary of Admiral C. Turner Joy at the Korean Armistice Conference* (Stanford: Hoover Press, 1978), pp. 32, 94, and see also 15 Jan. 1952 entry, detailing UN concern over North Korean airfields for this reason.

17. See Levie, "The Nature and Scope of the Armistice Agreement," pp. 886-888, and for more on this, see Chapter 9.

18. See Donald Wittmann, "How a War Ends: A Rational Model Approach," *Journal of Conflict Resolution* 23 (1979), p. 750.

19. C.R. Mitchell, *The Structure of International Conflict* (London: Macmillan, 1989), p. 173.

20. Janice Gross Stein, "The Termination of the October War: A Reappraisal," in Nissan Oren (ed.), *Termination of Wars* (Jerusalem: Magnes Press [The Hebrew University], 1982), p. 234.

21. William T. R. Fox, "The Causes of Peace and Conditions of War," in Fox (ed.), *How Wars End*, p. 6.

22. I. William Zartman and Maureen Berman, *The Practical Negotiator* (London: Yale University Press, 1982), p. 55.

23. See Nissan Oren, "Prudence in Victory," in Oren (ed.), *Termination of Wars*, p. 151.

24. Fox, "The Causes of Peace" in Fox (ed.), *How Wars End*, p. 9.

25. See A.H.M. Kirk-Greene, *Crisis and Conflict in Nigeria: Volume II -- A Documentary Sourcebook 1966-1970* (London: Oxford University Press, 1971), pp. 66-71 and 247-314, for documents and details on the conference.

26. To use the terms "Nigerian" and "rebel" to refer to the protagonists of this particular war would have been both incorrect and emotive. While the term "Biafran" also has emotive content, it is still preferable if only because that is how the anti-government belligerent in this case referred to itself. The terms "Federal" and "Biafran" will therefore be used.

27. Adam Curle, in an interview with the author on 19 September 1991, and see C.H. Mike Yarrow, *Quaker Experiences in International Conciliation* (London: Yale University Press, 1978), pp. 208-211, for a detailed account.*

28. Colonels Adekunle and Utuk, in Kirk-Greene, *Crisis and Conflict in Nigeria*, p. 64.

29. See Yarrow, *Quaker Experiences*, pp. 208-211, and see also "Interview with Yakubu Gowon, 24 August 1968, shown in BBC programme "Twenty-Four Hours," 26 August 1968," and reprinted as doc. 174 in Kirk-Greene, *Crisis and Conflict in Nigeria*, p. 316.

30. *The Times*, 2 March 1982.

31. *The Daily Telegraph*, 8 March 1982.

32. Interview with Hashemi Rafsanjani, 8 March 1982 (*Summary of World Broadcasts* [BBC World Service], ME/6974/A/2); Ayatollah Khomeini's speech to soldiers, 9 March 1982 (*Summary of World Broadcasts*, ME/6975/A/6); and see Rafsanjani's comments, 14 March 1982 (*Summary of World Broadcasts*, ME/6979/i).

33. *The Guardian*, 8 April 1982.

34. See *The International Herald Tribune*, 3-4 April 1982.

35. *Summary of World Broadcasts*, ME/7001/A/2 (11 April 1982).

36. Statement by the Government of Iraq, SCOR, 37th yr, doc. S/15196 (10 June 1982).

37. Efraim Karsh, "The Iran-Iraq War: A Military Analysis," *International Institute of Strategic Studies Adelphi Paper* 220 (1987), p. 25.

38. *Mid-East Economic Digest (MEED)*, 2 July 1982.

39. *Summary of World Broadcasts*, ME/7067/A/7 (2 July 1982).

40. See Abt, p. 91, for his analysis of this problem in the First World War.

41. Thomas Pickering, the US Representative to the UN, noted on 18 January that "Iraq can avoid further destruction by unconditional, immediate and complete withdrawal from Kuwait" (*International Herald Tribune*, 18 January 1991); David Hannay, the UK Representative to the UN, noted on 26 January that "our sole objective is the liberation of Kuwait" (*The Guardian*, 26 January 1991); US President George Bush outlined his conditions for cease-fire on 6 February, stating that only a "totally convincing Iraqi withdrawal" and the return of the legal government of Kuwait would result in a cease-fire (*International Herald Tribune*, 6 February 1991).

42. *The Guardian*, 19 February 1991.

43. *The Times*, 20 February 1991.

44. *The International Herald Tribune*, 20 February 1991.

45. *The Financial Times*, 19 February 1991.

46. *The Times*, 21 February 1991.

47. *The Independent*, 22 February 1991.

48. Efraim Karsh and Inari Rautsi, *Saddam Hussein: A Political Biography* (New York: Macmillan Free Press, 1991), p. 254.

49. Revolutionary Command Council announcement, *Summary of World Broadcasts*, ME/1005/A/6, 22 February 1991.

50. SCPV, doc. S/PV.2977, p. 296.

51. Ibid., resumption 3 (23 February 1991).

52. *The International Herald Tribune*, 23/24 February 1991.

53. *The International Herald Tribune*, 25 February 1991.

54. SCPV, doc. S/PV.2977, 4th resumption (25 February 1991), p. 356.

55. Karsh and Rautsi, *Saddam Hussein*, p. 262.

56. SCPV, doc. S/PV.2977, 4th resumption, pp. 356, 362.

57. Ibid., pp. 373-75, 361, 393-395.

58. On 28 January, UK Defence Minister Tom King concluded that fulfilling UN Resolution 678 required the dismantling of the Iraqi "war machine" (*The Financial Times*, 28 January 1991), and UK Foreign Minister Douglas Hurd declared on 30 January that "Kuwait has not just to be physically freed ... but it has to be freed in the sense that it's also freed from fear of attack" (*The Guardian*, 30 January 1991).

59. This depends, of course, on how one interprets the clause in Resolution 678 authorizing member states to "restore international peace and security in the area."

60. *The Times*, 27 February 1991.

61. Karsh and Rautsi, *Saddam Hussein*, p. 262.

62. Ibid., p. 263.

63. SCOR, doc. S/22273, 27 February 1991.

64. SCOR, doc. S/22274, 27 February 1991.

65. *The Times*, 28 February 1991.

66. SCOR, doc. S/22275, 28 February 1991.

67. Golda Meir, Israeli home service, 1828gmt, 10 October 1973, in *Summary of World Broadcasts*, ME 4422/A/1 (12 October 1973).

68. While recognizing the existence of the other major belligerent in the war (Syria), the power relationships in this case are most easily examined by looking solely at Israel and Egypt. This was a war taken at Sadat's initiative, and it is likely that even without Syrian assistance, Egypt would have waged war in any case. Moreover, there is little data available on either Syrian objectives or decision making processes, which makes the study of the field highly speculative. In the Egyptian case there is a significant body of information.

69. See *UN Yearbook, 1973* (New York: United Nations Office of Public Information), p. 193.

70. See Sydney D. Bailey, *Four Arab-Israeli Wars and the Peace Process* (London: Macmillan, 1990), pp. 288-89.

71. David Hirst and Irene Beeson, *Sadat* (London: Faber & Faber, 1981), pp. 151-152; and see Sydney D. Bailey, "The Prospects for Real Peace," *Survival (Strategic Forum: The Middle East Conflict, 1973)*, January-February 1974, p. 8.

72. See, for example, "Directive from President Sadat to the Commander in Chief of the Armed Forces on October 1, 1973," in Anwar el-Sadat, *In Search of Identity* (London: Collins, 1978), p. 327.

73. Sadat, *In Search of Identity*, p. 249.

74. Henry Kissinger, *Years of Upheaval* (London: Weidenfeld and Nicolson, 1982), p. 460; and see Bailey, *Four Arab-Israeli Wars*, p. 310.

75. For further details on the first day's fighting, see Bailey, *Four Arab-Israeli Wars*, p. 307, Howard M. Sachar, *A History of Israel* (Oxford: Basil Blackwell, 1977), pp. 759-760; Donald Neff, *Warriors Against Israel* (Vermont: Amana and Battleboro, 1988), p. 163, and General Saad el-Shazly, *The Crossing of Suez: The October War (1973)* (London: Third World Centre for Research and Publishing, 1980), pp. 149-156.

76. Moshe Dayan, *Story of My Life* (London: Weidenfeld and Nicolson, 1976), p. 478.

77. Major-General Avraham "Bren" Adan, in Neff, *Warriors Against Israel*, p. 163.

78. Kissinger, *Years of Upheaval*, pp. 475-476.

79. Sadat, *In Search of Identity*, p. 253.

80. Abba Eban, *An Autobiography* (London: Weidenfeld and Nicolson, 1978), p. 506.

81. Bailey, *Four Arab-Israeli Wars*, p. 309.

82. Ibid., p. 311.

83. See Kissinger, *Years of Upheaval*, p. 481.

84. Sadat, *In Search of Identity*, pp. 253, 254.

85. Kissinger, *Years of Upheaval*, p. 489.

86. Any earlier support would be seen to be ratifying territorial gains made through the use of force. Kissinger wanted a return to the *status quo* before cease-fire. (See Kissinger, *Years of Upheaval*, p. 471).

87. See Bailey, *Four Arab-Israeli Wars*, p. 315.

88. Edgar O'Ballance, *No Victor, No Vanquished: The Yom Kippur War* (London: Barrie and Jenkins, 1979), p. 174; *Time* magazine (No. 107, 12 April 1976, p. 39, claimed that bombs had been assembled and rushed to waiting aircraft, but before triggers were set, the battle turned in Israel's favour.

89. Kissinger, *Years of Upheaval*, pp. 492-93.

90. Ibid., pp. 495-96.

91. *Strategic Survey* (1973) (London: International Institute of Strategic Studies), p. 18.

92. Galia Golan, *Yom Kippur and After* (Cambridge: Cambridge University Press, 1975), p. 83.

93. *UN Yearbook 1973*, p. 193.

94. Mohamed Heikal, in Neff, *Warriors Against Israel*, p. 176.

95. See Bailey, *Four Arab-Israeli Wars*, p. 318.

96. Ibid., p. 319.

97. Kissinger, *Years of Upheaval*, p. 509.

98. Golda Meir, *My Life* (London: Weidenfeld and Nicolson, 1975), p. 368.

99. Eban, *An Autobiography*, p. 515.

100. Stein, "The Termination of the October War," in Nissan Oren (ed.), *Termination of Wars*, p. 241.

101. Eban, *An Autobiography*, p. 519.

102. Kissinger, *Years of Upheaval*, p. 539.

103. Eban, *An Autobiography*, p. 520; and see Meir, *My Life*, p. 431.

104. See O'Ballance, *No Victor, No Vanquished*, p. 159.

105. Kissinger, *Years of Upheaval*, p. 527.

106. Ibid., p. 531. Sadat made a major speech to the Egyptian people on the same day in which he said that a cease-fire would be acceptable if Israel withdrew to their *pre*-1967 boundaries, but this was hardly a credible cease-fire proposal (see Anwar Sadat, People's Assembly address, broadcast 1100 gmt, 16 October 1973, in *Summary of World Broadcasts*, ME/4427/A/8, and O'Ballance, *No Victor, No Vanquished*, p. 186).

107. O'Ballance, *No Victor, No Vanquished*, pp. 242, 253.

108. Sadat, *In Search of Identity*, p. 262.

109. Chaim Herzog, *The War of Atonement* (London: Weidenfeld and Nicolson, 1975), p. 233. Hirst and Beeson make a similar claim. (See Hirst and Beeson, *Sadat*, p. 156.)

110. See Golan, *Yom Kippur and After*, p. 112, for details.

111. Sadat, *In Search of Identity*, p. 259.

112. Ibid., pp. 262-263. Hirst and Beeson claim the decision to get in touch with Kosygin was made at 0300 hrs, 20 October (Hirst and Beeson, *Sadat*, p. 164).

113. Herzog, *The War of Atonement*, p. 234.

114. Sadat, *In Search of Identity*, p. 261.

115. Though Sadat may deny it (p. 263), Egypt was receiving Soviet aid. According to the *Strategic Survey* (1973, p. 27), Arab forces received about 15,000 tons in 934 round trips (and see Golan, *Yom Kippur and After*, p. 86). These figures do not include the sealift figures. According to Dismukes and McConnell, who base their figures on released Soviet documents, the sealift to Egypt amounted to 23,090 tons by 22 October, with an additional 24,980 tons by 9 November. They put the airlift figure for Egypt at 6,380 tons by 26 October (Bradford Dismukes and James McConnell [eds.], *Soviet Naval Diplomacy* [New York: Pergamon, 1979], pp. 208-209). American airborne aid to Israel amounted to about 23,000 tons in 566 round trips, supplemented by a further 5,500 tons in El Al aircraft (*Strategic Survey* [1973, p. 27]). Egyptian Chief of Staff General Saad el-Shazly (*The Crossing of Suez*, p. 187) puts the American sealift supply figure at 33,210 tons.

116. Herzog, *The War of Atonement*, p. 234; and see Neff, *Warriors Against Israel*, pp. 260-61.

117. Kissinger, *Years of Upheaval*, p. 553.

118. Resolution 242 had been adopted unanimously on 22 November 1967, and although expressing a range of opinions and two specific directions (to appoint a UN Special Representative to promote settlement, and to report progress), "no part of the resolution was intended to have mandatory or binding effect." States interpreted the resolution in many ways (see Bailey, *Four Arab-Israeli Wars*, pp. 283-4).

119.   Kissinger, *Years of Upheaval*, p. 554; Bailey, *Four Arab-Israeli Wars*, p. 327; see Yaacov Bar-Siman-Tov, *Israel, the Superpowers, and the War in the Middle East* (London: Praeger, 1987), pp. 219-221.

120.   See Sachar, *A History of Israel*, pp. 780-81.

121.   Meir, *My Life*, p. 369.

122.   Bailey, *Four Arab-Israeli Wars*, pp. 310,415.

123.   Eban, *An Autobiography*, p. 511.

124.   Ibid., p. 513.

125.   Dayan, *Story of My Life*, p. 543.

126.   For detailed treatment of the story of the 22 October cease-fire violations, see Herzog, *The War of Atonement*, pp. 246-48, Kissinger, *Years of Upheaval*, pp. 568-71, Sachar, *A History of Israel*, p. 781, and Milton Viorst, *Sands of Sorrow: Israel's Journey from Independence* (London: I.B. Tauris & Co, 1987), p. 166.

127.   Meir, *My Life*, pp. 370, 374.

128.   Kissinger, *Years of Upheaval*, pp. 568-69.

129.   Herzog, *The War of Atonement*, p. 246.

130.   Kissinger, *Years of Upheaval*, p. 571.

131.   O'Ballance, *No Victor, No Vanquished*, pp. 256-257, and see p. 257 for the direct apportioning of blame ("The fact that the Israelis broke the cease-fire ...").

132.   Herzog, *The War of Atonement*, p. 247.

133.   Ibid., p. 250.

134.   Adan, in Neff, *Warriors Against Israel*, p. 275.

135.   Hirst and Beeson, *Sadat*, p. 164.

136.   Kissinger, *Years of Upheaval*, p. 576.

137.   Ibid., p. 573.

138.   See Bar-Siman-Tov, *Israel, the Superpowers, and the War*, p. 228; Bailey, *Four Arab-Israeli Wars*, p. 330; Kissinger, *Years of Upheaval*, p. 573.

139.   Neff, *Warriors Against Israel*, pp. 276-77.

140.   UN Resolution 339 (S/11039), 23 October 1973.

141.   Meir, *My Life*, p. 372.

142.   Kissinger, *Years of Upheaval*, p. 576.

143.   Ibid., p. 579.

144.   UN. doc. S/PV.1749, p. 2 (24 October 1973).

145.   Hirst and Beeson, *Sadat*, p. 165.

146.   Henry Kissinger, "Excerpts from the Press Conference of Secretary of State Henry Kissinger, 25 October 1973," *Survival (Strategic Forum: The Middle East Conflict, 1973)*, January-February 1974, pp. 28-34.

147.   Kissinger, *Years of Upheaval*, p. 588.

148.   Ibid., p. 599.

149.   Ibid., p. 582. O'Ballance (*No Victor, No Vanquished*) argues that sporadic fighting continued until 27 October (p. 263).

150.   UN Resolution 340 (S/11046/Rev.1), 25 October 1973.

151.   Kissinger, *Years of Upheaval*, p. 598.

152.   Ibid., pp. 601-603.

153.   Ibid., p. 604.

154.   See pp. 24-25, this chapter.

155.   Meir, *My Life*, p. 371.

156. Kissinger, *Years of Upheaval*, p. 604.

157. Ibid., pp. 605, 608-09.

158. Stein, "The Termination of the October War", in Nissan Oren (ed.), *Termination of Wars*, p. 241.

159. Rabin, in Viorst, *Sands of Sorrow*, p. 170.

160. In fact, the apogee in its power gains had probably come earlier in the war, but Egypt had expected the gains to continue.

161. See Hedley Bull (ed.), *Intervention in World Politics* (Oxford: Oxford University Press, 1986), p. 1. For similar definitions, see Max Beloff, "Reflections on Intervention," *Journal of International Affairs* 22(2) (1968), p. 198, and Neil S. Macfarlane, "Intervention and Regional Security," *Adelphi Paper* 196 (Spring, 1985), p. 2.

162. Because the focus here is on how intervention can affect the possibilities for cease-fire negatively, intervention which goes to increase the chances of cease-fire will not be discussed (although it is acknowledged that this can happen).

163. Political recognition is generally not a factor in interstate war, although it can be occasionally (where the legitimacy of the ruling regime is in doubt). It is most often a factor in civil and internal conflicts, where at least one of the belligerents is fighting to create a politically independent area within a sovereign state, or to create a completely separate sovereign state. Chapter 6 in part concerns the overall question of how a failure by one belligerent to accept the political legitimacy of the other can make it difficult to achieve a cease-fire, but the problem of political legitimacy surfaces here also: political recognition by a third party of a belligerent whose political legitimacy is in doubt can have an effect on that belligerent's assessment of its relative bargaining power and willingness to cease fire. It is for this reason that it is considered "intervention."

164. See Raph Uwechue, *Reflections on the Nigerian Civil War* (New York: Africana Publishing Co., 1971), pp. 88,89.

165. See the Statement by the Zambian Foreign Minister issued in Lusaka, 10 May 1968 (Zambia House Press Release No. 750/1968), and reprinted as doc. 155 in Kirk-Greene, *Crisis and Conflict in Nigeria*, pp. 220-221.

166. Markpress Overseas Division Press Release, 10 May 1968, in Kirk-Greene, *Crisis and Conflict in Nigeria*, p. 41.

167. President Nyerere in *The Observer*, 28 April 1968, and reprinted as doc. 149, in Kirk-Greene, *Crisis and Conflict in Nigeria*, pp. 211-213; see also "Statement by the Government of Tanzania," 13 April 1968, and reprinted as doc. 148 in Kirk-Greene, Ibid., pp. 206-211, and also in Zdenik Cervenka, *The Nigerian War 1967-70 (History of the War and Selected Documents)* (Frankfurt am Mein: Bernard and Graefe, 1971), p. 343.

168. See John J. Stremlau, *The International Politics of the Nigerian Civil War (1967-70)* (Princeton: Princeton University Press, 1977), p. 128.

169. John de St. Jorre, *The Nigerian Civil War* (London: Hodder and Stoughton, 1972), p. 195.

170. Chukwuemeka Odemegwu Ojukwu, *Biafra: Selected Speeches of Ojukwu* (New York: Harper and Row, 1969), p. 355, and reprinted as doc. 168 in Kirk-Greene, *Crisis and Conflict in Nigeria*, pp. 247-272.

171.   Uwechue, *Reflections*, pp. 88,89; for examples of Lagos' reaction, see the unattributed editorial, "Biafra: Les Contradictions de l'Afrique," *Revue Français d'Etudes Politique Africaines* (May, 1968), pp. 12-14.

172.   Ntieyong U. Akpan, *The Struggle for Secession 1966-1970* (London: Frank Cass, 1971), pp. 110-111.

173.   Suzanne Cronje, *The World and Nigeria: A Diplomatic History of the Biafran War 1967-70* (London: Sedgewick and Jackson, 1972), pp. 195-98.

174.   Ibid.

175.   See Bernard Lewidge, *De Gaulle* (London: Weidenfeld and Nicolson, 1982), p. 340.

176.   Cervenka, *The Nigerian Civil War*, p. 115.

177.   Curle, interview. Stremlau (p. 230) argues that these military actions were completed before the arrival of French arms, but the issue here is not what Biafra was able to do with the arms *per se*, but the effect they had on Biafran morale (see Stremlau, *The International Politics of the Nigerian Civil War*).

178.   Stremlau, *The International Politics of the Nigerian Civil War*, p. 224.

179.   Cronje, *The World and Nigeria*, pp. 195-98.

180.   See Kirk-Greene, *Crisis and Conflict in Nigeria*, pp. 77-78.

181.   Janice Gross Stein, "The Termination of the October War," in Nissan Oren (ed.), *Termination of Wars*, p. 227. She argues that the theory of rationality is problematic for this reason, but as we have seen, it is only problematic if one assumes belligerents in isolation; it is their tacit agreement about the balance of power which ends the war, not their individual assessment of their own or their enemy's power.

3

The Avoidance of Weakness and the Search for Strength: *"WE will look weak"*

When people who make the more important decisions in war are trying to work out what they ought to do, and how they ought to behave, one of the things they try to *avoid* doing is appearing weak; instead, they look for strategies which convey an image of strength. It is not at all difficult to find examples of this behavior pattern, because history is littered with them. After a number of successful campaigns in the Russo-Japanese war of 1905, Japan refused to offer to end the fighting on the grounds that it would be "improper." During the World War I armistice negotiations, Marshal Foch, the allied "generalissimo," at first denied that the allies were there to make armistice proposals at all. Instead, he waited until the German representative made it clear that *he* was asking for the peace before Foch presented allied terms. The French Minister for Indochina commented in 1952 that "France does not refuse to negotiate with the Viet Minh, but we will not take the first step." Even after the devastation of Dien Bien Phu, the French declined to ask for a cease-fire for fear of appearing weak.[1] Finally, when Si Salah, FLN leader of the Algiers *wilaya* (an FLN political subdivision of Algeria), negotiated in secret with de Gaulle in June 1960, one of his primary concerns was that a cease-fire not appear as FLN capitulation. One effort made to achieve this goal, therefore, was to ensure that under any agreed cease-fire, FLN weapons would be "deposited for safekeeping" with the local gendarmerie -- specifically avoiding handing the weapons over to the French army.[2] Where does this behavior pattern come from? There are many answers to the question but in general the explanations fall into two broad groups: the psychological and the pragmatic.

To begin on the psychological side, it is clear that avoiding the image of weakness is primarily a *preventative* behavior, taken in advance in order to forestall the potential negative psychological effects (which in themselves may have practical consequences).[3] It is a problem related to what psychologist Ralph K. White terms the "virile self-image." Being in a competitive situation creates anxiety over one's status and prestige and this is "manifested by the double symptoms of assertion of strength and fear of humiliation should there be any retreat."[4] In more colloquial terms, "[b]eing the *first* to move towards peace negotiations is shunned because it is equivalent to crying 'uncle'."[5] As Adam Curle puts it, [t]ake a risk, however slight, for the sake of a peaceful settlement, and you are accused of cowardice or stupidity."[6] At base, it is about saving face. One reason the Angola-Namibia Accords came about when they did, for example, was that Castro, nearing the thirtieth anniversary of his revolution, and having just won a major military victory against UNITA at Quito Cuanavale, "was clearly in a triumphant mood and was clearly not apprehensive that the withdrawal of his troops from Angola, provided it was staged over a long enough period, would risk any loss of face."[7] The "virile self-image" is also closely connected with a rationalized pride in the qualities of one's own group:

> [i]n many situations, people are convinced by leaders (or manage to convince themselves) that their group or nation's reputation as a strong-but-wise, tough-but-peace-loving entity is at stake and that this, rather than the actual details of any current problem, is what matters.[8]

In a given war, then, strategies and actions which convey the impression of weakness are avoided because of the potential humiliation, loss of pride, and damage to self-image (the leader's or the belligerent party's) that might occur as a result.

As for the pragmatic explanations of the behavior, to convey the appearance of weakness to one's enemy is seen as dangerous because of the potential practical consequences. First, if a belligerent sees its enemy as weak, that belligerent may escalate the war, and its enemy (knowing this) therefore avoids appearing weak in the first place, *i.e.* "if we appear to be weakening, they will think we are losing, so they may escalate the war in order to win."[9] The fear is grounded in reality. In March 1985 during the Iran-Iraq war, Iran, apparently under Iraqi military pressure, suddenly made what seemed at first to be a dramatic announcement: it was dropping the demand that Saddam Hussein be removed, something Iran had been demanding from as far back as 1982. The announcement had an unintended effect: Iraq noted the change in priorities and then attempted to exploit what it must have seen as a weakness by threatening to escalate the civilian bombing unless Iran came to the negotiating table. In the words of the Iraqi ambassador to the UN, "enough is enough": the UN had failed in its efforts, and there would be no halt in civilian bombing now unless it were part of a comprehensive settlement. Moreover, before negotiations could take place, there would have to be a comprehensive cease-fire with no preconditions whatsoever.[10] Thus, one major consequence of appearing weak is that the perceived weakness may result in increased enemy demands and efforts to win the war.

The second practical consequence of appearing weak is that one's enemy may expect and therefore demand more from any future negotiations (such negotiations not necessarily being related to the war). That is, the appearance of strength is sought, and the appearance of weakness avoided, specifically to affect one's future bargaining position. There is a belief that being seen as weak leads the enemy to expect more than it is entitled to, or at least more than if one is seen as strong; the enemy will expect less from a strong opponent in negotiations. During the Soviet intervention in Afghanistan, for example, Pakistan's Yaqub Khan resisted a second draft of a cease-fire agreement, arguing that Pakistan could not be seen to be "knuckling under to Soviet pressure."[11] During the Algerian War of Independence, it was General Charles de Gaulle's belief that a military solution to the Algerian problem was unlikely, and that Algerian independence should be the ultimate French aim. In order to achieve that end, however, de Gaulle makes it very clear in his memoirs that it would be necessary for France to negotiate from a position of strength: it had to be "France, eternal France, who alone, from the height of her power, in the name of her principles and in accordance with her interests, granted [independence] to the Algerians."[12] For de Gaulle, there could be no other way. To grant either the right of self-determination or independence to Algeria before France was in complete control and before France could only be seen as magnanimous by allowing Algerian independence, was inconceivable. As long as France looked weak in any way, shape or form, she would be determined to keep Algeria under her control. It was a way of ensuring that France's negotiating position would be a strong one. With France in control, the FLN would be unable to demand more than France was willing to offer.

Finally, belligerents consider the potential effect that looking weak may have on parties not directly involved in the war. In a war where one belligerent appears weak, a potential enemy uninvolved in the war may take note of that weak behavior. Then, in a future (and as yet only possible) conflict with the apparently weak-willed belligerent, the potential enemy may expect a great deal more than it would have had the weak-seeming belligerent behaved strongly in the first place. That is, a belligerent who courts with strategies which convey an impression of weakness gains a reputation as being a weak bargainer, and this affects the future strategies and expectations of all its current and potential opponents.

In all these cases, the belief is that any strategy or action which conveys the impression of weakness is to be avoided because that perceived weakness will be exploited by somebody at some time. As the examples have shown, there is nothing to say that this belief should in any way be considered an unreasonable one. One may argue, as Curle does, that "whatever the circumstances and however discouraging the conventional military wisdom, it is almost always sensible, and not a sign of weakness, to accept a proposal to negotiate ... "[13] but it nevertheless remains the case that it is only natural to avoid an action which it is believed could result in harm, and the potential consequences of looking weak are simply seen as too damaging; for a belligerent decision-maker, an action which might convey weakness is to be avoided at all costs.

At the beginning of the Nigerian Civil War, for example, initial mediation feelers were refused. According to Curle, Gowon "was particularly afraid that the rebels, as he called the Biafrans, might get the impression that he was losing his nerve and looking for some escape route from the conflict."[14] As far as Uwechue was concerned, the key to a cease-fire in the war rested primarily on finding a formula which was both practical and which saved the face of both parties.[15] In one of his transcripted conversations with belligerent leaders, Curle attempted to point out that the leader's enemy ("General Y") did not believe in that leader's sincerity when it came to wanting peace. He then suggested that the leader do something to demonstrate his sincerity. When asked to be more specific, Curle recommended doing "something you don't want to do." The idea would be to show that he was "sufficiently sincere in [his] peaceful protestation to do something that in some way puts [him] at a disadvantage." The leader responded very negatively, pointing out that General Y's response to that kind of action "would be that I was either crazy or scared stiff and pleading for peace at any price. And so would mine be if he committed an equal absurdity."[16]

The Iran-Iraq war, too, provides a general illustration. Saddam Hussein freely admitted on 29 October 1980 that he would not be seen to be negotiating from a position of weakness, and when UN Secretary-General Perez de Cuellar managed to secure an agreement from Iran and Iraq in June 1984 to refrain from attacking civilian zones, Iran went to great lengths to ensure that everyone understood that it was not considering a wider peace. Rafsanjani said the agreement had "nothing to do with the war in general. There will be no negotiations on the war." The government generally was "extremely sensitive" to suggestions that the agreement constituted a first move to end the war, and the Iranian news agency reported on 2 July 1984 that the agreement "was *misrepresented* by the Western press as a gesture of conciliation by Iran and *even* as a kind of retreat from war" (emphasis added).[17]

The avoidance of the appearance of weakness, and the complementary search for the appearance of strength, are belligerent behavior patterns which both have psychological and practical explanations. The explanations themselves are in turn founded on natural and perhaps unavoidable beliefs about the avoidance of harm or embarrassment, and the desirability of presenting a good image, and achieving security. It should perhaps be accepted, therefore, that the avoidance of the appearance of weakness is based on a normal -- and even sensible -- belligerent belief structure which may not only be beyond the control of third parties, but may be beyond the control of the belligerents themselves. Admittedly, these behavior patterns do not occur in isolation. As with any behavior, outside agents may impinge on the process, but there is nevertheless a marked tendency for belligerents to behave in such a way as to avoid appearing weak.

Given that this is the case, however, it poses particular problems for anyone interested in stopping a war. The problems arise because strategies chosen in order to avoid the appearance of weakness and cultivate the appearance of strength are often incompatible with the strategies necessary to reach the point of cease-fire. It is a case of having two highly desirable goals, but where the attainment of one may preclude the attainment of the other.[18] While avoiding looking weak and wanting and end to the fighting are often desired simultaneously,[19] strategies needed to achieve one may be incompatible with, or may exclude, strategies needed to achieve the other. Often, it seems that the more desirable goal is the avoidance of appearing weak, and cease-fire is therefore precluded.

First, even before belligerents have decided that the time has come to end the war, strategies used to avoid the appearance of weakness can have an affect on a belligerent's ability to end the war when it wishes to. Because one way to avoid looking weak is to cultivate the appearance of strength, belligerents have a tendency to use strong and inflexible language in any communication which its opponent may receive. The trouble with this, however, is not just the effect this may have on the opponent, but the effect it may have on other recipients of the communication. The belligerent which believes it must appear strong, and therefore makes strong statements (usually in the form of "We will never ... " or "We will always ... "), may affect the receiver in ways the originator may not have intended, and may give the impression that it is more intransigent and more inflexible than it actually is. Expectations about what a country's leadership is and is not prepared to do "ever" are taken to heart, to the point that when the time does eventually come to settle, and even if the originally stated goals have not been reached, a belligerent may be unable to cease-fire because of the effect that offering to cease-fire could have on its own army, inner circle or domestic population, any of whom could now revolt in some manner. That is, strong statements may lead, one way or another, to at least one form of the political and cognitive dissonance problem (the subject of the next chapter). Domestic populations may come to expect more than was intended, or leaders themselves may find that they cannot go back on their words for the exact reason they uttered them in the first place: they will appear weak. It is a cruel circle.

Moving on to the case where a belligerent believes the time has come to settle, and assuming that the decision can be made without fear of internal revolt of some kind, the belligerent is still faced with a dilemma. Where a belligerent is winning, for example, and believes the time has come to cease fire, it may avoid offering (or even accepting an offer of) a cease-fire if it believes that the action will be seen as weakness. Again, this may be because its opponent may demand more at the negotiating table, it could affect the behavior of third parties, or -- if it is not seen as winning by a decisive margin -- its opponent could see the offer (or acceptance of an offer) of cease-fire as tangible evidence of a loss of confidence in the enemy's ability to win, and could therefore result in the losing side becoming even more determined to continue the struggle. (The dilemma disappears where the belligerent is seen to be winning by a decisive margin -- the offer can *usually* be made in safety.)

Taken from the other point of view, where a belligerent is losing and believes the time has come to settle, the outcome is no more hopeful. When losing, to offer a cease-fire or accept an offer of cease-fire (and thereby admit to weakness) could result in excessively harsh peace terms, could affect future negotiations with as yet unknown parties, or could result in an escalation of the war. Even where the war is stalemated, it is seen as unsafe and dangerous to offer or receive the offer of a cease-fire. Again, the act is perceived as weakness, and again the potential consequences (escalation, loss of bargaining power) are unacceptable. Also, it is worth remembering that whether any of these undesirable results would actually occur is beside the point; the belligerents *believe* they will (or could) be the result, and these beliefs affect the decision of whether or not to cease fire.

The dilemma is apparent. If a belligerent is thinking about ceasing fire, it may want to offer to cease fire, or to accept an offer of cease-fire from the other side. Either action, however, might convey the impression of weakness, and the weakness might be exploited. If on the other hand it takes no action, neither offering to cease fire nor accepting an offer, it may lose the war, may win it but at an unacceptable cost, or may find itself in a seemingly endless stalemate with ever-increasing costs. This has been called the "bargainer's dilemma": how to offer a concession (in this case a cease-fire) while "retaining the appearance of being unyielding, so as not to weaken one's bargaining position."[20] It is important to realize how complex this dilemma gets, however, as *both* belligerents are faced with the same problem.

Strategies for Coping with the Dilemma

Faced with this kind of quandary, belligerents have developed strategies in order to manage it effectively. Some are more productive than others, some are counterproductive, but all attempt to deal with the reality facing belligerents at war: that eventually the war must end, and it is desirable for it to end on the most favorable terms possible.

Perhaps surprisingly, the least effective tactic would appear to be the most common one: attempting to force a cease-fire through an endless barrage of threats of or actual coercion and/or escalation. (These actions are taken in addition to whatever military action is going on.) In what might be considered the "reflex" reaction to the dilemma of being willing to consider cease-fire but not wanting to appear weak in achieving it, belligerents frequently resort to the use of threats and coercive strategies. This is particularly ironic, because doing so may be entirely counterproductive. Belligerents seem to forget that they are not the only ones wishing to avoid the appearance of weakness; their opponents want to avoid it as well.[21] It would seem inevitable that where coercive strategies succeed, they will almost always result in the victim of coercion appearing to lack strength of will,[22] and therein lies the irony: one side wants to settle, but does not want to appear weak, and therefore resorts to threats and coercive strategies to achieve a cease-fire; its enemy also wants to settle, but does not want to appear weak, and must therefore react negatively to the threats and coercive strategies. As Mitchell notes, the trouble with coercion is that "it tends to bring forth a response of counter-coercion plus increased hostility, to be met in turn by increased coercion and further hostility."[23] One of the reasons for this must be belligerents' mutual desire to avoid the appearance of weakness.

Where the situation is desperate enough, belligerents may sometimes go ahead and take the risk of offering a cease-fire, usually hoping (but not expecting[24]) that the offer will be accepted and that they will not look weak by having made it. One way belligerents attempt to do this is by sending ambiguous messages in the hope that genuine intentions will be discerned by the receiver. The trick -- and it is a difficult one -- is to make messages ambiguous enough such that they can be denied if the need arises, but clear enough that they can be interpreted correctly by the receiver. A successful result means that channels of communication remain open, and moves toward negotiated settlement can be made without the fear of looking weak. An unsuccessful result, however, means that the message may not be received, may be misunderstood, or the receiver may attempt to take advantage by ignoring initial messages in the hope that clearer messages may be sent which can not later be denied.[25]

It is especially interesting to note how belligerents react if an offer to cease fire is refused, or circumstances arise which suddenly make the proposor want to withdraw the offer. If an offer is made and refused, or made and then seen as unnecessarily made, the interest of avoiding the appearance of weakness once again takes precedence, and belligerents immediately go out of their way to once again appear strong -- it is an attempt to restore "lost face."[26]

In September 1968, during the civil war in Nigeria, Biafra was in a militarily precarious position, and on the verge of defeat. Sylvanus Cookie, Commissioner of Commerce and Industry and a trusted lieutenant of Ojukwu, expressed interest in a cease-fire, and the Quaker mission attempted to arrange one. Cookie had been authorized by Ojukwu (who was busy conducting a major battle) to speak for him. Despite a number of difficulties (such as travel impeded by roadblocks and the military situation), Quaker mediator Walter Martin eventually managed to convey the information to Gowon, who was "very pleased." A meeting was convened to decide how best to meet the Biafran leadership: "[t]he meeting had hardly started when one of [Gowon's] aides came in with a transcript of an intercepted radio announcement by Ojukwu. Very tough ... saying that they would never give up, that Biafra would remain independent to the end;" the infusion of French arms had bolstered morale and gave Biafra the means to continue the struggle. The most interesting point about this move for our purposes, however, is the Biafran reversal of their offer of cease-fire: "They were very sorry that they might have spoiled the show by appearing to be weak and frightened and ready to yield -- which they were."[27] In this case, then, an offer of cease-fire had been made, but when it became evident that it had been unnecessary, there was a great deal of concern that the offer would have conveyed the appearance of weakness, and the struggle was entered into with even more vigor than had previously been the case. (Part of the reason this had to happen was that the initial message had not been ambiguous enough and could not be denied.)

Where tactics such as coercion, or the sending of ambiguous messages fail or backfire, other tactics can be more successful. These latter tactics tend to rely on belligerents' mutual acceptance of the idea that neither party should be made to appear weak by offering or accepting the offer of a cease-fire. Belligerents may phrase the *offer* of a cease-fire as a *response*.[28] In the Korean War, General Matthew Ridgeway, Commander in Chief of United Nations Command,[29] sent a message to his North Korean counterpart (in June 1951) in which what was really an offer of peace came across as a response to an offer: "I am informed that you may wish to discuss an armistice ... " Ho Chi Minh's offer to the French in Vietnam in November 1953 was similarly phrased: " ... if the French Government has drawn a lesson from the war they have been waging these last years and want to negotiate an armistice in Vietnam ... the people and Government of the DRV are ready to meet this desire."[30]

Belligerents (or third parties) may also attempt to deal with concerns about not appearing weak by means of carefully worded peace or cease-fire proposals. When these fail, it is usually not because the proposals themselves are bad ones, but because avoiding looking weak is never the only goal belligerents have. During the Iran-Iraq war, a non-aligned movement proposal for cease-fire came in early November 1980, during the first months of the war. The proposal envisioned a return to the 1975 border treaty to share the Shatt waterway and provided that Iraq not be made to "rescind its unilateral abrogation of the treaty which started the war ... nor would Iran be obliged to recognize the Iraqi action."[31] In effect it was a way for Iraq to admit, at least tacitly, that it had made a mistake in invading and back out without looking weak by doing so. It would be a return to the *status quo ante bellum* -- the situation as it was prior to the war -- and it would be as if nothing had happened. Unfortunately, returning to the *status quo* accomplished nothing. After all, if the *status quo* had been so acceptable to Iraq, it would not have gone to war in the first place. For Iraq, there could be no return to the *status quo*; having chosen war as a means to achieve its ends, at least some of those ends would have to be attained before the war could end. Thus, as could be expected, the plan was rejected. In this case, then, while the proposal may have allowed Iraq to escape without losing face and without appearing weak, the fact that Iraq had more than this one interest ensured the rejection of the proposal. Avoiding the appearance of weakness is always a belligerent interest, but it is not the only interest, and cease-fire proposals need to take account of all of them (or as many as possible) if they are to have any chance of success. It is necessary to deal with belligerent perceptions of weakness and strength, but it is not sufficient.

The Gulf War of 1991

One of the main difficulties in the Gulf War was that both Saddam Hussein and George Bush were avoiding the appearance of weakness and seeking the appearance of strength. Because they were both doing this, a cease-fire was a highly unlikely outcome. Where both belligerents are trying to appear strong, neither can take any action -- such as offering cease-fire -- which might convey weakness.

From Saddam Hussein's point of view, it is not unreasonable to suggest that he wanted out of Kuwait after 17 January (the beginning of coalition military action) and possibly even earlier. He had multiple war aims,[32] it is true, but it is reasonable to assert that leaving Kuwait, preferably having achieved as much as he could given the unexpected circumstances in which he found himself, was a high priority. That is, having misjudged the international reaction to his invasion,[33] and experiencing the result, leaving Kuwait after the achievement of as many goals as possible was probably highly desirable. Just when the decision to get out of Kuwait would be taken was unclear, but whenever it was taken, a necessary condition would have to be met: there could be no withdrawal if that action made Hussein appear weak. Announcing his intention to withdraw, for example, would have conveyed this impression, especially if such an announcement followed threats and ultimatums. Even if Hussein could have either won or stalemated the war (highly unlikely), or if Saddam could have achieved some of his war objectives (more likely), and if he then wanted to leave Kuwait, it is likely that he still would not have done so if this action would have been seen as weakness. It not unreasonable to suggest, therefore, that at least one of the reasons he took so long to comply with Security Council resolutions was that he believed doing so would have made him appear weak.

Saddam Hussein is a pragmatist whose prime concern is remaining in power.[34] Consequently, any action which he believed would place his position in jeopardy could not be considered. For Saddam, withdrawing from Kuwait under allied pressure, and more particularly under American threats and ultimatums, was out of the question.[35] In a letter read on Baghdad radio, only hours after the beginning of the war, Saddam Hussein castigated Bush for his "arrogant style," "hysterical statements threatening terrible consequences," and accused him of not understanding Iraq or its people. He also made it very clear that threats were not the way to approach this matter:

> [w]hen we call for peace, we abide by what God says, not out of fear ... You who have forgotten God imagine that threats will make our people kneel before you ... you are seemingly enjoying the threats and intimidation, as you have shown no desire to opt for dialogue and prudence that may lead to peace."[36]

Why threats were not the answer is made clear by Hussein's response to Gorbachov's 18 January plea to commit to a withdrawal: "we should not be asked to make statements that would make the United States appear to be shaking our steadfast will."[37] Saddam Hussein would not withdraw and would not respond to threats if doing so made him appear weak.

Saddam's response to American attempts to appear strong also make this clear. By the time of the 23 February closed Security Council meeting (five days before the end of the war), Hussein had been under massive military pressures to withdraw,[38] and the session opened with an announcement by the Soviet representative that Saddam Hussein was ready to withdraw unconditionally from Kuwait. The US representative, Thomas Pickering, laid down American conditions, insisting on full compliance with all Security Council resolutions. A ground war would not be initiated if Iraq began withdrawal by noon on 23 February. Conditions were laid out, including a one week time limit on withdrawal, and 48 hours to get out of Kuwait city and release prisoners of war.[39] President Bush had already outlined the ultimatum publicly,[40] but Saddam Hussein simply could not submit to the American ultimatum; it would be "tantamount to signing his own death warrant."[41] Thus, in a Radio Baghdad broadcast the next day, he called the ultimatum "shameful."[42] The ground war had not yet begun, and however desperate the military situation, still better in Hussein's view to continue to appear strong to his people. Bush's ultimatum could in no way allow Saddam to save face; any withdrawal now would look like a retreat under threat. (One wonders what would have happened had the deadline been kept secret, and communicated only from Bush to Hussein.) Moreover, the ultimatum was physically impossible to implement unless Hussein was willing to leave behind masses of military equipment, and at this point he was simply unwilling to do this. The deadline passed, and the ground war began eight hours later, at 0400 Baghdad time on 24 February.

It is worth pointing out that had military force been accompanied by gestures and words which would have allowed Saddam to save face and leave Kuwait with what he considered to be "honor," the task of getting Iraq out of Kuwait might have been that much easier, and could have been accomplished that much more quickly. At least one obstacle would have been removed -- Saddam Hussein would not look weak by leaving Kuwait. Of course, that the United States would have considered such a strategy is highly unlikely. George Bush, it seemed, was intent on Saddam's humiliation.[43] He, like Saddam, was intent on appearing strong, and avoiding the appearance of weakness, and there came a point in the war, therefore, after which no attempt would again be made to allow him to save face.[44] To have employed a face-saving strategy may not even have been the "just" thing -- some may have seen it as a reward for aggression. This is arguable, but will not be debated here. The point is simply that Saddam's concern with looking weak was an obstacle to cease-fire, and allowing him to save face could have removed that obstacle.

In the end, Saddam Hussein probably saw himself in a Catch-22 situation from which only the allied forces could help him escape. He wanted to get out of Kuwait, perhaps not only because he recognized that he would be unable to accomplish his goals, and that he might be faced with a long and devastating war, but because he risked losing power in Iraq. Yet he could not leave if this meant losing face and looking weak (which it undoubtedly would were he to submit to allied pressure to withdraw); this, too, would have threatened his domestic position. Thus, either course appeared to spell out his political, if not physical, demise. Without coalition acquiescence to a face-saving formula which would allow a withdrawal, he had only one choice open to him: to stay and fight as long as it took to prove Iraqi "steadfastness," and then to get out quickly, portraying the withdrawal as a victory of Iraqi will and a magnanimous decision. Such was the decision he took, and it explains why events happened the way they did during the war. Saddam Hussein did not opt for attempting a military victory in the war, he opted for conveying the appearance of strength.

The Bush ultimatum of 23 February was an attempt to appear strong, but the allies, like Saddam Hussein, were also extremely concerned about not appearing weak. The 31 January joint Soviet-American cease-fire offer is of interest, for example, as it would appear that the US had taken a number of deliberate steps to prevent the offer from appearing as allied weakness. The statement was not issued by either Bush or Gorbachov, but issued jointly by US Secretary of State James Baker and Soviet Foreign Minister Aleksandr Bessmertnykh. It was thus relatively easy to then claim (as the US did) that President Bush had not in fact seen the statement before its release, that White House was in "disarray," and that is was close to repudiating the offer.[45]

If this portrayal was deliberate -- and if the offer was genuine -- the hope would be that coalition forces could communicate to Hussein what it would take to cease-fire, while at the same time avoiding looking weak by making the offer a kind of unauthorized surprise. Hussein would see through the ruse, realize the statement was an official position and a genuine offer, and take the way out. In fact, and even if the moves to avoid appearing weak had not been deliberate, the offer could have been -- and perhaps was -- interpreted as Saddam Hussein as evidence of weakness. First, there had been the CNN interview with Saddam Hussein the day before, in which Hussein declared his continuing resolve and in which he estimated his doubts about winning at "not one in a million."[46] Second, the offer came just after the first series of Iraqi ground attacks, the most serious of which occurred in the Saudi town of Khafji, where allied troops suffered their first casualties (including 12 American marines).[47] Finally, the coalition position with regard to a cease-fire -- that there simply would not be one -- had been made abundantly clear; the offer was a clear reversal of that position. What all this adds up to is that the offer to cease fire if Iraq made "an unequivocal commitment to withdraw from Kuwait"[48] would likely be seen by Hussein as a lack of commitment to continue the war. It would be seen as evidence of allied weakness.

The allied concern for avoiding the appearance of weakness is also evidenced in their dealings with the Security Council. Amid increasing calls for a Security Council meeting to declare a cease-fire early in the conflict -- coming from Iran, Morocco, Libya, Mauritania, Tunisia, Algeria and India and others -- the allies demanded a statement of Iraq's intention to withdraw. At this point, however, both the meeting and a cease-fire were seen as inappropriate. A US official at the UN noted that such a meeting "would not be useful or productive and could be open to misinterpretation by Saddam."[49] It was clear that the allies saw both the possibility of a cease-fire and a Security Council meeting as unacceptable because of the message they could send to Baghdad: the allies are not committed, are not serious, and are not willing to continue the fight. As in so many other wars, the appearance of strength was of paramount importance. As it turned out, international pressure would eventually result in a Council session (on 14 February), but it is clear that the allies undertook this unwillingly; the session was a closed one to avoid any possible negative public reaction.

Commentary at that closed session (on 14 February) is also instructive. The Kuwaiti representative noted that

> there should be no cessation, no cease-fire whatsoever, before the complete liberation of Kuwait and the restoration of its legitimate government, because such a move would be counter-productive, a negative message from the Security Council to the Iraqi leadership.

The Belgian representative concurred, arguing that

> a cessation of military operations would be interpreted by the government of Iraq as a sign of weakness on the part of the international community and that government would use it to bolster new arguments to justify its contempt for the Council's resolutions and take it as evidence of an illusory tactical advantage in the field. It is therefore likely that any kind of truce would have an effect contrary to the one hoped for and that it would ultimately serve to prolong hostilities rather than to cut them short. Only a new element would allow the Council usefully the interruption of hostilities. We all know what that element should be: Iraq's unequivocal commitment to withdraw from Kuwait ... [50]

It is probably safe to assume that both these nations were stating the accepted allied line; outside the session, and as far as the George Bush was concerned, "The goals have been set. I'm not going to give."[51] A willingness to cease-fire was nowhere indicated.

The Gulf War is a prominent example of what can happen when both belligerents are intent on avoiding weakness and seeking strength. Offers of cease-fire will be rare, and where they occur, they may be heavily disguised by rhetoric and, if mis-timed, may backfire. Actions which could lead to settlement are not taken if they make one belligerent appear weak or, if they are taken, they are taken unwillingly. Attempts at appeasement made by one belligerent (in this case made by Iraq under military pressure) may be refused on the basis that they make the accepter appear weak (although there may be other reasons as well), and the jilted proposer, now believing he has been humiliated or looks weak, responds to the refusal with more threats and more intransigent rhetoric in order to regain lost ground and appear strong. The circle continues, and cease-fire will likely be out of the question until one of the belligerents achieves a complete military victory.

From this example, and from others presented, it is clear that the belligerent tendency to deliberately to avoid taking actions which might convey the appearance of weakness, and instead opt for those actions which convey strength, poses particular problems for stopping wars. Many common strategies used to achieve cease-fire are singularly incompatible with those used to avoid looking weak, and avoiding the appearance of weakness generally assumes the higher priority in belligerent decision-making processes. Belligerents (not to mention intervening third parties) therefore need to seek alternate strategies which will satisfy both interests simultaneously.

Notes

1. Paul Pillar, *Negotiating Peace: War Termination as a Bargaining Process* (New Jersey: Princeton University Press, 1983), pp. 66, 67, 88.

2. Alistair Horne, *A Savage War of Peace*, (London: Macmillan, 1977) p. 390; John Talbott, *The War Without a Name: France in Algeria, 1954-62* (New York: Alfred A. Knopf, 1980), p. 194. It has been argued that this procedure would nevertheless have looked like surrender (Talbott, p. 193), but this is not the point: it is the subjective view of the belligerent which counts in this case. If Si Salah saw this as a way of avoiding appearing weak, then a cease-fire could have been concluded.

3. See Bert R. Brown, "Face-Saving and Face-Restoration in Negotiation," in Daniel Druckman (ed.), *Negotiations: Social-Psychological Perspectives* (London: Sage, 1977), pp. 275-99. The article is also an excellent resource for other relevant psychological literature.

4. Ralph K. White, in Bryant Wedge, "The Individual, the Group and War," in John Burton, *Conflict: Readings in Management and Resolution* (London: Macmillan, 1990), p. 95, and see Brown, "Face Saving" in Druckman (ed.), *Negotiations*, p. 276.

5. Pillar, *Negotiating Peace*, p. 7.

6. Adam Curle, *Tools for Transformation: A Personal Study* (Stroud: Hawthorne, 1990), p. 69.

7. G.R. Berridge, "Diplomacy and the Angola/Namibia Accords," *International Affairs* 65(3) (1989), p. 465.

8. C.R. Mitchell, *The Structure of International Conflict* (London: Macmillan, 1981), p. 101.

9. Fred Charles Iklé, *Every War Must End* (London: Columbia University Press, 1971), p. 85; see also Robert Jervis, *The Logic of Images in International Relations* (New York: Columbia University Press, 1989), p. 123.

10. *The Times*, 23 March 1985; *The Daily Telegraph*, 29 and 30 March 1985.

11. Selig S. Harrison, "Inside the Afghan Talks," *Foreign Policy* 72 (Fall, 1988), p. 43.

12. General Charles de Gaulle, *Memoirs of Hope* (translated by Terence Kilmartin) (London: Weidenfeld and Nicolson, 1971), pp. 45,46; and see Jean Lacouture, *De Gaulle: the Ruler* (translated by Alan Sheridan) (London: Harvill, 1991), pp. 159, 185, 240, and 330.

13. Adam Curle, *In the Middle: Non-Official Mediation in Violent Situations*, Bradford Peace Studies Paper (New Series No. 1), 1986, p. 7.

14. Curle, *Tools*, p. 41.

15. Raph Uwechue, "Des Concessions Réciproque pour une Paix Juste et Durable," *Revue Français d'Etudes Politique Africaines* 49 (January 1970), p. 24.

16. Curle, *Tools*, pp. 68-69.

17. *The Financial Times*, 29 October 1980; *Summary of World Broadcasts*, ME/7668/A/2 (11 June 1984); *Daily Telegraph*, 13 June 1984; *The Guardian*, 30 June 1984; *Summary of World Broadcasts*, ME/7686/A/2 (2 July 1984).

18. Psychologists often refer to this as an "approach-approach" dilemma.

19. Berenice A. Carroll, "How Wars End: An Analysis of Some Current Hypotheses," *Journal of Peace Research* 6(4) (1969), p. 309.

20. J. Podell and W. Knapp, quoted in Brown, "Face Saving," in Druckman (ed.), *Negotiations*, p. 277.

21. Mitchell, *The Structure of International Conflict*, p. 230.

22. See James T. Tedeschi and Thomas V. Bonoma, "Measures of Last Resort: Coercion and Aggression in Bargaining," in Druckman (ed.), *Negotiations*, pp. 235, 237.

23. Mitchell, *The Structure of International Conflict*, p. 63.

24. Belligerents, too, can sometimes understand that if their enemy is winning, he may have little incentive to stop fighting.

25. Jervis, *Logic*, pp. 125, 130, 132.

26. For a general discussion on restoration of "lost face," see Brown, "Face Saving" in Druckman (ed.), *Negotiations*, pp. 275-99.

27. Curle, interview.

28. Pillar, *Negotiating Peace*, p. 78.

29. from 11 April 1951 to 28 April 1952.

30. Pillar, *Negotiating Peace*, p. 78.

31. *The Sunday Times*, 16 November 1980.

32. These included the annexation of the Bubiyan and Warba islands and other territories along the Iraq/Kuwait border, and the installation of an acceptable puppet regime in Kuwait – thereby securing Iraq's economic and strategic future. See Efraim Karsh and Inari Rautsi, *Saddam Hussein: A Political Biography* (New York: Macmillan Free Press, 1991), pp. 194-216 *passim*, 213, 218*ff*, and Bob Woodward, *The Commanders* (New York: Simon and Schuster, 1991), p. 252.

33. Apart from Hussein's fundamental misperception of the West, evidence suggests that Iraq was inadvertently (some argue deliberately) misled as to what reaction would be forthcoming from the United States if he invaded Kuwait. For a variety of evidence which could be used to support either view, see Karsh and Rautsi, *Saddam Hussein*, pp. 215-216, Woodward, *The Commanders*, pp. 212 and 215*ff*, especially p. 217 and 221, and "Speech by Philip Agee" (a former CIA operative) available on CRTNET, or through Mike Cole, University of California, San Diego.

34. See, for example, Karsh and Rautsi, *Saddam Hussein*, p. 2, and Woodward, *The Commanders*, p. 257.

35. See Karsh and Rautsi, *Saddam Hussein*, p. 221.

36. *Summary of World Broadcasts*, ME/0973/A/1, 0726 gmt, 17 January 1991.

37. *Summary of World Broadcasts*, ME/0977/A/3 (21 January 1991).

38. See Karsh and Rautsi, p. 254.

39. UN doc. S/PV.2977, resumption 3 (23 February 1991).

40. *The Times, The Independent*, 23 February 1991.

41. Karsh and Rautsi, *Saddam Hussein*, p. 261.

42. *International Herald Tribune*, 23/24 February 1991.

43. For more on this point specifically, see Steven Greffenius and Jungil Gill, "Pure Coercion vs. Carrot-and-Stick Offers in Crisis Bargaining," *Journal of Peace Research* 29(1) (1992), p. 49.

44. In fact, Bush personally was against allowing Hussein to save face as early as 30 November 1990. Though Bush did not elaborate on the comment, he said during the Gulf crisis that there would be "an enormous price to pay if we try to help him save face" (Woodward, *The Commanders*, p. 338).

45. *The Daily Telegraph, The Independent*, 31 January 1991, 1 February 1991.

46. Reported in SCOR, 46th yr., doc. S/22188 (1 February 1991); see also *Daily Telegraph*, 29 January 1991.

47. *The Times, The Financial Times*, 31 January 1991.

48. *The Daily Telegraph*, 31 January 1991.

49. Ibid., 25 January 1991.

50. UN doc. S/PV.2977, pp. 22, 107.

51. *The Times*, 20 February 1991.

4

Political and Cognitive Dissonance:
"WE'd never get away with it"

Defining the Trap

For a number of reasons, belligerent leaders in wartime will often make forceful, uncompromising, and truculent public statements. There is, first, the desire to avoid looking weak and to seek the appearance of strength, a behavior which we have already discussed. Second, there is the desire to heighten civilian and military morale, an integral part of war-fighting strategy (particularly where the enemy is more powerful militarily). Third, the belligerent leadership may have a strong expectations of victory (another obstacle which we have dealt with), and this expectation can lead naturally to statements which vocalize the expectation. Fourth, the belligerent leadership may have a "fight to the finish" mentality -- sometimes a result of a lack of criticism in the belligerents inner circle[1] -- which almost automatically leads to a hard-line opening position. Finally, where extreme distrust exists between belligerents (sometimes caused by misinterpretation of messages), there may be a desire to "play it safe;" the leadership starts with a "safe" uncompromising position from which they believe they can climb down in the event the opposition is less intransigent than appears to be the case at the outset. For any or all of these reasons, then, belligerents will make strong and hard-line public statements during wartime.

Being public statements, they also have multiple audiences, and the words used convey different messages to each of those audiences. To the enemy and potential enemies, the message is "Don't play games with us; see how strong and determined we are;" to allies, it is "We are worth being allied to; we would never let you down;" to the domestic population and to its own army, it is "Your leadership is fighting for you. See what a good government we are; we won't fail you."

That the making of strong public statements occurs is explicable, and not necessarily a problem in itself. Where this becomes a problem is when initial war aims change or the war begins to go badly for some reason, and the belligerent leadership needs to back away from the stated opening position. As the war progresses, the original statement -- which is almost always positional in character *e.g.* "We will never do X" or "We will always do Y"[2] -- often becomes an end unto itself, and the position will have to be defended even long after its author has realized that the position is untenable, and that it no longer serves that belligerent's interests. Backing away from that position (and certainly reversing it) will be precluded even where the military situation makes this the rational course. The making of strong and aggressive public statements, no matter why they are made, leads directly to a psychological and political trap with few means of escape.

The psychological trap is commonly associated with the theory of *cognitive dissonance*: the attempt to strive for consistency in one's cognitive processes leads to "irrational" behavior. In this case, it leads to an individual defending a position stated publicly long after that position has ceased to be supportable. The *individual's* prestige, or ego, or "face," becomes directly identified with the stated position, and the more often it is stated, and the greater the perceived audience, the more difficult the individual may find it to back away from that position. People seek justification for their behavior, and evidence which contradicts their justification therefore tends to be ignored.[3] Moreover, and perhaps even more worrying, is the tendency to ignore evidence which contradicts early suppositions and assumptions about the enemy. Belligerents will have a certain views of each other, and usually the image is biased and wholly negative. That negativity is then reflected in the public statements. As psychologists phrase it, "the outgroup that is seen as threatening some goal or value of the reference group becomes perceived as personifying a clever and amoral force bent on damaging one's own group as a principled purpose." This is the so-called "enemy image," and as the conflict wears on, the image is reinforced by continued public statements and forceful propaganda such that there will be a "striking tendency to perceive only those items which would sustain the enemy image and be blind to evidence that would contradict such views."[4] An unwillingness (one might even say inability) to back down from an initial position is thus at its base a psychological phenomenon, and backing away therefore has certain psychological consequences: the leader who retreats from a publicly-stated position risks losing face, risks appearing weak, risks his/her sense of personal prestige, ego, and pride. Moreover, leaders may not even realize that backing down is an option; they may become victims of their own propaganda. It is apparent that cognitive dissonance exists, but without access to the workings of the mind of a wartime leader, actual evidence for it can *usually* only be inferred. It is thus that the remainder of this discussion will focus primarily on the political trap created by the making of uncompromising public statements.

Backing away from a publicly defended position can eventually have serious political consequences. Apart from the ever present fact that reneging on a commitment damages reputations,[5] a leader or government also risks being driven from power by a domestic population which has come to expect the position to be defended at any cost. Even worse, they may risk being driven from power by their own military forces, or even a powerful political "inner circle" who have also come to expect the position to be defended. That is, the public statements, if repeated often enough, lead the domestic population and the belligerent's own military to expect certain things from their leaders (usually including a complete military victory), and if those things then fail to materialize, the leadership will be held directly responsible. The leadership, aware of the consequences, will therefore continue to cater to the expectations of the military and the domestic population, even where this comes into direct conflict with the requirements to end the war. Kuniaku Koiso (Japanese Prime Minister until 1 April 1945), in commenting on the reason Japan continued to fight a lost war in 1944, admitted that

> [i]f the government, being aware of the fact that were fighting a losing war, had immediately ventured to sue for peace, it would have been compelled to surrender under merciless terms, and [that] would have given rise to internal disorder, because the people, who had been led to believe that the war was being won, would probably have become indignant over such a surrender.[6]

Thus, even in the case where a leader has the strength of character to allow his own loss of face, or to accept a fall in prestige, and even where he realizes his position is untenable, unless he is also willing to risk the wrath of a "win-or-die" military or domestic population, the untenable position will continue to be maintained. This can be termed a *political dissonance* trap, the dissonance here being between policies, words and actions needed to end the war, and those needed to maintain domestic harmony and good civil/military or inner circle relations (see Figure 4.1).

Let us look at the problem of political dissonance in more detail, and most particularly at how it relates to the difficulties of cease-fire. There is little doubt that decision-makers are influenced by domestic and organizational/bureaucratic politics, and this is perhaps more the case in the modern world than ever before. Thus, despite the fact that the decision about whether or not to continue the war generally remains concentrated in the hands of a small group of people (a council of ministers, a cabinet, a single individual),[7] that small group is subject to external forces which may lead them to take the opposite action to that which they would take in the absence of such forces. This was perhaps most clearly stated in a

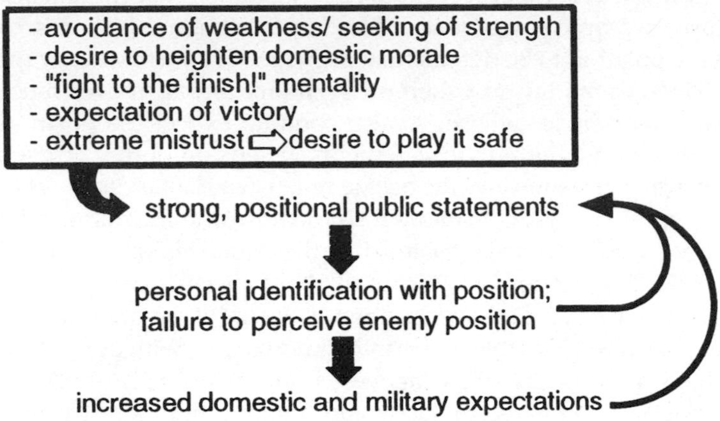

- avoidance of weakness/ seeking of strength
- desire to heighten domestic morale
- "fight to the finish!" mentality
- expectation of victory
- extreme mistrust ⇨ desire to play it safe

strong, positional public statements

personal identification with position;
failure to perceive enemy position

increased domestic and military expectations

FIGURE 4.1: Political and Cognitive Dissonance.

report of the United States Strategic Bombing survey in 1946:

> ... while defeat is a military event, the recognition of the event is a political act. The timing of the political recognition of the military realities is only partly determined by the actual situation on the fronts. The international situation, the domestic balance of power, the interests and antagonisms of relevant political groups -- they all weigh heavily when the grim realities of the armed contest have to be translated into the blunt language of capitulation[8]

(and this is almost certainly as true for cases of stalemate as it is for cases where defeat is apparent). It was clear during the Iran-Iran-Iraq war, for example, that even absent other difficulties, achieving a cease-fire early in the conflict without suffering the effects of political dissonance would have been unlikely. Despite the fact that this was a personal struggle between the leaders of two nations -- Saddam Hussein of Iraq, and Ayatollah Khomeini of Iran[9] -- and despite the fact that in the end it would be a combination of war weariness and international pressure which would help bring the fighting to an end, the effect of political dissonance was not unimportant. Political dissonance was a powerful force at work in the Iran-Iraq war, most evident in the summer of 1982 with at the point when Iraqi forces were finally expelled from Iranian territory. Instead of opting for cease-fire, the Iranian government chose to continue the war, a decision which was taken in large part because of the fear of what might happen if they did not do so.

It is important to understand that at the outset of the war, stated Iranian aims appeared at first blush to be somewhat modest. Iran's initial demands in the war said nothing about carrying the war to Iraqi territory, for example, only that Iran would fight to remove the aggressor. Less than a week into the war, President Bani-Sadr took the position that "so long as Iraq is in violation of our territorial sovereignty ... we see no use in any discussion, directly or indirectly, concerning the conflict between our two countries."[10] Ayatollah Khomeini, too, stated bluntly that Iran would not compromise and would not stop fighting until all Iraqis were driven from Iranian soil.[11] Given these declarations, there seemed to be hope that once Iraq had been repelled, some kind of peace could be negotiated. Indeed, as late as the Spring of 1982, Iranian authorities were denying that the war would ever cross the border. Khomeini remarked on 2 April 1982, for example, that ."..so far we have engaged only in self-defence ... We have never had any intention of committing aggression against other countries."[12] The Iranian Prime Minister, Mir Hosayn Musavi, announced the same day that "we do not covet a single inch of the territory of any country,"[13] an assertion oft repeated.[14] On 20 April 1982, and according to the National Voice of Iran, Iran's conditions for cease-fire still consisted of an Iraqi withdrawal, payment of reparations, and identification of the aggressor.[15]

Yet while denying that the war would cross the border, Iran did two things which would ensure that it would have no choice but to do so. The first was to hint at, and then declare openly, that one (non-negotiable) war aim was the fall of Saddam Hussein (and by extension the Ba'ath regime) -- a situation which would likely necessitate the use of force within Iraq.[16] Prime Minister Musavi, for example, while denying on 1 April 1982 that Iran would carry the war to Iraq, stated in the same breath that Iranian victories "will certainly continue until the destruction of Saddam's regime." About seven weeks later, he reiterated his assertion that one condition for peace would be the overthrow of Saddam Hussein. Khomeini was fairly clear on 12 June that peace with the Ba'ath party still in power was impossible.[17] The second, and more important, action taken by Iran which ensured that the war would have to move to Iraq was to engage in rhetoric which turned the war into a revolutionary crusade. The power of this latter rhetoric was in fact so strong and so endemic to the conflict that it would soon supersede the political declarations which indicated that the war would stop at the border.

The rhetoric of revolution had been present from the outset of the conflict. Less than a week into the eight year war, Ali Khamenei, Ayatollah Khomeini's representative to the Iranian Supreme Defence Council, stated bluntly that Iran's forces were "determined either to die or to achieve total victory ... reconciliation is impossible between an Islamic regime and a despotic arrogant regime." It was to be a war between "right and falsehood."[18] They were words calculated to place the war within a framework of religion and revolution, a framework which would entertain no compromise and inflame public opinion. Khomeini strengthened the concept of a war against evil and for the religion of Islam:

> [y]ou are fighting to protect Islam, and he is fighting destroy Islam ... There is absolutely no question of peace or compromise, and we shall never have any discussions with them; because they are corrupt and perpetrators of corruption. ... this is a rebellion by blasphemy against Islam.[19]

The effects of all the rhetoric were also clear. Even by 29 October 1980, public opinion had already been aroused to such an extent by this repeated stating of hard-line positions that a number of diplomats pointed out that even if both sides had wanted to cease-fire, it was now politically impossible.[20] A month later Olaf Palme, who (on 11 November) had been appointed as a special UN representative to the area, had had preliminary discussions with both parties, and noted that public opinion was "not responsive in either of the nations."[21] It is not unreasonable to conclude that the latter condition was a result of the continued public proclamation of the former.

It should have come as no surprise then, that with the expulsion of Iraqi forces from Iran in the summer of 1982, peace did not come to the region. On 20 June 1982, Saddam Hussein announced his "withdrawal" from Iran, a manoeuvre which he said would be completed within ten days. Khomeini, and in keeping within the framework of a war of revolution, responded this way:

> ... if the war between Iran and Iraq continues, and if in the war Iran defeats Iraq, Iraq will be annexed to Iran; that is, the nation of Iraq, the oppressed people of Iraq, will free themselves from the talons of the tyrannical clique and will link themselves with the Iranian nation. They will set up their own government according to their own wishes -- an Islamic one.[22]

Exactly how this was to be achieved was not clearly spelled out, perhaps primarily because there was now a debate occurring within the Iranian hierarchy about whether or not to now cease fire, or whether to carry the war to Iraq.[23] No clear public statement was forthcoming while the debate raged. Iran, having successfully repelled the aggression, was clearly in an advantageous position to accept a cease-fire (which Saddam Hussein offered on 10 June). Moreover, and as we have seen, it had stated that the war would not be extended. In the end, however, the decision was made to continue the war. In a foreign ministry statement on 29 June, Iran set its new course:

> Iraqi forces ... leave nothing behind but piles of destruction and misery ... The Islamic Republic of Iran cannot remain indifferent and witness the martyrdom and wounding every day of some of its citizens. It will, therefore, continue its honorable war against Saddam's regime ... [24]

The aggressor was no longer to be merely repelled, but tried and punished.

There are several explanations for Iran's decision, including its newfound ability to win the conflict (a factor which was discussed in the opening chapter). More important, however, was the political dissonance factor. The Iranian public, armed forces, and indeed much of the government had been forced to see the war in terms of religious duty and revolution -- to back away and stop fighting before that revolution was complete would have required explanations which the Iranian hierarchy was not willing try and invent. Thus, despite the early declarations that the war would not cross the border, religious duty was seen as the ultimate duty. Indeed, justificatory statements were everywhere in the press in the first weeks of July 1982.[25] Moreover, once the decision had been made, the idea that this was still a war of revolution was additionally reinforced by the claim that Iran was entering Iraq to make their way to Jerusalem. The Israeli invasion of Lebanon provided a convenient excuse for the Iranian regime, Ayatollah Montazeri commenting that

> [t]he most natural route to the Qods [Jerusalem] front to liberate the Al Asqa mosque from the occupation of the racist Zionists is through Iraqi territory ... we are certain that the Muslim millions masses will support our sacred aim.[26]

Khomeini added that "If Iran forgets its war with Iraq, it will lose both Iraq and Lebanon. So we must go toward Lebanon by defeating Iraq."[27] The war, then, came to serve as a symbol of the Islamic regime's "continuing vigor" -- and given the successes at the front, which supported the idea that the war was indeed a holy war, it would certainly be difficult to seriously challenge the legitimacy of the regime.[28] Had the decision been made to stop at the Iraqi border, however, it seems likely that the opposite would have been the case: an Iranian cease-fire might have been viewed as a betrayal of religious duty, putting the legitimacy of the regime in jeopardy.

In this case, then, political dissonance was a clear problem, most particularly at the time of the Iraqi withdrawal from Iran. Whatever the prevalent problems of the war, including Khomeini's own personality, political dissonance was a difficulty which would have to be overcome before the war could end. As we shall see later, a combination of factors would come into play in 1988 which would help to overcome the problem, but the point remains: while political dissonance was not prevalent throughout the war, it was a powerful force which likely served to decrease the possibilities of cease-fire early on in the conflict.

Unlike in early stages of the Iran-Iraq war, where internal considerations contributed to the continuation of the war, domestic and organizational processes can of course work in the opposite direction. Randle has highlighted a number of factors which may lead a public to demand peace, for example,[29] and Peter Lieurance has argued that during the Vietnam War, the efforts of the "Negotiation Now!" movement went a long way towards influencing the United States administration to attempt to arrange both a cease-fire and a political settlement in Vietnam.[30] Even in the Iran-Iraq war, Karsh reports that volunteers dropped steadily after 1984, and by 1985 there were large scale demonstrations against the war.[31] In part, Cuba and South Africa agreed to withdraw from the Angola/Namibia conflict in 1988 because the war was unpopular at home.[32] In spite of all these examples, however, the point is that domestic and organizational processes *can* prevent the decision to cease-fire from being made, not that they will always do so.

The decision to cease fire (or to terminate or begin the war, for that matter), then, is not purely a matter of belligerent recognition of objective conditions. It is not dependent merely upon recognition that a particular struggle is lost, or that it will remain stalemated for the foreseeable future. Even where belligerents are willing to contemplate a cease-fire, they may see themselves as unable to do so because of the impact made on the decision-making process by those normally external to that process. Sufficient and effective political will may thus be inhibited. In a wartime situation, an exacting and intolerant public can often be a creation of decision-makers' propaganda efforts, and this public can in turn come to have a strong impact upon decision-makers' perceptions of (or at least ultimate actions with regard to) questions of victory, defeat, and of course cease-fire.[33] Mitchell points out that the general rule appears to be that

> the higher the sacrifices involved, the more the people will feel that some significant gains must be achieved in the final settlement to make up for all they have endured. The more prolonged the conflict, the more difficult it becomes for the leaders to accept anything short of a significant improvement on the pre-conflict situation as a final settlement.[34]

Fisher phrases the problem in somewhat different terms -- "[t]here is a common tendency to treat sunken costs as invested capital"[35] -- and others have noted the tendency also.[36] What applies to the domestic population applies equally to the military, as can perhaps most clearly be seen in the Algerian War of Independence; the more an army puts in to a war, the more they will expect to get out of it.

The Algerian War of Independence

"France will not leave Algeria any more than she will leave Provence or Brittany. Whatever happens, the destiny of Algeria is French."[37]
Jacques Soustelle, 1956

The Algerian War of Independence offers up a stark lesson in political dissonance. In this case the trap was entered and acknowledged, but instead of being firmly confronted it was handled duplicitously, and the results were nearly catastrophic. The war shows the possible consequences of a given leadership having a public position which differs from its private position or, more precisely, the consequences of a leadership promising its military that which it knew it could never deliver, and then reneging on that promise. A conflict would inadvertently be set up, and then knowingly engendered. Positions would be taken by successive French governments on the issue of the Algerian war, and those positions would be declared and defended publicly and often. The military would come to expect the position to be defended, and whenever the government attempted a retreat, the army intervened. In the end, the political environment made it necessary to back away from the position, and when this occurred the government was the target of an attempted coup.

On 12 November 1954, not quite two weeks into the war, French Premier Mendès-France declared that

[o]ne does not compromise when it comes to defending the internal peace of the nation, the unity and integrity of the Republic. The Algerian departments are part of the French Republic ... Between them and metropolitan France there can be no conceivable secession. ... Never will France -- any French government, or parliament, whatever may be their particularist tendencies -- yield on this fundamental principle.[38]

François Mitterand, then French Interior Minister, added that France's only negotiation would be war.[39] Nearly three years later, in October 1957, Prime Minister Félix Gaillard of France (after the fall of Pierre Mendès-France, Edgar Faure, and Guy Mollet) rejected a peace proposal put forward by Tunisian and Moroccan leaders. Gaillard boldly stated that "whatever

the terms and the periphrasis, we shall never accept Algerian independence."[40] These statements, from two French governments, were typical
of those made throughout the war, and they encapsulate perhaps the single
most important problem in the Algerian war: the public French face of
"no compromise" which not only confused the FLN, but misled the French
public, *pied noir*,[41] and in particular the French army -- who eventually
saw any contemplated negotiation with the rebels as absolute and
indefensible betrayal.

At the outset of the war, and given the statements of Mendès-France,
Gaillard and others, it seemed as if French aims were clear: there could
be no compromise with the FLN, and France was to hold on to Algeria
at any cost. This in turn made the army's objective clear: to defeat the FLN
on the battlefield of Algeria. In fact, it is more than likely that this public
face was only a ruse. Horne and Talbott, among others, have advanced
the proposition that many French politicians were privately aware that
independence would come eventually, and chose "no compromise" only
as an opening position (and because of the very fact that they were the
face of French government).[42] Mendès-France, for example, immediately
after resigning in May 1956, delivered a speech whose keynote was
"dialogue," and dialogue "on the scene, even if it is difficult":[43] a radical
departure from his comments as French Prime Minister. Of course he, like
all those who followed him, was in a difficult position. By 1954, there were
at least a million *pied noir* in Algeria, and their lobby -- which opposed
Algerian autonomy or independence of any sort -- was a powerful one.
Pied noir demonstrations in Algiers in February 1956, for example, forced
French Prime Minister Mollet to rescind his nomination of General Georges
Catroux for the next governor-general for Algeria. Catroux was reputed
to be more conciliatory towards Algerian nationalist sentiment, and the
reception Mollet received in Algeria left no doubt as to the feelings of the
French colonists: demonstrations and violence broke out, and his entourage
was assailed by a variety of projectiles, including garbage and stones.[44]
It was undoubtedly the case that any weak French government not wishing
to endanger its rule was more or less forced to take a strong anti-
independence stance when it came to the Algerian question.

We will not dwell at length on the trials of the successive and unsuccessful
governments which preceded the de Gaulle government of 1958, nor on
the effect that the statements of these governments had on public opinion
and opportunities for peace (although that, too, makes a strong case for
the political dissonance trap). The important point for the purposes of this
discussion is that from the outset of the war, not only the French public,
but the French army particularly, were given to believe that France was
fighting to retain Algeria. In fact, the French army was in Algeria for entirely
different reasons: they were there to allow France to give Algeria away

while it was in control of the battlefield, to allow it to negotiate from a position of strength. If this was not the case from the outset of the war, then it was certainly true from 1 June 1958 with the coming to power of de Gaulle, the point at which the French government's private position can be clearly discerned.[45]

The story of de Gaulle's handling of the situation he faced between 1958 and 1962 is an intricate but illuminating one. It is a story whose moral is that the aims of a belligerent government, and the aims of that belligerent's army, must coincide. It seems likely that armies do not only need to be given reasons why they must fight, they must be given the *true* reasons, lest the result be near or actual catastrophe, as it was for France in the Algerian War.

After coming to power on 1 June 1958, the strategy of General Charles de Gaulle was a complex one. Despite his post-World War II commitment that "France, whatever happens, shall never abandon Algeria,"[46] by the summer of 1955 he had decided that independence for Algeria should be the goal towards which France should strive.[47] As we now know, having decided on that course, by the time he came to power he had also settled upon a strategy: it had to be France, in control of the situation on the battlefield, granting that independence.[48] The French army, in other words, was to win the Algerian war militarily so that France's withdrawal from Algeria could be an honorable one. To anyone who understood the plan, and more particularly to any French military man, its logic must have seemed tortured and utterly incomprehensible: the French army was to win the battle, in order that France could lose the war.[49]

So, in the words of Ferhat Abbas, first president of the Provisional Government of the Republic of Algeria (GPRA), and one of the most moderate of FLN leaders, "[t]o arrive at peace, General de Gaulle made war."[50] In 1959, de Gaulle and the new Prime Minister, Michel Debré, were demanding swift military successes from the new Algerian Commander in Chief, General Maurice Challe, "for France is beginning to get bored with the war."[51] We already know how important it is that sacrifices at least appear to be justified in some way. In this case, the opposite was occurring: the French leadership expected their army readily to give up what they had fought so hard to gain. The army was told to "win the match" (*gagner la partie*)[52] and Challe busied himself at his task, successfully and statistically defeating the FLN by the time of his departure in April of 1960. By June, for example, the army was claiming that the FLN forces were a mere fraction of their original number and that FLN units had been "smashed up" into small, ineffective formations. "To many soldiers," wrote one journalist, "the rebellion appears to be militarily on the verge of collapse."[53] De Gaulle, on the other hand, faced with the growing successes of the FLN at a political level, began to consider proposals which attempted to find a formula for cease-fire which the FLN would not regard as an act of surrender (or weakness), but which would nevertheless lead to negotiations.[54]

The results of de Gaulle's overall strategy would backfire tragically in 1961. In a speech delivered on April 11 1961, de Gaulle made a devastating announcement:

> Algeria is costing us -- to say the least -- more than she is worth to us ... France envisages with the greatest composure a situation in which Algeria would cease to belong to her ... and will offer no objection should the people of Algeria decide to organize themselves into a State which would take over responsibility for their country ... decolonization is in our interest and, consequently, our policy.[55]

In a single statement, de Gaulle had reversed the policy France had clung to for over six long years of war, and although de Gaulle believed that he had paved the way for that announcement,[56] nine days later the army would revolt and he would face a coup led by his own generals.

The coup attempt came on 20 April 1961, and was led by a group of four generals (Challe, Salan, Jouhaud, and Zeller), and a relatively small group of higher level officers. The reasons for the coup were more than obvious: the army believed that de Gaulle had betrayed them. General Challe announced over Radio "France" (it had been Radio Algeria moments earlier) that "I am in Algiers, together with Generals Zeller and Jouhaud, and in touch with General Salan so as to keep the army's oath to ensure a French Algeria, so that our dead shall not have died in vain."[57] Challe's intentions were not the overthrow of de Gaulle himself (although that was the aim of Salan and his followers), but to, at a minimum, ensure the complete defeat of the FLN.[58]

De Gaulle reacted quickly, and in a speech on 23 April 1961, he pleaded with the people in a style which can only be de Gaulle's:

> [i]n the name of France I order that every means, I repeat, every means should be employed to bar the way against these men until they can be crushed. I forbid every Frenchman, and first and foremost every soldier, to carry out their orders ... Frenchwomen, Frenchmen, help me![59]

In Algeria, "a million transistors were tuned in."[60] The vast proportion of enlisted men, more and more officers, and especially conscript soldiers, would either refuse to carry out orders or re-defect in support of de Gaulle. Whether as a reaction to de Gaulle's speech, or because the majority of the French Army in Algeria were conscripts who wanted the war to end, not continue, the coup fell apart in a matter of days.[61] By 26 April it was over. All in all, about 40,000 men took part in the revolt (about 1 in 10), but action was taken against only 600 of these in the end, and most would eventually be granted pardons.[62] De Gaulle had played his hand and won, but the coup was not the only problem which he would face. The Organisation de l'Armée Secrète (OAS), a virtually private anti-FLN army under Salan and Jouhaud "used deserters and fanatics who were the scum of the army"[63] and would eventually kill indiscriminately over 12,000 people in the year after the coup was put down.[64]

The coup of 1961 and the subsequent actions of the OAS could certainly have been predicted, for the army's predilection for involvement in French political affairs had been growing steadily since the war's beginning.[65] Indeed, by 1959, "the army had assumed almost unlimited powers."[66] Perhaps the first clearly visible sign of the army's potential for control lay in the story surrounding the arrest of Mohammed Ben Bella, one of the original founders of the FLN. FLN representatives had been secretly meeting with French officials since April 1956, and five meetings had taken place by the end of September. The final one had been important, as it decided that the next meeting would be to draft a paper publicly announcing the intention of both parties to enter into full scale negotiations. That meeting never took place. Ben Bella had his plane hijacked by the French authorities, was arrested in Algiers, and spent the next several years in a French prison.[67] The real question about that hijacking appears to be whether it was ordered by the French *government*, or by the French *military*. Ben Bella himself believed it was the latter (in collusion with disaffected French officials who supported a French Algeria):

> peace was in reach when, without the knowledge of Guy Mollet, [Robert] Lacoste [French governor in Algeria] and the Army perpetrated this act of international piracy. The French government faced with the *fait accompli*, weakly accepted it. By doing so, they gave into the army and, with its own hands, buried all hope of the peace which it had wanted. ... What bloodshed and what suffering could have been avoided if the French government had stood firm! The Algerians would have been spared six years of war and the appalling losses which resulted.[68]

That the army was responsible seems an inevitable conclusion. They had been given to believe that Algeria was to remain French, and were determined to ensure that goal. Certainly the government itself had nothing to gain by spoiling peace negotiations. Moreover, subsequent events would certainly go to support the indictment of the army.

The next visible sign of growing and ominous army power came in the Spring of 1958 with the set of events which brought de Gaulle to power. Yet another government (that of Gaillard) had fallen and France was, for over a month, leaderless. The army began to hand out warnings. In May, General Salan sent a telegram to General Paul Ely, then Chief of Staff. It had been drafted by Generals Salan, Jouhaud, Allard, Massu, and Admiral Auboyneau, and declared that

> The present crisis shows that the political parties are profoundly divided over the Algerian question. The press permits one to think that the abandonment of Algeria would be envisaged in the diplomatic processes which would begin with negotiations aiming at "cease-fire" ... The army in Algeria is troubled by recognition of its responsibility towards the men who are fighting and risking a useless sacrifice if the representatives of the nation are not determined to maintain *Algerie français*. ...
>
> The French army, in its unanimity, would feel outraged by the abandonment of this national patrimony. One cannot predict how it would react in its despair ... [69]

There were even plans to invade Paris in the Spring of 1958 if the new French government was not to their liking. On 24 May, French paratroops took over Corsica and called for the return of de Gaulle, and police sent to the island to quell the revolt joined them in their demand.[70] Pierre Pfimlin, who had agreed to form an interim government, resigned on 25 May, and on 1 June, de Gaulle formed the new government. Ironically, it was widely believed, by French colonists and particularly in military circles, that de Gaulle would be the one man who would never give up Algeria, a man who would sell out neither the *pied noir* nor the army.[71]

It was certainly true that de Gaulle was personally well aware of the feelings of the army. Touring Algeria after coming to power, he recalls:

> [r]eceiving reports from the local commanders wherever I went, invariably calling the officers and often the NCOs together in order to say a few words to them and question several of their number, I had no difficulty in discovering what they were thinking. By and large, this great body of men, by nature concerned with the short term rather than the long, clung to the idea that France should keep possession of Algeria ... [72]

In addition, French officers had made public statements such as "We won't have our men killed in order that the Algerians may be given the right to vote FLN," and General Massu had also publicly attacked de Gaulle's strategy, warning in January 1960 that "So far (the army) has not shown its power ... At the right moment it can impose its will."[73]

It is also true that de Gaulle took steps to counter the potential threat to his plans for an independent Algeria. He reduced the budget of the "Fifth Bureau" (the army's psychological warfare branch), which had been a prime source of the army's political power. He had reorganized the Algerian administration such that final decision-making power would lay in mainland France. Finally, he recalled General Paul Ely and gave him the task of "scattering the army plotters," who would be quietly moved in twos and threes from Algeria to new posts in France and elsewhere. Hundreds of officers were reassigned to France, Germany, or as "technical advisors" elsewhere in France, and "one by one, key administrative posts in Algeria were filled with hand-picked civilians and army officers."[74] As far as de Gaulle was concerned, "[t]he upholders of French Algeria were certainly not capable of forcing me to maintain the status quo, nor the Communists of compelling me to grovelling surrender."[75]

Despite all these efforts, however, unrest in the army continued, and the reason is hardly surprising. While taking efforts to counter the army's power, de Gaulle nevertheless continued to encourage the army to believe that France was out to retain Algeria. He never made clear to the army that what the FLN was losing on the battlefield, the rebels were winning at a political level both on the ground in Algeria, and in forums such as the UN, elsewhere in Africa, Asia, and even in some Western countries. In a speech to the army in January 1960, for example, de Gaulle proclaimed that " ... in your mission there is no room for any equivocation or interpretation, you must liquidate the rebel force, which is seeking to drive France out of Algeria."[76] He justified his actions this way:

> ... failing to perceive that, while leading France towards disengagement, I also wanted our forces to remain masters of the territory until such time as I deemed it advisable to withdraw them, [the press] represented the rousing words which I addressed to the combat units as a sudden reversal of my policy. For, quite naturally, I told these soldiers ... that the struggle was not yet over, that it might continue for many more months, and that as long as it lasted the adversary must be everywhere sought out, reduced, and conquered.[77]

Perhaps it came "quite naturally" to de Gaulle to speak his words of encouragement to the army, but those words were not taken as mere morale boosters. They were received as clearly defined goals towards which the French Army must strive. The army took de Gaulle's entreaties to heart, and sincerely believed that they knew what de Gaulle wanted from them. This was certainly true of General Challe, who was convinced that de Gaulle wanted a military victory over the FLN in order to keep Algeria French.[78] It was only slowly that suspicion of de Gaulle's true intentions dawned, and when it did, the army made its own position absolutely clear. On 11 November 1960, for example, Marshall Alphonse Juin, one of de Gaulle's *confidantes*, let it be known that "despite a friendship of fifty years' standing with General de Gaulle, he must protest, both in his capacity as the highest dignitary in the Army and as an Algerian against the idea of deserting our Algerian brothers". General Salan declared in the press: "I say No!

to this Algerian Algeria ... From now on, every man must face up to his responsibilities ... The time for evasions is over."[79]

There was more to be taken into consideration. Apart from the strong army belief that de Gaulle wanted a victory in Algeria, a number of students of the war make the assertion that, psychologically, the French Army *needed* a victory.[80] The assertion is a plausible one: they had lost in Indochina, Morocco, Tunisia, and Suez; Algeria was the "last outpost of a once vast empire that many had spent their entire careers defending."[81] According to Talbott, for example, French paratroopers (who constituted the bulk of the actual fighting forces in Algeria) were "haunted by the memory of the Vietnamese allies they had abandoned," and arrived in Algeria "determined to stay." These troops constituted the bulk of the revolting troops in 1961.[82] Add to this the fact that statistically, even by 1960, the FLN looked defeated,[83] and that the army had also pledged on its honor to defend any of the Muslim population who sided with them against the FLN,[84] pulling French forces back from the brink of a clear military victory must have seemed madness to those in combat. From this perspective, the attempted coup hardly seems surprising. "Nevertheless," said de Gaulle in his memoirs, "I continued to hasten things forward."[85] The events of April 1961, and the subsequent formation of the OAS,[86] were two results.

The Algerian War of Independence offers at least one lesson in terms of political dissonance: that to ignore the existence of the trap can be inherently dangerous. In this case, a public position was taken regarding the war -- that Algeria would be defended to the last. That position was repeated and defended publicly, despite the private plans of the government regarding the final outcome of the war. There followed years of army warnings concerning what might happen should the initial position be backed away from. De Gaulle, while admittedly taking some steps to counter the potential consequences of reversing his position, nevertheless continued to foster in the army the impression that the position would never change. Thus, when it finally became necessary to back down from the position, the result was an attempted coup.

Entering the Trap Deliberately

The political dissonance trap is not unknown to those who fight and lead wars (though they may not put a name to it). Thus, apart from those cases where belligerent leaders suddenly find themselves victims of political dissonance, it is in fact the case that they will sometimes enter the trap deliberately. Here it is used as a conscious strategy of wresting from their enemy that which they desire. It is a way of making a threat, a way of saying in effect, "In case we are not sufficiently committed to impress you, now we are. We hereby oblige ourselves. Behold us in the public ritual of getting ourselves genuinely committed."[87]

The Algerian War can once again provide a vivid illustration of this point, this time from the point of view of the FLN. Abderazzak Chentouf, an Algerian political leader, once noted that the Algerian mentality "is characterized by the right angle. There are no contours or compromises."[88] From the very beginning of the Algerian war, the FLN made it absolutely clear that Chentouf's assessment was entirely correct. In the war-opening proclamation of 1 November 1954, the FLN boldly stated that "our movement of regeneration presents itself under the label of: FRONT DE LIBERATION NATIONALE thus freeing itself from any possible compromise."[89] There was to be no intermediate position in this war; moderate reformers would be rejected, and compelled to choose one side over the other.[90] True, negotiations would be offered -- but only on the basis of a prior recognition of Algerian sovereignty.[91] At the FLN congress in the Spring of 1956 in the Soummam valley, for example, it was declared that a cease-fire would be contingent upon prior "recognition of the indivisible Algerian state," "recognition of the independence of Algeria and of its sovereignty in all matters," and "recognition of the FLN as the sole organization representing the Algerian people and as the sole partner in negotiations."[92] All attempts by the French government in Algeria to strike a compromise were consequently predestined to be rejected. A French offer of cease-fire in March 1957 was refused, for example, on the basis that no cease-fire could be contemplated before the proclamation of Algerian independence.[93] According to Ben Bella,

> Soustelle's [governor general in Algeria from January 1955 to February 1956] plan was to secretly encourage a moderate nationalist government which would advocate some of the same objectives as ourselves, but which were only to be achieved through legal and constitutional means. ... We lost no time in telling them in plain terms that their political game would only be tolerated by us insofar as it could further our own activities.[94]

Later, in a direct order from the FLN leadership, the FLN was told to "liquidate all personalities who want to play the role of *interlocuteur valable* ... Kill any person attempting to deflect the militants." Even Ferhat Abbas, the influential moderate intellectual who had declared in 1936 that he "would not die for the Algerian nation, because it does not exist," was forced to join the FLN after they killed his nephew and after the "tentative hand" that he had extended to the French government was rebuffed.[95] Abbas would eventually become the first president of the GPRA and, in a speech in Cairo on 25 April 1956, publicly declared that there would be neither peace, respite, nor armistice "until France agreed to negotiations with the

FLN and accept its terms"[96] -- meaning, of course, no negotiations until the recognition of Algerian sovereignty.

Benyousef Ben Khedda, president of the GPRA in 1961, and one of the original group of nine FLN leaders, argues that the FLN's strategy of eliminating all potential compromisers and mediators within Algeria was actually a factor for peace:

> [i]t is because it found in us a credible *interlocuteur* that France could negotiate with the FLN. Negotiation by two who, at a stroke, rendered useless all mediation at one level and *a fortiori*, eliminated all risk of internationalization.[97]

In a sense, this was true. By deliberately ridding themselves of any possible rivals, and by putting themselves in a corner from which there could be no escape, the FLN made it impossible for France to anything but deal with them and them alone. But there could be no turning back. The entire war was a gamble, and the FLN placed itself in a win or die situation with no compromise possible. In that sense, the FLN were very lucky. They were lucky because they did manage to win the war, at least politically, and therefore never realized how precarious their position really was. They would never realize that had they not been able to achieve all their goals, they would not be in a position which allowed a compromise which might have let them at least achieve some of them. As far as that goes, they were doubly fortunate, for the French had placed themselves in a similar position, suffered the consequences, and survived; when the time came to back down, the French were able to do it.

Deliberately entering the political dissonance trap is, in effect, a way of playing international "chicken," and while this may be effective (as the Algerian case shows), it often results in a position being defended even long after its author has realized that it is untenable, and that it no longer serves that nation's interests. There may come a time in the war, for example, when the situation is such that there is no possible way for a belligerent to expect its enemy to meet the initial demands made of it, but because the belligerent has deliberately entered the political dissonance trap, there is no choice but to continue to make the demand, even though this may be completely irrational in terms of the logic of the war. The question now becomes one of the regime's political survival in the domestic environment, as well its survival in the environment of the war being fought.

The Nigerian Civil War provides a salient, though troubling, example. In this case, the Biafran population (not to mention much of the international community), through constant exposure to especially strong anti-Federal propaganda, had come to believe that federal forces were attempting to commit genocide. Once convinced of this belief, any attempt to dissuade them of it was a non-starter: "nothing on earth could convince them to the contrary."[98] That the dissemination of anti-federal propaganda was a conscious choice is made clear by Akpan, who recalls that there was a tremendous effort afoot within the civil service:

> [t]he best literary talents and intellectuals were found in the propaganda directorate and the ministry of information. They were drawn from the universities, the professions, and the civil service. ... They had about fifty specialist groups all concerned with different fields and aspects of propaganda.... Even more effective than the literary output and programmes were the emotional songs composed by the many talented musicians discovered in the country since the war began. There were dramatists, artists, actors and actresses devoted to touring the fronts ... to inspire the people.[99]

Another notable effort included the formation in the United States of the Biafran Committee for the Prevention of Genocide, and references by the papal envoy to the area added to the weight of evidence.[100] Finally, there were the comments of Ojukwu himself, of which the following constitutes only a small sampling:[101]

1. For our part, we know that victory for Gowon would mean continued genocide for our people, bestiality, disease, and anarchy, ignorance, poverty and desecration of our religion. (29 September 1967)

2. We in Biafra have been fighting to protect ourselves and our institutions against a plunder that is most brutal, a tyranny that is monstrous, and a genocide that is total. (28 January 1968)

3. This is a war of survival. It is so, because every day it has become plainer to us that the enemy we have to fight is an enemy intent on destroying every one of us ... Our people are fighting with vigor, because we have our backs to the wall and death stares us in the face. (Umuahia, 18 April 1968)

4. ... when will world statesmen awaken to the fact that the Biafran race is being systematically wiped out? Can they, being responsible and honorable men, sit back and wait until genocide is completed before they realize that it is actually being committed with impunity? (international press conference, 18 July 1968)[102]

It is of course clear now that there was no attempt by federal forces to commit genocide. Such was the conclusion of the international team of observers,[103] which would also be later supported by reports from the OAU, the personal representative of the UN Secretary-General, and reports and evidence given by other international observer teams and academics.[104]

Finally, the completely non-standard end to the war, which included a great deal of emotional reconciliation between the parties, completes the evidence.[105] Despite this, and despite Uwechue's charge that "sovereignty or collective suicide" was a slogan which serious and humane ruling classes would neither stomach nor encourage,[106] the genocide strategy was clearly a very good one. As Curle notes, "it succeeded in dividing the world, and [Ojukwu] wasn't about to give that up."[107]

The point about all of this for our purposes, however, is that there are many who believe that Ojukwu did not really have the *choice* to give up the genocide strategy, and that he became a victim of his own propaganda. One member of this latter group includes one of Ojukwu's most outspoken critics, Ntieyong Akpan:

> Ojukwu almost certainly did not initially believe in secession, but in the unity of Nigeria ... But he made himself a helpless prisoner -- a prisoner of his personal glory, ambitions and idiosyncrasies, a prisoner of the will and caprices of those he trusted and upon whom he heavily relied, a prisoner of fear and self-deception, and finally, a prisoner of the mob.[108]

John de St. Jorre, a serious journalist of the war, also believes that Ojukwu became a captive of his own propaganda after June 1966, and that thereafter it became a kind of Frankenstein, out of his control. He asserts that the mood in Biafra in September 1968, for example, came down to "We have no alternative; if we surrender or are defeated, the Nigerians will wipe us out, so we might as well die fighting." De St. Jorre also reports a story that Ojukwu was presented with a detailed memorandum arguing against secession, to which he allegedly responded, "It's too late to go back now, they'd kill me if I did."[109] Even as early as February 1968, the papal delegation had noted that "[o]n every occasion, the deep conviction of the Ibo people that they are fighting for survival against a campaign of genocide manifested itself in forests of placards held aloft and poured forth in every address of welcome."[110]

In the final analysis, Ojukwu found himself in the classic political dissonance trap -- but on this occasion it was not unexpected. Instead, it was deliberately invoked as a strategy from the war's outset -- but it would backfire. Ojukwu's constant propaganda had resulted in a population unwilling to surrender, and when opportunities to settle arose, Ojukwu was unable to take advantage of them. This may seem an academic point, for even in the absence of propaganda, the evidence indicates that Ojukwu was unwilling to negotiate in any case. Moreover, it would appear that Ojukwu himself came to believe his own speeches (thus providing evidence of cognitive dissonance as well). He wrote in 1989 that "I firmly believe that I did my best to protect a people threatened with genocide."[111] In the end, then, does that fact that Ojukwu could not back down make a difference if we know that he did not want to anyway? It does, because the political dissonance problem was in this case a latent one which, in the absence of the more prevalent and obvious difficulties, could have prevented cease-fire. If, for example, Ojukwu had been killed, or the attempted army coup of 1967 had succeeded,[112] it is highly unlikely that a new military leadership could have negotiated with Gowon as they had planned to without risking a domestic uprising or some other kind of civil unrest.

Escaping the Trap

As we have seen, there are multiple ways into the trap, but there appear to be no ways out. The reason for this is that while the trap can be escaped, this happens only rarely, and only with great difficulty. While many examples exist of belligerents falling into the trap, or jumping in deliberately, few exist of belligerents being able to escape unscathed. Nevertheless, some strategies are available to those who would escape the effects of political dissonance.

First, belligerents may attempt to reverse the entire propaganda campaign which brought the problem about in the first place. This can be especially tricky, but can work. After all, if propaganda and rhetoric can be used to inflame public opinion and get it firmly in the camp of the war-fighting leadership, surely it can be used to douse the flames and convince a domestic population that a cease-fire is the desirable goal. The Iran-Iraq war provides an illustration.

On 3 June 1988, Rafsanjani (who had been appointed a day earlier as acting Commander-in-Chief of Iranian armed forces) began a speech by admitting a number of recent Iranian defeats, and it was noted that Iraq was embarking on large scale operations, having learned from their mistakes. Then, somewhat euphemistically, he noted that "under these conditions, we must prepare ourselves to confront the existing situation." The real enemies were "the nasty superpowers," and he warned that "certain things, bitter or sweet, may happen to us ... The people must assume that no one will lift a finger to help them in this world which is governed by evil powers."[113] Statements like these, from one so highly placed, and which contradicted nearly every public utterance the Iranians had made since the beginning of the war, must have been intended to soften the blow of the peace which was to come. Although Rafsanjani still warned that there would be "no compromise, no surrender,"[114] and notwithstanding the fact that minor victories would continue to be played up in the press,[115] the rhetoric of victory was decidedly less noticeable in the weeks which followed. The positions of the past seven years would be completely reversed. It was now no longer a war of revolution; instead, the war would be ended to *save* the revolution. Now, "shameful conspiracies"[116] would prevent a victory, and insistence on continuing the war would lead to "extraordinary losses" which were not seen as "advisable."[117] Highlighting "world blasphemy and arrogance"[118] offered a convenient way of sidestepping the intransigent position of the past and helping to bring the war to a close. Thus, the language of cease-fire came to be couched in terms of "saving the revolution," sentiments of "isolation and exposure to superior forces" would be played upon, and a brutal campaign of suppression of internal dissent would be launched in which hundreds, and possibly thousands, were executed.[119]

Second are the accidental escapes. The domestic populations of the warring nations may come into contact with one another in a non-violent manner, and undo the work of the propaganda to which they have both been subjected (as seems to be the case in the Nigerian Civil War). Alternatively, a significant event, such as a natural disaster or international incident, can serve to deflect the attention of the nation from the war, or allow for some readjustment of goals and purposes to which the domestic population will not be hostile. Of course, neither belligerents nor third parties are generally in control of such events; it would be difficult to arrange them as a means of bringing about a cease-fire, so these escapes are perhaps less interesting. Again the Iran-Iraq war is a good example.

On 3 July 1988, the US Navy apparently mistook an Iranian passenger aircraft for an Iranian warplane. Two missiles were fired, the plane was destroyed, and all 290 people on board were killed. The tragedy led to renewed calls for cease-fire from around the world,[120] and undoubtedly aided what anti-war feelings may have existed in Iran. "It gave Iran's leaders precisely the moral cover of martyrdom and suffering in the face of an unjust superior force, to cover the comprehensive defeat of their political goals."[121] A number of statements in the days which followed attempted to make clear to the Iranian people that the *real* war was no longer with Iraq, but was some place else. Ayatollah Hussein Ali Montazeri -- "Grand Ayatollah" since 1984 and Khomeini's named successor -- called for plans to be drawn up for a "principled fight against the main enemy, *i.e.* America, on the political, economic, cultural, and military fronts," and even Ayatollah Khomeini told the nation that "[o]ur war is the war waged by Islam against all inequalities in the capitalist and communist world ... We must all go to the fronts for an all-out war against the U.S. and its lackeys."[122] The Security Council met at Iran's request on 12 July to discuss the tragedy, again an unprecedented event, as Iran had virtually ignored the United Nations since the beginning of the war.

Finally, there is the strategy of avoidance, which is usually only taken in the case where defeat is predictable. A belligerent who finds itself drawn in to a war where defeat seems more likely than victory (which is normally not a situation entered into consciously) may be particularly circumspect about the rhetoric it uses. The bold public statements are still made, and are made for the same reasons, but there is a difference: war goals are more amorphous. The reasons the war is being fought, the goals and aims of the nation at war, are deliberately blurred and made indistinct to allow for major shifts in policy. The strategy is only effective pre-emptively, however; it is impossible to use once goals and aims have been clearly set and publicly defended. Here, the 1991 Gulf War provides the clearest illustration.

Unlike many other wars, it was clear from the outset of military action in the Gulf War, and even before, that any victory to be achieved by Saddam Hussein was not to be seen in terms of the military defeat of coalition forces. For Saddam Hussein, if he could find a way to withdraw from Kuwait having delivered at least a "bloody nose" to coalition forces, remain in power, and avoid losing face, he would have "won."[123] The rhetoric of the war makes this abundantly clear. There was, for example, a complete lack of Iraqi rhetoric which made any reference to *military* victory over coalition forces. True, pre-war Iraqi rhetoric had made reference to the United States facing "a second Vietnam" (implying Iraqi victory), but once it seemed as if war were inevitable, all that changed.[124] The closest Saddam Hussein ever came during the war to publicly stating that Iraq would win militarily came in the first hours of the war: "God is with the patient, struggling, steadfast believers. He will definitely grant them victory, God willing."[125] It is unlikely that even this refers to military success, however, because from that point on, victory would be framed only in terms of Iraq's ability to withstand the assault, to hold fast and weather the storm. On 30 January, for example, in the now famous interview with CNN correspondent Peter Arnett, Hussein noted that

> [w]inning and losing does not hinge on winning or losing a battle quickly, because winning depends on gaining the satisfaction of the one and only God and the hearts of the people. Have they won God's satisfaction, and have they won the hearts of the people through their resolutions? This is the criteria we follow.[126]

It was clear that for Hussein, then, the battle was not only with coalition forces; it lay in securing the support of the Iraqi people to ensure his own political survival. Rhetoric would be used to convince the population that victory was not contingent upon defeating coalition forces militarily, but defeating them morally by holding out and proving the superior Iraqi will to the world:

> the defeat of America will, above anything else, be a moral defeat, particularly after the sons of Iraq have proved their legendary steadfastness in the face of the forces of darkness and evil assembled against them from all corners.
>
> The Iraqi's will in steadfastness and patience will be the superior one and that of the infidels will be inferior, God willing. It is only a matter of time before the enemy becomes convinced that it has done all it can and that the Iraqi's are determined to confront it and triumph over it ... It is only a matter of time before the invaders leave.[127]

Saddam Hussein held no illusions about his ability to defeat the coalition on the battlefield. Even if he privately believed that any kind of military victory was possible, his doubts were sufficient to ensure that he would in no way jeopardize his powerful position by leading his people to believe that Iraq could triumph through force of arms. If Saddam Hussein managed to stay in power after the war, one of the main reasons may have been that he obviated the political dissonance trap.

Conclusions

Political dissonance imposes great obstacles to cease-fire. The leadership of a nation at war, unwilling to face the loss of power which could result from a change in position, may continue to defend the position and this is done to the detriment of the nation, which is constantly being subjected to the costs of the war. The effects are discernable: even where it appears rational for a nation to cease fire it will not do so. Where the trap is ignored, and a nation reverses position, offering cease-fire or negotiation, the leadership may be subject to military coup, internal dissent, civil war, and almost certainly its own demise. The trap is not inescapable. Its effects can be reduced through the use of the propaganda system which created it in the first place, it can be avoided, or it can be escaped from by accident. Unfortunately, only the first of these escape mechanisms is under the control of the belligerent once the trap has been entered, and that mechanism is not entirely reliable. Finally, it should be clear that if cognitive dissonance was not a problem before entering the trap, it may easily become one once the trap is entered. Cognitive and political dissonance feed off one another and support each other, although it is usually only the latter which can be readily detected.

Notes

1. See Chapter 5.

2. A good example is Ojukwu's, "Under no circumstances will this republic of Biafra surrender or negotiate its sovereignty" (Chukwuemeka Ojukwu, "Broadcast from Enugu," *Summary of World Broadcasts*, ME/2541/B1 [10 August 1967], and reprinted as doc. 125 in A.H.M. Kirk-Greene, *Crisis and Conflict in Nigeria: Volume II -- A Documentary Sourcebook 1966-1970* [London: Oxford University Press, 1971], pp. 153-55).

3. For cognitive dissonance theory generally, see the work of Leon Festinger, *A Theory of Cognitive Dissonance* (London: Row, Peterson and Co., 1957), and as it applies to international relations, see Robert Jervis, *Perception and Misperception in International Relations* (Princeton: Princeton University Press, 1976), pp. 382-406.

4. Bryant Wedge, "The Individual, the Group and War," in John Burton, *Conflict: Readings in Management and Resolution* (London: Macmillan, 1990), p. 104.

5. Jervis, *Perception and Misperception*, p. 387, and Robert Jervis, *The Logic of Images in International Relations* (New York: Columbia University Press, 1989), p. 74.

6. Leon V. Sigal, *Fighting to a Finish: The Politics of War Termination in the United States and Japan, 1945* (London: Cornell University Press, 1988), p. 133.

7. Evan Luard, *War in International Society* (London: I.B. Tauris and Co., Ltd., 1986), pp. 222, 224.

8. US Strategic Bombing Survey (Pacific), "Effects of Strategic Bombing on Japan's War Economy," Report No. 53 (Washington, D.C., 1946), p. 57, in Sigal, *Fighting to a Finish*, p. 4.

9. See former Iranian President Bani-Sadr's comments on their relationship, for example, in Abol Hassan Bani-Sadr, *My Turn to Speak* (Washington: Brassey's, 1991), pp. 61-66.

10. Letter from President Bani-Sadr to the Secretary-General, SCOR, 35th yr., doc. S/14203 (29 Sept. 1980).

11. *The International Herald Tribune*, 2 October 1980.

12. Khomeini's 1 April speech on the anniversary of the founding of the Islamic Republic, *Summary of World Broadcasts*, ME/6994/A/9 (2 April 1982).

13. *Summary of World Broadcasts*, ME/6994/A/10 (2 April 1982).

14. For some examples, see *Summary of World Broadcasts*, ME/6997/A/7 (6 April 1982), ME/7012/A/5 (27 April 1982), ME/7029/A/3 (18 May 1982).

15. NVI broadcast of 20 April 1982, reprinted in *Summary of World Broadcasts*, ME/7008/A/5 (22 April 1982).

16. Efraim Karsh, "The Iran-Iraq War: A Military Analysis," *International Institute of Strategic Studies Adelphi Paper* 220 (1987), p. 25.

17. *Summary of World Broadcasts*, ME/6994/A/10 (2 April 1982); ME/7030/A/3 (19 May 1982); ME/7051/A/24 (14 June 1982).

18. *Summary of World Broadcasts*, ME/6536/A/14 (30 Sept. 1980).

19. Ayatollah Khomeini's Address to the Nation, 30 Sept. 1980, in *Summary of World Broadcasts*, ME/6538/A/3 (2 October 1980).

20. *The Guardian*, 29 October 1980.

21. *The Guardian*, 28 November 1980.

22. Ayatollah Khomeini, 21 June 1982, *Summary of World Broadcasts*, ME/7059/A/8 (23 June 1982).

23. Karsh, *Adelphi Paper*, p. 25.

24. Iranian Foreign Ministry Statement, 29 June 1982, *Summary of World Broadcasts*, ME/7066/A/22 (1 July 1982).

25. See, for example, *Summary of World Broadcasts*, ME/7072/i (8 July 1982), ME/7073/i (9 July 1982), 7074/A/i and 2 (10 July 1982), 7075/1-2 (11 July 1982).

26. Ibid.

27. *Financial Times*, 10 July 1992.

28. Ralph King, "The Iran-Iraq War: The Political Implications," *International Institute of Strategic Studies Adelphi Paper* 219 (1987), pp. 20-21.

29. Robert F. Randle, "The Domestic Origins of Peace," in William T.R. Fox, ed., *How Wars End: Annals of the American Academy of Political and Social Science*, Vol. 392 (Philadelphia: Academy of Political and Social Science, 1970), pp. 76-85.

30. See Peter R. Lieurance, "'Negotiation Now!': the National Committee for a Political Settlement in Vietnam," in David D. Smith (ed.) and Robert F. Randle (commentary), *From War to Peace: Essays in Peacemaking and War Termination* (New York: Columbia University Press, 1974), pp. 171-195.

31. Efraim Karsh, "From Ideological Zeal to Geopolitical Realism: The Islamic Republic and the Gulf War" in Efraim Karsh (ed.), *The Iran-Iraq War: Impact and Implications* (London: Macmillan, 1987), p. 34.

32. Robert S. Jester, "The 1988 Peace Accords and the Future of Southwest Africa," *International Institute of Strategic Studies Adelphi Paper* 253 (1990), p. 30.

33. See Sigal, *Fighting to a Finish*, p. 302.

34. C.R. Mitchell, *The Structure of International Conflict* (London: Macmillan, 1981), pp. 18-181, and see Fred Charles Iklé, *Every War Must End* (London: Columbia University Press, 1971), p. 41.

35. Roger Fisher, *Basic Negotiating Strategy* (New York: Harper and Row, 1969), p. 38.

36. See Stuart Albert and Edward C. Luck (eds.), *On the Endings of Wars* (London: Kennikat Press, 1980), p. 4; Jervis, *Perception and Misperception*, p. 396.

37. Jacques Soustelle, Governor General in Algeria from January 1955 to February 1956, in his first policy speech, 1956, quoted in Edward Behr, *The Algerian Problem* (London: Hodder and Stoughton, 1961), p. 77.

38. Alistair Horne, *A Savage War of Peace* (London: Macmillan, 1977), pp. 98, 249, and see John Talbott, *The War Without a Name: France in Algeria, 1954-62* (New York: Alfred A. Knopf, 1980), p. 39, and Michael K. Clark, *Algeria in Turmoil: A History of the Rebellion* (London: Thames and Hudson, 1960), p. 120.

39. Behr, *The Algerian Problem*, p. 68, and see also the comments of Jacques Soustelle, quoted in Behr, *The Algerian Problem*, p. 77, and also in Clark, *Algeria in Turmoil*, p. 133.

40. Horne, *A Savage War of Peace*, pp. 98, 249.

41. Algerian colonists of European (mainly French) origins.

42. Horne, *A Savage War of Peace*, p. 98; Talbott, *The War Without a Name*, p. 39.

43. Jean Lacouture (translation by George Holoch), *Pierre Mendès-France* (New York: Holmes and Meier, 1984), p. 366, and see also p. 390.

44. For various accounts, see Behr, *The Algerian Problem*, pp. 90-95, Clark, *Algeria in Turmoil*, pp. 268-79, Don Cook, *Charles de Gaulle* (London: Secker and Warburg, 1984), p. 314, Martha Crenshaw Hutchinson, *Revolutionary Terrorism: The FLN in Algeria, 1954-1962* (Stanford: Hoover Institution Press, 1978), p. 13, Lacouture, *Mendès-France*, pp. 362-63 and Talbott, *The War Without a Name*, pp. 58-60. In an interview with Lacouture, Catroux, when asked what would have happened had he landed in Algiers, replied with a broad smile, "Those people would have killed me, my friend..." (Lacouture, *Mendès-France*, p. 478).

45. For a detailed account of de Gaulle's coming to power, see Lacouture, *De Gaulle*, pp. 163-181.

46. de Gaulle, August 1947, quoted in Talbott, *The War Without a Name*, p. 139.

47. General Charles de Gaulle, *Memoirs of Hope* (translated by Terence Kilmartin) (London: Weidenfeld and Nicolson, 1971), p. 45, and Lacouture, *De Gaulle*, pp. 159, 185, 240, and 330; for definitive evidence that this was his view by April 1958, see Lacouture, *de Gaulle*, p. 163. He may have changed his initial position even earlier than June 1955 (see Talbott, *The War Without a Name*, p. 140).

48. See de Gaulle, *Memoirs of Hope*, p. 46.

49. See Lacouture, *De Gaulle*, p. 188, for de Gaulle's comment on this.

50. Ferhat Abbas, *Autopsie d'un Guerre* (Paris: Editions Garnier Frères, 1980), p. 269 (my translation); (*"Pour arriver à la paix, le Générale de Gaulle fait la guerre"*).

51. Raymond Aron in Horne, *A Savage War of Peace*, p. 331.

52. Abbas, *Autopsie d'un Guerre*, p. 269 (my translation).

53. John Wallis, reporting from Oran in the *Daily Telegraph*, 28 June 1960.

54. Horne, *A Savage War of Peace*, pp. 337, 342.

55. de Gaulle, *Memoirs of Hope*, p. 104; Talbott, *The War Without a Name*, p. 204.

56. This was due to such things as, for example, his "self-determination" speech of 16 September 1959 (see Lacouture, *De Gaulle*, p. 248, for an account of the speech).

57. Lacouture, *De Gaulle*, p. 281, and Horne, *A Savage War of Peace*, p. 450.

58. Talbott, *The War Without a Name*, pp. 205-206, and see Lacouture, *De Gaulle*, p. 278.

59. de Gaulle, *Memoirs of Hope*, p. 107, and see Talbott, *The War Without a Name*, p. 208, and Lacouture, *De Gaulle*, pp. 283-84.

60. de Gaulle, *Memoirs of Hope*, p. 107, and see Lacouture, *De Gaulle*, p. 284.

61. See Behr, *The Algerian Problem*, p. 178; Talbott, *The War Without a Name*, p. 210.

62. See Edgar O'Ballance, *The Algerian Insurrection* (London: Faber and Faber, 1967), p. 181, and Lacouture, *De Gaulle*, p. 286n.

63. de Gaulle, *Memoirs of Hope*, pp. 121-122.

64. Even after the cease-fire agreement was signed at Evian, the OAS announced that "M. de Gaulle's cease-fire is not that of the OAS!" (Lacouture, *De Gaulle*, p. 319).

65. Their involvement had perhaps even begun before, as argues Behr, *The Algerian Problem*, p. 135f.

66. O'Ballance, *The Algerian Insurrection*, p. 104.

67. For an account of the episode, see Behr, *The Algerian Problem*, pp. 123-5, Horne, *A Savage War of Peace*, pp. 160-61, William B. Quandt, *Revolution and Political Leadership: Algeria, 1954-68* (Massachusetts: MIT, 1969) pp. 104-105; Richard and

Joan Brace, *Ordeal in Algeria* (Princeton: D. van Nostrand Co., 1960), pp. 142-47, Clark, *Algeria in Turmoil*, pp. 348-49, Talbott, *The War Without a Name*, p. 72.

68. Ben Bella (translated by Camilla Sykes), *Ben Bella (transliterations of recordings made by Ben Bella by Robert Merle)* (London: Michael Joseph, 1967), pp. 109-110; Quandt, too, blames the army (*Revolution*, p. 105). See Talbott, *The War Without a Name*, p. 73, for a refutation of the claim that war could have ended had the episode not occurred.

69. Horne, *A Savage War of Peace*, p. 282; for alternate translations with the same sense, see Brace and Brace, *Ordeal in Algeria*, pp. 206-07, and Lacouture, *De Gaulle*, p. 166.

70. For an account of the plans, see Talbott, *The War Without a Name*, pp. 126-27, and Brace and Brace, *Ordeal in Algeria*, pp. 241*ff*.

71. O'Ballance, *The Algerian Insurrection*, pp. 101-107, 111, 112-113; Behr, *The Algerian Problem*, p. 132.

72. de Gaulle, *Memoirs of Hope*, p. 50.

73. Behr, *The Algerian Problem*, pp. 143, 145.

74. See O'Ballance, *The Algerian Insurrection*, pp. 114-115; Talbott, *The War Without a Name*, pp. 144-45.

75. de Gaulle, *Memoirs of Hope*, p. 83.

76. General Charles de Gaulle, "Address to the European insurgents and the French Army in Algeria," 29 January 1960, reprinted in Behr, *The Algerian Problem*, pp. 250-54.

77. de Gaulle, *Memoirs of Hope*, p. 86.

78. General Maurice Challe, in Talbott, *The War Without a Name*, p. 145.

79. de Gaulle, *Memoirs of Hope*, p. 92.

80. See, for example, Cook, *Charles de Gaulle*, p. 313, Brian Crozier, *De Gaulle: the Statesman* (London: Eyre Methuen, 1973), p. 453, Alexander Harrison, *Challenging de Gaulle: The OAS and the Counterrevolution in Algeria, 1954-1962* (New York: Praeger, 1989), p. 39, Horne, *A Savage War of Peace*, pp. 174-175, Lacouture, *De Gaulle*, p. 165, and Talbott, *The War Without a Name*, pp. 64, 197, 207.

81. Harrison, *Challenging de Gaulle*, p. 39.

82. Talbott, *The War Without a Name*, pp. 64, 207, and see also p. 197.

83. Horne, *A Savage War of Peace*, p. 337; Talbott, *The War Without a Name*, p. 186, and see John Wallis, reporting from Oran in the *Daily Telegraph*, 28 June 1960.

84. See Harrison, *Challenging de Gaulle*, p. 49, and "Algeria deadline," by William Millinship, reporting in *The Observer*, 6 September 1959.

85. de Gaulle, *Memoirs of Hope*, p. 92.

86. Harrison, *Challenging de Gaulle*, p. 56.

87. Thomas C. Schelling, *Arms and Influence* (London: Yale University Press, 1966), p. 50.

88. Horne, *A Savage War of Peace*, p. 50.

89. See doc. 13 in Mohammed Harbi, *Les archives de la révolution algérienne* (Paris: les éditions jeune afrique, 1981), pp. 101-103, or Horne, *A Savage War of Peace*, p. 95.

90. Horne, *A Savage War of Peace*, pp. 40-41.

91. See Clark, *Algeria in Turmoil*, p. 113, and Horne, *A Savage War of Peace*, pp. 40-41.

92. See Harbi, *Les archives de la révolution algérienne*, pp. 346-47.

93. Dr. Lamine-Debaghine, FLN spokesman, quoted in Behr, *The Algerian Problem*, p. 125.

94. Ben Bella, *Ben Bella*, pp. 94-95.

95. Horne, *A Savage War of Peace*, pp. 135, 140-41. Ironically, the French themselves may have been somewhat responsible for this kind of FLN intransigence. Horne (p. 39) argues that it was a direct consequence of the French breaking up the traditional families of Algeria in the 1800s.

96. Clark, *Algeria in Turmoil*, p. 255.

97. Benyousef Ben Khedda, *Les Accords d'Evian* (Publisud-OPU, 1986), p. 10 (my translation); (*C'est parce qu'elle a trouvé en lui un interlocuteur crédible, que la France à pu négocier avec le FLN. Négociation, à deux qui, du coup, a rendu inutile toute médiation d'un tier et <<a fortiori>>, éliminé toute risque d'internationalisation*).

98. Ntieyong U. Akpan, *The Struggle for Secession 1966-1970* (London: Frank Cass, 1971), p. 107.

99. Akpan, *The Struggle for Secession*, p. 109, and see, for example, Sir Louis Mbanefo's comments in his speech at Kampala, 23 May 1968, reprinted as doc. 157 in Kirk-Greene, *Crisis and Conflict in Nigeria*, pp. 229-232.

100. See Kirk-Greene, *Crisis and Conflict in Nigeria*, pp. 47-48.

101. For more, see "Ojukwu's Address to Consultative Assembly", 27 January 1968, doc. 142 in Kirk-Greene, *Crisis and Conflict in Nigeria*, pp. 192-199, and his remarks in the address to the Addis Ababa Peace Talks on 5 August 1968, reprinted in Chukwuemeka Odemegwu Ojukwu, *Biafra: Selected Speeches of Ojukwu* (New York: Harper and Row, 1969), p. 355, and also reprinted in Kirk-Greene as doc. 168, pp. 247-272.

102. 1) Ojukwu, in a broadcast from Enugu, 29 September 1967, and reprinted as doc. 136 in Kirk-Greene, *Crisis and Conflict in Nigeria*, p. 175; 2) Chukwuemeka Odemegwu Ojukwu, *Biafra* (New York: Harper and Row, 1969), p. 93; 3) Ojukwu, *Biafra*, p. 28; 4) Ibid., p. 31.

103. See the report by the international observer team (2 October 1968), available from the British Foreign and Commonwealth Office (and also reprinted as doc. 184 in Kirk-Greene, *Crisis and Conflict in Nigeria*, p. 331).

104. See Kirk-Greene, *Crisis and Conflict in Nigeria*, p. 81; S.G. Ikoku (an Ibo), for example, noted that in the Lagos region more than 50,000 Ibos lived and worked unmolested, and that half a million more were in a similar situation in the Mid-West State. See S.G. Ikoku, "La sécession Biafran: mythes et réalités," *Revue Français d'Etudes Politique Africaines* 49 (January 1970), pp. 56-57.

105. See Kirk-Greene, *Crisis and Conflict in Nigeria*, pp. 143-44; but for more radical Biafran comment on all this evidence, see Arthur Agwuncha Nwanko and Samuel Udochukwo Ifejika, *The Making of a Nation: Biafra* (London: C. Hurst & Co., 1969), pp. 279-87.

106. Raph Uwechue, "Des concessions réciproque pour une paix juste et durable," *Revue Français d'Etudes Politique Africaines* 49 (1970), p. 33.

107. Adam Curle, interview with the author, 19 September 1991.

108. Akpan, *The Struggle for Secession*, p. xvi.

109. John de St. Jorre, *The Nigerian Civil War* (London: Hodder and Stoughton, 1977), pp. 113, 116, 222.

110.   The Papal Mission of Peace and Relief to the Ecclesiastical Province of Onitsha, 7-12 February 1968, unpublished report, p. 5, in John J. Stremlau, *The International Politics of the Nigerian Civil War (1967-70)* (Princeton: Princeton University Press, 1977), p. 122. Of course it was not only propaganda which fed the belief. Federal forces -- whatever their intentions -- had essentially cut Biafra off from outside aid, resulting in the death by starvation of hundreds of thousands.

111.   Chukwuemeka Odemegwu Ojukwu, *Because I Am Involved* (Ibadan: Spectrum Books, 1989), p. 168.

112.   See the following chapter.

113.   *Summary of World Broadcasts*, ME/0170/A/4-6 (3 June 1988).

114.   Ibid.

115.   See, for example, *Summary of World Broadcasts*, ME/0179/A/4, ME/0183/A/3.

116.   Iranian General Command Headquarters Address, *Summary of World Broadcasts*, ME/0207/A/10 (18 July 1988).

117.   Rafsanjani, *Summary of World Broadcasts*, ME/0208/i(a) (20 July 1988).

118.   Ibid.

119.   See Hanns Maull and Otto Pick, *The Gulf War: Regional and International Dimensions* (London: Pinter Publishers, 1988), p. 69. The effectiveness of the campaign was noteworthy: President Rafsanjani (in Maull and Pick, p. 72, n24) was confident enough of its success to state in February 1989 that "War till victory was never a slogan of the Revolution"!

120.   *The Daily Telegraph*, 5 July 1988.

121.   Maull and Pick, *The Gulf War*, p. 15; and see Thomas L. McNaugher, "Walking the Tightropes in the Gulf" and Chaim Herzog, "A Military-Strategic Overview," both in Efraim Karsh (ed.), *The Iran-Iraq War: Impact and Implications* (London: Macmillan, 1987), pp. 191, 266.

122.   Ayatollah Khomeini, *Summary of World Broadcasts*, ME/0195/i (6 July 1988) and see ME/0197/i, ME/0198/1-2, ME/0199/1-4, for further examples of the deflection of political goals.

123.   See Karsh and Rautsi, *Saddam Hussein: A Political Biography* (New York: Macmillan Free Press, 1991), pp. 248, 262-63.

124.   Karsh and Rautsi, *Saddam Hussein*, p. 241.

125.   *Summary of World Broadcasts*, ME/0973/A/1, 0418 gmt, 17 January 1991.

126.   *Summary of World Broadcasts*, ME/0986/A/2 (30 January 1991).

127.   *Summary of World Broadcasts*, ME/0995/5 (12 February 1991); ME/0979/A/1 (25 January 1991).

5

Making the Decision to Stop Fighting: *"WE didn't consider it; THEY wouldn't listen; WE couldn't agree"*

The decision-making structures of belligerent leaderships differ. Some are totalitarian or oligarchic, where decisions are generally made by one person or a small group of people, and criticism is generally neither offered nor tolerated. An example of this would be the leadership structure of Iraq during the Iran-Iraq and Gulf wars. Others are coalition structures with weak central leaderships, such as the early governments of France during the Algerian War of Independence, as well as their counterparts in the FLN. Although there is usually central leader, sometimes elected, the decisions are generally made by the group; group consensus is often a conscious goal. Finally, there are the so-called democratic structures, where an elected central leader is surrounded by colleagues and advisors. In general, decision making power ultimately rests with one person, but criticism of policy, or at least discussion, is generally accepted and expected.[1] Most Western governments fall in to this final category.

Whatever the structure of a belligerent leadership, the interaction between the leader or group of leaders and their "inner circle" -- those responsible to and closest to the ultimate decision-makers -- has a great effect on the consideration of the question of cease-fire. This is primarily and obviously a question of group dynamics and decision-making, about which there is a large body of literature. Most of that literature will not be discussed or evaluated here; that is a task which has not only been extensively undertaken by others, but is an unwieldy topic impossible to detail in as complete a way as might otherwise be desirable. Moreover, the group dynamic as it relates to cease-fires may by situation-specific; the process may in many cases be unique. For these reasons, the focus will therefore be on how, specifically, the structure of belligerents' inner circles contributes negatively to the effectuation of cease-fires.

Inner circle structures have a great effect on the possibilities for cease-fire. Moreover, identifiable structures can be related to specific effects. Again, the fact that a given structure *may* lead to a particular effect does not mean it will always do so -- the relationship is only quasi-deterministic in this sense. The point remains, however, that some structures are more readily associated with the negative effect which they have on cease-fire effectuation than others. As a general rule, there are only three types of relationships which can be distinguished in belligerent leadership-inner circle structures (see Figure 5.1). In all cases, the existence of an intransigent and generally closed-minded ultimate leadership is assumed. That is, the chapter focuses cases where the ultimate leadership has no sufficient will to cease fire, but those who surround him may, and discussion centres on their relation-

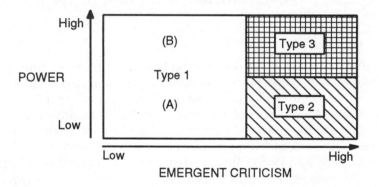

FIGURE 5.1: Belligerent Inner Circle Structures. The structure of inner circles -- and the consequent likelihood of their being able to help end the fighting -- is dependent primarily on two factors: the amount of power they wield, and their willingness to criticize.

ship to the leadership and the possibilities it offers for cease-fire.[2] It should further be remembered that the structures are not set for the duration of the war. They are fluid, and a change in structure may be effected, for example, by an increase in the power of the inner circle.

The first of these structures is characterized by an inner circle unwilling or psychologically unable to criticize the leadership. Their power -- the influence which they may bring to bear on the ultimate decision-maker or decision-making body -- may be either high or low. For ease of discussion, call this structure *Type 1*. The negative result of this kind of relationship is that the leadership, left to its own devices, develops a "fight to the finish" mentality which is difficult to overcome. The second structure (*Type* 2) concerns those cases where the inner circle, although willing to criticize, has little or no power. The negative results of this relationship are either that criticism is ineffective, or it is dealt with so severely that the group reverts to the previous, non-critical Type 1 relationship with the leadership.

Finally, there are those cases where the inner circle is willing to criticize and has moderate or high power (*Type* 3). One negative result here is that discernible divisions appear to outsiders, and confused instead of compromise positions emerge. Obviously, all of these relationships can have positive as well as negative consequences. In a Type 2 or Type 3 relationship, for example, where the leader is open to criticism, and willing to discuss all possibilities rationally, an inner circle with grave doubts about the course of the war and the desirability of cease-fire can raise those doubts, and a cease-fire may be the result. Again, however, the focus here is on obstacles to cease-fire, and the possibility of an open-minded or peace-desiring leader is not assumed.

Type 1 Structures: "*We didn't (dare) consider it*"

The Type 1 structure of belligerent inner circles is characterized by variable inherent power and an unwillingness or psychological inability to criticize. Thus, given a situation in which a leader -- which hereafter may be taken to mean a single individual or group of individuals (in all cases the ultimate decision-making body) -- is pressing for victory at any cost, and even where it is obvious to the inner circle that such a goal is unattainable, the possibility of cease-fire will not be raised. In the end, the leader's own position -- that force is still the best way to accomplish goals -- is the only one which emerges. A Type 1 relationship is really two relationships, the first of these (IA) where emergent criticism is low, and power is low. The second (IB) is where emergent criticism is low, and power is high. The two, although separable in terms of their origins, are characterized together as Type 1 relationship for the reason that the relevant factor in this behavior is not the power of the inner circle per se, but the relative quantity of emergent criticism. In either case -- whether the circle has high or low power -- the result is the same: a lack of criticism of a leadership unwilling to consider cease-fire.

Turning first to the Type 1A (self-suppression) relationship, where both power and emergent criticism are low, the single most common factor preventing leadership exposure to criticism concerns the penalties assumed to be attached to such actions, especially pronounced in wartime: "*We (the inner circle) didn't dare consider it.*" It is a notorious problem facing belligerents that those who have the nation's interests clearly in mind are reluctant to speak up when the directed course of the war goes against such interests. The critics suppress themselves, mostly because there are perceived penalties attached to revealing one's doubts in wartime, and things that need to be proposed are not proposed because of those penalties (which can be as mild as mere embarrassment or humiliation, or as severe as the loss of one's life).[3] It is thus that "no individual or faction within any party will relish being the first to advocate that goals be abandoned and defeat accepted."[4] In the same way, no individual or faction will enjoy proposing that the time has come to cease fire, even if only temporarily.

Leon Sigal, in his detailed study of the Japanese/American efforts at war termination in 1945, notes that Japanese officials whose duties could be presumed to include planning for eventual cease-fire, were nevertheless reluctant to do so "lest they appear to undercut the war effort and leave themselves open to accusations of treason by those whose only conception of war's end was victory."[5] This problem is certainly not unique to the Second World War. A journalist who spent time with FLN forces noted that the least transgression or sign of disloyalty usually resulted in the death of the offender.[6] Si Salah, the FLN leader of the Algiers *wilaya*, informed the GPRA that he had over 400 ALN guerrillas killed for their part in a "plot" aimed at a negotiated cease-fire with the French. These tactics were probably rare,[7] but they undoubtedly had their effect. In his account of his role in the Algerian War, Ferhat Abbas noted that the idea of negotiations with the French "was a taboo subject ... a sacrilege";[8] it was something simply not brought up for discussion, perhaps due to the perceived consequences of doing so. Later, during the Vietnam War, it was only after the Tet offensive that senior officials in the US administration began to voice doubt about America's role in Vietnam, doubts which they had apparently held for years.[9] In Iraq during the Iran-Iraq war,

> [t]he first rumblings of discontent ... came in the summer of 1982 ... Although this feeble criticism did not reflect any organized opposition within the ranks of the military, [Saddam] Hussein took no chances. Some thirty high-ranking officers were executed, along with a small number of Party officials; others were purged ... To dissent was to commit suicide.[10]

As Iklé notes, fear of moral condemnation, fear of being thought of as "traitor" (and we might add fear of death), "deters senior officials and government officials from taking steps to end a war, even if they know full well that further fighting will do more harm than good." Thus, even actions which are clearly not in the interests of the nation often fail to be criticized, even in the case where the very existence of the nation may be in jeopardy. It may indeed the case that the only way to salvage something from the ruins of war is to have the leader of a particular nation resign, but fear of potential consequences of making that suggestion prevent the suggestion from ever being made: "One cannot debate regicide in the presence of the king."[11]

It must be said that although there are similarities, this kind of behavior is markedly different to that of cognitive and political dissonance. First, cognitive and political dissonance arise from actions taken by the leadership in order to forestall negative domestic or military reaction. Here, doubts of senior officials over policy are suppressed because of the perceived penalties -- psychological or physical -- which may be imposed *by* the ultimate leadership or officials of similar ranking. That is, and in general, Type 1A inner circles suppress doubt out of fear of penalties from *above*, whereas cognitive and political dissonance arise out of fear of penalties from *below*. Second, whereas cognitive and political dissonance are self-focused ("*I* said this, so now *I* can't go back on it."), the "self-suppression" behavior of Type 1A inner circles is other-focused ("*They*, the ultimate leadership said this; how can *I* say anything without being attacked?"). Thus, for example, the plight of American officials who also contemplated the end of the Second World War:

> anyone who tried to change America's war aims unilaterally had to undo an oft-stated policy that had overwhelming domestic political support, leaving himself open to attack from right and left. Even bringing the issue up for discussion inside the government was risky; opponents might leak word of it, arousing public antipathy and congressional consternation.[12]

The example is not of a leader fearing being driven from power by going back on his word (political dissonance), but of senior officials fearing going against their superiors' stated policies and thereby suffering the consequences -- Type 1A inner circle self-suppression behavior.

The Type 1B inner circle structure (consensus, or *"We didn't consider it"*) occurs when inner circle power is high, but emergent criticism is low. The inner circle, while maintaining at least some power or influence over the leader, chooses not to exercise that power. There is consensus about the course of action being taken in the war, and discussion about the possibility of cease-fire is precluded. There is, in this case, a collective denial of the realities of the military situation, and a collective desire for overall victory. The general reasons for this emergent viewpoint have been discussed in detail in the opening chapter, and also find explanations in cognitive dissonance theory, but need to be briefly mentioned here due to their obvious connection to the structure of the inner circle.

The fact that consensus emerges about the decision to continue to prosecute the war and avoid consideration of cease-fire is generally explicable in one of four ways. First, the leadership and the inner circle may have been misled (deliberately or inadvertently) about the truth of the military situation. Second, although fully aware of the present and future military situation, they may consciously choose to continue the war because of the domestic situation which demands it. Third, they could be fully aware of the military situation, but simply unwilling to give up everything that had been fought for by ceasing fire; there may still be the belief that somehow, some way, it is possible to win -- a point about which we have already said a great deal.

Finally, there is the phenomenon of what Irving Janis calls "groupthink." Here, the leader wants, and may even encourage criticism, but "subtle constraints, which the leader may reinforce inadvertently, prevent a member from fully exercising his critical powers and from openly expressing doubts when most others in the group have reached a consensus." Group members striving for unanimity "override their motivation to realistically appraise alternative courses of action."[13] Such behavior may have played a part in American decision making during the Gulf crisis. Paul Wolfowitz, American Undersecretary for Defence responsible for policy during the crisis, concluded that Bush's inner circle -- Secretary of State James Baker, Secretary of Defence Dick Cheney, National Security Advisor Brent Scowcroft and Chairman of the Joint Chiefs of Staff General Colin Powell -- "was perhaps a little too close knit." Their discussion and meetings, which Wolfowitz believed ought to be a forum for discussing alternatives, was of a different character entirely: [t]here was no feedback from Cheney, and if there was any kind of organized debate .. it was done without the benefit of staff."[14] Janis sees the phenomenon of groupthink as inexplicable: "the search for an explanation forces us to tread through a quagmire of theoretical issues in still largely uncharted areas of human motivation ... no well-established theory is generally accepted by behavioral scientists." Having said that, however, at least two directional markers exists: concurrence-seeking behavior probably has its roots in, first, cognitive dissonance theory and, second, as a way of dealing with the stresses of decision-making.[15] Whatever the explanation, it is enough for our purposes to note that the problem exists: a leadership and its inner circle will sometimes strive for consensus and continue to prosecute the war even where it may not be rational to do so.

Type 2 Structures: *"They (the leadership) just won't listen"*

The Type 2 inner circle structure is characterized by a moderate to high emergent criticism, but low inner circle power. In such cases, an inner circle opting for a cease-fire makes their position clear to the leader, who may or may not have asked for the inner circle's views. Because the group has little or no power, however, the leader is not bound to listen to this criticism, and may even take action to prevent it from arising again. Depending on the strength of that reaction, the inner circle may revert to a Type 1A self-suppression structure. That is, if the leader reacts negatively to the criticism, humiliating, chastising, embarrassing, or perhaps even killing some or all of the critics, those who remain may revert to a strategy of suppressing all doubts or dissent. Those fears and doubts evidenced in a Type 1A structure come to life, and result in a shift from a Type 2 (open criticism) to a Type 1A (self-suppression) structure. Alternatively, the inner circle may counter-react with an attempt to gain the power they need to put their position into action; some means of removing the leader from power, by means of a coup or other such action, may be undertaken when the inner circle realizes that their criticisms are not being taken to heart. A "successful" result here -- *i.e.* the inner circle's counter-reaction achieves its goals of a change in leadership -- produces a Type 1B structure (consensus) which, other factors notwithstanding, would lead to a cease-fire.

One variant on the structure takes place in leaderships by coalition. In these cases, and although one member of the decision-making body may be elected as a figurehead, actual decision-making is left in the hands of the group. In such cases, the distinction between "leader" and "inner circle" is really just a distinction between those opting for cease-fire ("doves"), and those opting to continue the war ("hawks"). If the doves have low power, however, they are still left with the same dilemmas as the inner circle in the standard Type 2 structure. They may voice their opinions, but steps may be taken to prevent further criticism, in which case the doves have the choice of either reverting to a Type 1 structure, or attempting to increase their power base.

A salient example of the Type 1 and Type 2 inner circle structures, and their effect on the possibilities for cease-fire, can be found in the Nigerian Civil War. Here, the inner circle structure on the Biafran side was in flux for most of the war, and alternated between Types 1 and 2. In general, the relationship was Type 1 in nature, where criticism and doubt was suppressed because of the fear of Ojukwu's reaction. Occasionally, however, civil and military staff were prepared to settle with the North, and were prepared to speak their minds. At the outset of the war, some even attempted a coup. Ojukwu's reaction to these criticisms, let alone to the attempts at removing him, however, generally resulted in an inner circle reversion to a Type 1A structure (self-suppression), and later dissent was inhibited. The difficulty here was not necessarily that there was a lack of inner circle criticism, but that the leader was unwilling to listen to it, and the inner circle had not the power necessary to effect a change.

In September 1968, and in view of Biafra's precarious military situation and the enormous casualties, a group of civil servants (including Uwechue) decided that the time had come to settle. Some of the group approached Ojukwu on the matter, but his reaction, according to de St. Jorre,

> was that of a king who suddenly feels his crown slipping. A furious telegram came back ... accusing the group of treason, stressing with an almost hysterical emphasis that Biafra's sovereignty was not negotiable under *any* circumstances.[16]

Uwechue was arrested and forced to resign over the matter. This incident is probably not representative of the inner circle structure in the war because, in general, Ojukwu's critics knew their place, and where they did not, their criticisms were repressed: the overall structure was Type 1 in nature.

Those who knew Ojukwu testified on many occasions after the war that his reaction to criticism was a tremendous problem. Ntieyong Akpan, head of the Biafran civil service at the time, recalls that the eventual result was that

> even when as happened at certain stages, people felt that a halt should be called to the war, nobody dared say so openly. The intelligence network was complex and interwoven. Fear of sabotage and saboteurs was always present, particularly when the area controlled by Biafra became so small and the Federal troops were so near. On the occasions when certain people tried to speak out freely, cries were raised that such people were planning to stage a coup.[17]

Ojukwu's fears were perhaps understandable, as he had been the target of an attempted coup in September 1967, whose aim was to make peace with the federal government. The coup plot was discovered, and the plotters were executed.[18] It was no wonder then, that Ojukwu's later relationships with his inner circle were based on the suppression of dissent.

Providing further insight into Ojukwu's relationship with his inner circle, Akpan recalls an incident in which he was personally involved which occurred at the outset of the war. Two thousand Biafran volunteers had been lined up, issued each with a gun and *four* cartridges, and sent off to the front in waiting trucks. (It was this action which finally convinced Akpan himself of the hopelessness of the situation.) Then, two officers came to collect their promised anti-tank weapons, only to find that they did not exist. They took Akpan aside and told him that some other means, by which they meant diplomatic and political means, was needed to solve the crisis. Akpan agreed, and went to consult with Ojukwu, who demanded only to know which of his officers had suggested surrender. Akpan comments that "[i]f I had known [their names] I would not have told the governor for fear of what might befall the officers concerned, whose principal interest, I was sure, was to save lives."[19] It was obvious that while critics in the civil service were in danger of losing their jobs if they stepped over Ojukwu's line, those in the military were in danger of losing more. The executions of 1967 made that perfectly clear, and Ojukwu's successor, Philip Effiong, who took over when Ojukwu fled the country in 1970, noted in an interview that

> Ojukwu was a dictator, you know. It wasn't always safe or easy to oppose his ways or will. The best you could do was point out the dangers to Ojukwu. But if you didn't know when to stop shooting your mouth he could easily throw you in detention.[20]

Critics of Ojukwu also had another problem. Ojukwu also had mass support, thanks to the massive propaganda effort[21] and because the masses "saw in him a leader with the necessary toughness and the will to challenge Lagos and avenge them for their bitter experiences and the massacres of [the pre-war coup of] 1966."[22] His critics, therefore, all lay in the military and civil service and lacked requisite popular support.

Even at the end of the war, it was Ojukwu himself who dictated policy; critics were cautious, if not silent altogether. By 9 January 1970, military defeat was obvious, and Ojukwu had the final meeting with his cabinet. The Nigerians had made the breakthrough the in December, when two federal divisions linked up, isolating food producing areas in the East and cutting Biafra in two. Everything went downhill from there. According to St. Jorre, at the cabinet meeting, several military leaders and other inner circle members urged Ojukwu to leave the country to allow them to sue for peace. Ojukwu agreed "meekly" that it would be best for all concerned.[23]

Akpan, however, gives an entirely different account of this meeting, saying that Ojukwu himself suggested his own departure after being informed of the military situation by Akpan and Effiong. Given all we know of Ojukwu's reaction to criticism, Akpan's account would appear to be the more credible one.[24] Akpan also suggests, however, that Ojukwu's intentions were not nearly so honorable as they might appear: "I have since met a number of those concerned who are very embittered towards Ojukwu, whose sudden departure they consider despicable, cowardly, and ignominious." Akpan himself called the act "cowardly," "selfish and ungallant" but despite all this criticism, he acknowledges that the act did end the war more quickly than it might have otherwise.[25] Ojukwu's departure allowed Effiong to sue for peace, a thing Ojukwu felt himself unable to do. As was the case throughout the war, Ojukwu's own position inevitably triumphed, and his act of self-dismissal at the end of the war must be considered not as evidence that Ojukwu gave into pressure, but only as evidence that Ojukwu himself finally understood the situation and was willing to act on it.

Type 3 Structures: *"We (the leader and inner circle) couldn't agree"*

A Type 3 inner circle structure is characterized by high emergent criticism and moderate to high power. The inner circle in this case not only believes that cease-fire is the proper course of action, they are willing to state this openly, and may have the power and influence to bring that goal about. The primary difficulty in this structure lies in the estimate of the relative power of the inner circle by those external to the process. Where the power is only moderate, but perceived by outsiders to be high, the other belligerent or third parties may take the views of those pushing for cease-fire as the emerging ones. They may fail to realize that the power of the critics is not as great as it appears, and when the critics are forced to a more hard-line position by their more powerful leaders, and a cease-fire fails to materialize, distrust of the critics and their leader increases.

Alternatively, where the power of the critical inner circle is *actually* high, but still insufficient to bring about the desired change in direction, the result is similar. Third parties as well as the other belligerent are unable to discern genuine intentions; divisions are evident, and it remains unclear what the dominant position will eventually be. No negotiations for cease-fire can be entered into on this basis.[26] In Type 3 structures where inner circle power is insufficient to bring about a change, the leader's position may emerge as the dominant but dissenting positions are present, perceived by third parties, and inevitably confuse the issue.

The divisions which may characterize a Type 3 structure not only have an effect on the other belligerent and on third parties, however. Where leadership divisions become evident, the domestic population and the belligerent's own military may also perceive the divisiveness. This has an obvious effect on morale, which is almost always affected negatively. Domestic populations and military personnel who did not question the logic of the war previous to that point may well begin to do so when they see that their own leadership is unclear about the purpose of continuing to fight. In one sense, then, a Type 3 structure is a positive factor for peace. Domestic populations and military personnel may begin to exert pressure for a cease-fire which may not have existed previous to the perceived divisions. Overall, however, a Type 3 structure will generally act as an obstacle to cease-fire as it either increases the distrust of the other belligerent, or prevents a clear compromise position from emerging.

The inner circle of Iran during the Iran-Iraq war, for example, can generally be classified as a Type 3 structure. It is an imperfect model, as most are, as it fails to illustrate all the consequences of a Type 3 structure, but it can nevertheless provide some indications as to its functions and effects. As is well known, the Iranian position was generally hard line; Ayatollah Khomeini retained his "victory at any costs" position right to the very end of the war, and it would take the combination of war weariness and superpower pressure (which came only as a result of the internationalization of the war) to finally convince him that the time had come to settle. From the outset of the war, however, critics felt they had enough power to make their doubts known. They felt their own power base to be strong enough to withstand Khomeini's reaction, and felt able to risk the possible consequences of criticism. The dominant position in this case was always Khomeini's, however. Critics pushing for cease-fire really never had enough power on their own to actually effect a change in policy. The effect these critics had, however, was nevertheless substantial. Iraq and third parties were subjected to what at first seemed hopeful signs at various points in the war. In each case the hopes were dashed as critics were reprimanded and the hard line position restated.

Even from the outset of the war, it was clear that there was criticism of Khomeini's policy. We have already discussed the opening hard line position of Iran. By 29 October 1980, that position was firmly entrenched, and public opinion had already been aroused to such an extent by the repeated stating of hard-line positions that a even if both sides had wanted to cease fire, it was now politically impossible.[27] Despite this, and while there were probably precious few in Iran who were interested in a cease-fire as long as Iraq retained Iranian territory, there must have been some: when the non-aligned movement announced that it had a peace proposal on 12 November 1980, it was Iran which asked for clarification.[28] It seems unlikely that it would do such a thing now when it was all too willing to openly reject a Security Council resolution.[29] It is logical to conclude that there were at least some within the Iranian hierarchy who were pushing for a cease-fire. The public face of Iran, however, was decidedly in favor of continuing the war.

That there were serious divisions in the Iranian hierarchy became clearer in 1981. On one side stood the Islamic Republican Party (IRP) which believed in a theocratic government. It was generally allied to those on the left, the Tudeh and the majority of the Fadayan, as well as to the Revolutionary Guard.[30] Ranged against them were other, less politically powerful and more moderate groups who believed that the clergy should not wield supreme executive power.[31] Included in the latter group was President Bani-Sadr, who took office in January 1980, and who would be driven from office before the year was out. The divisions ran deep: Bani-Sadr, for example, considered the IRP "a greater calamity for the country than the war with Iraq." The feelings were mutual, the IRP apparently believing that it was "preferable to lose half of Iran than for Bani-Sadr to become the ruler."[32] The whole matter would be complicated by the Marxist-Islamic *Mujahadeen*,[33] who (in June 1981) assassinated not only Ayatollah Beheshti, the leader of the IRP, but (in August) the new president (Mohammed Rajai) and the Prime Minister (Javed Bahonar) as well.[34] As for Ayatollah Khomeini himself, he was at most times allied to the IRP and other groups which had set themselves against Bani-Sadr and his allies. This was not always the case, however, and Khomeini sometimes disapproved of IRP policy, motivated in part by his desire to avoid alienating those whom Bani-Sadr represented (such as the more moderate Islamic groups and the intelligentsia).[35]

The divisions, then, were well-entrenched. The varied comments which followed the "official" Iranian statement of conditions for cease-fire on 2 March 1981 more than made this clear. On 3 March, Iran's chief of the armed forces, General Valcollah Fallahi, announced that "this issue needs a very short stage of cease-fire and then immediately, and without any conditions, the aggressor should leave our territory." (Fallahi was taking the "cease fire, then negotiate" position, but Saddam Hussein was remaining with "negotiate, then cease fire." Just to dig himself in more, Hussein also added that he would retain this position "even if the war dragged on for 20 years."[36]) Whatever Fallahi's own beliefs, the official position of Iran had not changed: there would have to be a withdrawal before a cease-fire.[37] Even this official government position, however, was open to question, Premier Rajai restating Khomeini's firm belief that "there cannot be any peace between Islam and blasphemy."[38] To confuse matters even more, Ayatollah Beheshti, the head of the Iranian Supreme Court, announced on 5 March 1981 that "Iraq must first clearly *announce its intention* to begin withdrawing at a specified time and then there would be a provisional cease-fire while this is being done"(emphasis added),[39] and President Bani-Sadr called for a *simultaneous* cease-fire and withdrawal, compatible in some ways with Beheshti's proposal, but not with anyone else's. Bani-Sadr also called for an adherence to the Algiers agreement of 1975 and condemnation of the aggressor.[40] The critics seemed to be everywhere, but not only did they disagree with Khomeini's own policy, they disagreed among themselves. In such a situation, and even though the critics felt themselves sufficiently powerful to publicly comment on the conduct of the war, their own divisiveness would ensure that the only position which could finally emerge would be Khomeini's.

Of course, the critics were in a difficult position, for Khomeini's position was for all intents and purposes unassailable. Shaul Bakhash, in his extensive study of the Iranian Revolution, notes that Khomeini came to be seen as the *bot-shekan*, the idol-smasher. To his people, he was *the* Imam, not only a religious leader, but a political one as well, and due in part to earlier writings of influential clerics and jurists, the powers of the Islamic government, and particularly those of the *imam*, were extensive. Its (and his) authority could supersede the law of the land.[41] Critics, then, had a seemingly impossible task: to go against the policies of their foremost religious leader without crossing a line which might well have been considered blasphemous. In addition to the difficulty of Khomeini's essentially unassailable authority however, critics faced another problem. According to Bani-Sadr, Khomeini deliberately used the divisions in his inner circle to his advantage. In a policy of "rule by dividing," he consciously supported some parties "merely to annoy others," and his targets included the IRP.[42] Given all of this, it is hardly surprising that Khomeini's intransigent, hard-line position would be the only one which could be clearly pointed to by observers. In May 1982, for example, Iranian forces recaptured the port of Khorramshahr. For a month following the event, the inner circle argued among themselves about whether or not to now extend the war to Iraqi territory. Khomeini settled the debate with an announcement (on 21 June) that Iran now sought the overthrow of Saddam Hussein, and the war was carried over the border.[43]

Despite the emergent and underlying Iranian intransigence, however, Iran did continue to accept mediation efforts. In early December 1982, for example, Algeria and the UAE approached Iran, and their efforts, combined with the visible effects of a failed Iranian offensive of 6-16 February 1983, appeared to have paid off: on 21 February the Algerian foreign minister announced that Iran had dropped its demand for the removal of Saddam Hussein.[44] The announcement was confirmed by Iranian Foreign Minister Ali Akbar Velayati on 24 February, and although face-to-face talks would still be impossible, negotiations towards a cease-fire did not now seem out of the question.[45] Unfortunately, Iranian politics were still creating difficulties: Rafsanjani crushed all hopes of impending negotiations on 25 February, announcing that the "rumor" that Iran was no longer asking for the fall of Saddam was "not true."[46] A 25 February statement issued by the Security Council president which called for a cease-fire was rejected.[47] Moderates in this case, while having made some definite advances in achieving a cease-fire, were put down by the more powerful hard line forces, and the war continued.

Iran clung to its hard line position tenaciously, at least in public. An *Economist* article of 12 April 1984, however, reported a weakening of Iranian will, political disaffection, and public demonstrations. It is unclear whether this political disaffection and public discontent was a result of perceived divisiveness, a reaction to a number of failed Iranian offensives -- or both -- but if it were all true, one would have expected that a particularly promising proposal put to the Iranians by Egypt, Yugoslavia, and India would have been accepted. The plan, announced 29 April 1984, called for a withdrawal of Iraq, a cease-fire, an international peacekeeping force on the Iraqi side, a NAM commission to determine war guilt, and a pan-Islamic fund to rebuild both countries.[48] Admittedly, not all the Iranian demands would have been met in full, but it could have been a good start. Instead, it went nowhere. Two explanations for this suggest themselves. The first is that despite the number of failed Iranian offensives to this point, there was still a perception within Iran that victory was attainable, and since Khomeini held the reins, little could be done. The alternative explanation is that internal divisions within the Iranian hierarchy were still preventing a reasoned consideration of proposals to end the war. Still too few were interested, and those who were interested were not in positions of power or had no power behind them. The *Economist* article mentions these possible divisions, and it would go a long way towards explaining the rejection of the 29 April proposal.

On 29 September 1984, Japan unveiled a plan that, like so many proposals before it, promised to bring the war to an end. The proposal called for Iraq to commit to halting the use of chemical weapons (a practice which outraged both Iran and the world generally), for both countries to allow freedom of navigation in the Gulf, and for Iran to permit the dredging and re-opening of Iraqi harbors. It was relatively simple strategy, having the intent to neutralize the strategic battleground of the war. It was thought that although there might still be "skirmishes" in the North, the bulk of the fighting would inevitably be halted.[49] The 11 October *Times* noted other reasons it might be accepted. In the first place, it dealt with "the immediate interests of both sides. Moreover, it dispensed with the need for formal negotiations, and "each country could satisfy its honor by interpreting some of the points, for domestic reasons, as an overt surrender by the other side, or choosing other points to remain as tacit understandings."[50] Iraq "welcomed" the proposal officially on 8 October,[51] but it was, as usual, rejected by Iran. The Japanese chose to blame this on Iranian disunity: "Iranian leaders could not present a united position."[52] It was a plausible explanation.

The expansion of the tanker war in 1986 eventually led to the damaging of a Soviet freighter on 7 May 1987, and on 17 May an Iraqi attack on a US warship, the *USS Stark*, killed 37 US servicemen. The incidents, the latter by all accounts an accident, added to the international momentum which was being created to attempt to force a cease-fire, and underlined the need to bring the conflict in the Gulf to a swift end. On 20 July 1987, the Security Council *demanded* a cease-fire,[53] a thing which has been rare in the past. It was a threat, no doubt, as "further steps" would be taken if the resolution was not obeyed, but it also offered much to Iran in the way of positive incentives. Iran's demand that Iraq be named as the aggressor was handled with a promise of an impartial inquiry into the responsibility for the war. Reparations demands were dealt with through a recognition of the need for reconstruction "with appropriate international assistance," and the resolution "deplored" the use of chemical weapons, something Iran had been demanding that the UN do for some time.[54] (Iraq was not explicitly named as the culprit, however.) Iraq, according to its UN ambassador, would accept the resolution,[55] but Iran reacted somewhat differently. Officially, it had not rejected the resolution -- "we have not given a flat rejection",[56] "we simply comment on its contents."[57]

It was evident that the Iranian leadership was unclear about what to do next. President Khamenei of Iran stressed that Iran would *never* accept a UN resolution calling for a cease-fire: "We will pursue the war ... until the elimination of the regime governing Iraq."[58] On the other hand, the fact that attacks on Gulf shipping had ceased[59] since the adoption of the resolution was probably not a coincidence, and Iran's behavior may have been modified in other ways as well: Velayati announced on 17 August that a visit by de Cuellar would be welcomed, and he referred to de Cuellar's 1985 proposals as "positive."[60]

This hedging by Iran paid dividends (which may, as an alternative explanation, have been the original intent). The USSR announced on 26 August 1987 that an arms embargo now would be "premature." It now wanted to wait until de Cuellar had his chance to mediate. Moreover, a meeting of Arab League foreign ministers agreed on the same day to postpone until 20 September discussion about what steps the group should take if Iran rejected the resolution.[61] De Cuellar, for his part, was understandably wary about attempting to make another effort. All his attempts in the past had been met by the traditional Iranian demands which had not been subject to negotiation, and he saw no point in going until the exact conditions of his visit had been outlined.[62]

Iran continued to stall for time and sort out its internal position, still insisting on 27 August that it neither accepted nor rejected the resolution.[63] Public statements by Iranian officials shed some light on the divisions. The deputy foreign minister categorically stated that Iran did not accept the resolution,[64] but Rafsanjani commented that if the UN Security Council "focuses its activities on condemning the aggressor" then Iran would be ready to cooperate.[65]

In the face of Iran's vacillation, and UN movement which could only be described as ponderous, Baghdad felt compelled to renew its attacks on shipping in the Gulf on 1 September 1987. Iraq further argued that the brief respite had benefitted Iran only (recalling the argument about making gains under a cease-fire). The accusation was probably not unjustified: Iran, in the absence of attacks on shipping, was apparently putting oil through the Gulf at the rate of 3 million barrels a day.[66] The move was nevertheless condemned by Britain, which now wanted an embargo placed on both countries.[67]

The United States said that a definite response to the UN resolution had to come from Tehran before 5 September.[68] In response, Iran formally invited Perez de Cuellar to Tehran on 3 September. De Cuellar accepted, but the Security Council made it clear that the visit would be to discuss only how the resolution should be carried out, not to re-negotiate it.[69] On 4 September, Iran's UN representative responded to the accusations of time-wasting, and held out some hope that de Cuellar might finally accomplish something: "we do not want to waste time, but want to speak to the UN chief honestly." He added that the resolution contained positive points and therefore had not been officially rejected.[70] In the end, however, it was. Any members of the inner circle who may have been pushing for acceptance were eventually overruled, and Iran simply restated its original conditions for cease-fire.[71]

In this case, then, and at many points during the war, inner circle critics of Iran's hard-line position were able to make their views known not only to the domestic population, but to Iraq and third parties as well. Their power, however, was never great enough to effect a change in leadership views; the hard-line position was always the emergent one. The problem of a divided leadership is a "domestic difficulty" which can prevent a cease-fire even where there exists a degree of political will to end the war. Factional infighting, and the struggle for control over the nation can prevent a clear compromise position from emerging. In the Iran-Iraq war, any group or individual pushing for peace would eventually be obscured by larger, more powerful groups and individuals, who wished to continue the war "until victory."

Conclusions

In any war in which a belligerent leadership is not amenable to the idea of a cease-fire, but in which a cease-fire would nevertheless seem the rational course, the structure of the belligerent's inner circle can have a negative effect on whether a cease-fire will eventually result. Type 1A structures (self-suppression) are most often evident in governments of strong dictatorships. The chances of the inner circle being willing or able to convince its leadership to cease fire are extremely low. This probability is even lower where a Type 1B structure (consensus) exists, because the rational course of cease-fire is generally not even considered by the inner circle. Type 2 structures, characterized by high criticism but low power, provide much greater opportunities for cease-fire, but the possibilities are determined by two factors: the willingness of the leader to listen to the criticism, and the leader's reaction to the criticism. An unwillingness to listen obviously negates all chances; but an ability to take even a small amount of advice is beneficial, as it encourages further criticism at later date, when the leadership may be more amenable to cease-fire. Extreme over-reaction to criticism (killing the critics) will likely result in the emergence of a Type

1A (self-suppression) structure. The result may be that later in the war, where criticism is again needed, it will not be forthcoming; critics may even encourage the leader to *continue* the war where even the leader may have doubts, on the basis that they believe it is expected. Finally, there is the Type 3 structure, characterized by high criticism and low to moderate power. This structure offers the best chances for an emergent cease-fire, as critics with enough power may actually be able to effect a change in policy by directly influencing the leader. Moreover, they may have an indirect effect, as domestic populations and military personnel may perceive the divisiveness and begin to question the war-fighting policy. Type 3 structures have their dangers, however. Critics with an insufficient power base to effect a change in policy, but a strong enough power base to make their views heard by third parties and the other belligerent, may only succeed in increasing distrust when the critics are later forced into hard line positions by their more powerful leaders.

Notes

1. Even in cabinet structures, this is often the case: the Prime Minister often has the power to dismiss those who oppose his or her policy, and the cabinet as a whole tends to follow his or her lead or, at a minimum, present a publicly united front.

2. It is acknowledged that the opposite situation can occur, *i.e.* where the leadership wants to cease fire, but the inner circle pushes to continue the war, but such cases appear to be far more rare and need not be discussed separately. In any situation where the inner circle has moderate or high power and influence *vis-a-vis* the leader, then the roles are in effect reversed, and the analysis below can still apply (*i.e.* the "leadership" becomes the "inner circle" wanting peace in the analysis and the "inner circle" becomes the "leadership" wanting to continue the war). Conversely, in those cases where the inner circle pushes for war but has little or no power or influence, there is no obstacle to cease-fire; the leader's desire for peace will emerge as dominant.

3. Thomas Schelling, "Internal Decision Making," in Nissan Oren (ed.), *Termination of Wars* (Jerusalem: Magnes Press [The Hebrew University], 1982), p. 14; Roger Fisher, *Basic Negotiating Strategy* (New York: Harper and Row, 1969), p. 40.

4. C.R. Mitchell, *The Structure of International Conflict* (London: Macmillan, 1981), p. 187.

5. Leon V. Sigal, *Fighting to a Finish: The Politics of War Termination in the United States and Japan, 1945* (London: Cornell University Press, 1988), p. 29.

6. Martha Crenshaw Hutchinson, *Revolutionary Terrorism: The FLN in Algeria, 1954-1962* (Stanford: Hoover Institution Press, 1978), p. 77.

7. Ibid.

8. Ferhat Abbas, *Autopsie d'un Guerre* (Paris: Editions Garniers Frères, 1980), p. 133.

9. Schelling, "Internal Decision Making," in Oren (ed.), *Termination of Wars*, p. 14.

10. Efraim Karsh and Inari Rautsi, *Saddam Hussein: A Political Biography* (New York: Macmillan Free Press, 1991), p. 191.

11. Fred Charles Iklé, *Every War Must End* (London: Columbia University Press, 1971), pp. 60-61, and see Sigal, *Fighting to a Finish*, p. 155.

12. Sigal, *Fighting to a Finish*, p. 95.

13. Irving L. Janis, *Victims of Groupthink* (Boston: Houghton Mifflin, 1972), pp. 3, 9.

14. Bob Woodward, *The Commanders* (New York: Simon and Schuster, 1991), p. 320.

15. See the previous chapter, Janis, *Victims of Groupthink*, pp. 202-03, and Robert Jervis, *The Logic of Images in International Relations* (New York: Columbia University Press, 1989), p. 77.

16. John de St. Jorre, *The Nigerian Civil War* (London: Hodder and Stoughton, 1977), pp. 229-230.

17. Ntieyong U. Akpan, *The Struggle for Secession 1966-1970* (London: Frank Cass, 1971), p. 112.

18. Ibid., pp. 102-104, and see A.H.M. Kirk-Greene, *Crisis and Conflict in Nigeria: Volume II -- A Documentary Sourcebook 1966-1970* (London: Oxford University Press, 1971), pp. 11-12.

19. Akpan, *The Struggle for Secession*, pp. 94-95.

20. Uwechue, *Reflections on the Nigerian Civil War* (New York: Africana Publishing Co., 1970), p. 148.

21. See Chapter 4.

22. Uwechue, *Reflections*, p. 148.

23. de St. Jorre, *The Nigerian Civil War*, p. 397.

24. Akpan, *The Struggle for Secession*, p. xi, 166, 173; Akpan's account is supported by others in attendance (see Zdenik Cervenka, *The Nigerian War 1967-70 (History of the War and Selected Documents)* [Frankfurt am Mein: Bernard and Graefe, 1971], p. 80).

25. Akpan, *The Struggle for Secession*, p. xi, 166, 173, 186.

26. However, third parties might very well consider finding means to support such a critical inner circle as a way of hastening the cease-fire. See, for example, Clark Claus Abt, *The Termination of General War* (PhD Thesis: MIT, 1965), pp. 93, 153-54.

27. *The Guardian*, 29 October 1980.

28. *The International Herald Tribune*, 12 November 1980.

29. UN Security Council Resolution 479 (28 September 1980).

30. Shaul Bakhash, *The Reign of the Ayatollahs: Iran and the Islamic Revolution* (London: I.B. Tauris & Co., 1985), p. 135.

31. See Ralph King, "The Iran-Iraq War: The Political Implications," *International Institute of Strategic Studies Adelphi Paper* 219 (1987), p. 21.

32. Shahram Chubin, and Charles Tripp, *Iran and Iraq at War* (London: I.B. Tauris and Co. Ltd., 1988), p. 37; and see *The Financial Times*, 17 March 1981, Bakhash, *The Reign of the Ayatollahs*, pp. 130, 136, and Abol Hassan Bani-Sadr, *My Turn to*

Speak: Iran, the Revolution, and Secret Deals with the U.S. (Washington: Brassey's, 1991), p. 76.

33. This was the case at least until late 1982, when a particularly brutal response by the Iranian authorities virtually destroyed their power base (see King, "The Iran-Iraq War", p. 21).

34. See King, Ibid., p. 21.

35. Bakhash, *The Reign of the Ayatollahs*, p. 146.

36. *The Guardian*, 3 March 1981.

37. *The International Herald Tribune*, 4 March 1981.

38. *The Guardian*, 3 March 1981. True, peace is a wider concept than a cease-fire, but Rajai's comments were specifically in reference to a cease-fire, not an overall peace.

39. *The Financial Times*, 5 March 1981.

40. *The International Herald Tribune*, 6 March 1981.

41. See Bakhash, *The Reign of the Ayatollahs*, pp. 19-20, 170-73. As an example of this, former Iranian President Bani-Sadr recalls that before boarding a flight to the United Nations in November 1979 -- carrying proposals which he believed would resolve the question of American hostages in Iran -- he heard a radio announcement by Khomeini forbidding the presence of any representative of Iran at the United Nations. The broadcast forced the cancellation of the trip (Bani-Sadr, *My Turn to Speak*, p. 24).

42. Bani-Sadr, *My Turn to Speak*, p. 127.

43. Bakhash, *The Reign of the Ayatollahs*, p. 232, and see the previous chapter, p. 78, for Khomeini's statement.

44. *The International Herald Tribune*, 21 February 1983.

45. *The Financial Times*, 24 February 1983.

46. *Summary of World Broadcasts*, ME/7270/A/1 (25 February 1983).

47. *Le Monde*, 25 February 1983.

48. *The Sunday Times*, 29 April 1984.

49. *The Guardian*, 29 September 1984.

50. *The Times*, 11 October 1984.

51. *The International Herald Tribune*, 8 October 1984.

52. *The Times*, 30 November 1984.

53. UN Security Council Resolution 598 (20 July 1987).

54. *The Observer*, 19 July 1987.

55. *The Guardian*, 23 July 1987.

56. Khorasani, Iranian Representative to the UN, *The Guardian*, 23 July 1987.

57. *The Daily Telegraph*, 13 August 1987.

58. *The Times*, 23 July 1987.

59. *The International Herald Tribune*, 25/26 July 1987.

60. *The Times*, 17 August 1987.

61. *The Independent*, 26 August 1987.

62. *The Guardian*, 19 August 1987.

63. Khorasani, *Summary of World Broadcasts*, ME/8567/A/7 (27 August 1987).

64. Iranian Deputy Foreign Minister Larijani, *Summary of World Broadcasts*, ME/8656/i (26 August 1987).

65. *Summary of World Broadcasts*, ME/8662/i (31 August 1987).

66.   *The Independent*, 25 September 1987. This figure, if accurate, is quite exceptional, as Iranian oil exports had been reduced (due to Iraqi attacks) to as little as 6-700,000 b/d in October 1986, and its "preferred" level of export was only 1.6 million b/d (see Chubin and Tripp, *Iran and Iraq at War*, pp. 134-137).

67.   *The Guardian*, 1 September 1987.

68.   *The Times*, 2 September 1987.

69.   *The Independent*, 4 September 1987; *The Financial Times*, 5 September 1987.

70.   Khorasani, *Summary of World Broadcasts*, ME/8664/A/7 (4 September 1987).

71.   *Summary of World Broadcasts*, ME/8674/A (16 September 1987); and see *The Guardian*, 14 September 1987; *The Times*, 15 September 1987.

6

Unbridgeable Divides and Uncontrollable Armies -- the Inability to Cease Fire:
"WE can't give them what they want; WE can't stop fighting"

So far we have seen a number of situations where, despite the existence of at least some will to stop the fighting, no cease fire occurred. There were the difficulties of avoiding appearing weak, the potential problems of going back on a publicly stated position, and there was the inability of those with the will to cease fire to persuade or coerce the ultimate decision makers that cease-fire was desirable. To these may now be added a fourth difficulty: a perceived or actual inability to cease fire. Even in situations where there is no danger of looking weak, where moves for peace can be made without severe domestic repercussions, and where there is consensus that a cease-fire is desirable, a belligerent at war may still conclude that it is unable to cease fire for at least two main reasons. First, and at a high political level, it may appear to the belligerent wanting to end the war that the gap between what it is willing to offer, and what the other side will accept, is simply too wide -- to the belligerent, interests may seem irreconcilable. In such a situation, cease-fire is seen as impossible. Second, and at a pure logistical level, a belligerent may actually be unable to cease fire because it cannot control the military forces which purport to fight for it.

A Bridge Too Far

Turning first to those cases where "unbridgeable divides" result in a perceived inability to cease fire, there is an obvious and important connection to the perceived interests of the belligerents. These subjectively-defined interests may be entirely opposed, or at the very least may be seen as opposed. Thus, the party desiring an end to the war may decide to continue to fight because there appears to be no point in making an offer; the other side will simply reject it. Admittedly, it may believe that it knows what the other side wants (and indeed may be right about this). However, if by giving the other party that which it desires some perceived vital interest will be sacrificed, no acceptable offer will be made, and the only proposals forthcoming will be those which do not sacrifice the "vital interests" of the belligerent: *"We can't give them what they want, so we must keep fighting."* Here, it is perhaps a matter of distinguishing between the will to make peace, and the willingness to suffer defeat or relinquish interests.[1]

It can be argued, of course, that belligerents in these cases can in reality cease fire -- all they have to do is stop (*i.e.* they *can* cease fire, they are just not *willing* to), but the matter is more complex. Whatever the semantics, and while it is acknowledged that it is almost always possible to just stop fighting, the point is that to the belligerents this is *seen* as impossible; it means conceding that which it is unwilling to concede. To cease fire is to invite some negative consequence which, whatever the costs of the war, the belligerent is unwilling to incur. (A good example of this is the belligerent leadership in the political dissonance trap, as we have seen. It may very well be considering cease fire, but the potential domestic repercussions simply preclude the possibility.)

Perhaps one of the main reasons for the development of unbridgeable divides is that belligerents often fail to define their interests in any meaningful sense. Any nation, for example, which states that "we are fighting to defend our interests" is simply using phrasing which is simply too vague to be of any use. A failure to define and clarify a nation's interests can lead not only to an unnecessarily prolonged conflict, but to cease-fire proposals which have little to do with what the belligerent really needs. Finally, and most importantly·for our purposes, it can lead to a situation in which the gap between belligerent interests cannot be closed -- a bridge between them cannot be built -- because their interests change quickly and often as the conflict progresses; victory may lead to increasing demands, and what may have satisfied a belligerent at one point in the conflict will not at a later time.

At worst, a belligerent may never know when it has achieved its objectives, and that the time has come to cease fire. This appeared to be the case in Korea, for example, where the failure of the United Nations to be completely clear about the purposes of the war allowed military events to dictate the objectives, rather than the other way around. According to Vice Admiral C. Turner Joy (first head of the UN delegation to the Korean Armistice Conference),

[w]e learned in Korea that crystallization of political objectives should precede initiation of armistice talks ... United States forces entered Korea ... to prevent an impending collapse in the South Korean government and to repel aggression against South Korea. When the North Korean aggressor was thrown back ... these two political objectives had been secured. Then United States policy shifted to the intent to unify Korea ... [and then] became the desire to avoid an all-out war with China. When the Soviets suggested an armistice, the political objectives in Korea became an honorable cease-fire. During the armistice negotiations, we took on a political objective of gaining a propaganda victory over Communism in respect to prisoners of war. Thus the political objectives of the United States in Korea weather-vaned with the winds of combat, accommodating themselves to military events rather than the goal to be reached through military operations.[2]

That the interests taken in Korea were ill-defined is made even more clear by statements of military commanders in the field early on in the conflict. On 12 March 1951, the British military attaché, Brigadier A.K. Ferguson, commented in a letter to London that

the reputed objective of U.N. forces in Korea which is "to repel aggression and restore peace and security in the area" is much too vague under present circumstances to give the Supreme Commander in the field a military objective, the attainment of which would bring hostilities to a close.

Putting the problem even more succinctly was General James van Vleet, then commander of the Eighth Army who, when asked by reporters what the goal of the United Nations in Korea was, replied, "I don't know. The answer must come from a higher authority."[3] Unfortunately for the men fighting that war, such answer was not forthcoming in that conflict, and failed to materialize in many conflicts since then. ("Restoring international peace and security" is a phrase the UN continues to use, for example.)

Bob Woodward, in *The Commanders*, gives a clear account of how a number of decisions were made in the US administration in the months preceding the Gulf War, and there seems to be a good case for concluding that interests and options were not often consciously considered. Just after the Iraqi invasion of Kuwait on 2 August 1990, a meeting with Bush's top military and civilian advisors was called. General Thomas W. Kelly, operations chief to the Chairman of the Joint Chiefs of Staff (General Colin Powell), recalled to Bob Woodward that Secretary of Defence Dick Cheney demanded "options" from the JCS to give to the president in response to the Iraqi invasion -- but Kelly did not know what he was supposed to do:

What was it they were supposed to offer a plan for? Reprisals against Iraq? Liberation of Kuwait? Defence of other Arab States? He hadn't seen any guidance from the political level -- from either the president or the Secretary of Defence. Absent a mission, discussion of options was pretty abstract.[4]

Even given National Security Advisor Brent Scowcroft's recommendation to the National Security Council on 3 August that they had to "examine what the long-term interests are for this country and for the Middle East if the invasion and taking of Kuwait become an accomplished fact," at NSC meetings Scowcroft himself seemed "unable or unwilling to coordinate and make sense of all the components of the Gulf policy ... Positions and alternatives were not completely discussed. Interruptions were common. Clear decisions rarely emerged." In fact, it was often the case that action was taken in the Gulf crisis without a clear understanding of *why* that action was taking place -- interests were not fully considered. Powell, for example, "was unable to pinpoint precisely" when the decision to begin a major deployment to Saudi Arabia had been made. Nothing had been written which set out alternatives or the decision itself, or its implications: "[t]here had been no clear statement about goals."[5]

What this kind of behavior generally means for the possibilities for cease fire is that rather than focus on its underlying interests, a belligerent will tend to put down conditions for cease-fire which are based on attaining specific objectives -- often dictated by military events -- which may be wholly unrelated to underlying political interests. As Fisher and Ury have so concisely pointed out, positions may be taken in conflicts in order to achieve some objective, positions which in turn are supposed to help defend some interest (usually vaguely defined); but when the position becomes untenable, it, rather than the interest behind it, is what is defended.[6] The difficulty with doing this is that cease-fire proposals may consist of specific conditions which may have little to do with the underlying interests in the conflict, and rather than change the ·conditions when a proposal is rejected, belligerents will defend them, rather than the interests they represent. In the end, positions may become utterly irreconcilable.

Even where belligererits have defined their own interests (or believe that they have), they tend to fail to define those of their enemies as well, and it may lead them to make entirely unacceptable cease-fire proposals. Conflict is generally defined only in terms of enemy behavior: "we look at what people do, not what they are doing it for; we then imagine that we can devise techniques to control what they do, and we are always surprised when the techniques fail."[7] What is true of conflict generally is also true when it comes to thinking about cease-fires. Belligerents tend to avoid consideration of what the enemy will accept, therefore not only avoiding granting what the enemy has stated it wants, but what the enemy actually wants; both enemy positions and interests are firmly ignored.

Much has been made in the mediation literature of the importance of making the distinction between positions and interests. Fisher and Ury argue that where the distinction can be made, solutions will be more easily arrived at. They argue that while positions are almost always irreconcilable, the interests behind them often are not.[8] The difficulty is, of course, that in some cases interests, too, may be irreconcilable; as we shall see shortly with the both the Iran-Iraq war and the Nigerian Civil War, the gap may simply be too wide to bridge.

Furthermore, and perhaps more importantly, interests are always subjectively defined. If, for example, a belligerent believes that security requires control over a piece of land, control over that land may *become* its interest. "Objective" third parties may attempt to point out that their "real" interest lies in achieving security -- which could be gained in other ways besides seizing territory -- but if there is an unshakeable belief that the only way security can be achieved is through control of a piece of land, the distinction between an interest and a position all but vanishes.

In the light of these arguments, it is worth examining both the Iran-Iraq War and the Nigerian Civil War in some detail. In the former conflict, Iraq, despite some will to cease fire at a number of points in the war, believed that to do so would have been to give up vital interests as it defined them. To Saddam Hussein, what Ayatollah Khomeini demanded was impossible to give, and it seemed as if the only option was to continue the fight. It is likely that this was a case where interests were really irreconcilable. Similarly in the second case, the Nigerian Civil War, positions were entirely opposed and, as far as the belligerent leaderships were concerned, were not negotiable. Thus, despite the efforts of third parties and inner circle members to reconcile what appeared to them to be the underlying interests, the attempts were unsuccessful. Belligerent leadership interests, subjectively defined, determined their actions. In both cases, despite the will to end the fighting, to actually cease fire was seen as impossible.

The Iran-Iraq War

During the Iran-Iraq war, and although Iraq appeared to have a genuine interest in a cease-fire for most of the war, its proposals in almost all cases failed to include Iran's own conditions and interests for cease-fire. The conditions for cease-fire which Iraq offered, and which on occasion were even reasonable taken in isolation, were always bound to be rejected as they ignored or failed to take into consideration the conditions and interests of the Iranians. As far as Iraq was concerned in this case, it had no choice in this: to have given in to Iranian demands, to satisfy Iranian interests, would have meant sacrificing vital -- and non-negotiable -- Iraqi interests. Thus, and while the will to cease fire was in place, Iraq saw itself as unable to stop fighting. The desire to avoid sacrificing vital interests simply overrode the desire for cease-fire.

First, it is almost certain that Iraq wanted to cease fire, even within the first weeks of the war, and on many occasions subsequently. As early as 26 September 1980, barely three days into the war, Saddam Hussein had asked in a letter to the Secretary-General "whether Iran is ready for a cease-fire and whether such was requested from it by you or whether Iran has expressed its views on it in any form."[9] Then, having appeared to have gained what territory it wanted by 2 October, Iraq announced that it would cease-fire unilaterally from 5-8 October. Western diplomatic "sources" commented that it was probably no more than an Iraqi ploy to consolidate ground forces in Iran, but there nevertheless appeared to be a genuine Iraqi interest in a cease-fire. The fact that more "unilateral" cease-fires were offered in later years, and that Iraq accepted all UN resolutions which called for an end to the fighting, also lend credence to the view.

In Iraq, then, there was a substantial amount of political will to cease-fire, if not at most points in the conflict, at least at many (either because Iraq had gained much or all of what it wanted, or because it was in danger of losing what it had gained). The evidence that Iran wanted a cease-fire, however, is much less clear. Iran constantly rejected Security Council resolutions, accused it of partiality, and all "offers" of cease-fire contained conditions which appeared to be designed to force their rejection by Iraq. Such conditions included the handing over of the city of Basra as compensation,[10] and the payment of $50 billion in war reparations by Iraq *before* Iran would consider negotiation.[11] Given that this is the case, it is reasonable to focus on Iraq's conditions for cease-fire laid out during the war, because if we accept that it had the political will to cease-fire, then its conditions and offers can be considered as genuine efforts to bring that about, and not merely as proposals which attempted to give the appearance that peace was desired. Before we do this, however, it is important to say something about the conditions Iran set for cease-fire, as well as the interests which lay behind them.

In general, Iranian conditions for cease-fire included the following: the withdrawal of Iraqi forces (until mid-1982, when Iraq was pushed back over its border), the resignation (or removal) of Saddam Hussein and his followers, reparations for war damage, and punishment (or at least condemnation and identification) of the aggressor. Iran's three conditions for cease-fire laid down in March 1985, for example, consisted of a halt to civilian bombing, a public admission by Iraq that it had started the war, and an announcement by Iraq that it was willing to pay reparations.[12] Again in 1987, Rafsanjani laid down conditions for cease-fire:

[f]irst the identification of the aggressor so that we may know that you have goodwill ... When that is done, then the way can be opened for the rest of the problems ... Our principle demand was that the aggressor be introduced and then a tribunal set up to determine the punishment of this aggressor. Naturally, war reparations is included in it.[13]

The positions were based on genuine Iranian interests, which included: the fear that Saddam Hussein was becoming the strongman of the region and attempting to destroy the Islamic fundamentalist revolution[14] (a security interest), a desire to maintain the international borders of Iran (another security and also political interest), the "fundamental and extreme sensitivity"[15] concerning the identity of the aggressor (an interest in seeing justice done), and the desire to repair the damage caused by the war (an economic interest). The conditions set by Iran were not the only ones which could have satisfied those interests but, as is so often the case, it was the conditions which were consistently defended as opposed to the interests which lay behind them.

It is also worth noting that even among the varied Iranian positions, the only one which appeared to count was that dealing with the removal of Saddam Hussein and the ruling Ba'ath party. Ayatollah Khomeini had the ultimate decision making power in Iran, and for him, reconciliation was impossible. As we have seen in previous chapters, his view was that this was a revolutionary war to protect Islam from corruption and blasphemy, and as the war progressed, nothing short of the removal of the Ba'athist party in Iraq would satisfy him.[16] This position *became* an interest and was, until the very end, non-negotiable.

Given what we know of Iranian conditions for cease-fire, and the interests upon which they were based, it is very clear that Iraqi proposals could not build either into its proposals. Indeed, to satisfy the main Iranian concerns would have resulted in the demise of the Iraqi regime. Given that there could be no more vital interest for the Iraqi regime than its own survival, the only option was to keep fighting, make proposals based on what it wanted, and hope for the best -- a strategy which it clung to at almost all points in the war. On 30 September 1980, for example, about a week into the war, Iraq laid down conditions for cease-fire which included that Iran recognize Iraq's "historic rights" to the Shatt-al-Arab waterway and "certain" border areas, and abandon occupation of three islands at the mouth of the Gulf.[17] Moreover, it demanded that Iran "abandon its trends of racism, aggression and expansion; ... its evil attempts to interfere in the domestic affairs of the region's countries." (Iraq had charged Iran with inciting Moslem uprisings within Iraq.)[18]

In July 1981 Tariq Aziz, the Iraqi foreign minister, told the International Conference on Solidarity that there were three "principles" which needed to be "realized" in order to lead to an Iraqi withdrawal:

> 1) renunciation of the use of force or the threat to use force in solving disputes among the states of the region, and the restoration to their legitimate owners all the legitimate rights which had been usurped by force or through the threat to use force, 2) mutual respect for sovereignty and non-interference in the internal affairs of other states, and 3) freedom of navigation in the Gulf and in the Hormuz strait.[19]

Neither of these proposals dealt specifically with Iranian concerns, and with the latter proposal, it could also be inferred that it was *Iraqi* perceptions of legitimacy which would be paramount in any settlement. It should have come as no surprise to Iraq, then, that its 6 November 1981 offer of a temporary cease-fire during the Moslem holy month of Muharram would be rejected by Iran. (A similar offer of cease-fire during Ramadan in July was also rejected.)[20] The Iraqi position would remain fixed, therefore going to defeat all new proposals and attempts at intervention. In June 1985, and after it was clear that Iraq's threat to escalate unless Iran came to the negotiating table had failed, Iraq made another proposal. It offered to halt civilian bombing if Iran would accept its 5-point settlement plan which called for a cease-fire, a withdrawal, an exchange of prisoners of war, negotiations for a peace treaty, and pledges of future non-interference and mutual respect for sovereignty.[21] The proposal consisted of nothing the Iranians had not seen before, and it was almost immediately rejected.[22]

Through all the years of war, there was only one exception to this rule. In the Spring of 1982, Iraq's conditions for cease-fire became much more flexible, even conciliatory. Recalling our opening chapter, on 14 April, Saddam Hussein offered a full withdrawal and a committee to establish war guilt if guarantees to end the war were available, and if Iran agreed that the war had ended.[23] Even more interesting, this suddenly conciliatory tone was even more pronounced by the summer. On 10 June, Iraq was ready to observe a cease-fire and accept arbitration,[24] and on 20 June 1982, Saddam Hussein announced that his troops were "withdrawing" from Iran. Finally, on 2 July Iraq called for a neutral peacekeeping force to patrol the border to monitor a cease-fire and a withdrawal, adding that the latter was really a moot point as its forces had already pulled back to international boundaries.[25] Hussein also reiterated the fact that Iraq was still ready to accept a fact-finding committee.[26] What is particularly striking about this exception is that it came, as we now know, at a time when Iran had been conducting a successful counteroffensive.[27] Pressure had forced Iraq to consider what it was that Iran wanted, and to offer at least some of those things in its proposals. Unfortunately, it is also clear that to do so is pointless. We know already that belligerents who expect victory will not consider cease-fire. What Iraq needed to understand is that if it was truly interested in a cease-fire, Iran's interests (or at least those that it could satisfy) should have been considered in a proposal while the military situation was stalemated or, even better, while Iraq was winning. That this did not happen here, and does not happen generally, is again understandable. Belligerents in a winning posture say to themselves, "We're winning. Why should we consider anything the enemy wants?" They often fail to answer, "because (excepting cases of an overwhelming victory) the party which is losing must accept the terms of the winning party if the war is to end."

In sum, in almost all cases where Iraq made proposals for cease-fire, not only were Iranian conditions not built in, but neither were Iranian interests. As far as Iraq was concerned, Iran was simply asking for too much. It asked for things Iraq felt unable to give (such as the resignation of Saddam Hussein). Even under extreme pressure, and while it might have been willing to give Iran some of what it wanted, the one thing that might have stopped the war -- the removal of Saddam Hussein -- was not and could not be offered. Overall, unable to satisfy Iran, Saddam's proposals for cease-fire focused exclusively on his own conditions and interests; as far as he was concerned, he was unable to cease fire.

The Nigerian Civil War

The Nigerian Civil War, for its part, offers a classic example of the difficulties that arise when interests are seen as irreconcilable. In this case, *both* parties desired a cease-fire, but this failed to come about, and it was in part due to the setting of conditions which failed to consider the needs of the other belligerent. Federal Nigerian interests were well-defined in this case, and a position was taken up to defend that interest. Nonetheless, it failed to consider the interests of Biafra. On the Biafran side, too, a position (personified in the person of Ojukwu) came to be defended and seen as non-negotiable. Each position in this case excluded that of the other belligerent; they were mutually exclusive. Thus, and even while it appeared to some that the underlying interests of the parties were reconcilable, that fact did little to help end the war.

Gowon and Ojukwu were the two main protagonists of the Nigerian Civil War, yet they only ever met face to face once, and that meeting took place before the war.[28] They never gave themselves the opportunity to actually sit down and discuss their views on the war, but even if such a conversation had taken place, there would likely have been no positive result. At least one thing becomes clear when their respective points of view are juxtaposed and analyzed: in their own minds, both Gowon and Ojukwu saw their own positions as non-negotiable.

Between September 1967 and March 1968, Gowon laid down the federal position. Like Ojukwu's, it would remain unchanged throughout the war; if anything positive can be said about the war, it is that unlike many other wars, the aims of both sides were clear and were adhered to for its duration:

> [T]he rebels must renounce secession ... the rebels should accept the present administrative structure of a Federal Union of Nigeria comprising 12 states ... a body of men should come forward from the East Central State [Biafra] willing to work for material reconciliation, peace and reconstruction ... we have no quarrel with the Ibos as a people. We are prepared to discuss with Ibo leaders how to bring about peace and heal the wounds of the nation. (28 September and 25 December 1967)

> There are only two ways of ending the rebellion -- through peace talks or military suppression. ... The Federal Government's position on peace talks is very clear. The rebel leaders must give up secession and accept the 12 States structure.[29] (31 March 1968)

Even behind the scenes, Gowon's position was remarkably consistent. According to Adam Curle, Gowon offered a cease-fire with a third party to police the lines in February 1968.[30] While on the surface it seemed a hopeful sign, subsequent events would erase any optimism. Curle saw Ojukwu on 9 March, and as it was clear that the Biafran leader wanted talks, nine days later Curle made his way back to Gowon. Gowon, while impressed that the Biafrans had not used Curle's visit for propaganda purposes, now put down two preconditions: the "rebels" had to renounce secession and accept the new 12 state division, the latter of which would be subject to modification. If these conditions could be met, there could be a cease-fire and talks.[31] The basic federal position was based on a belief that the country had to be kept together -- the federal interest was clearly in Nigerian unity.

As for the Biafran position, it, too, was remarkably consistent. At the Kampala peace conference in May 1968[32] and then in subsequent conferences and public speeches, Ojukwu laid down the law:

1. Brave and valiant Biafrans, we our fighting for our survival as a nation. (20 July 1967);
2. Under no circumstances will this republic of Biafra surrender or negotiate its sovereignty ... (10 August 1967);
3. ... Gowon will not willingly agree to the cessation of hostilities and the negotiation of a peaceful settlement. It is clear that he feels no concern for the misery and destruction which the continuation of the war is causing (31 March 1968);

4. I addressed this joint meeting five weeks ago ... I also indicated the stand which our delegation would take at the talks: insistence on a cease-fire before meaningful discussions on the settlement of the conflict. ... Nigeria went to Kampala not to seek a peaceful end to the war but to achieve an accelerated imposition of its genocidal aims. She went to Kampala as a "conqueror" (30 June 1968);

5. If we agree in principle that a cease-fire is necessary, then it is a conference talking point ... I believe there is no question of a cease-fire on the present lines unless the enemy pulls back to the boundaries proclaimed Biafra (10 December 1968);

6. ... past and current experiences do nothing but show that [a permanent cease-fire] might be too much to expect of Nigeria, whose sole intent is that of a military solution. ... four and a half months ago, on Saturday, August 3 1968, I unilaterally ordered a truce for the duration of the abortive Addis Ababa talks. Nigeria's response to that well meaning gesture was to intensify their aggressive activities by land, air and sea. Nigeria has, of course, consistently spurned every idea and suggestion about a truce or cease-fire.[33] (December, 1968)

Gowon's response to repeated Biafran demands for cease-fire and withdrawal is instructive:

1. The rebels demand immediate cease-fire together with the immediate removal of the economic blockade of rebel-held areas and the withdrawal of Federal troops to what they call pre-war boundaries. This means in effect that the Federal Government should not only order a cease-fire but withdraw its troops from the two minority states, Rivers State and South-Eastern, and more than half of the East-Central (Ibo) State which the Federal troops have already taken over. The political condition inherent in the rebel proposal on these terms, is an implicit acceptance of the so-called republic of Biafra by the Federal Government;

2. A unilateral cease-fire by the Federal Government without any prior commitment by the rebel leaders will give the rebels the opportunity to re-group and re-arm and prepare for a bloodier conflict. It will also give them a diplomatic advantage since such a unilateral cease-fire will guarantee the continued existence of the rebel regime in rebel-held areas;

3. The difficulty in a cease-fire without any agreement by the secessionist leaders to retract and remain part of Nigeria, is that Ojukwu and his foreign backers will certainly use the cease-fire pause to re-arm and prepare for a bloodier conflict in which more innocent lives will be lost;

4. ... to agree to an unconditional cease-fire without the rebel leaders' prior commitment to give up their so-called sovereignty will be totally unacceptable to the Nigerian populace. That would be a cease-fire between two sovereign countries.[34]

Of course, as de St. Jorre notes, the positions taken up by both belligerents had their own inner logic. Federal Nigeria based its position on the battlefield situation where they had taken over nearly half of Biafra. Major towns, airports, industrial centres and an oil refinery had all been captured. Thus,

> it would have been madness to accept the Biafran conditions for a cease-fire, during which it would have been impossible to enforce an effective arms embargo [the cease-fire required a withdrawal to pre-war positions], with absolutely no guarantee that the subsequent talks would have led to a permanent and acceptable political settlement.[35]

Looked at from the Biafran point of view, on the other hand, and especially from the view of those who aspired to independence, it was equal madness "to give up everything they had suffered and fought for."[36] Again, however, the fact that each side's positions were perhaps reasonable taken in isolation ignores the fact that it is the willingness to consider the *other* side's positions and interests which will determine the probabilities of cease-fire.

In sum, the respective positions of the belligerents in the Nigerian Civil War were these:[37]

The Biafran (Ojukwu's) Position

Our goal, our *interest* as I define it, is secession. The Nigerians are intent on genocide, and we must secede in order to be safe from this threat. So many lives are being lost, we absolutely cannot negotiate until there is a cease-fire. In fact, they should withdraw to pre-war boundaries as well. We have offered peace many times, but the response has always been negative. It is obvious to us that they do not want peace, and are not interested in negotiations. When they do show up to negotiate, it is only a smokescreen to stall other countries who were considering recognising Biafra. They are interested only in a military solution. We are interested in negotiations and want the war to end.

The Nigerian (Gowon's) Position

Our goal, our *interest*, is a united Nigeria. We are not intent on genocide. In fact, we are deliberately limiting our military action because we are fighting our own people. There is no need for the East Central State [Biafra] to secede. We cannot cease fire unless they renounce secession and accept the current 12-states structure. They will use a cease-fire to re-arm, re-group, and will gain diplomatically because their regime survives under any cease-fire. We cannot withdraw as this would mean giving up almost half of the East Central State which we have liberated.

It would be tantamount to political recognition of Biafra. We are interested in negotiations and want the war to end.

What was reasonable to one side was completely unreasonable to the other. The result was a stalemate and a great deal of frustration at how unreasonable the other side was being.

What is interesting in this particular case is that if we examine the underlying interests of both sides, as others both inside and outside Nigeria have defined them, and in opposition to the positions Gowon and Ojukwu presented and defended, a solution to the conflict appears. First, if we deconstruct the Biafran position, it becomes clear that a number of elements of the position were based on false premises. This in turn made the entire position unreasonable and unworkable. The Biafran goal was secession, but that appeared not to be their underlying interest, however. The Biafran interest seemed to lie in security, not sovereignty, but this fact got lost (or was deliberately misplaced) somewhere along the way. The result was that the position (secession) came to be defended instead of the interest (security), heedless of the fact that the Nigerian interest in unity was emphatically not incompatible with the Biafran interest in security. Uwechue comments:

> Right from the start the problem that faced the Ibos in Nigeria was one of security. Sovereignty was only a means to attain this end. As the struggle progressed, it became evident that the chose means was obstructing progress towards the desired end — *security*. When this fact became clear, many friends inside and outside Biafra began to urge a compromise solution that would recognize Nigeria's territorial integrity but at the same time grant the Biafrans adequate local autonomy and security. The failure of Biafra's leadership to acknowledge the absolute necessity for a compromise, even in the face of overwhelming odds, not only prolonged the war but ensured that it ended the way it did.[38]

The result, then, was that sovereignty, a means of achieving security, became an end in itself. Second, and as we have discussed earlier, there was no intent to commit genocide. Federal attempts at post-war reconciliation support this, and it probably could have been seen at the time. However, massive popular exposure to devastating propaganda fed the belief, as did the fact that federal forces had essentially cut Biafra off from outside aid (resulting in the death by starvation of hundreds of thousands). These factors combined and had the result that to Ojukwu and to the majority of the population, any solution which envisaged security under a federal Nigeria was anathema. The belief that secession was the desired goal, and that the Nigerian intent was genocide, conspired to create a wholly unshakeable position which would prevent a cease-fire.

As we saw in the previous chapter, however, there were many in the Biafran inner circle who did see past Biafra's own demands, and were able to see the conflict from the point of view of federal Nigeria. They would argue, for example, that Biafra's security did not hinge on sovereignty, but security, which could still be achieved in a federal structure.[39] There were other reasons to be critical of Ojukwu's policy. Ntieyong Akpan, an Ibo and head of Biafra's civil service, said that it was "unrealistic and fatuous" for Ojukwu to speak of Federal withdrawal. Moreover,

> Biafra had no moral or legal right to expect the Federal Government to withdraw from areas which were not foreign but its own territory de jure and de facto, areas which they regarded as liberated from the rebels ... Many of us were under no illusion about these [sic], but dared not express it except in private and to the most intimate circles.[40]

Raph Uwechue, one of those who, on 7 September 1968, wanted to settle with the North and was later arrested and forced to resign over the action,[41] is another outspoken critic of Ojukwu's positional tactics, defending Nigeria's position:

> [o]n both occasions [at Kampala and Addis Ababa] we failed to be positive. We only insisted on a cease-fire. How realistic is it to hope to obtain a meaningful cease-fire from an opponent who was at that time militarily at an advantage without any reliable hint, even through trusted third parties, that we were prepared in exchange for their stopping the war to reconsider at least the question of sovereignty?[42]

Despite all this, this critical inner circle simply had not the power necessary to get Ojukwu to compromise, however, and their views would not be heard. The important point here is that the one voice which had power and authority, and which would be heard by federal Nigeria -- that of Ojukwu -- was the one voice which ignored not only its own (apparent) interests, but the interests of federal Nigeria.[43] As is so often the case in non-participatory government structures, the leader's perceptions are paramount, and sovereignty, as far as Ojukwu was concerned, was the Biafran interest and was therefore non-negotiable.

That this was the case was unfortunate, for there was one point in the conflict where a proposal to end the fighting had a real chance of success: at the Addis Ababa negotiations in August 1968. Behind the inflammatory rhetoric of the talks, which resulted in a stalemate,[44] Eni Njoku, the chief Biafran negotiator, made his behind-the-scenes cease-fire offer through Adam Curle:

Njoku said, "What we really need is safety, and we could get this with two conditions." The first required that Biafra be allowed some kind of armed force, even a local militia which would be lightly armed. The second condition required that Biafra be recognized internationally *in some way*. This latter condition was very flexible, Njoku making clear that its intent was "to make sure that if anything terrible happened in Biafra, the world would know about it."[45]

Even something as minimal as arranging for a seat on some kind of international commission (Njoku had in mind the example of Québec which has a seat in New York) -- it didn't seem to matter which one -- apparently would have satisfied the Biafrans. Whether this would have satisfied Ojukwu, however, is another matter. Curle believes that this was a genuine offer from Ojukwu, and even given that Ojukwu wrote in 1989 that "the Biafran aim was not secession per se. It was the exercise of the inalienable right of a people to self-determination,"[46] it seems unlikely that Ojukwu was really considering remaining within Nigeria. All the evidence points to the fact that Ojukwu's concentration lay almost exclusively with the goal of secession, the position which had been taken up since the war's outset. Moreover, and even if this was a genuine offer, it was highly exceptional; the overwhelming trend in the case of Biafra was towards the defence of a well-developed position of secession. Finally, it is noteworthy that although the offer was communicated, it was not taken up, primarily because federal forces were about to launch an offensive which was intended to end the war.

The example of the Nigerian Civil War is interesting for several reasons. First, and as with the Iran-Iraq war, it shows the tendency for belligerents to concentrate solely on their own perceived positions and interests rather that those of the other belligerent, which can minimize possibilities for cease-fire. It underlines once more the problems faced by a powerless but critical inner circle which may indeed have the "true" interests of the belligerents in mind and, finally, it shows how the belief that what the other side wants is impossible to give results in the belief that there is no option but to keep fighting.

Armies out of Control

Beyond those cases where there is a perceived inability to cease-fire, there are also times when, for very practical reasons, there is an actual inability to cease-fire, primarily due to a belligerent lack of control over their military forces. There are occasions on which the political leadership will discover that while they have the political will to cease fire, they may not have control over those who fight their battles, either because of poor communications, or because they are unable to exert their authority. In either case, however, control is necessary if all the fighting is to stop.[47] During the Dutch "police action" in Indonesia (1947), Indonesian Republican forces stated that a cease-fire would be difficult because they were not in control of all their forces. The problem surfaced in Palestine also, where irregular forces on both sides considered themselves exempt from the provisions of the cease-fire. Count Bernadotte, the UN mediator at the time, proposed that the Arab and Israeli authorities be made responsible for their respective irregular forces, but this proved impractical, as some groups, in particular "dissident terrorist" groups, were effectively out of control of the authorities.[48]

Interestingly, there is precedent under international law for concluding cease-fire agreements in cases where no cease-fire appears to be possible because of the existence of uncontrolled or independent forces. According to Oppenheim,

> small parts of the belligerent forces and small parts of the theatre of war may be specially excluded without detracting from the general character of the armistice, *provided that the bulk of the forces, and the greater part of the region of war, are included.* (emphasis added)[49]

Provided that it can be proven to the satisfaction of the other party to the conflict that these units are out of command, or *in communicado*, then no real difficulties in concluding an agreement should arise. (A third party would be instrumental in ascertaining the validity of such claims.)[50]

Despite the fact that it may be theoretically possible to conclude agreements where forces are out of control, it nevertheless remains the case that this option is not always considered or practicable. The wars in the former Yugoslavia provide clear examples of this problem.[51]

The Yugoslav Wars

On 25 June 1991, the Yugoslav Republics of Slovenia and Croatia declared their independence from the federal state. The result was an attempt by the federal government to keep the country together by force, and federal troops moved first within Slovenia, and then in Croatia in an attempt to re-establish their authority. In each republic, they came into conflict with the local Territorial Defence forces, as well as with groups of armed irregulars, and war was the result. Throughout both phases of the conflict -- and indeed as the conflict spread into Bosnia-Hercegovina in March 1992[52] -- there were concerns about control *over* as well as control *within* the military, not to mention the equally important question of who had control over irregular forces; whatever precedent there may have been to conclude a cease-fire under those conditions, until control had been established, cease-fire proved impracticable. Agreements might be signed, but they could not be fully implemented.

Regarding control over the military, this had been an issue even from the outset of the Slovenian phase of the conflict. Slovenian President Milan Kućan, for example, had commented on 2 July that "No one has control of the army in Yugoslavia. If there is no control of the army the agreements have no meaning."[53] On the same day, Federal President Stipe Mešić (a Croatian), had warned that there had been threats of a coup,[54] and by the end of August, had decided that the Yugoslav federal army (YA) was out of control.[55] Finally, the fact that the YA was brought in as a party to later cease-fire negotiations is not merely an acknowledgement that cease-fire is more than a political task, it was also an acknowledgment that cease-fire would require direct YA *participation;* no agreement could be concluded without considering the YA as a party with an agenda essentially separate to that of the federal political leadership.

Control within the military, and control over irregular forces, was also at issue at several points. After the first cease-fire agreement had been negotiated on 28 June, fighting continued in at least one area (Rožna Dolina) after the 2100 hrs deadline, and by 2200hrs, Matjaž Kek, the Slovenian Deputy Information Minister, while admitting that the situation in Slovenia was now "much calmer," noted that the army had not completely halted its actions:

> [m]ore precisely, while representatives of the military leadership have agreed to a cease-fire, we have information that low-level commanders have not yet given the cease-fire command. They allegedly defend themselves by saying that they have not heard from the central command. In our view, however, they do not want to obey.[56]

The cease-fire agreement of 2 September, too, was apparently broken on all sides,[57] but many of the "violations" were carried out by individual units out of control of their military and political masters. This was certainly the opinion of Joop van der Valk, head of the then 75 strong European observer mission.[58] The language used in the cease-fire agreement signed at Igalo on 17 September also made it clear that control within the military was at issue. The agreement was signed by Slobodan Milošević (the Serbian President), Veljko Kadijević (federal Defence Minister and Army General), Franjo Tudjman (the Croatian President) and Lord Carrington (the European representative). The involved parties pledged that: "everyone within our control and under our political and military influence should cease fighting immediately."[59] A few weeks later, after that agreement had failed, the cease-fire of 8 October (while being generally observed) was being violated by Serbian units apparently out of control of their respective political and military authorities, and actions were being taken in and around Vukovar.[60] A distraught Miljenko Minaeric, logistical organizer of a failed European food convoy, noted on 14 October that "Nobody trusts nobody. Nobody is under the control of anybody. Anybody can shoot you."[61]

As far as the conduct of irregulars was concerned, then UN Secretary-General Perez de Cuellar's report to the Security Council on 11 December further noted that despite the agreed cease-fire of 24 November, there had been "credible reports" of advances by both federal and irregular units. Significantly, however, he also noted that it was his representative's view that "all sides, *and especially the irregular forces*, have been wanting in observing the 24 November Geneva Agreement in respect of the cease-fire" (emphasis added).[62]

Even as late as 4 February 1992, control was still an issue. The new UN Secretary-General, Boutros Boutros Ghali, noted that although the cease-fire (of 3 January) appeared to be holding, there were still a number of violations. This he blamed on uncontrolled military forces: "irregular armed elements who are not fully under the control of the established military commands ... have been responsible for a substantial proportion of the alleged cease-fire violations."[63] On this occasion, Ghali's comments may have been motivated by the desire to avoid blaming the federal army and allow for the emplacement of UN peacekeeping troops,[64] but (as subsequent events in Bosnia-Hercegovina would show) control over irregulars and their local leaders was a constant problem throughout the various stages of the Yugoslav conflict. Despite the Croatian and Serbian agreement to the emplacement of UN force deployment, secured on 2 January 1992, for example, that deployment was jeopardized by Milan Babić, the Serbian leader of the self-proclaimed "Krajina Republic" located in Croatia.

Babić opposed UN deployment on the basis that it provided insufficient guarantees for minority Serbs in Croatia.[65] Apparently exercising control over military forces in the area, he noted on 20 January that without his agreement, the UN mission was "condemned to failure."[66] He threatened to authorize a "general uprising" if UN troops attempted to deploy,[67] and the result was a meeting on 31 January between Serbian regular and irregular forces to "discuss" UN deployment, a meeting at which Babić was subjected to extreme pressure to accept the UN plan.[68] Babić's continued resistance, however, eventually resulted in his relegation to the backwaters of political life in Krajina. By 15 February, the Secretary-General was informed by Borisav Jović, President of the State Committee established in Belgrade to assist the UN on peacekeeping matters, that resistance by Babić no longer had "undue significance."[69] Coercion and political manipulation were ultimately successful in re-establishing control in this particular case, but it is clear that control over military (and sometimes political) forces continually undermined peace efforts in the Croatian phase of the conflict. It was, in fact, only with the establishing of Serbian military control over various regular and irregular forces, that the cease-fire of 2 January came into effect.[70]

Conclusions

Even given the best of intentions, it is sometimes the case that belligerents can not cease fire. Sometimes this is a only a perception; there is a belief that to cease fire would lead to an unacceptable political consequence or the relinquishing of some perceived vital interest; interests may be ill-defined or overrated unnecessarily. Alternatively, what the enemy asks for may actually be beyond the belligerent's capability to deliver; interests may be irreconcilable, and the gap may simply be too wide to bridge. Finally, military forces may be beyond the effective authority of the political leadership, or out of communication with them, and there is a real inability to cease fire. In all cases, it is clear that the existence of political will to stop the fighting simply does not guarantee cease-fire.

Notes

1. As argues Lewis Coser, "The Termination of Conflict," *Journal of Conflict Resolution* 5(4) (1961), p. 352.

2. Joy, V.A. C. Turner, *How Communists Negotiate* (New York: Macmillan, 1978), pp. 173-174.

3. Max Hastings, *The Korean War* (London: Pan Books, 1987), pp. 236, 249.

4. Bob Woodward, *The Commanders* (New York: Simon and Schuster, 1991), p. 234.

5. Woodward, Ibid., pp. 236-37, 259-260, and see also pp. 265, 281, and 318.

6. For a discussion of the positions/interest dichotomy in conflict generally, as well as an example of successful interest-based negotiation, see Roger Fisher and William Ury, *Getting to Yes* (London: Hutchinson Business, 1981).

7. Berenice A. Carroll, "War Termination and Conflict Theory: Value Premise, Theory and Policies," in William T.R. Fox (ed.) *How Wars End: Annals of the American Academy of Political and Social Science* (Philadelphia: Academy of Political and Social Science, Vol. 392), p. 25; see also Gilbert R. Winham (ed.), *New Issues in Crisis Management* (Boulder: Westview Press, 1988), p. 5.

8. See Fisher and Ury, *Getting to Yes*, pp. 3-14, 41-57.

9. SCOR, 35th yr., doc. S/14199 (26 Sept. 1980).

10. *The Financial Times*, 30 Sept. 1980.

11. *The International Herald Tribune*, 10 March 1983.

12. *The Times*, 23 March 1985.

13. *Summary of World Broadcasts*, ME/8672/A/5-6 (10 September 1987).

14. *The Guardian*, 21 February 1981.

15. Khamenei, to de Cuellar, *Summary of World Broadcasts*, ME/8673/A/1 (15 September 1987).

16. See Ayatollah Khomeini's Address to the Nation, 30 Sept. 1980, in *Summary of World Broadcasts*, ME/6538/A/3, and also the letter from President Bani-Sadr to the Secretary-General, SCOR, 35th yr., doc. S/14203 (29 Sept. 1980), and *The International Herald Tribune*, 2 October 1980, for examples of the rhetoric.

17. SCOR, 35th yr., doc. S/14210 (6 October 1980); *The Financial Times*, 30 Sept. 1980.

18. SCOR, 35th yr., doc. S/14210 (6 October 1980); *The International Herald Tribune*, 30 Sept. 1980; *Summary of World Broadcasts*, ME/6536/A/9 (30 Sept. 1980). This is undoubtedly the case: Iranian activity to destabilize the Ba'ath regime was a primary cause of the war. (See Efraim Karsh, 'The Iran-Iraq War: A Military Analysis." *International Institute of Strategic Studies Adelphi Paper* 220 [1987], pp. 11-13).

19. Tariq Aziz, in a speech to the International Conference on Solidarity, 17 July 1981. See *Summary of World Broadcasts*, ME/6777/A/4 (17 July 1981).

20. *The International Herald Tribune*, 6 November 1981.

21. *Summary of World Broadcasts*, ME/7979/A/2-3 (14 June 1985); *The Times*, 15 June 1985.

22. *The Guardian*, 18 June 1985.

23. *Summary of World Broadcasts*, ME/7001/A/2 (11 April 1982).

24. Statement by the Government of Iraq, SCOR, 37th yr., doc. S/15196 (10 June 1982).

25. *Mid-East Economic Digest (MEED)*, 2 July 1982.

26. *Summary of World Broadcasts*, ME/7067/A/7 (2 July 1982).

27. See *The International Herald Tribune*, 3/4 April 1982.

28. The meeting took place at Aburi, 4-5 January 1967.

29. Yakubu Gowon, *Official Speeches: Faith in Unity* (Lagos: Ministry of Information); see also A.H.M. Kirk-Greene, *Crisis and Conflict in Nigeria: Volume II -- A Documentary Sourcebook 1966-1970* (London: Oxford University Press, 1971), pp. 22, 167.

30. Adam Curle, in C.H. Mike Yarrow, *Quaker Experiences in International Conciliation* (London: Yale University Press, 1978), p. 197.

31. Yarrow, *Quaker Experiences*, p. 200.

32. See Yarrow, *Quaker Experiences*, p. 206, Kirk-Greene, *Crisis and Conflict in Nigeria*, p. 43ff.

33. 1) Broadcast from Enugu, *Summary of World Broadcasts* ME/2522/B1 (20 July 1967), and reprinted as doc. 121 in Kirk-Greene, *Crisis and Conflict in Nigeria*, pp. 148-150; 2) Broadcast from Enugu, *Summary of World Broadcasts*, ME/2541/B1 (10 August 1967), reprinted as doc. 125 in Kirk-Greene, Ibid., pp. 153-55; 3) Ojukwu, broadcast of 31 March 1968, in Kirk-Greene, Ibid., p. 32; 4) Ojukwu, at a joint meeting of the consultative assembly of the Council of Chiefs and Elders, 30 June 1968, in Chukwuemeka Odemegwu Ojukwu, *Biafra: Selected Speeches of Ojukwu* (New York: Harper and Row, 1969), pp. 273-75; also reprinted as doc. 237 in Kirk-Greene, Ibid., p. 237. In an interview with Dutch, Canadian, and Danish parliamentarians and journalists in Umuahia on 13 November 1968, Ojukwu offered a cease-fire,

to be followed by negotiations (Ojukwu, *Biafra* (New York: Harper and Row, 1969), p. 98); 5) Ojukwu, *Biafra*, p. 99; 6) 1968 end of year message, Ibid., p. 95; and for similar comments, see John Stremlau, *The International Politics of the Nigerian Civil War (1967-70)* (Princeton: Princeton University Press, 1977), p. 90.

34. 1) Gowon, *Official Speeches*, in his address to the OAU at Naimey, 16 July 1968 (also reprinted as doc. 162 in Kirk-Greene, *Crisis and Conflict in Nigeria*, pp. 238-242); 2) Ibid; 3) Ibid.; 4) Gowon, in his address to the OAU at Naimey, 16 July 1968, reprinted as doc. 162 in Kirk-Greene, Ibid., pp. 238-242.

35. John de St. Jorre, *The Nigerian Civil War* (London: Hodder and Stoughton, 1977), p. 201.

36. Ibid.

37. These summations are my own, based on a careful reading of the public and private writings of Gowon, Ojukwu and others, much of which has been presented above. Adam Curle, who has read them, believes them to be accurate representations, and see also Zdenik Cervenka, *The Nigerian War 1967-70 (History of the War and Selected Documents)* (Frankfurt am Mein: Bernard and Graefe, 1971), p. 94.

38. Raph Uwechue, *Reflections on the Nigerian Civil War* (New York: Africana Publishing Co., 1971), p. 134, and see Uwechue, "Des concessions réciproque pour une paix juste et durable", *Revue Français d'Etudes Politique Africaines* 49 (1970), pp. 33-57.

39. See, for example, Uwechue, *Reflections*, p. 134, and see Uwechue, "Des concessions," pp. 33-57.

40. Ntieyong Akpan, *The Struggle for Secession 1966-1970* (London: Frank Cass, 1971), p. 138.

41. See Kirk-Greene, *Crisis and Conflict in Nigeria*, p. 78.

42. Uwechue, *Reflections*, p. xxv.

43. There is little evidence to support the proposition that Gowon was subjected to similar pressures to change his position -- federal inner circle structures appeared to strive for consensus. Having said this, however, it is clear that Gowon did wield the same kind of power as Ojukwu -- government structures were not primarily democratic.

44. See Kirk-Greene, *Crisis and Conflict in Nigeria*, pp. 66-71, 247-314, for documents and details on the conference.

45. Curle, interview with the author, 19 September 1991.

46. Chukwuemeka Odemegwu Ojukwu, *Because I Am Involved* (Ibadan: Spectrum Books, 1989), p. 167.

47. Barry Schneider, "Terminating Strategic Exchanges: Requirements and Prerequisites" in Stephen J. Cimbala and Keith A. Dunn (eds.), *Conflict Termination and Military Strategy: Coercion, Persuasion, and War* (Boulder: Westview Press, 1987), p. 116; and see also James L. Foster, and Gary D. Brewer, "And the Clocks Were Striking Thirteen: the Termination of War," *Policy Sciences* 7 (1976), p. 228.

48. See Sydney Bailey, *How Wars End: The United Nations and the Termination of Armed Conflict, 1946-1964* (2 vols.) (Oxford: Clarendon Press, 1982), Vol. II, pp. 19, 197.

49. L. Oppenheim, in H. Lauterpacht (ed.), *Oppenheim's International Law*, vol. 2: *Disputes, War and Neutrality* (7th ed) (London: Longmans, Green & Co., 1952), p. 548n2.

50. See Chapter 9 for further discussion on this point.

51. Primarily because events in Bosnia continued unabated at the time of writing, this book examines only the first two complete phases of the conflict (Slovenian and Croatian), which effectively ended with the UN-sponsored cease-fire of 3 January 1992. Analysis takes into account events in these areas to 7 April 1992. It is more than likely that the later, Bosnian phase, could be analyzed in the same way (the reason some examples are included here). The Bosnian phase as a discrete event is not considered in great detail here primarily because it lies generally outside the methodology used. This book looks primarily at two-party wars -- Bosnia is obviously a more complex situation, and deserves a detailed and separate treatment. Moreover, most of the cease-fires in Bosnia have been local (what we termed "suspensions of arms" in Appendix 1), and the interest in this book is in broader agreements.

52. The conflict later spread into Bosnia-Hercegovina after that republic, too, declared its independence (on 1 March 1992).

53. *The Guardian*, 2 July 1991.

54. *International Herald Tribune*, 3 July 1991.

55. *International Herald Tribune*, 30 August 1991.

56. *Foreign Broadcast Information Service* (FBIS)-EEU-91-126 (1 July 1991).

57. This according to Henri Wijnaendts, the Dutch ambassador to France, who was in Yugoslavia personally observing the hostilities.

58. *The Times*, 13 Sept 1991. The mission had been established on 7 July, and was intended to monitor implementation of the cease-fire agreements.

59. Statement by Lord Carrington, the Presidents of Croatia and Serbia, and the Minister of National Defence at Igalo, Yugoslavia, on 17 September 1991.

60. *The Observer*, 13 October 1991.

61. *The Guardian*, 15 October 1991.

62. "Report of the Secretary-General Pursuant to Security Council Resolution 721 (1991)," UN doc. S/23280 (11 December 1991).

63. "Further Report of the Secretary-General Pursuant to Security Council Resolution 721 (1991)," UN doc. S/23513 (4 February 1992). Although not dealt with specifically in this book, the problem was also evident in the third (Bosnian) phase of the conflict. The Secretary-General noted on 30 May 1992, for example, that uncertainty about political control "has further complicated the situation," and that the word of federal officials could not be held as binding on irregular forces (see "Report of the Secretary-General Pursuant to Paragraph 4 of Security Council Resolution 752 (1992)," UN doc. S/24049 [30 May 1992]).

64. See James Gow and J.D.D. Smith, "Peacemaking, Peacekeeping: European Security and the Yugoslav Wars," *London Defence Studies* 11 (London: Brassey's for the Centre for Defence Studies, May, 1992), p. 40.

65. See "Further Report of the Secretary-General Pursuant to Security Council Resolution 721 (1991)," UN doc. S/23513 (4 February 1992), and *The Independent*, 9 January and 11 January 1992.

66. *The Independent*, 21 January 1992.

67. *The Independent*, 1 February 1992.

68. Babić accused federal generals of subjecting him both to physical and verbal abuse to force him to agree to UN deployment (*The Independent*, 4 February 1992).

69. "Further Report of the Secretary-General Pursuant to Security Council Resolution 721 (1991)," UN doc. S/23592 (15 February 1992).

70. Gow and Smith, *Peacemaking, Peacekeeping*, p. 35.

7

The Cease-Fire
Proposal -- Construction,
Acceptance, and Failure:
"WE can't make/accept the offer;
the agreement didn't work"

There comes a time in every conflict when belligerents will finally decide that it would be a good idea to offer (or demand) a cease-fire. It may see itself as having won, lost, or believe that the conflict will end in stalemate. It may simply be tired of the war, may be under internal or third party pressure, or may wish to at least give the appearance that it wants peace. At least four general obstacles stand in the way of a willingness to cease fire translating into an acceptable and workable cease-fire proposal or agreement.[1] First, there may be an absolute refusal to communicate with the opponent, in which case proposals may not even be made, or when made by the opponent, will be ignored. Second, and even where proposals are made and listened to, it is frequently the case that the proposal (which can either be a demand or an offer) will be flawed in some way, and will be rejected.[2] As shown earlier, the proposer often tends to focus only on its own perceived needs (which may be ill-defined), and/or may fail to consider or fully understand the needs and interests of its enemy; in either case, the proposal may be rejected or be seen as impossible to accept. Third, and as a general rule, proposals are often seen as either too political, or not political enough, and are rejected for that reason. Finally, and perhaps most importantly, where any cease-fire proposal is accepted, and where a cease-fire agreement results, if such agreement fails to be specific enough it will often break down or -- in the worst cases -- fail even to come into effect.

The Failure to Communicate

It is sometimes the case in war that despite the fact that it seems the right time to propose peace, no proposal will be made. Or, if proposals are made, they come in the form of a demand -- usually communicated through the mass media. The reason for this is usually that one belligerent is refusing to communicate directly with its enemy. According to Mitchell, at least four major difficulties arise with regard to communications between parties in conflict -- including, for example, a failure to read intentions properly or to send accurate signals -- but perhaps surprisingly, none of these difficulties include the simple refusal to communicate.[3] The refusal to talk to the enemy may lead to a situation in which one side comes to believe that the other has no interest in ceasing fire, even where that belief has no objective justification. During the Vietnam War, for example, President Johnson rejected proposals from his advisors to refrain from bombing North Vietnam and enter into negotiations, primarily due to his belief that the enemy would be unwilling to negotiate. He later wrote that the United States had to "wait until the Communists realized that their military ambitions were unattainable"[4] before peace talks could begin. In this case, Johnson was not only failing to communicate effectively, he was failing to communicate *at all*.

It may well be asked how an agreement between belligerents can come about if they refuse to talk to each other.[5] In July 1915 during the First World War, a British Member of Parliament asked the Prime Minister if the government would consider "taking steps to find out the terms of peace which the enemy governments [would] entertain." Not only did the government refuse to take such steps, but questions were raised as to whether doing so could be "detrimental to the public interest."[6] At the end of the Second World War, the failure of the United States to communicate directly and effectively with Japan probably prolonged the war's end in the Pacific theatre. Sigal's evidence indicates that in June 1945, the United States chose to concentrate on four different approaches to Japan, none of which contemplated direct communication with her in order to determine which means would be most effective. Once a course had been decided upon, the U.S. moved in two directions at once -- escalating the conventional bombing campaign while at the same time vaguely hinting that it might consider the retention of the Emperor if Japan surrendered. The moves confused the Japanese as to American intentions, and the message itself [the Potsdam declaration] was communicated by means of the mass media and this, combined with its phrasing, led the Japanese to dismiss it and reject it as propaganda.[7] American efforts were fruitless primarily because, and although Sigal himself does not put it this way, they chose to use inappropriate methods to decide on an inappropriate message which was sent by an inappropriate medium. Japan, for its part, also failed to engage in direct communication until the final week of the war. In part, however, this was because they believed such an approach was pointless given the American failure to explicitly indicate a willingness to negotiate over crucial Japanese interests (including the retention of the Emperor); the vagueness of the Potsdam declaration only served to support this belief.[8] During the Nigerian Civil War, Gowon at first refused to have anything to do with Ojukwu at all. In his attempts at bringing the parties together subsequently, Ethiopian Emperor Haile Selassie stressed the importance of convincing Gowon that communication with Ojukwu was a necessary first step:

> we must find a way of communicating with the other side which is conducting the hostilities against the Federal Government of Nigeria. ... my personal opinion is that in order to discharge effectively the mandate [of finding a peaceful solution] we hold, it is necessary to somehow ... communicate with Col. Ojukwu.[9]

In conclusion, one difficulty in arriving at acceptable cease-fire proposals is the lack of communication between belligerents: "one must be able to understand the perspective of the opponent if one is to conceive of terms to which he might be agreeable short of a Carthaginian peace."[10] An underlying failure to communicate effectively (or at all) with the enemy, can lead very easily to conflicting and unacceptable terms for cease-fire. As Luard notes, "though communication in itself cannot ensure that a peaceful settlement will be reached, without it disputes cannot be discussed at all."[11]

The refusal to communicate, or to communicate effectively, may itself occur for a variety of reasons, some of which we have discussed (such as the fear of looking weak, for example[12]). One more serious reason is that direct communication would imply political recognition of the opponent. This is generally not a problem in international war (although it can be), but comes up rather more often in civil wars, and very often in guerrilla or low-intensity intra-state conflict; at least a brief discussion is in order.

A cease-fire may be precluded not because either party does not wish to talk, but because it is felt by one party that even agreeing to talk about a cease-fire gives political legitimacy to its enemy.[13] Objectively valid or not, it is a belief that can become a major sticking point. As we have noted, this is a situation which arises primarily in intrastate wars between the ruling government and either "rebel" forces (Algeria/FLN) or other non- or extra-state actors (Israel/PLO; Turkey/Kurds; Britain/IRA). Governments involved in these conflicts do not want to give their opponents the "advantage" of political legitimacy, and therefore refuse to communicate terms for cease-fire, even in cases where it is desired by both sides. Peace talks nearly broke down during both the Vietnam and Indochina wars, when disputes arose as to the status of "rebel" organisations.[14] During the Nigerian Civil War, Gowon made it clear that "the Federal Military Government will not negotiate with Ojukwu as the rebel leader."[15] More recently, the government of Pakistan "refused to recognize the Najibullah regime, and thus made direct, face-to-face talks impossible."[16]

On 20 November 1959, during the Algerian war, Charles de Gaulle specifically rejected an FLN offer to negotiate on the basis that their representatives would be political representatives currently held in French detention (which included Ben Bella).[17] De Gaulle wanted to have discussions "with those who fought and not with those who [were] 'out of combat'."[18] This position arose primarily due to de Gaulle's desire to avoid political recognition of the FLN. Earlier that year, de Gaulle's foreign minister, Antoine Pinay, received word through the editor of a Swiss newspaper that "responsible leaders" of the FLN would be willing to open talks with the French government. De Gaulle refused, telling Pinay: "I don't want it; because the day after you've seen them they will say that I have recognized the FLN government."[19] De Gaulle's firm position was backed up by his deputies. In June 1959, Michel Debré, the French Prime Minister, threatened to break off diplomatic relations with any nation which recognized the "so-called" Algerian government.[20] Later attempts at negotiation were spoiled for the same reasons.[21] All of these refusals, then, were based on the same underlying assumption: that any communication with FLN representatives would imply political recognition of the FLN, and that, to de Gaulle, was unacceptable. Thus, while de Gaulle might meet military representatives, public meetings with GPRA officials would be out of the question. Despite the FLN insistence that they were the only valid spokesmen for Algerian rights,[22] he consistently and categorically rejected their claims "to assume power by virtue of the submachine gun alone [and] on the ground that they were already to all intents and purposes 'the government of the Algerian Republic.' Such a republic 'will one day exist, but has never yet existed'."[23]

The difficulty of a refusal to communicate based on a desire to avoid political recognition is clear: if belligerents will not talk to each other long enough to convey their cease-fire terms -- either directly or indirectly through third parties -- and apart from the case where there is a decisive victory, how do they expect to come to some kind of settlement? In November 1989, Peter Brooke, then British Secretary of State for Northern Ireland, made statements to the effect that if the IRA were to desist from acts of violence, the government might be prepared to negotiate with Sinn Fein, the political arm of the group. The political infighting these statements invoked was immediate, and its tone distinctly negative. Official government reaction was less than encouraging, and Reverend Ian Paisley, leader of the Democratic Unionists, went so far as to say that any suggestion of talks was "treachery and surrender."[24]   Paisley's reaction is a common one, as Sigal notes:

> [t]hose who think about ending wars often treat the enemy like a rival boxer to be pummelled into submission rather than like a politically unstable coalition to be threatened, cajoled and helped to reach some mutual accommodation.[25]

This is not to say that governments which refuse to negotiate with their opponents do not have valid concerns, but whether or not negotiating with an opponent actually confers political status, there is a strong tendency to *believe* that it does, and this in itself makes the question worthy of consideration.

The matter is complex, however. There is a strong belief among belligerents, for example, that even *agreeing* to negotiate cease-fire terms, let alone actually beginning those negotiations, can confer status on an opponent and, in addition, "can have profound implications for subsequent negotiations through a recognition that the discussions must include some representatives and issues previously ignored."[26]   This was the case in the Algerian war, as we have seen. Admittedly, and as Mitchell notes, the acknowledged status of the parties to the conflict has a very close connection with the very definition of the issues to be discussed, and therefore with the eventual outcome of the negotiations. In Cyprus after 1964, for example, any Turkish acknowledgment Turkish Cypriots as "rebels" would have led not to discussions about the need to work out new political arrangements between them and their Greek Cypriot counterparts, but to discussions about how the Turkish "rebels" could be returned to the Greek-dominated community.[27]

As for actually concluding an agreement, as opposed to merely agreeing to negotiate, it has been argued that this would appear to "almost inevitably" confer status. Mitchell asserts that

> [h]aving signed a peace treaty with Israel, the Egyptian government [could] hardly deny Israel's right to exist, no more than the British government, having concluded the Anglo-Irish Treaty in 1921, could deny the representative status of Sinn Fein and the Dail Eirann.[28]

Strictly speaking, of course, Mitchell's assertion is incorrect. Concluding a cease-fire agreement or even a peace treaty with another party is not recognition that that party has a *right* to exist -- only recognition that it *does* exist. This is a crucial distinction. In the Egypt-Israel case, it is true that the distinction was acknowledged and made explicit: by Art. III.I.a and b of the 1979 peace treaty, Egypt did recognize Israel's right to exist.[29] However, it is important to understand that in the absence of that clause, the agreement would have only been an acknowledgment of Israel's existence, not its right to that existence.[30] There is a great deal of difference between acknowledging that X exists, and acknowledging that X exists *legitimately*. Ultimately, belligerents who fail to make this distinction (and most of them do -- particularly in intrastate conflicts) see agreeing to negotiate as an acknowledgment of legitimacy, and they therefore refuse to deal with their opponents in any way whatsoever.

Interestingly enough, where the distinction *is* made, it may be much easier to arrive at a cease-fire. In the armistice agreements concluded between Israel and Arab states in 1949, rights and duties were assumed in the name of "the Parties" with a final clause reading: "No provision of this Agreement shall in any way prejudice the rights, claims and positions of either Party hereto in the ultimate peaceful settlement of the Palestine Question." The intention of the wording was precisely to avoid a situation in which Arab states would have to recognize the political legitimacy of Israel in order to conclude an agreement. It is noteworthy that during the Algerian war, even when de Gaulle relented and opened negotiations with the FLN, the invitation was vague and deliberately sidestepped the question of political recognition. De Gaulle offered to discuss only the "fate of the combatants" and "an honorable end to the fighting."[31] The *Spectator* of March 1961 noted that the opening communiqué for the first talks at Evian "managed not to mention the FLN at all."[32] Then, when an agreement finally came about at Evian, France concluded the cease-fire with "the combat forces of the FLN."[33] Once again, all of these moves go to indicate that France was not recognising the *political* legitimacy of the FLN, only recognising it as a *military* force -- an entity which existed and had to be dealt with.

Thus, where recognition of belligerents as political entities is politically impossible, it would appear to be perfectly feasible to conclude cease-fire agreements between military commanders, who have no political legitimacy merely by virtue of their existence, but do have authority over their respective armed forces. Belligerents concluding agreements in such cases take it for granted that the act of ceasing fire is "military, functionally oriented, and necessitated by the exigencies of warfare, [and therefore] does not entail the recognition of any party with which such an agreement may be concluded."[34] The agreements concluded in Korea were along these lines. The United States did not recognize the North Korean government, and the cease-fire agreement was therefore concluded between the Commander in Chief, United Nations Command, the Supreme Commander of the Korean People's Army, and the Commander of the Chinese People's Volunteers.

For lack of a better phrase, this technique can be called *semantic juggling*, and what it involves is using very precise language – either in the agreement itself or in public statements -- in an effort to avoid disputes over political legitimacy in cease-fire agreements. Admittedly, this whole process of semantic juggling in order to avoid any kind of political recognition can seem absurd at times. In Vietnam, for example, a number of rather peculiar arrangements had to be made to bring the agreement into force. The United States had to conclude an agreement with the Government of the Republic of Vietnam on one page, followed by an agreement between the Government of the Democratic Republic of Vietnam and the Provisional Government of the Republic of South Vietnam on another, followed by an agreement between the United States and the Government of the Democratic Republic of Vietnam (again on a separate page) to finally bring the whole agreement into force. Sadat's willingness to negotiate a more permanent peace with Israel in the spring of 1971 was in large part a result of the fact that he was able to claim that negotiations were being conducted with the United States, and not Israel.[35] Belligerents themselves undoubtedly recognize the word games that are being played here, but the point is that semantic juggling, however absurd it may appear, can lead to cease-fire agreements which otherwise might not have come about.

In sum, a major difficulty in arriving at acceptable cease-fire proposals is the refusal to communicate with the enemy. That refusal may be motivated by valid concerns about appearing weak, or providing political legitimacy to an unacceptable opponent. Whatever the reasons, however, the refusal to communicate, or to at least come to the conclusion that the other belligerents exists and is a force which has an effect, can lead to a situation where no negotiation takes place, or where the only cease-fire terms forthcoming are unacceptable ones.

The Flawed Proposal

When offers and demands for cease-fire are made, it certainly seems to be the case that those offers and demands may be flawed, and are frequently rejected on the basis of those defects. Apart from a failure to communicate, one of the major reasons for this (as we have seen in the previous chapter) is that belligerents often focus only on what *they* want or need from a cease-fire. This is only natural; nations have objectives in war and want to see those objectives fulfilled. One difficulty that arises, however, is that nations often fail to be clear about what exactly it is that they want; their interests are ill-defined, leading to demands which are unacceptable to the enemy. Moreover, the content of a proposal will almost inevitably avoid consideration of what the enemy will accept. The assumption is that *"what WE want is reasonable; what THEY want is not"* and once that assumption is made, proposals are thereafter created on that basis. At the outset to a conflict, this is understandable behavior; after all, if the enemy's demands had been reasonable, they would likely have been granted in the first place. The difficulty is, of course, that if demands and offers change during the war, even if they become more flexible, they still may not be considered by the enemy if they continue to ignore its interests. A belligerent failure to consider the point of view of its enemy will often lead it to make proposals which are considered unacceptable, and this is an obstacle to any cease-fire.

That belligerents fail to communicate with their enemy, concentrate on their own positions and interests, and fail to concentrate on those of their enemy, may suddenly appear somewhat irrational if it is realized that in any given war, it is the *recipient* of a cease-fire proposal who, in the final account, is the last to decide whether or not there will be an end to the fighting. This is because for any cease-fire to occur, all parties to the war must agree to cease fire, they must believe that all other parties will agree to do it and, finally, they must all believe this at the same time.[36] Just as it takes two (or at least two) to end a war,[37] so it takes two to effect a cease-fire; unlike love, no cease-fire can be unrequited. As long as one side sees fighting as more beneficial than not fighting (or conditions make it such that that side believes it has no choice but to fight), and apart from the unusual case where one side is simply able to abandon the field without fear of pursuit,[38] there can be no cease-fire (assuming, of course, that all belligerents still have the capacity to keep fighting).

Even in a case where one party offered "unconditional" surrender, or unilaterally ceased fire, the fighting could continue if the second party refused to accept such surrender or cease-fire.[39] This was the case in Nicaragua, for example, where Daniel Ortega ceased fire "unilaterally," but attacks by the Contras continued nevertheless, forcing further confrontation.[40] The cease-fire ended in October 1989 because, in Ortega's words, "We do not consider it an acceptable cease-fire when we cease and they fire."[41] During the Iran-Iraq war, too, Iraq initiated unilateral cease-fires on at least three occasions (5 Oct. 1980, 20 June 1982, and 14 June 1985); none of these cease-fires were accepted by Iran. In the Yugoslav conflict as well, there were two occasions of declared unilateral cease-fire, the first on 28 June 1991, when the Yugoslav federal army declared Slovenian borders secure, and the second on 7 August, again declared by the federal government.[42] Neither brought a halt to the fighting.

Thus, it is the recipient of the offer who has to make the final determination as to which terms are acceptable and which are not. As Quincy Wright wrote in 1951, "a conflict is solved by *definitive acceptance* of a decision by *all* parties."[43] So too with cease-fires. It is a question of recognizing that "no solution [is] possible without the participation of the other party." There is a condition of "mutual veto" over the question of a solution.[44] Where both belligerents fail to come to that conclusion, cease-fire may be precluded, even where it is desired by both sides.

Proposals and Politics

As we have seen, cease-fire proposals may be prevented because of a failure to communicate, or may be flawed because of a failure to include (or consider) one's own or enemy interests in the cease-fire proposal. The behavior in either case is explicable, and may arise out of an unwillingness to recognize the opponent, or a failure to recognize that the enemy often has a say in the final decision about when to cease fire. The end result, however, is always the same: an unacceptable cease-fire proposal, or an unacceptable demand for cease-fire. Apart from these general difficulties, however, there is one additional common defect among many cease-fire offers and demands: they will either be too political (including conditions for the overall political settlement of the conflict) or, more commonly, will not be political enough (suggesting only that the parties cease fire and little more). Perhaps most common of all is the case where the proposals of each side are flawed in both ways. That is, one side will see its enemy's proposals as too political, while the enemy will see the first sides's proposals as not political enough. This results in the side which sees it as too political demanding that all negotiations toward political settlement be dealt with after the cease-fire, whereas for the side which sees the proposal as not political enough, political negotiations are seen as a necessary adjunct or precursor to any cease-fire. These arguments also raise the question of the "unconditional" cease-fire.

Where proposals are too political, it is often a matter of the unwillingness of belligerents to accept even temporary political arrangements in the interests of achieving a cease-fire (a problem directly linked to the failure of belligerents to understand each other's perspectives). This may be a significant problem primarily because belligerents often believe that political effects may be an unavoidable concomitant to any cease-fire agreement, particularly if any kind of guarantees are to be included.[45] Conversely, and more commonly, agreements are not political enough. Belligerents may *demand* that political settlements be included the cease-fire agreement. As usual, the settlement proposed will not necessarily be a just political settlement, but a settlement which advances only one party's interests. In fact, belligerents have a marked tendency to attempt to link political progress with the conclusion of any cease-fire agreement.[46] China rejected cease-fire proposals during the Korean War in January 1951 on the grounds that they failed to include a political settlement.[47] Janice Stein, in her account of the 1973 October War between Israel and Egypt, noted that after 16 October the war was being fought "almost exclusively to determine the framework and terms of post-hostilities bargaining,"[48] rather than to actually end the hostilities themselves. Such linkage between the conclusion of an agreement, and political settlement, was evident in all Bailey's case studies as well.[49]

The opposing demands of two belligerents, where one wants political guarantees, and the other does not, most commonly lead to the case where one belligerent wants a cease-fire prior to negotiations (a non-political cease-fire), while the other wants negotiations prior to the cease-fire (a political cease-fire).[50] Once again, to each belligerent its own terms are acceptable, while those of the enemy are not, and a cease-fire is therefore precluded. We have detailed already the positions taken up in the Nigerian Civil War, and it is clear that in that case, for example, one of the fundamental problems in achieving a cease-fire was the federal demand for Biafran renunciation of secession before cease-fire, balanced against the Biafran demand of a prior cease-fire.[51] Which should come first -- negotiations for political settlement, or cease-fire?

The logic underlying the positions taken in the "which first?" debate are interesting. The side wanting cease-fire first may have several objectives and motivations. The demand could arise purely or partially from humanitarian motives; their overriding objective could be to stop the killing. Alternatively, the reason could be a practical one. In a situation where battle continues, and where the results of military action are varied, they can affect political negotiations both positively and negatively for both sides at different times, often resulting in a situation where the negotiations go nowhere. Korea is the best example of this, with armistice negotiations continuing for over two years. On the negative side, however, there is the difficulty that neither side will be willing to enter into negotiations unless they see that the situation on the battlefield is in their favor, or stalemated (and unlikely to change). Finally, it could be a desire to avoid political settlement in the enemy's favor which leads to the demand. If there can be a cease-fire, particularly if that cease-fire can be guaranteed in some way (through the use of peacekeeping troops, for example), then there will be no compulsion to discuss a permanent political settlement after cease-fire. If the dispute was over territory, for example, a guaranteed cease-fire on the then current battle line provides a *de facto* political settlement, and from the point of view of the party having gained new territory, there is no need for political discussion.

It is exactly this type of situation that the belligerent demanding political negotiations prior to cease-fire is trying to avoid, however. Belligerents often see cease-fire not as a pause in which more rational debate over political settlement can occur, but as an end to the war and a giving up of war aims. (While this may be true sometimes, it is not so always.) Given this view of a cease-fire, belligerents will tend to demand as much in the way of political settlement as possible before cease-fire, out of fear that post-cease-fire negotiations will not bring them the goals they seek.

The alternative logic used by belligerents demanding political negotiations prior to cease-fire is that they are the only way to stop the fighting. Sir Zafrullah Khan, during the dispute over Kashmir in 1948, took the position that the negotiations for permanent settlement should take priority on the grounds that the *only* way to stop the fighting was to settle the original dispute.[52] This latter logic is deceptive. In essence, Khan's argument is that because it was the dispute which gave rise to the violence, it follows that the violence can only be ended by solving the dispute. It also would appear to follow that as long as there is a dispute, there will be violence. While it is certainly true that there would be no violence in the absence of the dispute, this does not necessarily mean that the dispute cannot exist in the absence of the violence. Conflict without violence occurs constantly in society; violence is only one means by which parties attempt to resolve those conflicts. Solving the dispute is not the only way to end the violence: it is more a question of finding a way to "de-escalate" from violent to non-violent conflict. This is exactly what happened in Yugoslavia, for example, when the UN-brokered cease-fire of 2 January 1992 came into effect in Croatia. The overall political settlement had not been reached, but the parties agreed to cease fire nevertheless; the conflict de-escalated from primarily violent to primarily non-violent ways of dealing with their conflict.[53]

Finally, belligerents demanding negotiations prior to cease-fire may have strong practical reasons for the demand. Where the morale of one belligerent is not strong, there is a belief that a cease-fire could spell the end of military force cohesion. Those who are tired of the war will not fight on should the cease-fire (or the negotiations which followed it) fail, and the war will be lost.

The Algerian War of Independence

The Algerian War of Independence can offer a salient example of the problems encountered and the motivations involved when one side demands cease-fire before settlement, and the other demands settlement before cease-fire. Guy Mollet (the French Prime Minister from January 1956 to May 1957) once told Alistair Horne that the peace which seemed to be in the offing with the Ben Bella episode[54] was unlikely, as "the FLN never accepted our basic thesis that there should be, first of all, a cease-fire."[55] Of course the French never accepted the basic FLN thesis that there should be a political settlement before a cease-fire, and these opposing viewpoints were to be the cause of a major deadlock in potential and actual negotiations. The FLN wanted to settle political negotiations first, and cease fire second, and the French wanted the cease-fire first, and negotiations to follow.[56] As is often the case, there was to be a collective failure on both sides to consider the point of view of the other side.

On 23 October 1958, de Gaulle made a genuine offer of cease-fire -- the so-called peace of the brave (*paix de braves*). One of the main difficulties with this offer was that, as far as the FLN was concerned, it went against a basic FLN proposition that negotiations aimed at a political settlement should occur before a cease-fire. As such, the FLN response was predictable. Ferhat Abbas declared that "the problem of a cease-fire in Algeria is not simply a military problem. It is essentially political and negotiation must cover the whole question of Algeria." He then renewed his appeal to the FLN for a war to the end.[57]

Abbas' interpretation of the offer is may have been misconceived, however. First, there was nothing in the offer which appeared to specifically exclude political negotiations of the kind Abbas was demanding. True, it asked for a cease-fire, but did not specifically say that political negotiations would be excluded from the process.[58] Moreover, Abbas knew that de Gaulle was ready to negotiate. From the previous summer, Abbas and de Gaulle had been communicating, somewhat tentatively, through Abderrahmane Farès, the former president of the Algerian Assembly, and as early as August Abbas had been informed that de Gaulle was ready to "open serious negotiations with the rebels."[59] The alternative explanation to the rejection of the offer is that there were serious divisions within the FLN, and the compromise position was prevented from emerging, but at its base, there was a basic difference in the positions from which neither side would back away.

When the first face-to-face talks between the FLN and France took place on 25 June 1960, they were quickly bogged down due to French insistence on a prior cease-fire, versus FLN insistence on prior (or at least simultaneous) political settlement, and it is with this episode that we glean something of the interest behind the FLN's insistent position. According to Horne, the FLN had two real reasons for sticking to this position. The first was sheer mistrust of the French.[60] The second is highlighted by a the views of FLN commander Belkacem Krim at Evian I. Despite France's now clear determination to rid itself of the Algerian problem, Krim refused to have a cease-fire until the negotiations had been completed. He called the proposal premature "from a military, psychological and political point of view."[61] Thus, from the FLN point of view, cease-fire was simply impractical: "once the military revolt [in Algeria] had been stood down, if for whatever reason the emergent solution proved unacceptable, it would be extremely hard to get it going again."[62] There was a practical interest in ensuring that political negotiations were begun before cease-fire, an interest which was never made explicit to the French, and which was probably not made clear even among the FLN leadership.

Of course the French were just as insistent. The primary intent of the FLN representatives at Melun (20 June 1960) was to arrange a meeting between de Gaulle and Ferhat Abbas, but de Gaulle's reply to the attempt was clear. He says (speaking of himself in the third person): "General de Gaulle would never confer with the rebel leader as long his soldiers were being fired on in Algeria."[63] The cease-fire simply had to precede talks over political questions.

Finally, the problem surfaced once again at the first Evian talks (May-July, 1961). The FLN refused to cease-fire without adequate political guarantees, one leader in Tunis declaring that "an effective interruption of the fighting can only be the result of a bilateral accord bearing on the overall political settlement."[64] Belkacem Krim, in an internal FLN document concerning the progress at Evian, noted that the GPRA would continue to refuse a truce until fundamental guarantees about sovereignty had been given. He also noted that the French "would like to discuss the truce first before all political negotiation." Krim concluded that the two parties remained with their positions, that the problem therefore remained in full, and that "an agreement will be very difficult to realize."[65]

In this case, each side took up a position diametrically opposed to that of the other. The French insisted on a cease-fire before negotiations, and the FLN on negotiations before cease-fire. Each position excluded the other, and progress towards the mutual goal of ending the war was precluded. Had either or both sides considered the other's interests earlier in this case, the result might have been different. This can never be proven, of course, but what is entirely clear is that the mutual intransigence and determination to remain true to one single position was a clear obstacle to any cease-fire. It is noteworthy that the problem was only solved when questions of cease-fire and of overall political settlement were discussed simultaneously. De Gaulle comments:

> In February 1961, in response to solicitations addressed to us from Switzerland by emissaries of the "Front," I deemed it advisable to send a semi-official spokesman to Lucerne [George Pompidou]; someone of whom there could be no reason to doubt that he expressed my point of view directly. In accordance with instructions, he could make it clear to his interlocutors that, far from wishing France to cling on to Algeria, my aim was to disengage her therefrom, and that this would happen in any event ... we proposed, and the Front agreed that real negotiations should begin at last on French soil, dealing simultaneously with the cease-fire, the conditions governing the final referendum, and the future of Algeria.[66]

Those negotiations led to both rounds of Evian talks in 1961, and although there would be FLN insistence on guarantees for political settlement at the first round, the second would lead to the eventual cease-fire of 19 March 1962. In the end, then, de Gaulle not only made his objectives explicit to the FLN, but he also came to the realization that FLN interests would have to be dealt with if the conflict were to end. That realization wavered at Evian I, but Evian II could never have succeeded without French willingness to deal with FLN concerns.

The answer to the question of the "which first" dilemma, and given the example of the Algerian war, is probably "neither" and/or "both," depending on the situation. The desire to end suffering, the desire to keep what one has gained to that point in the war, the desire to avoid negotiating while fighting: for all these reasons and more, one belligerent will insist on a cease-fire prior to negotiations. The belligerent insisting on negotiations first also has its reasons, including the drop in morale which a cease-fire could bring, the assumption that any cease-fire will be a *de facto* end to the war, and the desire to use fighting to gain additional bargaining power at the negotiating table. These interests all need to be taken into account when attempting to achieve a cease-fire. It is possible that both sides' interests can be achieved through simultaneous negotiations and cease-fire, or simultaneous negotiations over political questions and questions of cease-fire. On the other hand, there is always the possibility that the interests are irreconcilable, in which case one belligerent will eventually have to accept the other's demands. On such occasions, belligerents and third parties may be left with no other option but to attempt to force belligerents to cease fire (the concern our final chapter). Despite all this, it remains the case that wherever possible the cease-fire should take priority; cease-fires save lives. If such a cease-fire can be arranged, every effort must be made to ensure that negotiations *do* occur when the fighting stops, and that the situation remains in stasis as far as that is practicable.

It is precisely because belligerents need guarantees about political settlement and post-cease-fire procedures that demands for "unconditional cease-fire" (not to mention demands for "unconditional surrender" or "unconditional withdrawal") are almost always considered as unacceptable by the recipient of the demand. There may indeed by reasons that the demand is made in the first place. Where allies have diverse underlying interests, for example, any collective cease-fire proposal may consist of no more than a demand for unconditional cease-fire on the basis that to offer more would be to jeopardize alliance unity.[67] Moreover, any time one belligerent considers its cause just or its power great, it may make an "unconditional" demand on the basis that the enemy is, as a collective, unjust or powerless, and therefore *nothing* they have to say is either just or of interest. (This was the coalition's general perception of Saddam Hussein in the Gulf War of 1991, for example.)

Regardless of why the demand is made, it is important to realize that a cease-fire which is *truly* unconditional will almost always be unacceptable. All belligerents, and particularly those which have "lost" conflicts, have concerns about what will happen to them after the war. They will need to know, for example, that genocide is not intended, and that their population will be well-treated. These are probably *minimum* conditions for cease-fire. There may be others in particular cases -- belligerents will want to know if their regime will be allowed to continue governing, for example -- but without at least *some* guarantees and *some* conditions, *why stop fighting?* It is a case of battling with the devil you know: "fight on no matter what, because they won't tell us what will happen if we stop." Abt argues, by way of example, that the domestic political conflict in Japan might have been resolved earlier had Japan understood *exactly* what unconditional surrender entailed. A US Strategic Bombing Survey had reported that 68% of the Japanese people expected brutalities, enslavement, starvation, and annihilation after surrender.[68]

The Missing Link: Getting the Words Right

There is one final difficulty with regard to a willingness to cease fire translating in to a workable cease-fire agreement, and it concerns what happens after such proposals are accepted, and a cease-fire agreement ensues. Even if the accepted proposal for cease-fire consists of nothing more than a "simple" non-political cease-fire (usually to be accompanied by negotiations towards political settlement), a failure to be clear about what is supposed to happen under the agreement may prevent it from coming into force, result in its breakdown shortly after it comes into effect, or at the very least cause major difficulties for cease-fire monitors or peacekeeping troops where they are present. The difficulty is compounded where the cease-fire is political in nature.

Historically, cease-fire agreements have been noticeably lacking in clarity. It is sometimes the case that no formal, written agreement exists at all, yet belligerents will declare a cease-fire. This was the case, for example, between the Sandinistas and the Contras between March 1988 and November 1989.[69] Apparently fed up with the failure of written agreements, General Sir Michael Rose (then UN Commander in Bosnia) negotiated a cease-fire on 10 February 1994 -- but "no agreement was signed. Deeds rather than signatures were to indicate intent."[70] The difficulties in determining when such verbal agreements have been violated are obvious, even in the case where both sides want to abide by its terms (which was clearly not the case in either of the above conflicts).

Even where written agreements exist, however, the situation does not improve. In Palestine, an agreement to demilitarize Mount Scopus was drafted on the back of an envelope, and included two differing maps of the area.[71] During that same conflict, a cease-fire order had been given in Jerusalem at the same moment as the affirmative reply to the UN call for cease-fire of 29 May 1948. "Complications" arose when the Arabs continued fighting after that moment.[72] These particular problems were caused primarily because of a failure to clearly specify the time and place of cease-fire (which must be considered the minimum content of an agreement)[73] but there is clearly a great deal more that can go wrong apart from questions of location and timing. The peace agreements in Vietnam (of January and June, 1973), for example, said nothing about the withdrawal of North Vietnamese troops from South Vietnam, and called for an end to foreign intervention but gave no deadline.[74] Such agreements simply leave too much room for misunderstanding or deliberate violation. One party could violate what it *knew* to be a tacit or unwritten condition of the agreement, for example, and it would be able to get away with this because the agreement did not specifically preclude the action.[75] Agreements are often too broad, and the result is that belligerents may take the position that any action which is not specifically excluded is permissible: "What is not forbidden is allowed." Such a position, while logically defensible, automatically creates a situation in which a signed agreement will be unlikely to come into force.

Admittedly, making agreements specific is time-consuming and may lead to rigid agreements which could quickly become obsolete.[76] Moreover, there may indeed be times that deliberate ambiguity must be included in an agreement (for this may allow an agreement to come about where no other is possible). Kissinger believed strongly that it was the "very lack of specificity that allowed the coming together of Egypt and Israel [during the October war]. Every attempt to discuss details ... might run the delicate agreement aground." Kissinger further argued that it was preferable, in this case, to work out the details of the agreement after it had been signed.[77] Despite these cases, however, a clear agreement must generally be considered preferable to an agreement which carries no weight, entails no obligations, and allows for the renewal of violence on even the slightest pretext. As an extreme (but probably not uncommon) example of this, Bernadotte recalls that during the Arab-Israeli conflict of 1948, and after the first cease-fire (of 11 June), Arabs complained that *a single Jewish plane* had circled over Damascus and tried to bomb it. Azzam Pasha, Secretary of the Arab League, reacted by stating that "the Arab states, in consequence of the Jewish action, must unfortunately regard the truce as broken."[78] Former UN Secretary-General Dag Hammarskjöld has noted that

> an assurance to comply with the armistice agreements has little practical bearing on the situation to the extent that any party can reserve for itself the right to give to the obligations its own interpretation, which may be different from the one which in good faith is maintained by the other party.[79]

Belligerents' interpretations, then, would appear to almost inevitably allow for their own actions, but to exclude those of other belligerents ("*What THEY do is impermissible; what WE do is permissible*"), and this can prevent a signed agreement from being implemented.

One might assume that the problem all but vanishes in the case where both belligerents have genuine political will to cease fire, and that any resultant problems can somehow be worked out simply because the belligerents now desire peace. There is certainly something to this argument, but one must ask how often such cases occur. The cases where both belligerents genuinely desire peace and are willing to work *cooperatively* with their enemies to "iron out" difficulties in agreements must be considered to be more rare than those cases where at least one belligerent is only ceasing fire due to internal or third party pressures, where ceasing fire is done only to establish the appearance of the desire for peace, and where any excuse to renew the fighting will be seized upon. Moreover, there is almost always extreme distrust between belligerents at war's end, and they are not often willing to accept that the enemy may have difficulties in implementing an agreement. More likely, the difficulties will be seen as deliberate attempts to avoid ceasing fire, and to continue the war.

In cease-fire agreements generally (and in forced agreements specifically) clarity must therefore be the watchword. Parties who are under no illusions as to just what it is they have agreed to will be unable to renounce the agreement on the grounds that its opponent "violated" it in those cases where the violation was a matter of interpretation. That is, defining what counts as a violation must be clearly spelled out in the agreement. Parties will always interpret agreements to suit them,[80] and while this is perhaps inevitable, it also demands that the language used in agreements be as unambiguous as possible, leaving little room for misunderstanding (wilful or otherwise). This is by no means mere semantic quibbling: parties need to understand precisely what it is they have agreed to do. Less than this usually results in misinterpretation and, in the case of a forced cease-fire, for example, allows them to evade the responsibilities placed on them by the third party.

Where gaps in an agreement exist, and belligerents interpret the agreement in ways which suit them alone, they may then undertake actions which the other side may consider to be violations of the agreement, and no cease-fire will take place.[81] The point here is that if an agreement fails to be specific, and one side then takes actions which the other side considers hostile, the "victim" will not implement the agreement (or accept that the other party has implemented it): there will be no cease-fire. The danger here is obvious, because for every agreement signed, but not then implemented, the task of constructing the next cease-fire probably becomes all that much more difficult. It is likely that distrust increases with every failed agreement, and the chances of implementing a durable cease-fire, let alone any kind of political settlement, decrease proportionally. Unclear agreements must be considered an obstacle to cease-fire.

The Yugoslav Wars

Perhaps the best example in support of the above argument can be found in the wars in the former Yugoslavia. In this case, the belligerents had the "assistance" of a third party -- the European Community -- in writing the agreements, but one of the main reasons that the numerous cease-fire agreements failed to be implemented is that they simply were not specific enough. Even where there was some willingness to cease fire on one or both sides, it was often not clear to either side what exactly it was they had agreed to. As a result, they made their own interpretations and undertook actions which the other side considered to be violations of the agreement. Furthermore, where actual violations did occur, there were no effective procedures outlined to deal with those violations, which inevitably meant that any actual violation held the potential of wrecking the cease-fire agreement and resulting in both sides having to start from scratch.

Turning first to the lack of specificity, what is entirely clear is that the cease-fire agreements were *not* clear. Part of the first cease-fire agreement (of 28 June) during the Slovenian phase of the conflict was that federal army troops return to barracks. While both sides had agreed to this, it had not been specified whether that return should be with or without equipment, and the belligerents had opposing views on this, possibly without even realising this when the agreement was made. The federal government obviously wanted the return of troops to barracks with their equipment while Slovenia, concerned about army control, wanted troops to return without it. The federal army was therefore blockaded and prevented from returning to barracks, and the federal government then took the position that the blockade amounted to a violation of the cease-fire agreement.[82] This would not be the last time the question of blockades would cause difficulties. Most agreements reached in Croatia failed because the issue of blockades was never dealt with in an acceptable manner.[83]

Some of the cease-fire agreements did get more specific as the crisis wore on. The Brioni agreement of 7 July, for example, did attempt to deal with one or two problems that had surfaced during implementation efforts of the first failed agreement in Slovenia. It answered the question of who was going to control the borders, for example, and it dealt with the question of whether the return to barracks was to be with or without equipment.[84] Other issues were left open, however. The question of who was to do what first (remove blockades, withdraw etc), for example, was not specified. Nor was the fact that the Slovenian parliament had to ratify the agreement taken into consideration; this resulted in a both sides making accusations of violations of an agreement which had not even legally taken effect!

Few of the lessons of the failed agreements in Slovenia were taken into account in subsequent agreements between Croatia and the federal government. Omissions in the first EC-sponsored agreement of 1 September, for example, while specifying which forces were to do what, failed to detail the order in which actions were to be taken: "hostile forces in direct contact shall separate and withdraw to locations at least out of range of small arms ... the Croatian National Guard reserve forces shall be demobilized, the [YA] should return to barracks."[85] Again, which forces were to take actions first was never specified. (Also note the word "should" in that particular clause, which can be misinterpreted. Just because someone "should" do something in no way obligates them to actually do it.) The result of these omissions and lack of clarity was an inevitable dispute over whether the federal army should return to barracks first, or after paramilitaries had disbanded.[86] As far as the disbanding of irregulars was concerned, for example, and although it was agreed that "all paramilitary forces ... and irregular units shall disarm and disband," no mechanism for the handing in of weapons was included, nor any means of overseeing the process.[87] In fact, according to Croatian President Franjo Tudjman, none of these "technical" questions were even discussed.[88]

The agreement of 17 September made at Igalo is also interesting from the point of view of specificity. Tudjman was optimistic,[89] and indeed, there seemed ample reason to be. This time, who was to do what was again specified and, in addition, "when" and "in what order" was also agreed, the "when" being "immediately," and the "in what order" being "simultaneously." Unfortunately, and given what we know already, the failure of this agreement could have been predicted. Croat forces would be unlikely to lift blockades simultaneously with the return of federal troops to barracks -- they would lose a powerful lever in the process, and expose themselves to what they saw as unacceptable risks. The use of the word "immediately" is also a problem. If parties are to cease fire "immediately," this does not even allow time for the cease-fire order to be communicated to military forces, and even if it assumes that adequate time will be allowed to communicate the order, how much time is "adequate"? How much time will be allowed for the order to filter down to front line troops? In the worst interpretation, *any* shooting which occurred after the agreement was signed could automatically have been considered a violation. It may seem far-fetched to say that a party which has signed an agreement would turn around and consider it null and void simply because there had been an incident five minutes after it was signed, but in cases where the agreement was only entered into under pressure, or where the political will to cease-fire is fragile and subject to disintegration at the slightest transgression, the importance of specificity cannot be understated.[90]

The 4 October agreement was more specific than that made on 17 September, but it too resulted in a disputes over the sequence of actions to be taken.[91] Tudjman and Kadijević exchanged a number of letters to attempt to clear up the differences, but to no avail. Tudjman's final communication concluded that

> [t]he Hague agreement is a continuation of agreements reached earlier ... the sequence of lifting the blockade on the barracks ... can function only under the conditions of cease-fire ... we are again advising you on our proposal on a simultaneous cease-fire, lifting the blockade, and a halt to the offensive actions which we presented in our letter of 5 October.[92]

Even this final communication failed to make clear whether the blockade was to be lifted simultaneously with the cease-fire, or occur later. Thus, this agreement also failed to be specific enough -- as did the resultant communications between the parties. Federal Yugoslav forces continued to attack Dubrovnik, and on 6 October, Tudjman called Croatia to arms.

The most specific European-backed agreement was that of 8 October, this time arranged between Croatia and the YA, and brokered by Dirk Jan van Houten, the new head of the European monitor team. It is worth noting that this was the first agreement put together by those on the ground fighting the war, and not by politicians or diplomats who may have been unaware of the specific military problems of cease-fire. The difference showed. For the first time, the agreement dealt with blockades in detail, specifying the order in which they were to be lifted. It further detailed arrangements which allowed the YA to leave all barracks in Croatia. Moreover, it made specific provision for federal units to leave with "their means of transport, technical material, weapons intact, military equipment, and other mobile military property."[93] On 9 October, the naval blockade began to be dismantled. Croatian forces were still unhappy about the YA being able to withdraw from barracks in Croatia with all their weapons -- one guardsman outside a barracks in Zagreb summing up the feelings of his comrades: "They should be allowed to take only their underpants and toothbrushes with them"[94] -- but at least the problem had been dealt with. Even this agreement failed because it was not specific enough, however. Incredibly, the federal army was able to claim on 11 October that it had made no agreement to withdraw from Croatia, and the claim could be made because the agreement had apparently been an verbal one; despite all the other specific provisions, there had been no written commitment to withdraw.

By 18 October, the agreement style was back to square one: it was short, unclear, and again resulted in interpretive arguments. In less than five dozen words, this document attempted to provide for an immediate cease-fire, and a lifting of base blockades and their subsequent evacuation.[95] Tudjman gave the appropriate orders, but made them conditional upon "simultaneously, the lifting the lifting of [federal] blockades on settlements, ports, roads, and air traffic." The condition, as far as Tudjman was concerned, was in keeping with "the spirit of the agreements." The federal presidency, however, stuck to the letter of the agreement, pointing out that Tudjman's condition was not agreed on in the Hague (although it acknowledged that he had put the proposal forward).[96] It may very well have been that Tudjman believed that his condition had been accepted (albeit tacitly) at the peace conference, and was therefore acting in good faith, but the fact that it was not written specifically into the agreement led to the inevitable dispute over its terms, and fighting continued.

What was missing from *all* these agreements, no matter how specific they seemed to be, were attempts to define what counted as a violation, and effective procedures to deal with violations when they occurred. These omissions are of paramount importance; if the agreement is to be implemented fully (and if it is to last), how perceived or actual violations are to be dealt with needs to be made as explicit as possible. This means not only dealing with obvious violations -- firing on units of the opposing army -- but also with actions taken under the cease-fire which, although not specifically prohibited by the agreement, could be considered to be hostile acts and violations of the agreement. Federal complaints of republic violations, for example, included the following: the blockade of YA units and bases by STD (Slovenian Territorial Defence) and CNG (Croatian National Guard) forces (an action considered to be a violation by the YA, but originally taken by STD and CNG forces to prevent violations by YA), the cutting of power and water to YA bases, the regrouping of STD and CNG forces, the existence of barricades on roads, the prevention of delivery of humanitarian aid to bases and the emplacement of tank traps and minefields outside barracks.[97] As an extreme example, Kadijević complained on 23 September that the latest cease-fire had been violated when a forest had been set alight around the naval sector command in Sibenek.[98]

Croatian and Slovenian forces had their own complaints, of course, including the federal refusal to re-open airspace, virtually *any* movement of YA forces, the fact that not all YA units were in barracks, that fresh reinforcements were being brought in, that reservists in Serbia and elsewhere were being mobilized, and the failure of YA to give advance warning of overflights.[99] What was permissible and what was not permissible was never fully specified in any of the European-brokered agreements, and the result was inevitably that one side would take actions seen as violations by the other side, which would then retaliate with hostile actions of its own, and the agreement would fail to be fully implemented. Once again, "what is not forbidden is allowed."

Even where obvious violations occurred, as they did on many occasions, there was simply no mechanism in place to deal with those violations. It was not that the need went unrecognized; Slovenian President Milan Kućan, to his credit, realized as early as July how many problems were not covered by the Brioni agreement, and said that "top-level negotiations on questions of principle have to be started to resolve specific issues of violations on both sides. An inter-government commission has to be set up."[100] The proposal was not taken up, and no agreement dealt with this question adequately. The problem is making arrangements for dealing with violations when they occur, and it is a task which belligerents in the midst of crisis have little time to contemplate rationally, if at all. Dealing with violations is a complex process which cannot be detailed overnight.

Even the relatively detailed agreement of 1 September left these questions open. As noted above, "which forces to do what" was dealt with in the agreement, but that was as far as it went. If separation, withdrawal, and other such activities were to occur simultaneously -- which can only be inferred -- this would cause the inevitable difficulty of forces coming into contact with one another in the process (as troops headed back to barracks or out of urban areas). Effective monitoring would once again be important, but the agreement dealt with this process in only two short clauses:

[i]n order to ensure a comprehensive and effective control of the cease-fire, parties agreed that monitoring activities will be conducted by the [YA] and the Croat authorities and representatives of the Serbian population in Croatia, involved in the hostilities.[101]

The European monitor mission was to *complement* this haphazard and dangerous arrangement, and violations were to be reported to the European monitors, but the difficulties this particular monitoring process would cause should be clear. The decision as to what counted as a violation was left to the discretion of the belligerents, and nobody knew what was going to count as a violation, let alone what procedure was to be followed where a violation was alleged.

As a final example, it is worth noting that the 17 September agreement -- while recognising that "when forces are closely intertwined, there are inevitable problems of provocation, real or imagined, and retaliation" -- failed to include effective monitoring procedures, and left unwritten answers to questions concerning procedures to be taken in the event of violation. Tudjman explained this away by noting that

> all three of us, all the signatories, have pledged to facilitate the control by EC observers. No reference was made to details but these details were mentioned in previous cease-fire agreements and in the memoranda providing for observers.[102]

It was clear, however, that neither the memoranda, nor any previous cease-fire agreement, had been specific enough about these issues to allow for adequate monitoring which would deal with the question of violations.

The multitude of failed agreements (twelve by 23 November) clearly resulted in increased cynicism and distrust on the part of the belligerents. When Tudjman faxed letters to Kadijević on 20 September 1991 accusing him of violating the latest cease-fire agreement, Kadijević responded angrily: "[y]our failure to observe the cease-fire declaration of 17 September 1991 was not the first case of your treacherous conduct ... instead of implementing the declaration your armed formations are continuing to launch attacks." He then reminded Tudjman that he was still willing to negotiate Tudjman met his obligations in the manner which had been agreed.[103] As shown above, however, there was constant confusion about precisely that matter.

As for Tudjman, he too became more cynical and distrustful as agreement after agreement failed. After the failure of the 4 October agreement, for example, he said that he had always doubted that it would be observed, and suggested international intervention. In addition, one of his reasons for failing to lift the blockade of federal bases was that the federal army would not cease fire, but would instead take up more advantageous positions, something he said they had done more than once.[104]

Certainly distrust had been on the rise before this. A Croatian Information Ministry spokesman, commenting on the 2 September agreement, remarked that "We've been cheated so many times. The Serbs were forced into this, it may be a trick,"[105] and Croatian foreign minister Zvonimir Separović bluntly stated on 17 September that "We do not trust that [the federal army] will obey what they promised."[106] By 16 November, with the arrival of the eleventh agreement, van Houten could state categorically that "no one believes in any cease-fire until we see it working."[107]

Lack of specificity, then, combined with the failure to provide specific provisions for dealing with violations, were major factors contributing to the failure to achieve a cease-fire -- not to mention increasing distrust -- in the Yugoslav conflict. For the most part, all that changed with United Nations involvement, a fact which should not be underemphasized. Whether it was because the UN has experience at cease-fire negotiation and peacekeeping, or whether it was merely that everyone was now aware of the difficulties, it is clearly the case that the UN-brokered cease-fire agreement of 2 January was remarkably more successful than its predecessors in achieving a lowering in the levels of violence. Although conditions in Croatia were admittedly now ripe for cease-fire,[108] an examination of the agreement itself provides an important part of the explanation for this phenomena. The parties did not merely agree to cease fire, but to "the complete cessation of all hostile military activity on land, at sea and in the air." This was further defined by specifying that there would be no firing across a party's forward lines, no movement forward by any units or individuals, no reinforcement of existing defences, and no redeployment of troops to "other and more advantageous ground." Other conditions were also agreed, but most impressive of all were the arrangements made to deal with violations and monitoring. Parties agreed to establish "joint liaison teams to resolve local incidents," to "cooperate fully with third-party monitoring mechanisms" and, perhaps most importantly, troops would be instructed not to return fire -- even if fired upon -- "without first taking recourse to the monitoring arrangements."[109]

This agreement, brokered by Cyrus Vance (UN Special Envoy as of 8 October 1991), was still imperfect, but it was by far the best which had been made in the region. It came into effect as planned at 1800hrs on 3 January, and more or less held from that point forward. True, there were violations, but as Boutros-Ghali noted in his report of 4 February, "the cease-fire has been generally observed," and it was irregular forces who were responsible "for a substantial majority of the cease-fire violations."[110] (That this was the case is noteworthy, for it once again underlines the importance of dealing with the question of irregular forces in the agreement.)

Conclusions

The content of the cease-fire proposal -- if a proposal is even considered -- can be a major obstacle to any cease-fire. Belligerents' refusals to communicate (for whatever reason), their concentration on their own perceived interests, and failure to concentrate on the interests of their enemy, all combine to lead to unacceptable cease-fire proposals being made, or to the rejection of enemy proposals. Offers may be too political, or not political enough, and a common result is that one side will demand negotiations before cease-fire, while the other demands cease-fire before negotiations. There appear to be at least two preconditions to arriving at acceptable cease-fire proposals. There must first be recognition that an opponent exists at least in fact -- that the enemy is a force which must be dealt with if a cease-fire is the desired result; this is also a recognition that belligerents have a mutual veto over final cease-fire proposals. Beyond this, there must also exist a willingness to communicate, even if only through a third party. Without either of these preconditions, acceptable cease-fire proposals are unlikely to result. The resultant proposal may not be sufficient to achieve a cease-fire, but it is a necessary component. Finally, when a proposal for a cease-fire has been accepted, and an agreement results, that agreement must be specific in every detail; the failure to do so may result in the agreement failing to come into force, an increase in distrust, and a decreasing likelihood that later proposals will be accepted.

It is also worth repeating that although underlying interests are not always reconcilable, they sometimes are, a fact which bodes well for the conclusion of cease-fire agreements. The trouble is, and as we have seen, belligerents themselves are often incapable of conceiving how the reconciliation of interests might be accomplished. Third parties may be invaluable in this regard. Where either belligerent seems to have forgotten or badly defined either its own or its enemy's interests, or where there is a stark refusal to communicate, a third party may be able to provide a necessary link or see the common ground. Achieving a cease-fire is, after all, a cooperative activity. There is a common goal (a cease-fire) requiring a common strategy (the ability to find a proposal both sides can accept), and it is certain that belligerents in conflict with one another have little if any experience of working together. They are, moreover, simply too involved in the conflict. The ability to see another's point of view can be all but impossible if that other is destroying your industry and killing your people. Third parties, uninvolved, and able to see both sides, may be able to help. They can help belligerents to identify their underlying interests, disengage them from positions, and come up with flexible, interest-based proposals which both sides will feel able to accept.

This is not always true, of course. As we have seen, there are always occasions on which there can be no common ground, and no interest-based formula will succeed. The conflict may be so deeply-rooted, or interests may be so diametrically opposed, that the only solution might be to continue the war until both sides are exhausted, or one side has won. Moreover, simply having the formula is no guarantee of a cease-fire. The content of the proposal is only one obstacle, and the fact that the third party may be able to remove that obstacle in no way guarantees that there will not be others. The point, however, is that third parties can sometimes hold the answers where belligerents on their own are unable to find them. William

B. Quandt, for example, concludes that Carter's role at Camp David was "central": "Left to themselves, Sadat and Begin would probably not have overcome their suspicions and would have broken off the talks over any number of issues."[111] In June 1982, with the Israeli launching of the war in Lebanon, it was US Ambassador Philip Habib who was to eventually have success in achieving a cease-fire between Israel and the PLO, getting the seige of Beirut lifted, and arranging the PLO withdrawal from Beirut.[112]

For a final, more detailed example, consider the negotiations which took place between Pakistan and the Soviet Union over Afghanistan. The Soviet Union demanded that Pakistan stop interfering in Afghanistan before negotiations could begin. Pakistan denied any interference. There were therefore completely opposing starting positions, stopping negotiation even before it had begun. What both nations failed to realize, however, was that their interests would allow for negotiations. The UN mediator, Cordovez, saw this and got negotiations started by arranging for mutual pledges of *future* good behavior: "without admitting to past or present misdeeds, both sides would make pledges, to be effective on a certain date, not to interfere in each other's territory."[113] This particular dispute was not over the content of a cease-fire proposal, but it is illustrative of the ability of third parties to reconcile interests.

Of course, third party success or failure depends on a number of elements. Intermediaries have their own difficulties when they become involved in cease-fire negotiations, and the way they conduct themselves has serious implications on their ability to be effective. Indeed, third parties may even be an obstacle to cease-fire -- the subject to which we will now turn.

Notes

1. These obstacles are not the same as those which stand in the way of a cease-fire. Here, we are concerned with those obstacles preventing the existence of a workable cease-fire proposal or agreement, which may or may not lead to an actual cease-fire. The acceptable proposal or agreement is a necessary but insufficient requirement for an actual cease-fire.

2. In the case where it is only the appearance of the desire for cease-fire which is sought, proposals may be deliberately defective. Such cases will not be dealt with here, however, because no genuine desire for cease-fire is present. The concern here is that even where a cease-fire is desired, proposals will either not be made at all, or will still be flawed in some way.

3. See C.R. Mitchell, *The Structure of International Conflict* (London: Macmillan, 1981), pp. 154-55.

4. L.B. Johnson, in Paul Pillar, *Negotiating Peace: War Termination as a Bargaining Process* (New Jersey: Princeton University Press, 1983), p. 46.

5. This point is also noted by Evan Luard, *War in International Society* (London: I.B. Tauris & Co. Ltd., 1986), p. 273. The word "communication" is here being used in a more narrow sense than Schelling, for example, would use it. For Schelling, actual formal talk ("communication" as it is used here) is only a small part of communication; it is *actions* that comprise the greater part of belligerent communications (see Thomas C. Schelling, *Arms and Influence* [London: Yale University Press, 1966], p. 136, n7). Primarily because cease-fire agreements consist of words, however, it is speech which will be here considered the more important *form* of communications. Schelling's assertion that speech forms the smallest *part* of belligerent communications will not be disputed here.

6. Fred Charles Iklé, *Every War Must End* (London: Columbia University Press, 1971), p. 76.

7. See Leon V. Sigal, *Fighting to a Finish: The Politics of War Termination in the United States and Japan, 1945* (London: Cornell University Press, 1988), pp. 117*ff*, 130, 143, 153, 303.

8. Ibid., pp. 82, 145. For an alternative argument, still based on communication difficulties, see Clark Claus Abt, *The Termination of General War* (PhD Thesis: MIT, 1965), p. 227, who argues that it the fault lay primarily with the Japanese, for while "American statements and broadcasts also had occasionally stated that unconditional surrender did not mean enslavement or destruction or even necessarily the loss of the Emperor, ... this information was suppressed, ignored, or distorted by the Japanese die-hards."

9. Haile Selassie, in John J. Stremlau, *The International Politics of the Nigerian Civil War (1967-70)* (Princeton: Princeton University Press, 1977), p. 100. Also note the careful language which avoids specifically naming Biafra as the other belligerent in this war, a move which some would have seen as political recognition.

10. Stephen Cimbala, "The Endgame and War," in Stephen J. Cimbala and Keith A. Dunn (eds.), *Conflict Termination and Military Strategy: Coercion, Persuasion, and War* (Boulder: Westview, 1987), p. 6.

11. Luard, *War in International Society*, p. 273.

12. See Chapter 3, and on this point specifically, see Berenice A. Carroll, "How Wars End: An Analysis of Some Current Hypotheses," *Journal of Peace Research* 6 (1969), p. 309.

13. See Mitchell, *The Structure of International Conflict*, pp. 209*ff*.

14. Pillar, *Negotiating Peace*, p. 74; Mitchell, *The Structure of International Conflict*, pp. 210-211.

15. Gowon, broadcast to the nation on 2 September 1967, reprinted as doc. 131 in A.H.M. Kirk-Greene, *Crisis and Conflict in Nigeria: Volume II -- A Documentary Sourcebook 1966-1970* (London: Oxford University Press, 1971), pp. 166-68.

16. G.R. Berridge, "Diplomacy and the Angola/Namibia Accords," *International Affairs* 65 (3) (1989), p. 468; see Robin Hay, "Humanitarian Cease-fires: an Examination of their Potential Contribution to the Resolution of Conflict" (Ottawa: Canadian Institute for International Peace and Security, 1990), pp. 22-23 for a brief example of the political legitimacy problem in the El Salvador Civil War.

17. Edgar O'Ballance, *The Algerian Insurrection, 1954-1962* (London: Faber and Faber, 1967), pp. 144-145; William B. Quandt, *Revolution and Political Leadership: Algeria, 1954-68* (Massachusetts: MIT, 1969), pp. 141-42.

18. Ferhat Abbas, *Autopsie d'un Guerre* (Paris: Editions Garniers Frères, 1980), p. 275 (my translation); (*"avec ceux qui se battent et non avec ceux qui sont <<hors combat>>"*).

19. Alistair Horne, *A Savage War of Peace* (London: Macmillan, 1977), p. 384.

20. *Manchester Guardian*, 5 June 1959.

21. Horne, *A Savage War of Peace*, p. 395, and see Jean Lacouture, *De Gaulle: the Ruler* (translation by Alan Sheridan) (London: Harvill, 1991), p. 259, for more of de Gaulle's comments.

22. See, for example, *The Times*, 29 September 1959.

23. General Charles de Gaulle, *Memoirs of Hope* (translated by Terence Kilmartin) (London: Weidenfeld and Nicolson, 1971), p. 90.

24. See *Christian Science Monitor*, 9-15 Nov. 1989, p. 6.

25. Sigal, *Fighting to a Finish*, p. 310.

26. Mitchell, *The Structure of International Conflict*, p. 210.

27. Ibid., p. 211.

28. Ibid., p. 327.

29. See "Egyptian-Israel Peace Treaty, March 26, 1979," reprinted in William B. Quandt, *Camp David: Peacemaking and Politics* (Washington: Brookings Institute, 1986), pp. 397, 403.

30. In this particular example, of course, the agreement would likely not have been signed had recognition not been explicitly included.

31. See *The Observer*, 26 June 1960.

32. *The Spectator*, 31 March 1961.

33. See the "Evian Accords," reprinted in Benyousef Ben Khedda, *Les Accords d'Evian* (Publisud-OPU, 1986), and see also R.R. Baxter, "Armistices and Other Forms of Suspension of Hostilities," *Recueil des cours de l'Académie de droit Internationale* 149 (1976), pp. 361-362.

34. Baxter, Ibid., p. 366. The Israel-Syria disengagement agreement of 1974 might also be examined with this idea in mind.

35. Saadia Touval, "Managing the Risks of Accommodation," in Nissan Oren (ed.), *Termination of Wars* (Jerusalem: Magnes Press [The Hebrew University], 1982), pp. 29-30.

36. Barry Schneider, "Terminating Strategic Exchanges: Requirements and Prerequisites" in Stephen J. Cimbala and Keith A. Dunn (eds.), *Conflict Termination and Military Strategy: Coercion, Persuasion, and War* (Boulder: Westview, 1987), p. 116; Janice Gross Stein, "The Termination of the October War: A Reappraisal," in Nissan Oren (ed.), *Termination of Wars* (Jerusalem: Magnes Press [The Hebrew University], 1982), pp. 226-227; and see Pillar, *Negotiating Peace*, pp. 53-55 for a good illustration of this point.

37. William T.R. Fox, "The Causes of Peace and Conditions of War," in William T.R. Fox (ed.), *How Wars End: Annals of the American Academy of Political and Social Science* (Philadelphia: Academy of Political and Social Science, Vol. 392, 1970), p. 5; Iklé, *Every War Must End*, p. 13; Mitchell, *The Structure of International Conflict*, p. 165; Thomas Schelling, "Internal Decision-Making," in Nissan Oren (ed.), *Termination of Wars* (Jerusalem: Magnes Press [The Hebrew University], 1982), p. 9 ("usually"); Schneider, "Terminating Strategic Exchanges" in Cimbala and Dunn (eds.), *Conflict Termination and Military Strategy*, p. 118; Donald Wittman, "How a War Ends: A

Rational Model Approach," *Journal of Conflict Resolution* 23 (1979), p. 744; H.A. Calahan, *What Makes a War End* (New York: Vanguard, 1944), p. 18, in Abt, *The Termination of General War*. p. 8.

38. Fox, "The Causes of Peace and Conditions of War," in Fox (ed.), *How Wars End*, p. 5; and see William O. Staudenmaier, "Conflict Termination in the Nuclear Era," in Stephen J. Cimbala and Keith A. Dunn (eds.), *Conflict Termination and Military Strategy: Coercion, Persuasion, and War* (Boulder: Westview, 1987), pp. 15-32, for such an example.

39. Carroll, "How Wars End", p. 308.

40. See the *Christian Science Monitor*, 2-8 November 1989, p. 4.

41. Daniel Ortega Saavedra, "Why I Ended the Cease-fire" (*New York Times*, 2 November 1989, p. 31).

42. Occasions where local unilateral cease-fires occurred for humanitarian reasons, such as at Vukovar on 18 October and Dubrovnik on 27 October, are not included in these figures.

43. John Burton and Frank Dukes, *Conflict: Readings in Management and Resolution* (London: Macmillan, 1990), preface.

44. I. William Zartman and Maureen Berman, *The Practical Negotiator* (London: Yale University Press, 1982), p. 57-59.

45. See, for example, the comments of General Paul Ely in Pillar, *Negotiating Peace*, p. 31.

46. Bertrand de Montluc, *Le Cessez-le-feu*, Ph.D. thesis (Univérsité de Droit et d'Economie et de Sciences Sociales de Paris), 1971, p. 246.

47. Sydney Bailey, *How Wars End: The United Nations and the Termination of Armed Conflict, 1946-1964* (2 vols.) (Oxford: Clarendon Press, 1982), Vol. II, p. 420.

48. Stein, "The Termination of the October War", in Oren (ed.), *Termination of Wars*, p. 234f.

49. Bailey, *How Wars End*, Vol. I, p. 112. The studies included Indonesia (1947-48), Kashmir (1947-49), Palestine (1947-49), Indonesia (1948-49), and Korea (1951-1953).

50. Both objectives ignore the obvious fact that the cease-fire *itself* may require negotiations.

51. See above, Chapter 6, and Zdenik Cervenka, *The Nigerian War 1967-70 (History of the War and Selected Documents)* (Frankfurt am Mein: Bernard and Graefe, 1971), p. 94.

52. See Bailey, *How Wars End*, Vol. II, p. 76.

53. This has also been the case in the Arab-Israeli conflict, where wars ended without political settlement, but where conflict remained nevertheless.

54. 27 Oct. 1956; see Chapter 4, p. 85.

55. Horne, *A Savage War of Peace*, p. 157.

56. John Talbott, *The War Without a Name: France in Algeria, 1954-62* (New York: Alfred A. Knopf, 1980), p. 22.

57. Horne, *A Savage War of Peace*, p. 307.

58. See the terms of the offer, in Edward Behr, *The Algerian Problem* (London: Hodder and Stoughton, 1961), p. 156.

59. Horne, *A Savage War of Peace*, p. 319.

60. Ibid., pp. 395, 466.

61. Behr, *The Algerian Problem*, p. 190.

62. Horne, *A Savage War of Peace*, pp. 395, 466; and see Behr, *The Algerian Problem*, p. 190 for similar comments.

63. de Gaulle, *Memoirs of Hope*, p. 88.

64. Horne, *A Savage War of Peace*, p. 470.

65. Mohammed Harbi, *Les archives de la révolution algérienne* (Paris: les éditions jeune afrique, 1981), doc. 84, pp. 391-92.

66. de Gaulle, *Memoirs of Hope*, pp. 98-99.

67. See Abt, *The Termination of General War*, p. 248.

68. US Strategic Bombing Report, "Effects of Strategic Bombing on Japanese Morale," in Abt, *The Termination of General War*, p. 23. One incident which can be attributed to these beliefs was the collective suicide of 84 Okinawan civilians (including 45 children) in 1945. They had been told by occupying Japanese troops that the Americans would slaughter everyone they found, and that it would be dishonourable to fall into their hands. When the Americans landed, most chose to kill themselves and their children (see *The Independent*, 11 July 1992).

69. *The Guardian*, 5 November 1989.

70. Roy Thomas, "Sarajevo UNMOs", *Esprits de Corps* 4(1), 1994, p. 9.

71. Bailey, *How Wars End*, Vol. II, p. 198.

72. See Count Folke Bernadotte, *To Jerusalem* (London: Hodders and Stoughton, 1951), p. 45.

73. See Madame Paul Bastid, "Le Cessez-le-feu," *Société Internationale de Droit pénal militaire et de droit de la guerre [Actes du]*, 6ᵉ Congrès internationale, La Haye, 22-25 Mai, 1973 (1974), p. 37.

74. See Robert Randles comments, in David S. Smith (ed.), and Robert F. Randle (comments), *From War to Peace: Essays in Peacemaking and War Termination* (New York: Columbia University Press, 1974), p. 51.

75. Fred Charles Iklé, *How Nations Negotiate* (London: Harper and Row, 1976), p. 9.

76. Ibid.

77. Zartman and Berman, *The Practical Negotiator*, p. 127.

78. Bernadotte, *To Jerusalem*, p. 83.

79. Dag Hammarskjöld, Report of the Secretary-General to the U.N. Security Council, 9 May 1956, in John F. Murphy, *The United Nations and the Control of International Violence: A Legal and Political Analysis* (Manchester: Manchester University Press, 1983), p. 34.

80. For a clear example of this, see Bailey, *How Wars End*, Vol. I, p. 34; vol. II, pp. 18-19, 22.

81. This does bring up the issue of the failure to detail procedures to handle violations in a cease-fire agreement, but this is a durability issue which is generally beyond the scope of this book.

82. See the comments of Slovene Defence Minister Janež Janša in FBIS-EEU-91-127 (2 July 1991), p. 60.

83. For the 23 September agreement, for example, see James Gow and J.D.D. Smith, "Peacemaking, Peacekeeping: European Security and the Yugoslav Conflict," *London Defence Studies* 11 (London: Brassey's for the Centre for Defence Studies, 1982), pp. 16-17.

84. Text of Brioni Declaration, FBIS-EEU-91-130 (8 July 1991).

85. "Agreement on Cease-fire," Belgrade, 1 September 1991, in 10 copies (available through United Kingdom Foreign and Commonwealth Office).

86. For the belligerents opinions on this question, see FBIS-EEU-91-172 (5 September 1991), FBIS-EEU-91-178 (12 September 1991).

87. "Agreement on Cease-fire," 1 September 1991.

88. Interview with Franjo Tudjman, Zagreb Radio Croatia Network, 0910gmt, 2 September 1991, in FBIS-EEU-91-170 (3 September 1991).

89. Franjo Tudjman, Zagreb HTV television interview, 1940gmt, 17 September 1991, in FBIS-EEU-91-181 (18 September 1991).

90. The media must play their part as well, and act responsibly when it comes to communicating the facts. There were many occasions during the Yugoslav conflicts where cease-fire agreements were signed, where the media took the time of signing as the time it was to come into effect, and where they responded to any firing that occurred after that time with, "Well, another cease-fire down the drain." They failed to realize that time was needed for the order to filter down, and it is even possible that the belligerents themselves -- who *do* watch television news reports off things like CNN -- saw these reports and considered the cease-fire broken even before it had come into effect.

91. *The Independent*, 5 October 1991.

92. See the exchange of communications between Tudjman and Kadijević, Zagreb Radio Croatia and Zagreb HTV, 1400gmt 5 October, 1630gmt 6 October, and 1400gmt 6 October, in FBIS-EEU-91-194 (7 October 1991), or see Gow and Smith, "Peacemaking, Peacekeeping," p. 20.

93. "Cease-fire memorandum of agreement," 8 October 1991, reprinted in FBIS-EEU-91-196 (9 October 1991), and see *The Independent*, 9 October 1991.

94. *Daily Telegraph*, 10 October 1991.

95. Facsimile of agreement reprinted as Annex III, "Report of the Secretary General Pursuant to Paragraph 3 of Security Council Resolution 713 (1991)," UN doc. S/23169 (25 October 1991).

96. FBIS-EEU-91-203 (21 October 1991), and FBIS-EEU-91-203 (21 October 1991).

97. See, for example, Ljubljana Radio Slovenia, 2059gmt, 28 June 1991; Belgrade TANJUG, 1559gmt, 4 July 1991, in FBIS-EEU-91-129 (5 July 1991), p. 38; Ljubljana Radio Slovenia, 1700gmt, 10 July 1991, in FBIS-EEU-91-133 (11 July 1991), p. 34; *The Independent*, 12 July 1991.

98. FBIS-EEU-91-184 (23 September 1991).

99. See, for example, Ljubljana Radio Slovenia, 2059gmt, 28 June 1991; Belgrade TANJUG, 1559gmt, 4 July 1991, in FBIS-EEU-91-129 (5 July 1991), p. 38; Ljubljana Radio Slovenia, 1700gmt, 10 July 1991, in FBIS-EEU-91-133 (11 July 1991), p. 34; *The Independent*, 12 July 1991.

100. FBIS-EEU-91-133 (11 July 1991).

101. "Agreement on Cease-fire," 1 September 1991.

102. Franjo Tudjman, Zagreb HTV television interview, 1940gmt, 17 September 1991, in FBIS-EEU-91-181 (18 September 1991).

103. See the exchange of communications between Kadijević and Tudjman, *Summary of World Broadcasts*, EE/1184/B/18 (23 September 1991).

104. Franjo Tudjman, 7 October press conference, *Summary of World Broadcasts*, EE/1198/B/9 (9 October 1991).

105.   *The Times*, 3 September 1991.

106.   *The Times*, 18 September 1991.

107.   *The Independent*, 16 November.

108.   There was a military stalemate, the federal army had low morale, Serbian irregulars had been brought under some kind of control, and domestic and international pressures on Serbia had increased (see Gow and Smith, "Peacemaking, Peacekeeping", p. 35).

109.   See "Implementing Accord," set out as Annex III, "Further Report of the Secretary-General Pursuant to Security Council Resolution 721 (1991), UN doc. S/23363 (5 January 1992).

110.   "Further Report of the Secretary-General Pursuant to Security Council Resolution 721 (1991)," UN doc. S/23513 (4 February 1992). Despite some minor violations, and one more serious incident in early September 1993, the cease-fire in Croatia was still holding as of 8 October 1994.

111.   William B. Quandt, *Camp David: Peacemaking and Politics* (Washington: Brookings Institute, 1986), p. 257.

112.   See Bernard Reich and Rosemary Hollis, "Peacemaking in the Reagan Administration," in Paul Marantz and Janice Gross Stein (eds.), *Peacemaking in the Middle East* (London: Croom Helm, 1985), p. 138. For a similar US role in securing agreement on withdrawal of foreign forces, see Reich and Hollis, Ibid., pp. 146*ff*.

113.   Zelig S. Harrison, "Inside the Afghan Talks," *Foreign Policy* 72 (1988), pp. 37-38.

PART THREE

Third Parties and War

8

Mediator Impartiality
and the "Two-Hat" Dilemma:
"YOU are not objective"

The major focus of this book concerns the question of why wars are so difficult to stop. The assumption so far has been that what obstacles to peace exist come primarily from the warring parties -- that they themselves are the architects of the barriers to cease-fire. In fact, this is not always the case. Major obstacles to any cease-fire can also arise when third parties become involved in the conflict. Even where third party assistance is desired, cease-fire may be prevented if third parties are not careful about how they intervene.[1]

A third party is often necessary in international conflicts. Parties to a dispute may be unable or unwilling to communicate effectively with one another, but may nevertheless want the fighting to end. Parties may desire to avoid looking weak, and might wish to make the offer of cease-fire through a third party. Conversely, proposals may be easier to accept if they can be said to have been made by a third party.[2] Belligerents may be under pressure from the international community to accept outside assistance. Whatever the reasons, belligerents do sometimes turn to third parties to help them find the way to a cease-fire. In fact, and as far as cease-fire negotiations are concerned, the presence of a third party would appear to be more than common: cease-fires arranged through direct communication are the exception rather than the rule.[3] What is interesting for our purposes, however, is not so much that intercession occurs, but whether it militates *against* settlement, despite the intention to promote it. When third parties intercede -- when they mediate -- can their conduct go to prevent agreement? What part of mediator conduct can act as an obstacle to cease-fire?

There are a number of qualities which have been assumed to be essential (or at least helpful) to effective and acceptable mediation. The extensive list of such mediator qualities has included "transparent honesty," trustworthiness, an ability to respect confidentiality, a good knowledge of the parties and their problems, an attitude of acceptance, and a professional knowledge of conflict resolution procedures. Other, more personal qualities have included a necessity to be friendly and feel genuine good will towards the parties, a "capacity for support," intelligence, stamina, energy, patience, and a sense of humor.[4] Finally, a great many practitioners and academics emphasize the importance of impartiality.[5] While all these qualities are useful, it is the intention of this chapter to argue that and above all other mediator qualities, the most important is the final one -- the ability of the mediator to be impartial or, more precisely, to be *seen* as such. Thus, one of the major obstacles to stopping a war is perceived mediator bias.

From the outset, this argument requires an unfortunate but necessary excursion into a debate in the world of international mediation generally, for a growing body of literature in that field apparently goes to indicate that "the assumption that it is essential that the intermediary be impartial ought to be discarded."[6] If this is indeed the case for international mediation generally, then it is likely that it is the case for cease-fire negotiations specifically. Thus, we need to examine the arguments of those who dismiss mediator impartiality as a requirement for successful mediation. In fact, this entire debate is both chimerical and pointless, and arises from a fundamental difference between two schools of thought regarding what constitutes "mediation."

Impartiality and "Mediation": What's in a Name?

For Saadia Touval, perhaps the most outspoken of the critics of impartiality, mediators are intermediaries who "*make suggestions* pertaining to the substance of the conflict, and *seek to influence* the parties to make concessions *by exerting pressures* and *offering incentives*" (emphasis added).[7] Jacob Bercovitch, guest editor for the *Journal of Peace Research* special issue on international mediation and critic of the requirement of impartiality, argues that a mediator

> engages in behaviour that is designed to elicit information and exercise influence. To exercise any degree of influence, mediators need "leverage" or resources. Leverage or mediator power enhances the mediator's ability to influence the outcome.[8]

What is evident in both these definitions is that they see mediation as a process involving the exercise of *power*. The mediator has power to reward, power to punish, and power to induce parties to reach the agreement the mediator wants them to reach.

Defenders of impartiality, however, have an entirely different view of mediation. Andrew Acland, involved in legal/commercial and international mediation, states that "[m]ediators help people to negotiate through careful listening, empathy, their ability to define and clarify issues, to think creatively and to work to build trust."[9] For John Burton, who has perhaps carried out the most extensive research into mediation processes generally, the role of the third party "is not to seek compromises. It is initially to facilitate analysis so that goals and tactics, interests, values and needs, can be clarified, and later to help deduce possible outcomes on the basis of the analysis made."[10] In both these definitions, and in the definitions of other defenders of the requirement of mediator impartiality, the exercise of power as a mediation tactic is absent.[11] Raymond Probst, a Swiss diplomat who has led a long and distinguished career in international mediation, concludes that the State which lends its good offices or which acts as mediator can use its influence to induce the parties to negotiate "of course, short of any political or military pressure, which would be tantamount to political intervention."[12]

So what we have here are two divergent concepts of third party roles and functions. Despite the fact that the end result may be the same, both use the same word -- mediation -- to describe processes which operate by wholly different means. There are other terms which could be used. "Conciliation," or "Good Offices" for example, could be used to describe the activities of third parties envisioned by Acland, Burton, and others, leaving the term "mediation" to apply to the activities of the third parties studied by Touval and Bercovitch. Acland, for example, notes that "the distinction between mediation and conciliation is seldom clear even to those using them,"[13] and Probst notes that good offices and mediation differ only in nuances.[14]

There are difficulties with distinguishing the terms on this basis, however. First, doing so would be in direct conflict with the Hague Regulations, which are absolutely clear about the definition of mediation: it is a voluntary, non-binding, non-coercive process wherein "the part of the mediator consists in *reconciling* opposing claims and appeasing the feelings of resentment which may have arisen between the states at variance" (emphasis added).[15] International law, then, supports the contention that mediation is free from power politics. Unless there can be a clear and unequivocal statement to the contrary in some internationally respected forum, that definition will continue to hold (and confuse). Second, and despite the Hague definition, researchers and mass media appear content to call nearly *any* form of third party intervention (short of the threat of or use of military force) "mediation." Bercovitch states that mediation consists of "third party activity, provided such activity as acceptable to the adversaries, and purports to abate, settle or resolve an international dispute without resorting to force or invoking authoritative rules,"[16] -- but note that this activity does not exclude using other coercive methods, such as an explicit or implicit system of reward and punishment. For Fisher and Keashly,

> mediation at the international level involves interventions by credible and competent intermediaries who assist the parties in working toward a negotiated settlement on substantive issues through persuasion, the control of information, the suggestion of alternatives, *and, in some cases, the application of leverage* (emphasis added).[17]

Lord Carrington, the EC representative in the Yugoslav crisis, was constantly referred to in the press as the EC "mediator," despite the coercive element present in the discussions.[18] Perhaps this is unavoidable. Because of the way the term is used, and even given the Hague definition, perhaps all that can be done now is to distinguish *styles* of third party intervention -- again short of the threat or use of force -- but placing them all under the generic banner of "mediation."

There are two basic axes along which mediator activity can be placed -- the first is their coercive potential (which is power-dependent): how many carrots and sticks can they bring to bear on a situation? The second axis is their stake in the outcome (which is in effect a measure of impartiality): what do they have to lose or gain by promoting one kind of settlement over another? Mitchell argues that any third party can be placed simultaneously anywhere along these two axes.[19] While that may be true, whatever their position there are still only two common styles of mediation. The first is the low power, low stake mediator -- that of Burton and Acland. The second is the high power, high stake mediator -- that of Touval and Bercovitch in which "mediators, like brokers, are in it for profit."[20]

In fact, and while it may be the case that many accept this distinction, perhaps the best attempt to define the two styles clearly comes from to Fisher and Keashly:

> *Mediation* (that is, "pure" mediation) involves the intervention of a skilled and experienced intermediary who attempts to facilitate a negotiated settlement to the dispute on a set of specific substantive issues ... and uses reasoning, persuasion, the control of information, and the suggestion of alternatives ... *Mediation with muscle* (or what might be termed "power" mediation) ... includes the use of leverage or coercion by the third party in the form of promised rewards or threatened punishments. In a very real sense, the third party becomes a member of a negotiating triad and bargains with each party, using carrots and sticks, to move them toward a settlement.[21]

(Fisher & Keashly's terminology will continue to be used here. I would also advocate their general use in future -- rather than suggest new terms and contribute to the problem.) What is interesting about these definitions is firstly that no pure mediation theorist has made the distinction -- primarily because for these theorists, power mediation is simply *not* mediation. For them, any third party which uses coercive methods of any kind, which uses any system of reward and punishments, is not mediating: "The essence of mediation is persuasion, not coercion."[22]

Moving on to the adherents of power mediation, they also generally fail to distinguish the two styles. Although Bercovitch does attempt to distinguish between facilitated mediation and more coercive mediation in his study of mediation effectiveness, all his case studies included "formal or institutionalized ... intervention."[23] The flaw here is that pure mediators will argue that pure mediation is only effective when it is *not* formalized, when it is out of the public eye.[24] When Touval questions whether impartiality is necessary for mediation, he operates from a power mediation framework, seeing mediators as powered bargainers,[25] yet he criticizes pure mediators who operate in an entirely different world to his own. His main targets, for example, are Oran Young and Elmore Jackson, both of whom see mediation as a process free of considerations of inducement through power. Young's "mediatory actions" consist of persuasion, enunciation, elaboration, interpretation, communication, and data collection[26] -- hardly coercive functions -- and Elmore Jackson is a Quaker who comes from a similarly non-coercive, "private" mediation framework. In sum, questions such as "Is impartiality necessary for effective mediation?" and "How effective is mediation?" are simply incomplete. More appropriately, the questions should be concerned with which type of mediation (pure or power) is more effective, and whether impartiality necessary to either form.

The answer to the question of the necessity of impartiality in mediation, then, is a simple one, and depends merely on whether one speaks of pure or power mediation. In power mediation, the answer is simply "no." Touval and Bercovitch are entirely correct. In power mediation, disputants often have little choice but to accept mediators, who have a number of resources at their disposal with which to induce agreement. They can "bang heads together" when they have to. Thus, in many cases disputants attend a mediation not so much out of choice, but because they may have *no* choice,[27] for threats may hover in the background should they fail to demonstrate appropriate will to enter negotiations. Dutch Foreign Minister Hans van den Broek, speaking on behalf of the EC mediating "troika" in the Yugoslav conflict, once said that, "We feel that certain pressures have to be carried out in order to obtain participation in good faith."[28] Unique logic, to be sure, but the point is that power mediators can reward and punish appropriate behavior, and their impartiality, while perhaps desirable, is unnecessary to secure an agreement.[29] Indeed, it can even be argued that any mediator who is perceived as a power mediator can never simultaneously act as an impartial pure mediator. As Princen notes, "[i]f a mediator's ability to bargain lingers in the background, disputing parties will condition everything they do by that bargaining possibility."[30] Moreover, even where power mediators are accepted, this is likely done not on the basis that they are impartial, but because the belligerents want access to the power and resources such mediators have available to them; the relevant characteristic for power mediators is their power, not their impartiality.

Pure mediators, however, while not having to face the possibility of disputants wanting access to their power, must accept the restrictions that that lack of power brings. Because they lack the coercive (or persuasive) resources of the power mediator, their position is a precarious one: their disputants have come of their own free will, may leave the negotiations at any time and, most importantly, may dismiss the mediators if they do something which parties dislike, find inappropriate or, most importantly, see as biased behavior. Pure mediators must rely on their skills in building trust, in communicating, and on their own personality to see them through to an agreement. Quaker mediators, who have a long history of pure mediation, have often commented that without at least the appearance of impartiality, they would never have been in a position to mediate in the first place.[31] Indeed, pure mediators would in all likelihood *refuse* to mediate any conflict in which they were perceived as biased. Probst, for example, comments that "Switzerland ... remains ready to render "Good Offices" in a spirit of international solidarity whenever such services are asked for *and can be offered without prejudice*" (emphasis added).[32] Following on these last points, it is entirely clear that impartiality or, rather, the appearance of impartiality, must be and is the *sine qua non* of pure mediation. Indeed, pure mediators *define* mediation in terms of impartiality. It is inextricably bound up in what they attempt to do.

The debate about whether impartiality is required for effective mediation is a non-debate. Those who say that it is *not* a requirement are entirely correct, for they perceive mediation as a process of punishment and reward in which mediators become a third bargaining force, arguing for one side or the other depending on where they believe settlement should fall. The relevant variable here is indeed power, not impartiality. Those who argue *for* impartiality are also correct however, for they see mediation as a voluntary process in which mediators have no coercive power over the disputants but who must be acceptable if they are to be given the opportunity to help the parties find a settlement they can live with. Where they are seen as biased, they will be dismissed, and no opportunity to continue (or perhaps begin) mediating will be given. The relevant characteristic in this setting, the defining characteristic, is impartiality.[33]

It is beyond the scope of this book to make a definitive judgment as to which style of mediation -- pure or power -- is more effective. Suffice it to say that both can be effective under certain circumstances, and for our purposes it is more important to understand that when pure or power mediators become involved in conflicts, both will face certain obstacles. Later, questions about coercion and its relationship to a forced cease-fire will be discussed, at which point the activities of power mediators become relevant. Here, however, and because the concern is with impartiality, pure mediation is more germane. If it is now clear that pure mediation is in large part defined in terms of impartiality, it is possible move on and specifically consider how a lack of impartiality, or perceived lack of impartiality, can act as an obstacle to peaceful settlement -- the question to which we now turn.

How to be Impartial: Avoiding The "Two-Hat" Dilemma

When pure mediators become involved in international conflict (and assume that we are speaking only of pure mediators from this point on), there arises an immediate distinction between what belligerents require from them, and what they desire from them. What belligerents desire from a mediator is the ability to help them achieve their goals -- in this case a cease-fire -- an end to the violence. If they fail to do this belligerents will be disappointed, but they will not (usually) deride or discredit the third party which acted on their behalf. The general question of why mediators cannot deliver what they are asked is too broad a topic to be discussed here; the answers lie in questions of process and the ability and characteristics of individual mediators. (It has a great deal to do with how well they match the list of rather saintly characteristics and qualities mentioned earlier). Despite this, something can be said about what belligerents *require* from pure mediators, for if the requirements are not met, no mediation effort will have the opportunity to succeed. A failure to meet belligerent requirements, then, must be considered a major obstacle to cease-fire.

As in international mediation generally, if there is a single belligerent requirement for a mediator interested in stopping the fighting, it is that the mediator be *objective* in the dispute. That is, the mediator must be seen to act in such a way as to promote an equitable settlement based on disputants' needs and interests as *they* have defined them.[34] It is clear, for example, that the declared status of the politically neutral nation has often allowed it to play a bridging role in international conflict. Sweden, for example, achieved "considerable success" in its attempts to mediate between the USSR and Finland in 1939, and Switzerland, thanks to its status as a neutral, remained as one of the few lines of communication between Axis and Allied powers.[35]

The critical variable here is belligerent perceptions of partiality.[36] Whether the mediator (or even the "neutral" nation) is *actually* biased is beside the point. Mediators who are in reality impartial will be dismissed if they are seen as biased, just as biased mediators will *not* be dismissed as long as they are *seen* as impartial. Thus, even in the case where the mediators are not outsiders (and therefore not neutrals as some would define them),[37] if they are still perceived as acting fairly, they will be allowed to get on with the job. This is probably not only the case in humanitarian cease-fires,[38] or in cease-fires generally, but in every kind of dispute at every conceivable level.

As we have argued earlier, there can be no effective mediation of a dispute where the pure mediator is perceived as biased. Detractors may point, for example, to Wehr and Lederach, who have argued that in Central America, there is a native Indian preference for an "insider" (and by the researchers' definition non-neutral) mediator,[39] but even here the relationship is based on trust (*confianza*) -- trust that the mediator will promote a fair settlement. The mediator in this case, then, while being partial towards one *party* in terms of feeling or emotional attachment, is nevertheless trusted to be impartial towards the issue of a *settlement*. It seems likely, then, that in almost all cases, pure mediators who fail to be objective in the eyes of the belligerents will be castigated by one or both of them, and they will automatically lose their credibility and status:

> [t]o the extent that an intervening party is perceived as partial to one side or the other, it loses its status as a true third party, and becomes more and more assimilated to one or the other of the protagonists for all practical purposes.[40]

During the Nigerian Civil War, for example, peace negotiations were affected negatively by Biafra's (justified) perception that the OAU was not acting impartially, and this perception led to the rejection of a British offer to mediate, as well as undermining all further OAU efforts[41] (a point to which we shall return in detail later). Any organization or individual attempting to act as a pure mediator and bring about a cease-fire therefore has the absolute and unswerving duty to attempt not only act impartially but, most importantly, to appear to act impartially, for it is always the disputants' perceptions of the ability of the mediator to be impartial which are most important. Andrew Acland recalls that in South Africa "wearing a short-sleeved shirt with epaulets ... was perceived to be an indication of pro-white sentiments."[42] In this case, and no matter how impartial a mediator might actually be, his fashion sense would dictate his success!

The real question is what belligerents consider to be an objective, impartial mediator. Certainly one requirement for objectivity is that the third party be non-judgmental. Any time a third party engages in overt criticism, and particularly if that criticism is public, it loses its status as a neutral. This is not so much because the criticism is undeserved or unfounded (although it may be), so much as that any criticism of one belligerent is taken for granted as *support* for its enemy: "if you're not with us, you're against us." This creates a special dilemma for those organizations who have more than one role in the dispute. If a regional or international organization has the duty not only to promote peaceful settlement, but to pass judgments, make pronouncements, or become otherwise involved in a given conflict, immediate difficulties arise. The organization wearing two or more "hats" has the difficulty that belligerents may be unable to make the distinction between the roles, or believe that the distinction exists.

Some nations, for example, believe that the role of the UN Security Council should be that of a neutral third party. When it fails to act in this manner -- by issuing resolutions which condemn one or another party to a conflict -- it loses that perceived status and damages its perceived reputation. Instead, it is considered a pawn to the interests of the states which compose it (usually the five permanent members). Worse, any representative of the United Nations attempting to mediate faces the same perceived lack of objectivity, being generally assumed to be acting not on behalf of some Platonic ideal of objective, impartial, helpful UN Security Council, but on behalf of the member states which make it up.

Perez de Cuellar, in his 1991 Report of the Secretary-General, noted that

> [o]ver long years, there has grown a view of the United Nations itself ... as a place of litigation that is likely to result in a negative verdict for one or the other party. I believe that we need now actively to foster the perception that, *except in cases of action with respect to breaches of the peace or acts of aggression* ... the United Nations is more an instrument of mediation that can help reconcile legitimate claims and interests and achieve just and honorable settlements (emphasis added).[43]

The Secretary-General's exception is important. It implies that where the United Nations *is* involved in enforcement actions, it cannot act impartially. When it takes actions under Chapter VII of the Charter (enforcement), this is undoubtedly the case, but further to this, even issuing a resolution which condemns one or another party means that it is acting in a judgmental capacity. It cannot therefore presume to act as a mediating influence. Any organization, therefore, which attempts to mediate but at the same time has the duty to make pronouncements or pass judgments on a conflict situation faces a conflict of interest which it must attempt to resolve if its efforts at mediation are to be considered credible.

De Cuellar's exception raises a further issue. Where the third party is engaged in peace *enforcement*, as distinct from peacekeeping or mediation efforts, it is seen by belligerents not as an objective third party, but often as an *involved* third party, and sometimes even as a third belligerent. This again applies most obviously to the UN, and most often when it acts under Chapter VII of the Charter. Where the UN becomes involved as a peace enforcer, it excludes itself from any possibility of effective mediation -- no belligerent will see it as an objective neutral. In both the Korean War and the Gulf War of 1991, for example, the UN was seen as a belligerent. Whether the UN was a legal belligerent in either case belies the point. In the Korean War, for example, on 15 December 1950, the Group on a Cease-Fire in Korea[44] attempted to arrange a cease-fire, but the attempt was rejected by the Chinese on the basis that it was to be the UN, itself considered to be a party to the war, which was to have sole responsibility for the supervision of the cease-fire.

Again, during the Gulf War of 1991 Iraq considered allied forces and the Security Council as cooperative partners in the effort being launched against it. On 14 February 1991 the Security Council met in closed session for the first time since military action began. The Council had come under increasing pressure to discuss the situation, and more particularly to discuss a cease-fire. At the meeting, the objectivity of the Council was not only questioned by Iraq, it was denied altogether:

> the Council is no longer an international security council. It has no credibility or legitimacy. It is merely the instrument for the covering up of the worst of international crimes, which is now being perpetuated in the heartland of the Arab nation.

Iraq's position with regard to a cease-fire was also put forward. The United States was the "great criminal" which attempted to "shoot down any peaceful initiative to solve the crisis." The war, for Iraq, was "actually an American, North Atlantic and Zionist immoral war of revenge against Iraq, its people, its army, its leadership, and its civilisation," and the United States would "continue its aggression even if the Security Council were to adopt a resolution on a cease-fire." Until the aggressors withdrew, Iraq would exercise its right and duty to "legitimate self defence against the attempts being made by the United States and its co-criminals to kill us off. In the end, God willing, we shall win."[45] It is likely that this attitude was present even before the war, and must have had an affect on de Cuellar's last-ditch mediation effort on 14 January, the day before the UN deadline to announce a withdrawal; he would not be seen as a helpful pure mediator, but as a representative of the organization attempting to force its compliance.

The point is clear. The UN, or any other organization involved in pure mediation efforts, cannot be seen to be playing two roles if its efforts are to be acceptable (and ultimately successful). It is either a peacemaker, a pure mediator which remains objective and attempts to help the parties settle in the way they want to settle, or it is a peace enforcer, delving into the world of power mediation and attempting to bring about a cease-fire through arbitrating, judging, and influencing the war through its actions. The roles are almost always mutually exclusive (if for no other reason that the belligerents themselves are seldom able to perceive that the roles could function independently). Both the Iran/Iraq war and the Yugoslav conflict illustrate the arguments. In the former case, Iran was unable to perceive the differences between the UN's mediatory and enforcement functions, and in the latter, it was only when the roles were clearly separated that a settlement resulted.

The Iran-Iraq War

Turning first to the Iran-Iraq war, and in an effort to halt the fighting, on 12 July 1982, the Security Council called for a cease-fire and a withdrawal of troops; blame for the war was laid at no one's feet, however. Although it seemed an impartial act, Iran's response was that in case a state decides to resort to force unilaterally (Iran's version of the war's beginning), "it is the duty of the Security Council to condemn that state for not having complied with the Charter ... Failing to do so means that the Council has not acted in accordance with the principles and purposes of the UN." Resolutions 479 (28 September 1980) and 514 had failed to do this and, by Iran's interpretation, the Security Council waited until "Iraq had killed as many Iranians as it wanted ... before stepping in to create a shield behind which the war criminals who are ruling Iraq could be safe from punishment that awaits them." Until the Security Council named Iraq as the aggressor, therefore, Iran would "dissociate itself" from (read "ignore") the actions of the Security Council.[46] In October of 1982, in a statement to the UN Secretary General from the Iranian representative to the United Nations, Iran asked,

[a]re we not justified in questioning the impartiality and objectivity of the [the Security Council], which has remained silent for over 22 months of Iraqi occupation of our territory and started deliberations only after the Islamic Republic of Iran was succeeding in forcing the aggressors to retreat?[47]

Moreover, it explicitly accused the Council of supporting Iraq in Resolution 522 (article 3 of which said that the Council "welcomes the fact that one of the parties has already expressed its willingness to cooperate [with Resolution 522])."[48]

Iran, it is clear, was unable to distinguish the two potential roles of the Security Council, confusing them both (perhaps deliberately), and resulting in accusations both that the Council was neither impartial when it took action, nor fulfilling its responsibility. By 1984, Iran's opinion of the Council had remained unchanged. In the opinion of Iran,

> ..it is the callousness of the United Nations and its blatant negligence of its constitutional responsibilities that has abetted the Iraqi rulers in their criminal perpetrations. The people and the government of the Islamic Republic of Iran therefore consider the Security Council partially responsible for the murderous action and devastation brought to the two Muslim nations of Iran and Iraq.[49]

The Council was explicitly accused of "patronage" towards Iraq.[50]

In 1985, the criticism was even more harsh. Iran complained once more of the "deafening silence" of the Security Council to the situation, complained also about members of the Security Council supplying weapons to Iraq (which they were), and of its failure to act concerning Iraq's use of chemical weapons. Regarding the latter grievance, Iran specifically charged that the UN waited months to send an investigatory mission after which it "shied away from identifying the culprit." It concluded that there was "little doubt about the malicious intentions of some of these mediators, who have been carrying olive branches in one hand, while supplying the aggressor with the most sophisticated weapons of mass destruction." The Security Council had "undermined its legitimacy."[51]

In his report to the Council after an abortive mediation attempt in the Spring of 1985, Perez de Cuellar specifically noted Iran's concern with UN partiality, which was "brought home to [him] forcefully."[52] Undoubtedly, as in the Gulf war, this must have had an affect on de Cuellar's ability to mediate effectively. Resolution 582 (of 24 February 1986) was still considered "one-sided" as it failed to condemn Iraq on a number of points, including its initial aggression and use of chemical weapons.

Iraq's response to a statement by the President of the Security Council in 1986 is particularly revealing. The statement read:

> The members of the Security Council ... Profoundly concerned by the unanimous conclusion of the specialists that chemical weapons on many occasions have been used by Iraqi forces against Iranian forces ... the members of the Security Council strongly condemn this continued use of chemical weapons ... [53]

Iraq's reply: "It is a cause of regret to the government of Iraq that the statement issued by the Council clearly lacks the required degree of balance."[54]

Iran's official position on Resolution 598 (of 20 July 1987) was familiar: the Council as a whole was seen as biased, and as a vehicle for US intervention. Perhaps surprisingly, Iran admitted that some members of the Council remained impartial (although it did not name them).[55] It is noteworthy of this particular resolution that for the first time since the war began, the Security Council was actually *demanding* a cease-fire, a rare action. It was a threat, no doubt, as "further steps" would be taken if the resolution was not obeyed, but it also offered much to Iran in the way of positive incentives. Iran's demand that Iraq be named as the aggressor was handled with a promise of an impartial inquiry into the responsibility for the war. Reparations were dealt with through a recognition of the need for reconstruction "with appropriate international assistance," and the resolution again "deplored" the use of chemical weapons, something Iran had been demanding that the UN do for some time.[56] (Unlike 1986, Iraq was not explicitly named this time as the culprit, however.)

It was really only with Resolution 598 that the Security Council made clear the role it was playing was not that of impartial pure mediator, but as (partial) arbitrator -- passing judgment on the situation. It went even further than this, however. When Iran invited de Cuellar to discuss the resolution with them, the Security Council said that any visit would be to discuss only how to implement the resolution, not to renegotiate it.[57] De Cuellar's normal function of "good offices" was being suspended, and de Cuellar himself began to function in a different role as a result. On 13 December, he announced that UN authority was being undermined, and it was time for a UN embargo[58] -- a judgmental act which could not be seen as impartial by Iran.

The confusion of roles was clear in this war. The UN, while attempting to act as mediator through the personage of Perez de Cuellar, and despite the latter's limited successes,[59] was considered to be acting in a biased and prejudicial manner both through action and inaction at various points in the war. The Security Council, concerned with making pronouncements and issuing resolutions, removed whatever appearance of objectivity it possessed. Its dual responsibility -- to react to the situation, yet remain impartial to aid mediation efforts -- at best confused the belligerents. At worst it resulted in the augmentation of their ability to evade serious negotiations for cease-fire by allowing them to decide which role the UN was not fulfilling, and to criticize it on that basis. It was only with Resolution 598 that its role became clear.

The Yugoslav Conflict

The wars in the former Yugoslavia provide an even clearer example than the Iran-Iraq war. In this case, it was the European Community[60] which confused the roles of pure and power mediator, and it was only after those roles had been separated -- with the UN taking over cease-fire mediation, and Europe concentrating on using power mediation to achieve political settlement -- that a successful cease-fire occurred.

When violence broke out in Yugoslavia in July 1991, Europe -- through a number of institutions concerned with European security -- became involved as a mediator at a very early stage. It is very clear, however, that there was a great deal of confusion as to the type of mediation Europe was intending to attempt. On the one hand, there were documents such as the Brioni declaration of 7 July, brokered by the "troika" of the past, present and coming presidents of the European Council of ministers, which noted that the "only the nationals of Yugoslavia can decide their own future"[61] -- a clear indication of pure mediatory intent. On the other hand, there were threats of sanctions and withdrawal of aid,[62] implementation of sanctions,[63] and various comments by European representatives including, "I don't want any more words; I want signatures"[64] and van den Broek's opinion that "certain pressures" had to be carried out in order to reach a settlement[65] -- the language of power mediation.

In fact, European involvement in Yugoslavia consisted of two roles: first, attempting to aid (or coerce) in political settlement and, second, to supply observers for monitoring cease-fires. The former role became coercive in its tactics, but from the outset, the latter function was initially intended by Europe to be wholly non-coercive. Yet even here there were concerns that there would be attempts at coercion. It was entirely clear that as far as the participants in the Yugoslav conflict were concerned, the monitoring mission -- not to mention the overall European role -- *should* have been a non-coercive one. On 3 September, for example, Branko Kostić, vice president of the federal presidency, complained that

> if the observer mission behaves like Mr. van den Broek, and if it is not prepared for dialogue and a detailed examination of the problems and a search for compromise solutions acceptable to both sides, then everything will fall apart rapidly and its futility will be revealed ... Van den Broek is acting in an extremely undiplomatic way.

Despite this wish, it seemed clear that Europe was not going to behave in the way Kostić wished them to. When the third European-brokered agreement was signed on 1 September, van den Broek apparently rejected any proposed changes: it was a document he had "brought along to be signed."[66]

The misunderstandings regarding the European role continued. On 7 September, an EC-sponsored conference in the Hague opened under the chairmanship of Lord Carrington, the EC-appointed "special envoy." Speaking the day before the conference opened, Serbian President Slobodan Milošević declared that the role of the EC "is to unbiasedly and through competent mediation, help to find solutions to the crisis, not to impose a solution."[67] Despite this perception (or hope) regarding Europe's role, Kostić had further complaints in October, arguing that

> as things moved along, Europe was behaving increasingly aggressively and with less and less unbiasedness ... Van den Broek used, or attempted to use [the 10 October] talks to establish new conditions which are unacceptable.[68]

On 28 October, Europe threatened to implement sanctions on 5 November unless Serbia accepted a new peace plan. Milošević reacted angrily to the ultimatum, arguing that the Hague conference could not unilaterally abolish Yugoslavia. As Milošević rightly pointed out, the EC's initial declaration at Brioni on 8 July was that "only the nationals of Yugoslavia can decide their own future," and Serbia therefore expected Europe to abide by this declaration. "Serbia," he said,

> will not accept ultimatums and considers that the Hague conference can achieve success only if all sides in the work of the conference participate on an equal basis and if the interests of all Yugoslav peoples and republics are equally taken into consideration.[69]

Milošević's position was even more clear by 5 November, three days before sanctions were actually imposed. The ultimatum was considered "an act of pressure and violence incompatible with the democratic order that we wish to build in Europe." In addition, his view of Europe's role was specifically laid out: the ultimatum was an act

> contrary to the stands that the Community itself has proclaimed regarding Yugoslavia, such as the role of the EC in the form of good services in seeking a solution acceptable to all republics and peoples, goodwill in accepting proposals and suggestions.[70]

There were, then, entirely different perceptions of Europe's role in this conflict. Those in dispute in Yugoslavia wanted help to find a settlement, but they did not want a settlement dictated to them. Europe, for its part, appeared to want to play the role of a well-intentioned but firm-handed uncle, and would flip back and forth between pure and power mediation depending on whether or not the parties were moving towards what *Europe* saw as the best solution.

The European Community in this case was attempting to fulfil both the role of the peacemaker, as well as the role of peace enforcer, and the mutual exclusivity of the roles ensured that it was unable to achieve this. Europe could not simultaneously attempt to force a political settlement through power mediation, and at the same time supply a pure mediation observer mission which would be seen as impartial, non-coercive, and separate from the political agenda. These difficulties would be compounded when it came to the question of peacekeeping troops. Milošević, for example, rejected any suggestion of Western or European peacekeeping troops.[71] One of the main reasons for this, especially considering his later willingness to accept UN troops, must have been that armed forces under the aegis of institutions intent on imposing a solution would have been considered by some not as peacekeepers, but as an occupying force, and this would be unacceptable.

The end result of this confusion of roles in Yugoslavia was that calls by belligerents for assistance in achieving cease-fire were increasingly redirected to the UN. Serbian Vice-President Budimir Kosutić, for example, commented on 25 November that the "participation of the United Nations Organization in the resolution of the Yugoslav crisis is more desirable than that of the European Community." His reasons were twofold: first, he believed that the emplacement of a peacekeeping force would help obviate obstructive tactics Germany appeared to be using at the Hague and second, would create the necessary conditions conducive to a diplomatic solution.[72] Croatian President Franjo Tudjman, too, saw the UN as a "guarantee for the way out of this war."[73] The EC failed, he said, because it "did not have the mechanism for it to be able to succeed in imposing its views on the solution of this crisis and ending the war in Croatia." It was not that the UN was taking over the role of the EC as such, but it would take it over "in the essential matter of ending the war."[74]

Even the UN, however, was initially uncertain as to the role it was expected to play. Resolution 713 (adopted 25 September) strongly urged all parties to abide by the cease-fire agreements of 17 and 22 September, and further encouraged them to settle their disputes peacefully and through negotiation. In the same breath, however, the role of pure mediator became that of power mediator: the Security Council made the decision to implement a "general and complete embargo on all deliveries of weapons and military equipment to Yugoslavia."[75] Cyrus Vance, too, appointed as the UN Secretary-General's personal representative on 8 October, was initially uncertain as to the prospective UN role. On 14 November, he noted that if any of the parties broke a cease-fire or fired on UN troops, then the organization would be "ready to exert pressure."[76] In the end, however, and at least as far as Croatian phase of the war is concerned,[77] it appeared that the UN managed to confine its role to that of a pure mediator, arranging a durable cease-fire by means of good offices and non-coercive methods -- a feat which it accomplished in Croatia on 3 January 1992. Part of the reason it was able to do this was undoubtedly that political questions were to be left to Europe and the Hague conference. As the new UN Secretary-General Boutros Boutros Ghali pointed out on 5 January 1992,

> [t]he purpose of a United Nations peace-keeping operation has been, since the outset, conceived as being to create favourable conditions for the necessary negotiations between the parties ... negotiations that have been proceeding in the [European] conference on Yugoslavia. In this way, the United Nations would be supporting the role and efforts of the European Community.[78]

The UN would be involved purely in cease-fire negotiations, separated from the more complex issues of political settlement; a separation of roles would be a major factor contributing to ultimate UN success in implementing a cease-fire.[79] In this case, while power mediation might have been effective in moving the parties toward overall political settlement, and in fact *because* power mediation was used at that level, negotiating cease-fire agreements, and subsequent monitoring and implementation, required the presence of a party who was seen by the belligerents as impartial and had only one role to play. Despite its failures in the Iran/Iraq war, the UN managed significantly better in the Yugoslav conflict, at least with regard to the Croatian phase of the war.

Who Should Mediate?

Since the UN and similar regional organizations see themselves as being (or hope to become) the primary instrument of international third party mediation, but since it is impossible for these organizations to mediate in a conflict in which they are themselves politically involved (or seen to be involved), the question arises: who can mediate such conflicts?[80] Apart from this particular "two-hat" problem, there is certainly a case that can be made for mediation by representatives of the United Nations and similar organizations -- the "public" mediators. These third parties gain credibility and acceptability by virtue of their association with the organizations they represent and, depending on the particular state they are also associated with, their credibility may be enhanced. This latter association, however, most often creates yet another two-hat dilemma. Any representative of an international organization almost always is simultaneously a representative of an identifiable state. Belligerents deciding whether or not to accept that representative as credible must therefore decide not only whether the chosen mediator is from an *organization* which is considered impartial, but whether the mediator is coming from a *state* which is considered impartial. All states have interests, and while a mediator appointed by an international body is supposed to represent that body, the fact that the mediator could also be representing particular state interests must enter the minds of belligerents.

It may also be the case that the perception is valid -- that mediators actually champion particular state interests, albeit as surreptitiously as possible. Handel has commented, for example, that "there are no honest brokers in the Middle East conflict. Every side is involved and can gain or lose from one or another agreement between the sides."[81] The Secretary of the Palestine Conciliation Commission once commented that the conduct of individuals appointed to a supposedly impartial UN body "could not fail to be dictated by the governments they represent."[82] After a study of Carter's role in securing the Camp David Accords, one writer has concluded that despite Carter's attempts to act as an impartial pure mediator, he was not seen as such. Instead, he was seen as a power mediator:

> [t]he fact was that Begin and Sadat were there to bargain, not just between themselves but with the USA as well. In fact, for both Israel and Egypt, the bargain was indeed with the USA, not each other. Carter carried the entire baggage of the USA, not just his predecessors' tactics, but also the undeniable carrots and sticks all US presidents have.[83]

Thus, unless mediators are perceived by belligerents as being able to divorce themselves from the interests of the states they represent, they may not be seen as either credible or objective.

The alternative to public mediators appointed by an international body is for belligerents to seek out individual mediators who, while retaining particular nationalities and possibly even representing particular organizations, nevertheless maintain the appearance of neutrality -- the so-called "private" mediators. These can be individuals who are mutual personal friends of both belligerent leaders, or who belong to organizations which have neither the ability nor the desire to coerce, judge, or force either party to cease fire. That is, the mediator comes from an organization which has only one role -- that of mediating the conflict and achieving a cease-fire; no other interest is perceived by the belligerents.

Examples of such organizations have included the international Red Cross (which usually involves itself in arranging humanitarian cease-fires), the World Council of Churches, and the Quaker Society of Friends. Dean Rusk, in a letter to Sydney Bailey, once wrote that in eight years as Secretary of State of the US he had "never encountered a negative impact from informal Quaker work for peace," except perhaps during the Vietnam War when a message to Hanoi implied that if they persisted they would win politically what they could not win militarily.[84] Other efforts of this type include those of the Permanent Conciliation Commission established between France and Switzerland in 1925, or the efforts of the recently established Foundation for International Conciliation, a non-political, independent body which stresses neutrality, non-coercion, and creative problem solving approaches to international conflict resolution.[85] The Foundation has been in existence since 1984, and has apparently had a number of successes in resolving international disputes (although the specifics of these disputes remain outside public knowledge due to the Foundation's insistence on confidentiality).

There are disadvantages to such private mediators. Mitchell argues that "customary channels through which intermediary offers may be initiated are often closed to private mediators." That is, private mediation is unofficial, and operates outside normal diplomatic procedures.[86] This "disadvantage," however, is also one of private mediation's main strengths. That peace and cease-fire negotiations are a public affair often results in a great deal of posturing by the parties, who must play to various audiences in the attempt to convince them that they are not going to "give the farm away." (This public posturing is also related, of course, to the desire to avoid appearing weak.)

During the Nigerian Civil War, for example, vehement posturing was undertaken by the leaders of both sides as well as their representatives. Specifically, the Addis Ababa talks which took place in August 1968 are a good illustration of this. Ojukwu had been confident that the talks would end the war, as he was prepared to offer concessions.[87] Unfortunately, not only did his opening speech not sound conciliatory,[88] the talks in general were apparently used for propaganda warfare than for any constructive purpose.[89] Mike Yarrow, a chronicler of Quaker mediation efforts, notes that they

> were a depressing succession of statements and counter-statements, with each side seeking to score points through personal attitudes or leaks to the press. Subtle elements of flexibility put forth in several statements from each side were lost in the clamor of debate.[90]

Ojukwu, for example, accused Gowon of genocide, duplicity, bad faith, and even went so far as to label him the "Hitler of Africa."[91] Despite this public castigation, however, Ojukwu's private opinion was somewhat different:

[p]eople make me laugh when they talk about an enmity between Yakubu Gowon and Ojukwu. That Gowon and I did not see eye to eye on a certain issue was a result of our different perceptions of the situation at the time ... In leading the war, we both postured. For anyone, therefore, to try and extend this posturing and make it permanent on the national stage, to my mind, is sterile.[92]

In one of Curle's transcripted conversations, too, the point that public posturing can prevent settlement comes through strongly. The belligerent leader in this case was "very disappointed" by the collapse of a peace conference. Curle asked him why he thought it failed, to which came the response that "[t]hey just shouted slogans at us; refused to discuss our proposals. There was no real negotiation whatsoever. ... I'm certainly not going to set up any more conferences just to improve their legal status." Curle then suggested the possibility of a secret and unpublicized conference, "no press, no communique, tight security." Participants would be second-level people, senior officials as opposed to ministers "who might not be so noticeable." The idea would be that the participants would not be so concerned with scoring political propaganda points, and be able to "get on with the business of detailed negotiations." The leader's response was positive.[93]

So public mediation has its disadvantages, most of which private mediation overcomes. There is first the problem of objectivity and the difficulty of the dual or multiple roles of appointed mediators and of the organizations they represent. Second, there is the public face of most international mediation, which results in belligerent posturing. Private mediation would appear to resolve these difficulties, in most cases for the former problem, and in almost all cases for the latter.

Curle argues for private mediation for these and other reasons:

since of most of today's approximately 30 wars are civil wars about which the UN and regional bodies such as the OAU are unable, at least officially, to take any action, there is considerable need for the non-official agencies to fill the gap. This is doubly desirable since many of these wars, though intranational, often have serious international implications.[94]

I think there has to be some public mediation going on, but I also think that private mediation is very important. Things can be said there that cannot be said in public, and the fact that they are carried out by "private" people and not "public" people is also an advantage. They are more credible, because it means that they are not serving the ends of their own governments, and they are making a serious attempt to solve the problem and not just trying to solve it in a way which would benefit their side. They can also be ignored if necessary, whereas if you ignore a public official, even if he [sic] is acting in a non-public way, this is always going to cause difficulties.[95]

In sum, private mediation would appear to resolve many of the difficulties associated with the provision of credible mediators in cease-fire negotiations. Even in the world of the private mediator, however, difficulties with perceptions of partiality arise. Both the Nigerian Civil War, and the efforts of Folke Bernadotte in the Palestine conflict of 1947, can serve to illustrate this point clearly.

The Nigerian Civil War

As we have noted earlier, one of the main attempts at mediation during the Nigerian Civil War came from the Organization for African Unity. That organization, however, regardless of its intentions in promoting peaceful settlement, was decidedly not perceived as objective, and was firmly on the side of the Nigerians.[96] The OAU Resolution of 14 September 1967 recognized the situation as "an internal affair," put their "trust and confidence" in the Federal Government, and sought to assure Gowon of the "assembly's desire for the territorial integrity, unity and peace of Nigeria."[97] This was a boon for Gowon, who used the organization's efforts to bolster his self-portrayal of reasonableness.[98] Biafra, of course, found little comfort in OAU statements, and only rarely and reluctantly accepted OAU peace efforts and mediators. Sir Louis Mbanefo, head of the Biafran delegation at a meeting of the OAU consultative committee, accused the organization of having "neither the ability nor a genuine desire to bring the war to an end ... They are more concerned with maintaining the legitimacy of Gowon's regime than stopping the war."[99]

Despite the failed OAU effort (among others), some mediation efforts had a great deal more success, most notably the efforts of the Quaker pure mediation mission which included Adam Curle, Walter Martin and John Volkmar. In this case, Quaker mediation had the advantage over other efforts in that it took place privately, out of the public eye, where both sides could state their positions clearly and truthfully without having to address more than one audience. At many points in the conflict, real positions had often been masked because the belligerents were attempting to please or appease more than one group, as we have seen.[100] Talks at Kampala and at Addis Ababa both failed, for example, primarily due to the public atmosphere of the talks.

Behind the scenes, and most specifically in the background at the Addis Ababa conference, however, Quaker mediators were able to help more than most people realized. In a private conversation with Adam Curle, and as we now well know, Njoku spelled out Biafran terms which it would not state openly for fear of looking weak: Biafra was willing to become part of a Nigerian union. The concept of sovereignty, which had become a hardened position, was now seen more as a symbol of defiance than as a political necessity, and it could be diluted "significantly."[101] The fact that Njoku would make such a proposal is highly significant in this case, for his public position at the talks was the complete reverse of his private position. In his concluding statement of 15 August 1968, Njoku stated categorically that "the millions of people in Biafra have tasted freedom and will not give it up. Biafra must be recognized as a free, sovereign and independent nation."[102] Privately, however, and by concentrating on the Biafran interest in security, as many apart from Ojukwu saw it, allowed a change in position: the underlying goal of security could be satisfied without achieving independence if that appeared to be the only way forward. Unfortunately, and as we recall from our second chapter, this proposal went nowhere. Although causing heated discussion in Lagos, federal forces had already decided on a military solution, and the proposal was rejected.[103]

It can be argued that all the mediation mission did in this case was carry a message privately which could not be carried publicly. While that may be true, it belies the point that a private mediator was able to achieve what public mediators could not, and that it was achieved primarily because the Biafrans saw them as trustworthy. They trusted that the message would be relayed accurately, without bias, and that Curle would not jeopardize their position by misinterpreting the proposal.

Moreover, it needs to be said that pure mediation has little to do with carrying messages. If all "mediators" do is carry messages, they are not mediating. Mediation is about changing perceptions,[104] or facilitating agreement despite perceptions. It is about getting both parties not only to fully understand the position of the other, but to enable them to view their dispute as a joint problem over which they need to -- somewhat paradoxically -- cooperate in order to resolve. As to the former object of changing perceptions, Curle probably managed to do this on a number of occasions during the Nigerian Civil war. Gowon's New Year message of 1968, for example, predicted that the war would be over by March. The war was not over by March, and his meeting with Curle on 19 March may have convinced him that it was nowhere near to being over. Curle told him that the Biafrans were not nearly as badly affected as reports had suggested. Moreover, their morale was high, there was broad support for Ojukwu, and the fear of genocide was firmly in place.[105]

Having said this, however, even the pure mediation mission in this case suffered at more than one point from a perceived lack of impartiality and the two-hat dilemma. The two hats in this case were mediation and humanitarian relief. The role of the Quaker mission was one of pure mediation, but an organization with which they had strong ties, the American Friends Service Committee (AFSC), was engaged in humanitarian relief. Under normal circumstances, this dual role should not have caused difficulties. Humanitarian relief is customarily offered to both sides, to preserve the appearance of neutrality, but in this case, aid to the Biafran side was considered of great political significance.

The AFSC's first mistake came in October 1968, with the publication of a mimeographed report entitled "General Situation in Nigeria/Biafra." The report was strongly criticized by the Nigerian ambassador in Washington, primarily for its use of the word "Biafra," as it implied political recognition. Moreover, it was felt that the report exaggerated the suffering of the Biafran community. On this occasion, the matter was smoothed over by a promise from the AFSC to be more careful about its choice of words. The incident had no effect on Quaker mediation efforts, but it was a sign of more serious things to come.

On 27 April 1969, "emotionally gripping"[106] reports of the suffering in Biafra were the subject of a three-quarter page advertisement in the New York Times. It had been placed by the AFSC to aid in its fund-raising activities, and despite major efforts by the AFSC to avoid appearing partial, the appeal nearly wrecked Quaker mediation efforts in Nigeria. The AFSC had made great attempts to appear impartial in this case. First, the text of the ad made no reference to the source of bombing and made no accusations. Moreover, a note at the bottom read, "Our work is directed to the victims of war without regard for geography or politics. We believe that all sides share responsibility for war's tragedy; we know that all sides suffer from it." These efforts, however, were to no avail.[107] As Curle recounts, the Federal Nigerians were furious:

> my colleague in New York was soundly berated by the Nigerian ambassador at the UN. Gowon referred to the affair sadly, in the terms of one who has been let down by a trusted friend. We thought the Quakers were impartial, was the theme, can we really trust them now? But one of the senior Nigerian's said, "When we are deeply hurt, we just keep quiet. When we are openly angry it means that the pain will pass." And after many explanations and apologies, it did, fortunately the relationship was fundamentally sound.[108]

In this case, a pure mediation effort was almost spoiled because of a two-hat dilemma. The federal side was unable to distinguish between the personal mediation efforts of Curle and his mission, and the humanitarian efforts of the AFSC. Had it not been for the long-standing Quaker reputation for impartiality, and the underlying trust which had been built up between Gowon and Curle, the effort would not have been allowed to continue.

Quaker efforts in the Nigerian Civil war were significant. They were able to explore options, change perceptions, and allow the belligerents to communicate in ways which could not have been done in any other forum. Even here, however, a perception of bias nearly destroyed all that had been achieved. Quaker efforts were allowed to continue throughout the war only because the belligerents believed in their sincere desire -- and overall ability -- to remain impartial. Had that belief not existed, the effort would have come to an abrupt end.

Count Folke Bernadotte in Palestine (1948)

While the conflict in Palestine in 1948 did not form one of the case studies for this book, it is worth discussing the efforts of the UN mediator in that instance, for his work clearly shows the effect that perceived partiality can have on mediator attempts to achieve cease-fire. In this case, a mediator who saw himself as a pure (and private) mediator was viewed as a power mediator with the weight and power of the superpowers and the United Nations behind him. Not only did this hamper his effectiveness, but his perceived bias -- in part a direct result of a two-hat dilemma -- eventually led to his assassination.

Count Folke Bernadotte was a Swedish diplomat appointed by the UN Security Council on 20 May 1948 as mediator to the dispute in Palestine. On 17 April 1948, the UN Security Council called upon "all persons and organizations in Palestine, and especially upon the Arab Higher Committee and the Jewish Agency" to cease fire. In its wake, a Truce Commission had been set up on 23 April by the UN to aid and implement and supervize the resolution, but it soon suffered from a perceived lack of impartiality.[109] In the opinion of Dr. Dov Joseph, for example, who was to be Israel's first governor of Jerusalem, members of the Truce Commission were far from objective.[110] Bernadotte, who arrived in the Middle East on 29 May, was therefore the only additional (and hopefully unbiased) influence that would have now an opportunity to mediate between the parties.

From the outset, Bernadotte believed that he had made every effort to at least appear impartial. Upon being appointed by the UN as mediator in May 1948, he rejected a suggestion that he go to New York to make himself familiar with the situation. He notes in his diary that "[i]t seemed to me quite wrong that anyone who had been appointed Mediator in a conflict in the Near East ... should make it his first business to go West to acquire information."[111] He refused to bias himself in advance by talking to those who observed the conflict (and undoubtedly had a stake in how it came out) instead of getting his information from the parties involved in the dispute.

Further to his attempts to appear impartial, Bernadotte notes that he wanted to avoid appearing as a representative of the Red Cross, an organization with which he was closely associated. Bernadotte believed that the Red Cross was regarded as pro-Jewish by the Arabs and pro-Arab by the Jews. Therefore he aimed to appear in the Middle East as a representative simply of Red Cross ideals: "I wanted to emphasize the fact that my mission had a strongly humanitarian background and that I wanted to be completely objective and neutral when I met the various representatives of the conflicting forces."[112] Quite simply, he wanted to appear as a "private" mediator.

Finally, in talks with various leaders, he did try to emphasize that he was not bound by UN proclamations (most particularly that on partition of 29 November 1947), and that he had a free hand in helping to come up with new options. As far as he was concerned, if he was "one hundred per cent. bound by the decision taken by the General Assembly ... I think that the Security Council should not have had a Mediator because no Mediator would have been necessary." The mediator, then, was to explore options, to reason, to persuade and to discuss options,[113] but, under no circumstances, to dictate them.

Bernadotte considered himself empowered to use good offices, which he defined as involving "offering friendly suggestions to facilitate adjustment of a controversy" -- this was hardly a coercive function. Indeed, as far as Bernadotte was concerned, "the mediator can achieve success only be achieving voluntary agreement between the parties. His decisions have no binding effect and his suggestions and proposals may be rejected at will by the parties."[114] Despite this, Bernadotte *was* a representative of the United Nations, acting under its instructions, and the UN -- assumed by all to be effectively under the control of the superpowers -- was believed to have numerous rewards to offer and punishments to inflict. The Egyptian Prime Minister, Nakrashi Pasha, kindly pointed this fact out in his first meeting with Bernadotte. "The Mediator," he said, "as an agent of the United Nations, would have to take the fact of the recognition of the Jewish Provisional Government by the United States and the Soviet Union into account ... "[115]

Moreover, the United Nations, and by extension Bernadotte himself, was considered to be biased. When the president of the Security Council attempted to clarify a Council Resolution of 29 May 1948, which again called for a cease-fire,[116] the clarification was rejected by Jewish Foreign Minister Shertok. Bernadotte recalls that

> [b]arely had I finished reading before he interjected in a very irritated tone that, as the President of the Security Council for the month of June was a Syrian and the telegram was consequently signed by a national from a country which was at war with the State of Israel, it was impossible for him to accept this ruling.[117]

That he personally was taken as biased was brought home to him forcefully on 17 June 1948. On a plane flight, after having had further discussions over the arrangement of the cease-fire (of 11 June), he was reading a Jewish paper, and he came across a particularly harsh and heavily critical article:

> I began to realize what an exposed position I was in. I also began to understand that all my efforts to think and act objectively would inevitably be misunderstood and misinterpreted by irresponsible and fanatical writers. I recalled what I had said to my assistants on my first visit to Tel Aviv ... that the friendliness that flowed towards me then would unquestionably turn to suspicion and ill will if, in my later activities as Mediator, I failed to study primarily the interests of the Jewish party but sought to find an impartial and just solution to the problem.[118]

Perhaps strangely, Bernadotte eventually concluded that he must be acting impartially because both the Jewish and Arab press were equally critical.[119] There may be some truth in this, but again, whether he was actually impartial was not the issue. He was perceived as biased, in part due to his association with the United Nations, and nothing he personally could do would help him out of that dilemma. As Bailey notes,

> [t]he Arabs thought of him as representing the hated United Nations, and wherever he went Arab crowds shook their fists and booed. Some Israelis were equally critical: Golda Meir (Myerson) claims that he became "extremely unpopular" because he was "amazingly lacking in neutrality." Bernadotte, she wrote, "never understood what the state of Israel was all about."[120]

Even in the Security Council, Bernadotte was similarly chastised. The Ukrainian SSR alleged that Bernadotte was taking orders not from the Security Council, but from the United States, France and Great Britain.[121]

Of course, Bernadotte's dual role was not the only reason he was perceived as biased. His plans for settlement were seen as unfair by all sides in the conflict.[122] On 27 June 1948, he published tentative proposals for settlement in which he had proposed the give Jerusalem to (Transjordan-annexed) Arab Palestine;[123] the move would certainly not be seen as satisfactory to the Jews, despite the fact that they were to retain Western Galilee (which they occupied in any case). There was little to comfort Arabs in the settlement either,[124] and Bernadotte's plan was ultimately rejected by both sides; Egypt in particular became convinced that the mediator was no more than a tool for British imperialism.[125] The response of the Political Committee of the Arab League to the plan was unenthusiastic: it was called "disappointing" as it guaranteed no Arab demands, and aimed "at the realization of all Zionist ambitions." The Jewish reply, handed over by Shertok on 6 July, was similarly negative. They were "deeply wounded" by the suggestions concerning Jerusalem's future, and concluded that "the Government did not find it necessary to comment on the other parts in

Bernadotte's suggestion, hoping that he might reconsider his whole approach to the problem. Bernadotte's second plan, of 16 September, was similarly ill-received. At the UN, on 15 November, Shertok stated that the plan did not even provide a basis for discussion, and the Arab delegation reacted similarly.[126]

It is perhaps a moot point whether or not Bernadotte was actually biased in his attempts to find a solution to the Palestine conflict. It seems likely, given his own perceptions, and given the evidence of other observers, that Bernadotte really did attempt to be impartial. Amitzur Ilan, Bernadotte's biographer, for example, concluded that "he was not "biased" in favor of any party to the dispute; it was not in his nature in such circumstances to be partisan."[127] The point, however, is how those in directly involved in the conflict received Bernadotte and for them, he was not impartial. After receiving details of the first settlement plan, David Ben-Gurion noted in his diary on 29 June 1948 that "those who suspect that he is a Bevin agent are not too far off the mark,"[128] and as we have seen, there were many who felt similarly. In the end, Bernadotte's perceived lack of neutrality led to his death. On 17 September 1948, on his way to continue discussions with both parties on implementing a cease-fire, he was assassinated by the extremist Jewish group LEHY (labelled by the British authorities as the "Stern Gang").[129] One of their leaders, Israel Eldad, commenting on the assassination, said:

> Bernadotte was seen as a very dangerous man. He was an international personality, designated by the Security Council. His plans meant the end of the hope of a Jewish State. We threw out the British ... and what Bernadotte wanted was in line with the British ... So the LEHY central committee decided to kill him ... I have no second thoughts about the killing of Bernadotte -- we saved Jerusalem.[130]

Those who look at this case may blame Bernadotte's failure for any number of reasons. In terms of lack of resources, he had been promised observers and personnel for the supervision of the 11 June cease-fire, for example, but these personnel were not in place when they should have been.[131] Touval (who, it should be noted, originally used this case to *support* the idea that biased mediators can be effective)[132] blames his failure in Palestine on a number of factors, including a lack of information about the Israel-Arab conflict, lack of personal charm, tact, and persuasive ability, and lack of resources with which to influence parties' positions.[133] Even he, however, admits that Bernadotte aroused Israeli suspicions

> to such an extent that it became very difficult for them to cooperate with them ... Had he merely been suspected of bias, Israel would probably have

tried to win him over ... But he was suspected not merely of bias, but of being in the service of Israel's foes.[134]

It is clear then, that Bernadotte attempted in every way he could to appear impartial, and that he himself saw his role as that of a pure mediator, helping the belligerents to explore options and come up with a settlement they wanted. To those he was attempting to mediate between, however, it was entirely clear that not only was Bernadotte biased, but he was a power mediator. Like Carter at Camp David, he was unable to dissociate himself from his power-laden background.

In this case, Bernadotte's two-hat dilemma was compounded, because not only did he have two roles in the sense of being both a mediator and an UN representative, he also had two mediatory roles: one which was mandated to achieve a cease-fire, and the other to achieve political settlement. The latter role had a decidedly negative effect on his ability to be successful in the former. Many comment on the success Bernadotte had in arranging cease-fires in the Palestine conflict.[135] The difficulty was, however, that these cease-fires were in constant danger of collapsing, and while Bernadotte may have been effective at holding them together, in the end he was denied the opportunity because of his perceived partiality when it came to achieving political settlement.

Moreover, Bernadotte was ineffective because while acting as a pure and private mediator, he was *expected* to act as a power mediator. As a pure mediator he could not be effective because he was perceived to be biased. As a power mediator, he could not be effective because he declined to use the carrots and sticks available to him through his association with the United Nations and the superpowers, and this did nothing but frustrate the belligerents and the effort as a whole. Blame for the failure to use the instruments of influence should not fall on Bernadotte's shoulders, however. Indeed, it is likely that he would not have even thought to use them, because of his own belief that he was there to act as a pure mediator. Wherever blame lies, however, it is clear that perceived bias in this case not only affected the possibilities of continued mediation and of cease-fire -- it resulted in the death of the mediator.

Conclusions

Where third party intercession is necessary to achieve a cease-fire, and where it consists of pure, as opposed to power, mediation, a necessary element to the success of the mediators' efforts is their perceived impartiality. Where the perception of impartiality does not exist, mediators will be rejected either out of hand, or at any point in the mediation at which they are perceived as biased. As a general rule, mediators will only be perceived as impartial if they refrain from passing judgments on the disputants, and if they are able to enter the conflict as a third party who has no more than one role. Pure mediators who have more than the single role which they are expected to fill -- that of helping disputants to come to a voluntary agreement of their own making -- will find that they will be accused of partiality and bias, and their efforts will be terminated. A pure mediator who is perceived as biased is an obstacle to cease-fire.

Notes

1. Readers should note that we are concerned here only with third parties who are intent only on stopping the war -- not with third parties attempting to profit from the war, or intervening on behalf of one or more of the belligerents.

2. Louis Kriesberg, "Formal and Quasi-Mediators in International Disputes: An Exploratory Analysis," *Journal of Peace Research* 28(1) (1991), p. 25.

3. Bertrand de Montluc, *Le Cessez-le-feu*, Ph.D. thesis (Univérsité de Droit et d'Economie et de Sciences Sociales de Paris), 1971, p. 148 (my translation); ("*La procédure de conclusion des accords de cessez-le-feu peut se dérouler sous les auspices des Nations Unies, de façon directe ou indirecte, ou en la presence d'un tiers étatique, les cessez-le-feu par entente direct étant, on l'a vu, hypothèse exceptionnelle*").

4. For "honesty": C.H. Mike Yarrow, *Quaker Experiences in International Conciliation* (London: Yale University Press, 1978), pp. 165-66; and see Adam Curle, *In the Middle: Non-Official Mediation in Violent Situations*, Bradford Peace Studies Papers (New Series No. 1) (New York: Berg, 1986), p. 11; "trustworthiness": Adam Curle, *Tools for Transformation: A Personal Study* (Stroud: Hawthorne, 1990), p. 37; "knowledge": John Burton and Frank Dukes, *Conflict: Practices, Settlement, and Resolution* (London: Macmillan, 1990), p. 199; Curle, *Tools*, p. 37; see Ronald J. Fisher, "Third Party Consultation: A Method for the Study and Resolution of Conflict," *Journal of Conflict Resolution* 16 (1972), pp. 67-94; "acceptance", see Fisher, Ibid.; "procedures": Fisher, Ibid.; Burton and Dukes, Ibid.; "good will": Curle, Ibid., and Curle, *In the Middle*, p. 11.; "support": Fisher, Ibid.; "intelligence," etc.: Jacob Bercovitch, *Social Conflict and Third Parties: Strategies of Conflict Resolution* (Boulder: Westview, 1984) in Jacob Bercovitch, J. Theodore Anagnosen, and Donnette L. Wille, "Some Conceptual Issues and Empirical Trends in the Study of Successful Mediation in International Relations," *Journal of Peace Research* 28(1) (1991), p. 15.

5. Andrew Acland, *A Sudden Outbreak of Common Sense* (London: Hutchinson, 1990), pp. 18, 196; Sydney Bailey, "Non-Official Mediation in Disputes: Reflections on Quaker Experience," *International Affairs* 61 (1985), p. 209; Curle, *Tools*, p. 37; R.J. Fisher, "Third Party Consultation", Ibid.; Raymond R. Probst, *Good Offices in the Light of Swiss International Practice and Experience* (Dordrecht: Martinus Nijhoff, 1989), p. 161; Yarrow, *Quaker Experiences*, pp. 164-165. For Burton and Dukes, who have perhaps done the most extensive cross-context research on mediation so far compiled, impartiality is so bound up with the definition and process of mediation, that it is all but taken for granted in their extensive "rules" and procedures for

facilitated conflict resolution (see Burton and Dukes, *Conflict: Practices, Settlement, and Resolution,* p. 189).

6. Saadia Touval, "Biased Intermediaries: Theoretical and Historical Considerations," *Jerusalem Journal of International Relations* 1(1) (1975), p. 68; for further examples, see Bercovitch *et al.,* "Some Conceptual Issues and Empirical Trends", p. 14, David A. Brookmire and Frank Sistrunk, "The Effects of Perceived Ability and Impartiality of Mediators on Time Pressure in Negotiation," *Journal of Conflict Resolution* 24(2) (1980), p. 327, and Paul Wehr and John Paul Lederach, "Mediating Conflict in Central America," *Journal of Peace Research* 28(1) (1991), p. 87. For views supporting the need for impartiality, see Acland, *A Sudden Outbreak of Common Sense,* p. 18; Bailey, "Non-Official Mediation," p. 209; Curle, *Tools,* p. 37, and see also Curle, *In the Middle,* pp. 11, 12; Oran Young, *The Intermediaries: Third Parties in International Crises* (Princeton: Princeton University Press, 1967), p. 81.

7. Saadia Touval, *The Peace Brokers: Mediators in the Arab-Israeli Conflict* (New Jersey: Princeton University Press, 1982), p. 4.

8. Bercovitch *et al.,* "Some Conceptual Issues and Empirical Trends," p. 15.

9. Acland, *A Sudden Outbreak of Common Sense,* pp. 32-33.

10. Burton and Dukes, *Conflict: Practices,* p. 198.

11. This may not be strictly true. In the latter, non-coercive style of mediation, power is a factor, but in an entirely different sense. Power here is *given* to the disputants. Non-coercive mediation is about enabling others -- empowering them -- to resolve their own dispute. Non-coercive mediators are not about carrots-and-stick power, because in their world, they are not attempting to move the donkey in a direction it does not want to go. In their world, the donkey wants to get somewhere, and mediators do their best to show it the easiest way.

12. Probst, *Good Offices,* p. 5.

13. Acland, *A Sudden Outbreak of Common Sense,* p. 18.

14. Probst, *Good Offices,* p. 20.

15. Arts. 4-6, Hague Regulations (1899, 1907) in Adam Roberts and Richard Guelff (eds.) *Documents on the Laws of War* (2nd. ed.) (Oxford: Clarendon Press, 1989).

16. Jacob Bercovitch, "International Mediation," *Journal of Peace Research* 28(1) (1991), p. 3.

17. Ronald J. Fisher and Loraleigh Keashly, "The Potential Complementarity of Mediation and Consultation Within a Contingency Model of Third Party Intervention," *Journal of Peace Research* 28(1) (1991), p. 30.

18. See below, and Chapter 9.

19. C.R. Mitchell, *The Structure of International Conflict* (London: Macmillan, 1981), p. 296.

20. Touval, *The Peace Brokers,* p. 321. Examples of the high power-low stake and low power-high stake mediator do exist, and other combinations are possible (see Mitchell, *The Structure of International Conflict,* p. 298), but the focus here is on general and common styles. The low power-high stake mediator is a rare combination, primarily because there is no incentive for belligerents to accept such mediators, who have nothing to offer except their (usually biased) version of a solution. Similarly, the high power-low stake mediator combination is rare as, first,

if they become involved but have no stake in the outcome, they are less likely to use the power available to them, even if asked to do so (thus they become for all intents and purposes a low power mediator) and, second, they are less likely in general to become involved in conflicts, as they have no incentive to embroil themselves in other people's troubles. (Admittedly, this discounts the possibility of mediation motivated by altruism -- but high power mediators are almost always representing state actors, whose altruistic motivations are seldom evident or believed.)

21. Fisher and Keashly, "The Potential Complementarity of Mediation and Consultation", p. 33.

22. Kjell Skjelsbæk, "The UN Secretary-General and the Mediation of International Disputes," *Journal of Peace Research* 28(1) (1991), p. 100.

23. Bercovitch *et al.*, "Some Conceptual Issues and Empirical Trends", p. 9.

24. Curle, interview with the author, 19 September 1991.

25. Touval, *The Peace Brokers*, p. 17.

26. Young, *The Intermediaries*, pp. 50-61.

27. Touval, *Biased Intermediaries*, p. 68; When Brookmire and Sistrunk "proved" the irrelevance of impartiality to effective mediation, the experiment took place under conditions where disputants had no choice but to accept the biased mediator, *i.e.* impartiality was not a factor because the option to refuse the mediator's services did not exist (see Brookmire and Sistrunk, "The Effects of Perceived Ability and Impartiality").

28. Hans van den Broek, in *The Independent*, 29 October 1991.

29. Impartiality is perhaps *desirable* in power mediation primarily for the reason that there is a limit even to what power mediators can do, and equally a limit to what the disputants will put up with.

30. Tom Princen, "Camp David: Problem Solving or Power Politics as Usual?", *Journal of Peace Research* 28(1) (1991), p. 68.

31. Landrum Bolling in Maureen R. Berman and Joseph E. Johnson, *Unofficial Diplomats* (New York: Colombia University Press, 1977), p. 80; Walter Martin, "'Quaker Diplomacy' as Peace Witness," *The Friend* 142 (1984), p. 973.

32. Probst, *Good Offices*, p. 15.

33. It is noteworthy that Touval's concept of "conciliation" closely matches the Quaker concept of mediation. Conciliation, he says, tries to "modify the parties' images of each other and to influence them to make concessions by clarifying to each his opponent's views and the bargaining situation that they both face" (Touval, *The Peace Brokers*, p. 4). How much needless debate could have been avoided had he realized that the objects of his criticism were, by his own definition, not "mediators," but "conciliators"!

34. This book uses the words "objective," "impartial," and "unbiased" interchangeably, though it is acknowledged that in other contexts, it could be argued that there are differences.

35. Efraim Karsh, *Neutrality and Small States* (London: Routledge, 1988), pp. 38-41.

36. Young, *The Intermediaries*, p. 81.

37. Wehr and Lederach, "Mediating Conflict in Central America", pp. 86-87.

38. Robin Hay argues that impartiality is a minimum requirement (in "Humanitarian Cease-fires: an Examination of their Potential Contribution to the Resolution of Conflict" [Ottawa: Canadian Institute for International Peace and Security, 1990], p. 36).

39. See Wehr and Lederach, "Mediating Conflict in Central America", pp. 87*ff*.

40. Young, *The Intermediaries*, p. 81, and see Mitchell, *The Structure of International Conflict*, pp. 293-296, for further.

41. Thomas N. Hull III, "The Organisation of African Unity and the Peaceful Resolution of Internal Warfare: The Nigerian Case," in David D. Smith (ed.) and Robert F. Randle (commentary), *From War to Peace: Essays in Peacemaking and War Termination* (New York: Columbia University Press, 1974), pp. 103, 110.

42. Andrew Acland, in a letter to the author, 30 April 1992.

43. Javier Perez de Cuellar, *Report of the Secretary-General on the Work of the Organization* (New York: United Nations, 1991), p. 10.

44. The group was included the President of the General Assembly Nasrollah Entezam of Iran, Lester Pearson of Canada, and Sir Benegal Rau of India.

45. UN doc. S/PV.2977 (14 February 1991), pp. 57, 61, 62, 67, 72.

46. SCOR, 37th yr., 2nd. Supp., doc. S/15292 (14 July 1982).

47. SCOR, 37th yr., 2nd Supp., doc. S/15448 (4 October 1982).

48. UN Resolution 522 (4 October 1982).

49. SCOR, 39th yr., doc. S/16384 (2 March 1984).

50. SCOR, 39th yr., doc. S/16604 (6 June 1984).

51. SCOR, 40th yr., doc. S/17084 (4 April 1985).

52. "Report of the Secretary General to the United Nations Security Council," SCOR, 40th yr., doc. S/17097 (12 April 1985).

53. SCOR, 41st yr., doc. S/17932 (21 March 1986).

54. SCOR, 41st yr., doc. S/17934 (23 March 1986).

55. SCOR, 42nd yr., doc. S/19031 (11 August 1987).

56. *The Observer*, 19 July 1987.

57. *The Independent*, 4 September 1987; *The Financial Times*, 5 September 1987.

58. *International Herald Tribune*, 12/13 December 1987.

59. One such success included the agreement to refrain from bombing civilian targets in June 1984.

60. Strictly speaking, involved institutions in this case were not always entirely bound to Europe or the EC (including, for example, the Conference on Security and Cooperation in Europe (CSCE), whose membership extends beyond European borders). Mediation efforts were, however, primarily left in the hands of European officials, and those efforts are therefore characterized here as "European."

61. Brioni declaration, reprinted in FBIS-EEU-91-130 (8 July 1991), pp. 22-23.

62. This was done on 30 June and 28 October 1991, for example.

63. These were imposed on 8 November 1991.

64. Gianni de Michelis, Italian foreign minister and member of EC troika, stepping off the plane in Yugoslavia, 1 July 1991 (see *The Independent*, 2 July 1991).

65. Hans van den Broek, *The Independent*, 29 October 1991.

66. FBIS-EEU-91-170 (3 September 1991).

67. Branko Kostić, FBIS-EEU-91-199 (15 October 1991).

68. FBIS-EEU-91-173 (6 September 1991).

69. Milošević, FBIS-EEU-91-212 (1 November 1991); and see the Brioni Declaration, reprinted in FBIS-EEU-91-130 (8 July 1991), pp. 22-23.

70. Milošević, speech in the Hague, 5 November 1991, and reprinted in FBIS-EEU-91-214 (5 November 1991).

71. *Daily Telegraph*, 30 August 1991.

72. Interview with Budimir Kosutić, FBIS-EEU-91-226 (22 November 1991).

73. Interview with Franjo Tudjman, Zagreb HTV television, 28 November 1991, FBIS-EEU-91-230 (29 November 1991).

74. Interview with Franjo Tudjman, Ibid.

75. "Report of the Secretary-General Pursuant to Paragraph 3 of Security Council Resolution 713 (1991)," UN doc. S/23169 (25 October 1991).

76. *The Independent*, 14 November 1991.

77. In terms of an in-depth case study, this book goes no further than the end of that phase.

78. "Further Report of the Secretary-General Pursuant to the Security Council Resolution 721 (1991)," UN doc. S/23363 (5 January 1991).

79. For a more complete discussion of European and UN roles in this conflict, see James Gow and J.D.D. Smith, "Peacemaking, Peacekeeping: European Security and the Yugoslav Conflict," *London Defence Studies* 11 (London: Brassey's for the Centre for Defence Studies, 1992), *passim*. It is worth considering that in the Bosnian phase of this conflict, the UN began to have similar difficulties, blurring this separation of roles (by attempting to force the belligerents to cease fire, for example), and its peacekeeping mission in both Bosnia and Croatia was threatened as it was no longer seen as either impartial or helpful.

80. States who hope to mediate suffer, of course, from the same dilemma.

81. Michael Handel, "War Termination -- A Critical Survey," in Nissan Oren (ed.), *Termination of Wars* (Jerusalem: Magnes Press [The Hebrew University], 1982), p. 67.

82. Sydney Bailey, *How Wars End: The United Nations and the Termination of Armed Conflict, 1946-1964* (2 vols.) (Oxford: Clarendon Press, 1982), vol I, p. 167.

83. Princen, "Camp David", p. 66, and for specific evidence of this, see William B. Quandt, *Camp David: Peacemaking and Politics* (Washington: Brookings Institute, 1986), pp. 213, 220, and 237.

84. Sydney Bailey, "Non-Official Mediation in Disputes: Reflections on Quaker Experience," *International Affairs* 61 (1985), p. 208.

85. See Anthony de Reuck, "The Foundation for International Conciliation; Theory and Practice of Conflict Resolution" (35th Pugwash Conference on Science and World Affairs, Campinas, Sao Paulo, Brazil, 3-8 July 1985).

86. See Mitchell, *The Structure of International Conflict*, p. 295.

87. See John Stremlau, *The International Politics of the Nigerian Civil War (1967-70)* (Princeton: Princeton University Press, 1977), p. 194f., and Yarrow, *Quaker Experiences*, p. 207ff.

88. Ntieyong Akpan, *The Struggle for Secession 1966-1970* (London: Frank Cass, 1971), p. 139; and see Chukwuemeka Odemegwu Ojukwu, *Biafra: Selected Speeches of Ojukwu* (New York: Harper and Row, 1969), p. 355, and reprinted as doc. 168 in A.H.M. Kirk-Greene, *Crisis and Conflict in Nigeria: Volume II -- A Documentary Sourcebook 1966-1970* (London: Oxford University Press, 1971), pp. 247-272.

89. See Kirk-Greene, *Crisis and Conflict in Nigeria*, pp. 66-71, 247-314, for documents and details on the conference.

90. Yarrow, *Quaker Experiences*, p. 208.

91. See Ojukwu, *Biafra: Selected Speeches*, or reprinted as doc. 168 in Kirk-Greene, *Crisis and Conflict in Nigeria*, pp. 247-72, and especially p. 271.

92. Chukwuemeka Odemegwu Ojukwu, *Because I Am Involved* (Ibadan: Spectrum Books, 1989), p. 158.

93. Curle, *Tools*, pp. 74-75; also in Curle, *In the Middle*, p. 46.

94. Curle, *Tools*, p. 40.

95. Curle, interview.

96. John de St. Jorre, *The Nigerian Civil War* (London: Hodder and Stoughton, 1977), p. 190; Kirk-Greene, *Crisis and Conflict in Nigeria*, p. 75.

97. OAU communiqué, issued at Kinshasa on 14 September 1967, and reprinted in Kirk-Greene as doc. 134, pp. 172-73; also in Stremlau, *The International Politics of the Nigerian Civil War*, p. 93.

98. See Yakubu Gowon, *Official Speeches: Faith in Unity* (Lagos: Nigerian Ministry of Information), and Gowon, in Kirk-Greene, *Crisis and Conflict in Nigeria*, p. 14.

99. Statement by Sir Louis Mbanefo, 20 April 1969 (Markpress Release No. Gen. 576), in Kirk-Greene, *Crisis and Conflict in Nigeria*, p. 110; see also Stremlau, *The International Politics of the Nigerian Civil War*, p. 105, for further commentary.

100. See Chapter 4.

101. Yarrow, *Quaker Experiences*, pp. 209-210.

102. Eni Njoku, in Kirk-Greene, *Crisis and Conflict in Nigeria*, p. 69.

103. Curle, interview, and see Yarrow, *Quaker Experiences*, pp. 208-211, for a detailed account; see Kirk-Greene, *Crisis and Conflict in Nigeria*, pp. 64, 72.

104. Anthony de Reuck would probably argue that changing perceptions is not the task of the mediator, and that trying to change them is risky and perhaps even improper (Acland, letter). While this may be true, it remains the case that mediators often change perceptions even if they are not seeking to do this; it may happen despite it not being a conscious goal.

105. Yarrow, *Quaker Experiences*, p. 202.

106. Ibid., p. 228.

107. For a detailed account, see Yarrow, Ibid., pp. 226-230.

108. Curle, *Tools*, p. 44.

109. The relevant Security Council Resolutions are 46 (UN doc. S/723, 17 April 1948) and 48 (UN doc. S/727, 23 April 1948).

110. Bailey, *How Wars End*, Vol. II, pp. 172-173.

111. Count Folke Bernadotte, *To Jerusalem* (London: Hodders and Stoughton, 1951), pp. 3-4.

112. Ibid., pp. 17, 44. One wonders why, however, if that was Bernadotte's intent, he chose to wear his red cross uniform in the initial stages of his mission (see Sydney Bailey, *Four Arab-Israeli Wars and the Peace Process* [London: Macmillan, 1990], p. 24).

113. Ibid., pp. 33, 171, 236.

114. "Report of the UN Mediator on Palestine to the Security Council," UN doc. S/888 (12 July 1948).

115. Bernadotte, Ibid., p. 25.

116. Security Council Resolution 50 (UN doc. S/801, 29 May 1948).

117. Bernadotte, *To Jerusalem*, p. 59.

118. Ibid., p. 107.

119. Ibid., pp. 158-59.

120. Bailey, *How Wars End*, Vol. II, p. 189.

121. Ibid., p. 205.

122. Golda Meir, *My Life* (London: Weidenfeld and Nicolson, 1975), p. 199.

123. Sune O. Persson, *Mediation and Assassination: Count Bernadotte's Mission in Palestine, 1948* (London: Ithaca Press, 1979), p. 176, and see Jon and David Kimche, *Both Sides of the Hill: Britain and the Palestine War* (London: Secker and Warburg, 1960), pp. 221-222.

124. See Persson, *Mediation and Assassination*, pp. 144-207, for details.

125. Kimche and Kimche, *Both Sides of the Hill*, pp. 221-222, and see Persson, *Mediation and Assassination*, pp. 144-207.

126. Persson, *Mediation and Assassination*, pp. 149, 153-54, and 210-211.

127. Amitzur Ilan, *Bernadotte in Palestine, 1948* (London: Macmillan, 1989), p. 252.

128. Persson, *Mediation and Assassination*, p. 112.

129. For direct allocation of blame, see Persson, *Mediation and Assassination*, p. 208, who states that the decision to kill Bernadotte was taken by the LEHY Central Committee, consisting of Nathan Friedman-Yellin (now Yalin-Mor), Dr. Israel Scheib (Eldad) and Yitzhak Yezernitsky (Shamir). The latter two now admit responsibility for the killing, though Yalin-Mor still denies it.

130. Persson, *Mediation and Assassination*, p. 4.

131. Bernadotte, *To Jerusalem*, p. 90.

132. Touval, *Biased Intermediaries*, p. 59.

133. Touval, *The Peace Brokers*, p. 52. Persson, *Mediation and Assassination*, too, argues that he suffered from a lack of resources (p. 237).

134. Touval, *The Peace Brokers*, p 52.

135. See, for example, Ilan, *Bernadotte in Palestine*, pp. 73-123, 145-75, and 253.

9

The Imposed Cease-fire:
"YOU can't make us"

There are times in almost every war where it appears to third parties that there is simply no hope of a negotiated cease-fire. The reasons for coming to that conclusion are varied: political will may be lacking with one or both parties, there may be a desire to avoid looking weak by making an offer, an inflammatory domestic situation, irreconcilable interests, an inability to make an acceptable offer, an intransigent belligerent leadership, or lack of a pure mediator who is perceived as impartial. In other words, there may be obstacles to peace which appear to be insoluble. Whether those obstacles could in fact be removed by other means is irrelevant here; there is a perception by third parties that no better option remains open to them than to attempt to force the warring parties to stop fighting; the time has come for negative intervention.[1]

To begin, it is important to understand that it is often assumed, both by belligerents and by third parties, that coercion will automatically bring the desired result where other means have failed: *"If they won't listen, we'll make them listen."* One might even go so far as to say that coercion may be the *preferred* strategy for any international actor with such means at its disposal. A Brookings Institute study in 1976 reported that the United States had deployed its military forces for a political impact abroad on at least 215 occasions since World War II.[2] The corresponding figure for the Soviet Union over roughly the same period was 187, and out of that number 155 were instances in which the researchers considered the use of armed force to be coercive.[3] This willingness to apply coercive tactics does say something about the perceived effectiveness of coercion: if it had been seen as *that* ineffective, it would not have been tried nearly so often. The use of coercion as a means of securing a goal has certainly been less noticeable in those international actors who have "peaceful settlement" as a primary objective. The United Nations, for example, despite its legal authority to order a cease-fire under Chapter VII of the Charter -- that section that deals primarily with enforcement -- has in the past failed to use that authority on most occasions.[4] Even here, however, that "reluctance" probably had more to do with disagreements among the five permanent members than any real desire to avoid using the coercive authority granted by the Charter. One need only look at the speed and willingness to use the provisions of the Charter to apply sanctions and authorize the use of force in the Gulf War of 1991 to see that even in the UN, the willingness to use coercion as a strategy -- particularly in clear-cut cases of aggression by one state on another -- may now become more common.[5] Thus, and in the so-called "new world order," the UN and other third parties may begin to use the option of an imposed cease-fire more often. Whether or not the imposed cease-fire becomes less exceptional, however, it is evident that coercion will be used as a means of attempting to end wars on more than a few occasions in the future. Given that, and ignoring the question of whether it is ethically acceptable to use coercion as a strategy,[6] it does make sense to question the basic assumption that coercion can achieve the desired result where other means fail. More specifically, it makes sense to what obstacles stand in the way of being able to force people to stop killing one another.

Coercion -- the Tools of the Trade

There are a wide variety of means open to those who would use coercion as way to stop a war. If we define coercion as "the use of means intended to compel another to do one's will," a number of strategies quickly come to mind. Those which attempt to use subtle or indirect pressure, or those which merely *imply* that something bad could happen if people don't do what they are told to do, may be called "indirect coercive techniques;" those means which involve direct and explicit threats, punishments, or the threat or use of force, can be called "direct coercive techniques."[7] Which technique a third party chooses to use depends primarily on its relationship with the belligerents. Third parties who are in the position of being power mediators rarely use direct coercive methods, and rely instead on more indirect means to reach their objectives. Third parties unconnected with the belligerents, or in a patron/client relationship with one of them, may use either indirect or direct means, and the choice in these cases is highly subjective -- the third party makes a decision as to just how much coercive power it wishes to exercise, and chooses a method accordingly. Like Herman Kahn's "ladder of escalation," coercive methods can therefore be scaled, with indirect coercion at the lower end of the scale, and direct coercion at the upper end. The further one goes up the scale, the more coercion becomes visible; more and more pressure is being applied in the attempt to force the belligerents to cease fire.

Indirect coercive techniques, at the lower end of the scale, include such things as "talking up the talks" and control over resources, and they are used most often, although not exclusively, by power mediators. These techniques are "soft" coercion; they are generally more subtle than the direct coercive options, and they allow an otherwise powerless third party to exercise some small degree of influence over the belligerents.

"Talking up the talks" is perhaps the softest of all coercive options, and it is probably used most often by power mediators. It is a technique mentioned by Berridge in his account of the Angola/Namibia accords, and it can be very effective -- provided that it is not used often and indiscriminately. The technique involves generating momentum by giving the impression that the peace talks are closer to success than they really are. This can be accomplished by doing something as limited as sounding optimistic at press conferences, to something as risk-laden as publishing partial agreements or texts concerning the progress of the negotiations. The object of the tactic is to create the impression that successful settlement is close at hand, such that "any party which deserted the talks or behaved in a manifestly obstructive manner would be the target of attack from many and influential quarters which ... favored a settlement." This requires, of course, the existence of influential parties which desire a settlement or, at the very least, belligerents who are sensitive to world opinion.

In the Angola/Namibia case, Berridge argues that using this technique probably made a bigger contribution to the success of the talks than did the setting of deadlines. Despite this, and as Berridge notes, talking-up the talks "cannot be done repeatedly or in circumstances where it is simply not plausible, or it will lose credibility."[8] During the Soviet war in Afghanistan, the UN mediator, Diego Cordovez, announced in April 1983 that the draft text of a cease-fire agreement was "95 per cent completed." Yaqub Khan, the Pakistani Foreign Minister, later criticized Cordovez for this remark which "made it necessary to slow down in order to placate apprehensions among the Afghan refugees and our allies that we were going to sell them out behind their backs." Talks broke down in June 1983. Despite the setback, it has been argued that it was primarily due to the persistence of Cordovez, who "fanned hopes for a settlement even when the outlook was in reality dismal," that an agreement between Pakistan, the Soviet Union, and the Afghan resistance was reached.[9]

Having some control over belligerents' resources can also be used in the attempt to force them to cease fire. It is generally most effective in those cases where the belligerents are lesser or weaker powers, and the interested third party is a greater or stronger power which has control over some resource on which the smaller power is heavily dependent. Being able to imply that those needed resources might be denied if the belligerent does not comply with the supplier's wishes can have the intended effect. The Angola/Namibia Accords of 22 December 1988, for example, were facilitated because this technique was employed by a number of third parties. The United States, which had been supplying arms to UNITA forces in Angola, had achieved a measure of control over those forces; that control was such that communicating its desire to UNITA that it come to some kind of settlement held out a number of implied threats which UNITA had little choice but to take seriously. Similarly, SWAPO was "militarily weak and heavily dependent on Cuban and MPLA support" and was therefore "in no mood to stand in the way of negotiations."[10] It is important to understand that in this case, the threat to withhold resources was only *implied*, and therefore an indirect coercive technique. If the threat had actually been made, or even carried out, then the action would have been categorized as direct coercion, the subject to which we will now turn.

Moving up the scale, it is clear that direct coercive techniques, like their indirect counterparts, can also be effective. They include the use of various forms of ultimatums -- such as the "fading opportunity," one kind of direct threat -- or the use of other forms of direct threats or direct action. (These techniques, although open to some power mediators, are rarely used by them.) To offer a "fading opportunity" is "to set deadlines, dates by which -- *on pain of some penalty* -- agreement must be reached or some important development must commence which presupposes prior agreement" (emphasis added).[11] What this amounts to is an ultimatum, and it is direct coercive technique, involving explicit threats and punitive measures for the target of the threat should it fail to comply with the wishes of the threatener. Suggested by Iklé and Fisher, among others, it seems unlikely that it was originally intended as a coercive method. More likely, it was suggested merely as a method of "maintaining diplomatic momentum."[12] Despite this, offering a "fading opportunity" is without doubt a direct coercive technique, and will be included as such here.[13]

As for other kinds of direct threats, as well as direct action, they too can be effective. Bailey notes that during "Operation Ten Plagues" in 1948, Israel launched an offensive on the night of 22/23 December, and that it was "strong US pressure rather than action by [a] now demoralized Security Council that induced the Israelis to call a halt."[14] Eight years later in the spring of 1956, when sporadic (though geographically widespread) violence threatened to lead to a renewed outbreak of fighting in the Middle East between Israel and its neighbors, Dag Hammarskjöld was sent to the area under UN auspices. In his capacity as Secretary-General, he had been requested by the Security Council to "arrange with the parties for the adoption of any necessary means which ... he considers would reduce existing tensions along the armistice lines." Provocative incidents, evasions, and allocation of blame continued throughout his mission. Even after having successfully gained both Egypt and Israel's assurances of compliance -- which had been accomplished without the use of threats -- the difficulties continued, and he felt compelled to resort to coercion. On 2 May, for example, in trying to extract assurances of compliance with the cease-fire from Lebanon, he threatened the government that a failure to respond positively to his recommendations would leave him no option but to report its non-compliance to the Security Council, a measure which could have resulted in punitive measures and impacted negatively on Lebanon's international reputation. He received the assurances he sought.[15]

More recently, in the Yugoslav conflict, and in an attempt to achieve a second cease-fire, the European mission threatened on 30 June 1991 that unless a cease-fire was implemented and unless Yugoslav federal forces returned to barracks, a US$ 1155 million aid program to Yugoslavia would be frozen. Although the resulting cease-fire did break down (for reasons we have already discussed), the threat did secure an agreement to cease fire. On 8 November of that same year, and after numerous failed cease-fires, the threat was carried out.[16] The coercers had moved up the scale of coercive techniques after less forceful methods had failed. As we shall see shortly in the October War, Kissinger used the same strategy in attempting to force Israel to cease fire in 1973.

The Problem with Coercion

The fact that both indirect and direct coercive techniques *can* be effective under certain circumstances tends to overshadow the potential negative effects which can be the result of such strategies. A number of theorists have found difficulty with the idea of attempting coercive strategies, some of these arguments less serious than others. De Montluc, for example, has noted that belligerents will often be "reticent" to obey an international organization which orders them to renounce the resort to the use of force.[17] "Reticence," however, is no reason not to attempt coercive strategies. Bank robbers are "reticent" to stop when a policeman tells them to, but this does not deter the policeman from threatening to shoot if his instructions are not obeyed.

Mitchell, too, sees problems with coercion as a strategy, and his objections are more serious. First, and drawing on the work of Milburn, he notes that parties to a conflict often have differing perceptions of the risk involved in failing to comply with a coercive tactic.[18] What the coercer *believes* may work on the target, the target *knows* will not, and *v.v.* Thus, any party contemplating the use of coercive strategies must always take into account the other's subjective evaluations of (a) what is threatened, and in what circumstances, (b) how it is valued, compared with the benefits to be gained from ignoring the threat and proceeding and (c) how credible is the threat.[19]

This is more a rule to accompany coercive strategies, rather than an argument against them, however. Second, and more seriously, frequent use of threats and coercive strategies may be counterproductive "if only because it brings into play another value in the adversary, namely the desire not to be seen giving into threats or abandoning goals under duress."[20] We have already discussed how belligerents will avoid looking weak at almost any cost,[21] but it is important to note that where coercive strategies succeed, they will almost always result in the victim of coercion appearing to lack strength of will. In this regard, the use of coercive strategies must be contemplated very carefully. Belligerents may prefer to avoid looking weak, and instead desire appearing as strong as possible, regardless of whatever penalties and consequences are threatened by the coercing third party.

Related to this are two final points, both highlighting the fact that coercion may be counterproductive in some circumstances. Edmead has noted that

by using coercive strategies to impose a high level of sacrifices on the opposing party, the coercing party may be increasing the value to the adversary of the goal pursued, thus making that party's abandonment of the goal less, rather than more, likely.[22]

This point was discussed earlier in connection with the political dissonance trap. There, it was argued that the mere fact that a belligerent recognizes that the war is lost may not be enough to bring the war to an end. Sacrifices need to be justified, and war may continue even where it is not rational to do so. Here, the point is also well taken. It is this very tendency for belligerents to achieve goals, to justify expended resources -- to pay for their dead -- that may militate against submitting to outside coercion to end the war.

Finally, the trouble with coercion is that "it tends to bring forth a response of counter-coercion plus increased hostility, to be met in turn by increased coercion and further hostility." Thus, coercion is an easy tactic to fall into, but difficult to escape from, as "the existence of major goal incompatibility between parties predisposes them to enter into a *malign spiral*, from which it is difficult to escape. Escalation becomes easy, de-escalation difficult."[23] Of course, if the coercer is the United Nations, backed up as it is by the collective armed forces of several nations, a response of counter-coercion is likely to be either impossible or ineffective, so the difficulty tends to be diminished. This does not mean that it disappears, however. Weaker powers under the coercive guns of greater powers may have little defence, but what defences they do have, they will be tempted to use. (Golda Meir's threat to mobilize Jewish-American public opinion in the face of Kissinger's threats in the October War are a good example.)[24] Coercion, then, like escalation, can get out of control and result in the opposite effect to that intended, *i.e.* an increase in intransigence rather than a willingness to cease fire. In their study of coercion, Blechman and Kaplan concluded that

> demonstrative and discrete use of the armed forces for political objectives should not be an option which decision makers turn to frequently, nor quickly, to secure political objectives abroad, except under very special circumstances ... over the longer term these uses of the armed forces were not an effective foreign policy instrument.[25]

The main arguments against coercion, then, would appear to be based on the idea that under some circumstances it may have the opposite effect to that intended, increasing rather than decreasing the willingness of belligerents to cease fire. With that in mind, it is worth discussing perhaps one of the most common *belligerent* techniques of forcing their enemy to agree to cease-fire -- the threat of or actual escalation in a limited war. The lessons of escalation are important, primarily because of what they can offer to any third party contemplating the use of direct action to force a cease-fire. Escalating a war to end the war involves the use of even more military force to, paradoxically, end the use of military force. In that respect, it has a parallel in third party attempts to end war -- the threat of armed intervention in a conflict to end the belligerents' use of military force (*"Stop shooting -- or we'll shoot"*). An examination of the general effects of escalation on belligerent willingness to cease-fire may therefore be able to offer more than a few warnings to third parties considering such an action.

"Bombing Them to the Table": Does Escalation Work?

There is a tendency among international actors to believe in the axiom that belligerents' peace terms will decrease in proportion to an increase in the costs of the war.[26] It is this belief which leads belligerents to choose escalation as a strategy, and which may lead third parties to choose coercive strategies. Escalation is used as a form of pressure to force the enemy to cease fire, or to at least begin negotiations. By the same logic, failure to escalate a war, or reducing the level of conflict, could prolong a war and decrease the chances of a cease-fire because it decreases the costs associated with continuing the war.[27] It is true that some students of international relations and even of conflict resolution support the idea of escalating a conflict in order to end it more quickly. Bloomfield and Leiss, for example, recommend four different strategies for conflict suppression and termination of war, one of which is the intensification of hostilities such that they end more quickly.[28] The strategy as a whole, however, is questionable. Iklé, for example, notes that

> the greater the enemy's effort and costs in fighting a war, the more will he become committed to his own conditions for peace: in World War I the destruction wrought by the Germans in Belgium and Northern France contributed to the French and British stance against a compromise peace with Germany.[29]

We have seen earlier how belligerents who have expended vast amounts of energy in the course of conducting a war must find a way to justify the expense. It does seem more likely, therefore, that terms for settlement would become considerably more harsh as the conflict is escalated. Escalating in order to bring about a cease-fire does seem impractical and counterproductive.

Choosing escalation as a strategy also tends to exclude certain other courses of action: overtures of peace are less likely to be received favorably in the case where the offeror is in the process of inflicting massive damage on the offeree. Bombing the opponent to the bargaining table can work, but as Iklé notes, "when escalation -- or the threat of it -- has succeeded in reversing the enemy's determination to fight on, it has consisted of an extraordinarily powerful move."[30] In their study of escalation in the Iran-Iraq war, Sabin and Karsh note that

> Iraq's initial attempt to obtain peace through escalation was a dismal failure ... which enabled the authorities in Tehran to consolidate their legitimacy and to unite the nation around an even more fervent struggle against the Ba'athists.[31]

Later attempts at escalation to end the war were equally ineffective. Admittedly, the authors did note that escalation in combination with a number of other important factors -- including clashes with the US Navy in the Persian Gulf, battlefield losses, and missile attacks -- did help to bring about a peace. Despite this fact, however, they conclude that while escalation can eventually lead to a peace, "the road may be very much longer and harder than initially hoped; individual escalatory actions ... are rarely enough in isolation to persuade the opponent to cease fire."[32] Thus, in cases where decisive victory cannot be guaranteed, escalation must, in most cases, be a considered a risk not worth taking. It could have the very opposite effect to that intended, increasing rather than decreasing the intransigence of the enemy. In this sense, asking whether it is morally justified may not even be necessary, as escalation is simply imprudent.

Even threatening to escalate can entail unacceptable risks in many cases. Threatening escalation is an attempt "to attain the benefits of cost manipulation without suffering losses of life or resources in the process."[33] Like actual escalation it, too, can be effective. Pillar argues, for example, that Eisenhower's threats to escalate in Korea in 1953 were instrumental in bringing the North Koreans to the negotiating table.[34] The problem with such a strategy, however, is that the bluff may be called, and if the threat is not carried out, it may result in the threatener appearing weak and indecisive, possibly jeopardizing future negotiations. (One could look at the entire history of the Yugoslav wars in this light. The number of threats made and never carried out by Europe and the UN were countless.) Moreover, if the threat *is* carried out, then the belligerent may find himself caught in a situation exactly opposite to what was intended. That is, instead of bringing the conflict to an end more quickly, it ends up being prolonged. Following through on a threat can end up being just as costly for the threatener as for the victim.[35] In early 1984, Iraq attempted to forestall an Iranian offensive by threatening escalation. Iran called that bluff, Iraq felt compelled to carry out its threat, and the result was the first "war of the cities." So not only did Iraq set in motion events it had not intended, it also failed to accomplish its original goal of preventing the Iranian offensive.[36]

Overall then, and if achieving a cease-fire is the desired goal, escalation is not a strategy which should be easily or often recommended. Its outcome is unpredictable and the fact that other alternatives exist which do not carry with them the same risks as escalation should relegate it to the category of last resort. Someone truly intent on settling a dispute requiring cooperation of a second party should probably not hit that party even harder as a means to that end. The lessons of escalation can therefore offer warnings to third parties considering military intervention to end a conflict.[37] If only a threat, the third party must be prepared to carry it out, lest the threat lose its coercive impact and result in belligerents choosing to ignore further threats of coercive action. If the threat of direct military intervention is actually carried out, third parties need to be aware that this will tend to be seen as a widening of the war. While the costs of the war increase, so too might belligerents' commitment to actually achieve what they have fought so hard for up to that point.

The October War

As already noted, a number of techniques are open to third parties attempting to force a cease-fire. These may range from the subtle and indirect, such as talking up the talks, to the forceful and direct, such as threatening to withhold needed resources, to intervene militarily, or even carrying out these threats. The choice will depend greatly on the circumstances, the relationship of the third party to the belligerents, and the coercer's perception of the amount of coercion necessary. The effectiveness of the technique depends primarily on the belligerent's perceptions of the coercer's intentions, willingness and ability to carry out an implied or actual threat. Beyond this, effectiveness depends on a belligerent's subjective judgment of its own ability to withstand the effects of any action taken and finally (as we are about to see), its subjective evaluation of priorities (*i.e.* deciding whether it is more important to give in or to continue fighting). To make all of this more clear, and before proceeding any further, it might be useful to look at one case of an imposed cease-fire -- that of the October War.

During that war, pressure was applied by the United States on Israel to end the war on 22 October, and when that failed, more forceful pressure was applied in the days which followed. That pressure was ultimately successful, but the success was a limited one. Israel pushed its relationship with the United States to its limits, resisting the coercive strategies for as long as it believed that by continuing to fight the interests of the nation were being served. It will become clear that although Israel did cease fire before it would have in the absence of coercion, a number of important goals had been achieved before it finally acquiesced to American demands. Thus, and as we shall see, Israel's ability and willingness to withstand the storm of US coercion underlines the limited effectiveness of coercive strategies in certain cases.

Recalling the story of the October War presented in the second chapter, it is clear that superpower pressure to end the war only began to surface when it appeared that one of the belligerents -- in this case Israel -- was beginning to win the war. Until that time, both superpowers had been cautiously waiting for the power balance between the belligerents to be established, and had restricted their activities to military support and diplomatic manoeuvre (although given its interest in the conflict, supply and support on the Soviet side was certainly less equivocal).[38] The Soviet Union had been supplying arms to Egypt to support its initial gains, and the United States began to supply Israel when it appeared that Israel might actually lose the war. The relationship between the superpowers and their clients in this war was perhaps a non-standard one. The Soviet Union, while having no particular objection to an Arab victory, was of course averse to an Arab defeat. The United States' relationship with Israel was more complex. While unable to sanction an Israeli defeat, the US was equally reluctant to sanction an Israeli victory; the interests of the United States in the October War lay in achieving the conditions necessary to aid the process of long-term political settlement. Those conditions did not include an Egyptian battlefield humiliation, as it had been that condition which had stifled diplomacy at the end of the 1967 war. In sum, and as the war progressed, both superpowers had an interest in preventing a crushing Israeli victory. As a rival patron, the Soviet Union would have a limited ability to pressure Israel into a cease-fire (although it did in effect drive America to coerce Israel through its threat to intervene militarily), and our focus will therefore be on US efforts to end the war.

The story of US pressure on Israel begins on 18 October, two days after the first Israeli forces crossed to the east side of the Suez Canal, and immediately after Meir's rejection of Kissinger's proposal to accept a cease-fire in place and linked to Resolution 242. This was the first turning point in US/Israeli relations during the war. There would be fewer American suggestions and appeals, and more threats and pressures. Meir's rejection of Kissinger's proposal prompted him to write in his memoirs that

> [w]e had seen Israel through two weeks of mortal peril. We had stalled at the UN ... we had proposed a cease-fire when Israel was ready; we had poured in supplies ... We could not now jeopardize relations with Europe and Japan, tempt an oil embargo, confront the Soviets, and challenge our remaining Arab friends either by forever delaying a cease-fire proposal, or by jettisoning Resolution 242.[39]

Accordingly, Kissinger warned Dinitz that Israeli objections could endanger the continuation of the US airlift, and trigger a confrontation with Nixon. He further recommended that any gains Israel wanted to make should be made within 48 hours, the longest time Kissinger believed a UN resolution calling for a cease-fire could be postponed.[40] Thus, while still supporting its client, the US had issued an implied threat, based on its control over a needed resource, in order to warn Israel that it ought to seriously begin to plan for a cease-fire.

Meanwhile, and as we are now aware, by 20 October Egypt had agreed to a cease-fire in place "activating" Kosygin.[41] Immediately prior to that event, however, the Soviet Union had already made the decision to begin to pressure the United States.[42] On 19 October, Kissinger was accordingly invited to Moscow at Brezhnev's invitation. The move which "shocked" Dinitz, but Kissinger persuaded him that Israel had nothing to worry about, as no conclusive outcome was expected before 21 October. By that time, Israel should have hopefully completed its operations, and he in any case promised to keep Israel informed of developments.[43] In fact, not only did Kissinger fail to keep Israel informed, but negotiations between the superpowers were completed much earlier than expected (in part due to Nixon's grant of complete negotiating authority to Kissinger, the absence of which would have allowed for a delay as Kissinger consulted with his president).[44] The superpower agreement, which became the substance of UN Resolution 338 (issued within the first few hours of 22 October), called for a cease-fire in place, and was linked with UN Resolution 242.[45]

Upon conclusion of the agreement, but before becoming a UN resolution, Nixon sent a message (drafted by Kissinger) to Meir, arriving at midnight on 21 October, in the attempt to persuade her to accept the terms. He argued that acceptance would leave forces where they were (allowing some Israeli gains, or at the minimum a restoration of the *status quo ante*). Moreover, the word "withdrawal" was not in the resolution -- a face-saving syntax. Finally, the agreement was the first of its kind in that it was a joint superpower agreement calling for direct negotiations without preconditions, a factor which highlighted the seriousness of an Israeli refusal.[46] As Bar-Siman-Tov rightly points out, however, and despite the seeming advantages, the message was perceived by Israeli decision makers as a "formidable constraint":

> Israel had been confronted with a *fait accompli* of the highest value complexity.
> ... The United States had not consulted Israel and had presented the proposal
> as a virtual ultimatum. Its acceptance by both Egypt and the Soviet Union
> rendered it highly unlikely that the United States would agree to rectify
> the text to meet Israeli concerns.[47]

Moreover, after the massive US airlift, Israel would be hard pressed to reject an explicit presidential request. After all, the need for US aid would not end with the cease-fire. Finally, there was the possibility that an Israeli rejection might trigger Soviet intervention.[48] Feeling betrayed, there was little Israel could do but accept the superpower agreement. UN machinery was set in motion, and the Soviet-American proposal developed into UN Resolution 338 on 22 October 1973. Israel signalled its acceptance the same day.[49] Thus, and from the Israeli point of view, the consequences of rejection (which had been laid out by means of a number of implied threats) made acceptance of the proposal the only feasible option.

Signalling acceptance of a proposal, however, is by no means the same as implementing that proposal. We have already discussed Israel's calculations that an impending victory was at hand. It was thus that the UN cease-fire resolution of 22 October would never have a chance; whatever implied threats lay in the background, the promise of victory was simply too strong to resist, and Israel would not let it slip through its fingers. The words of Mordechai Hod, commander of the Israeli air force in the 1967 war, perhaps best encapsulate the Israeli attitude:

I'm an expert on the history of another war, and posterity will never forgive us if we let the war end like this. Those of us right here can take the responsibility on ourselves. If the Egyptians are violating the cease-fire, we'll cut off the Third Army, and then let them shout their heads off![50]

As Hirst and Beeson recall in their biography of Sadat, UN Resolution 338

had made no provision for policing the complex, uncertain cease-fire lines, and Israel, alleging (inventing according to Shazly) violations, lost no time in pressing home the encirclement of the Third Army to the east of the Canal,[51]

a story which we have already detailed in our second chapter. (In fact, UN observers would not be on their way until 24 October, and would not arrive until 25 October).[52]

The effect of that continued Israeli defiance of American will, however, was such that at just after noon on 23 October, Nixon received a message from Brezhnev, urging him to take decisive measures in tandem with the Soviet Union to impose a cease-fire. As Hirst and Beeson note,

the Russians were furious. They thought they had been double crossed, that, after agreeing to a cease-fire in Moscow, Dr. Kissinger ... had encouraged the Israelis to believe that they could finish off the job they had begun.[53]

That anger had a motive, of course. Some argue, for example, that the Soviet move was a way for of exploring the possibility of regaining a military foothold in Egypt,[54] but it may simply have been to avoid a humiliating Egyptian defeat. Whatever the motivation, however, they would shortly become even angrier, but in the meantime Nixon attempted to placate them with the assurance to the Soviet Premier that the United States would take responsibility for ensuring Israeli compliance.[55] A potential conflict with the Soviet Union was looming, even more so after the Israeli drive to encircle the Egyptian Third Army.

The American position became even more precarious. Informed of the possibility of another impending UN resolution which would again call for a cease-fire, Meir sent to the US what Kissinger called a "blistering communication" stating that Israel would disregard the pleas for an end to the war.[56] Perhaps strangely, Dinitz informed Kissinger later that day that Israel would in fact accept the new resolution. That resolution (339) was passed on 23 October, and accepted by both Egypt and Israel.[57] As it turned out, however, the situation would almost be identical to that on 22 October, and Meir's emphatic statement to the effect that Israel would not accept a peace was accurate. Israel would accept the resolution, but

military events would create the conditions under which it would be able
to continue operations regardless. On the excuse that violations were
occurring -- which they may well have been -- Israel would continue its
operations. Dinitz informed Kissinger on the morning of 24 October that
the Egyptians were attempting to break out of the Israeli encirclement,
and Israel was defending itself and "blocking" the offensives.[58] It is clear
that the looming prospect of a devastating Egyptian defeat had temporarily
overridden American wishes. The client was ignoring the desires of its
patron in the face of the perceived ability to achieve a major objective.

Thus, on the evening of 23 October, Kissinger again pressed the Israelis
to cease fire. He told Dinitz bluntly that the art of foreign policy was to
know "when to clinch one's victories." He stated further that there were
limits beyond which the United States could not go, and one of those limits,
despite the US friendship with Israel, "was to make the leader of another
superpower look like an idiot." Dinitz replied only that Israel would cease-
fire if Egypt did, a move which Kissinger considered to be only a "time-
wasting device."[59]

Israeli operations continued, and the bleak future of the Egyptian Third
Army was coming ever closer. While such an outcome was highly desirable
from the Israeli point of view, from the American perspective, the
development was inflammatory. As Kissinger notes, it was "almost certain
to bring about a confrontation with the Soviets."[60] This perception, combined
with new violations of the recent cease-fire, resulted in a continuation of
Kissinger's diplomatic assault. He again warned Israel of the potential
confrontation with the Soviet Union, and again demanded full compliance.
Israel made some concessions, but even were there now to be a cease-fire,
the question of the resupply of the Third Army would arise in its stead.

Sadat meanwhile, had sent letters to both leaders requesting joint action,
and Zayyat had called for intervention in the Security Council on the evening
of 24 October.[61] The height of the crisis came at 2135 hrs that evening
with the telegram from Brezhnev to Nixon warning that if joint action to
guarantee the cease-fire was not forthcoming, the Soviet Union would have
no choice but to act unilaterally. Golan argues that the idea behind the
message was to force the US into more forceful bullying of Israel to cease
fire, and not as a pretext for gaining some kind of foothold in Egypt,[62]
but the United States regarded the threat of Soviet intervention very
seriously. Soviet airborne divisions had been assembled on a "ready-to-move"
alert,[63] and there had even been reports that a Soviet ship carrying "nuclear
material" passed out of the Black Sea and into the Mediterranean.[64] At
midnight, US forces were placed on "DefCon III" alert, the highest state
of peacetime military alert and a state which includes the activation of
strategic nuclear forces.

The Soviet move probably instigated the second turning point in US behavior towards Israel. Despite Kissinger's assertions to Dinitz that the United States had no intention of coercing Israel in response to a Soviet threat,[65] the coercer was nevertheless being coerced, and the blame would be laid at Israel's door. By 25 October, and despite the Soviet Union's retreat from the brink of confrontation with the United States, a new Resolution had been tabled at the UN. (The timing of those two events is probably not coincidental.) Resolution 340 *demanded* a cease-fire,[66] and this, combined with Kissinger's continued warnings, apparently had the desired effect. Israel would agree to the ordered cease-fire of 25 October. It is noteworthy, however, that by the time of that cease-fire, the Third Army had been cut off, and this in itself was a substantial victory which Israel knew it could exploit to great advantage in any subsequent negotiations.

All hands had been played -- or so it seemed. The Soviet Union could not allow the crushing defeat of Egypt, and had made moves which would galvanize the United States into controlling Israel. The United States, on the basis of a possible confrontation with the Soviet Union, and because the long term prospects of a political solution in the Middle East demanded it, decided that it could not allow the Third Army's slow starvation, and pressure on Israel increased. Primarily due to the prospects of a victory over Egypt, Israel in turn had defied the will of its patron until such time as it appeared as if that relationship might dissolve. Again it seemed at that point that Israel was left with little choice. If it desired continued US support in the post-war environment, it now had to accede to US demands.

Amazingly, however, this failed to materialize. Israel's only concession was to allow, on 25 October, a single convoy of supplies through to the besieged Third Army, and even that was only granted after renewed and oft-repeated statements by the US that a failure to grant the resupply would result in Israel finding itself in a crisis with the United States.[67] Clearly, Israel did not take the US threat to abandon it seriously enough to warrant abandoning what it considered to be a powerful bargaining position *vis-a-vis* Egypt.

By the afternoon of 25 October, the new Security Council resolution demanding the cease-fire had been passed, and the Israeli failure to lift the siege of the Third Army resulted in American contemplation of direct punitive action against it. The United States was considering moving up the scale again, this time from direct threats to direct action. On 26 October, the possibility of ending the airlift and of resupplying the Third Army itself again entered American discussions.[68] For Kissinger, and the US generally, the destruction of the Third Army "was an option that [did] not exist."[69] Although the plan for resupply never actually materialized, Kissinger nevertheless made a direct threat on the evening of 26 October. Speaking to Dinitz on behalf of Nixon, Kissinger first warned that the United

States would not permit the destruction of the Egyptian Third Army. He then threatened that unless Israel gave "some sort of positive response" to the question of resupply by 0800 hrs 27 October, the United States would be forced to support a UN resolution calling for enforcement action against Israel -- a clear case of a fading opportunity.

Still Israel did not immediately comply. Meir responded with a threat of her own, arguing that the powerful Jewish lobby in America could be mobilized against the administration;[70] the attempt at coercion had resulted in an attempt at counter-coercion.[71] Nevertheless, on 27 October, the final showdown was averted by the Egyptian offer to hold direct talks with Israel. The offer had undoubtedly been a response to the Israeli offer of direct talks of 26 October, and its only conditions were a complete cease-fire and granting passage to a single supply convoy to the Third Army.[72]

In this case, Israel had defied the will of its patron until the very end. In Israeli eyes, the expected victory over Egypt simply outweighed the advantages to be gained by compliance with US wishes. True, it did agree to cease fire, but circumstances allowed them to continue fighting well after the cease-fire had come into effect and to complete the encirclement of the Third Army. At that point, it was again willing to agree to cease fire because one of the main goals it sought, apart from a military victory, was face-to-face negotiation, and that goal could be achieved without continuing the battle. Again after the encirclement Israel held out until the last. It defied its patron and the international community, risking confrontation and future support, until it got what it wanted. As Kissinger recalls,

> Israel was about to enter the first direct talks between Israeli and Arab representatives since the independence of Israel. It retained control over the access route to the Third Army even while the UN almost unanimously was pressing for Israeli withdrawal back from that to the October 22 line. All this in return for permitting one convoy of non-military supplies to pass.[73]

The point here is that although Israel did yield to pressure, it did the absolute minimum it could to help ease that pressure while at the same time pursuing its goals. Every concession the United States wrung from the Israelis was only achieved through the most intense bullying, and every concession could be granted without fear that overall Israeli goals would be compromised. In the end, Israel knew it would have to compromise -- if it wanted the aid of the United States in future. When Nixon asked congress for $2.2 billion in military aid to Israel on 19 October, for example, he made it clear that one reason for the aid would be to "achieve stability."[74] The utter defeat of Egypt would not serve that goal. The point remains, however, that although American coercion of Israel did pay off in the end,

Israel was able to avoid compliance until it believed a number of its own goals had been satisfied: "one is struck" Bailey observes, "by the power of the weak and the impotence of the strong."[75]

The October War is a fascinating example of the use of (and limits of) coercion to achieve a cease-fire. In this case, the relationship between the belligerent and the third party coercer was one of patron-client. Given the traditional dependence of a client on its patron, one would have expected the ability of the United States to force Israel to cease fire to be high. It had a number of sticks with which to threaten, some hidden, some blatantly brandished. Probably precisely because it was dealing with a client state, the United States began by using indirect coercive methods, and only slowly, as those methods failed to be effective, did it move up the scale and use more direct techniques. Despite eventual American success in this case, Israel held out far longer than might have been expected. Its subjective assessment of American willingness to carry out its threats, and its overall desire to secure what it saw as vital Israeli interests, resulted in continued defiance of coercive attempts.

Having argued this, it must be said that in comparison with other possible conflict situations, the imposed cease-fire which resulted in this case was relatively *easy* to establish. First, the relationship between coercer and coerced was that of patron-client. There were therefore obvious means of control which could be exercised, including the threat to withhold resources; other third parties attempting to force a cease-fire may not always have such obvious options. Second, the other belligerents -- especially Egypt -- *wanted* a cease-fire; there was therefore no need to use coercive methods to obtain their agreement to end the war. It is more often the case that all parties to the war want to continue, and forcing a cease-fire is obviously more difficult in such cases. Finally, it is clear that by the time Israel agreed to cease fire it had achieved much of what it wanted out of the war; it was therefore less intransigent than it might have been. Again, in many wars this is not the case.

Imposing the Peace: Can It Be Done?

So what happens when the relationship between coercer and belligerent is *not* patron-client, when none of the belligerents wants a cease-fire, and when virtually none of the goals of the belligerents have been achieved at the point where coercive methods are employed, or where they have secured belligerent acquiesence to cease fire? How likely is it that a durable cease-fire can be imposed in such cases? In fact, cease-fire in such cases is unlikely, for the task is more complex and difficult than might at first be imagined. Any third party considering imposing a cease-fire in the difficult case we have just outlined must be concerned not only with all the potentially negative effects of using coercive strategies, but the extreme difficulty of the task involved. There are obstacles to imposed cease-fires.

It is here that it is important to make the distinction between an imposed cease-fire, and an imposed cease-fire *agreement*, for it is relatively easy to coerce belligerents into taking the latter action -- signing a document -- than it is to get them to take the former -- actually ceasing fire. There is a great difference between an agreement to cease fire, and an actual cease-fire. The former is a declaration of intention, and the latter the action which proves the intention. As we saw in the October War, and as we shall shortly see in the Yugoslav case, the signing of an agreement to cease fire by no means leads to a situation where the fighting stops.

It is certainly possible, and relatively easy, to force parties to agree to cease fire. Where threats of sanctions and/or intervention in some form or another are credible (*i.e.* coming from a third party with considerable power over the belligerents), belligerents will in many cases agree to cease fire -- as Israel did on 22 October, and as various parties did at many points in the Yugoslav conflict. The problem, therefore, is not that it is impossible to force people to agree to cease fire; it is forcing people to actually implement their agreement. As Lord Carrington so accurately pointed out in the war in Bosnia in August of 1992, "none of them really meant any of this to work. That's the truth of the matter. None of them. You can't go on negotiating cease-fires which nobody has any intention of keeping. I mean, they'll all agree to anything and sign it, but they don't mean it." Things were no better for Lord Owen, attempting to mediate in May 1993: "I am sick and tired of agreements being signed like confetti."[76] What this means is that if a third party is going to force belligerents to cease fire, it needs to ensure that it has a means -- and is willing to use that means -- to guarantee that belligerents do what they said they would do. The coercer, by imposing the cease-fire, in many ways takes full responsibility for it, and this means that any imposed cease-fire needs to be guaranteed by the coercer.

In Palestine in 1948, for example, the UN Security Council ordered a cease-fire on 15 July. A number of difficulties arose immediately, and it was fairly clear that at least one of the belligerents, Israel, felt that the order had no substance. Eventually, Bernadotte was forced to communicate these facts to belligerents in Palestine on 7 August: first, that "no party may unilaterally put an end to the truce"; second, that "only the Security Council is competent to decide what measures should be taken against the violator of the truce."[77] The trouble in this case was primarily that the coercer responsible for ordering and forcing the cease-fire agreement refused to take responsibility for guaranteeing it. The United States had, it is true, warned the parties that violation of the order could lead to enforcement action under Chapter VII, but it was never clear how serious the U.S. was about carrying out this threat and, furthermore, David Ben-Gurion, in the result, took the view that the threat was only a threat, and no more. Beyond this, when the cease-fire order was violated, and the fighting renewed, little action was taken to enforce the order (thus substantiating Ben-Gurion's beliefs). The U.N. mediator, now Ralph Bunche (after the assassination of Bernadotte), "sought to persuade the parties to respect the Council's decisions," and Britain and China recommended that non-military sanctions be considered,[78] but beyond this, little else was done. In this case, then, the Security Council ordered a cease-fire, but was unwilling to take actions to ensure its implementation.

There is an additional difficulty to be taken into consideration. Where coercing third parties fail to guarantee agreements they have brokered, not only is there no incentive to comply, but belligerents often find it extremely easy to claim that they were simply unable to implement the agreement. They may claim that domestic pressures forced them to ignore the agreement or, alternatively, that they are not in control of all their military forces, or that the enemy provoked them into violating the agreement. Even where the claims are not valid, they may still be made, and any third party imposing a cease-fire agreement but not guaranteeing that agreement is left in the position of being unable to invalidate the claims. Where the claims are valid -- and they may well be on occasion -- third parties refusing to guarantee a coerced agreement have done nothing productive: they have forced belligerents to sign a piece of paper which has no meaning on the ground.

Regarding the question of control over military forces, for example, third parties imposing cease-fire need not only to be aware whether or not problems of control actually exist, but that it may very likely become their responsibility to ensure that such forces respect the cease-fire or, at the very least, that the belligerents themselves take responsibility for such forces. It was earlier argued that it is theoretically possible to conclude cease-fire agreements where problems of control exist.[79] Even if such agreements are rare, however, issues of control do not vanish. It is unlikely that independent or uncontrolled forces should be allowed to operate freely, for example. Nor is it likely that parties who have ceased fire should be expected to refrain from defending themselves if they are attacked by such forces. Conditions under which such attacks would be considered "violations," as well as what responsibilities and duties lie on the belligerent allied to such forces, would therefore have to be spelled out in the cease-fire agreement to a great an extent as is practicable under the circumstances. Again, however, the distinction between securing an agreement to cease-fire and an actual cease-fire arises. The belligerent who is forced to sign an agreement to cease-fire, but does not have control over all its forces, is in a position to say to the coercer, "It's not my fault" if the agreement cannot be implemented. Similarly, where a belligerent makes the claim that his forces are out of control, a third party needs to be in a position to validate (or invalidate) the claim. The coercer truly interested in achieving an actual cease-fire must be willing to take responsibility for the agreement and guarantee it as far as that can be done.[80] (The point here is that *some* body must take responsibility for those uncontrolled forces where they exist: either the belligerent itself, or the coercing third party. Where this fails to occur, victims of attacks by such forces have every right to defend themselves, and those defensive actions can by no means be considered a violation of the cease-fire.)[81]

At a practical level, guaranteeing a cease-fire requires one of two related things: adequate monitoring or adequate peacekeeping. To discuss either of these is to begin to delve into an entirely different set of problems -- those of maintaining the durability of the cease-fire. This book is concerned with stopping wars, with getting to the point of cease-fire. What happens after that -- whether the implemented agreement lasts or not -- is not the primary concern of this book (although its extreme importance is granted), and the requirements of space must limit the discussion. Having said that, however, it would be entirely proper to discuss the importance of having adequate observer forces to aid in reaching the point of cease-fire.

Any third party attempting to ensure that a coerced agreement to cease-fire is carried out generally has two choices: either intervene militarily, using military force to stop the use of military force -- a questionable and paradoxical tactic -- or force the emplacement of observers or monitors to ensure that the cease-fire order is given and carried out. This latter option is more practical, but again, this is only the case if the coercer is willing to institute a system of monitors and observation on a large scale. A few observers, scattered over various parts of the country, will simply be unable to determine whether the agreement to cease-fire is being adequately observed. Without them, however, difficulties are inevitable, and can lead to comments like those of Major-General Lewis MacKenzie, a UN commander in Bosnia in 1992: "God protect us from cease-fires. It seems whenever we have a cease-fire, the level of fighting goes up."[82] The problem of inadequate force levels has a long history. In Palestine (1948), a number of incidents threatened an already fragile cease-fire, and lack of adequate supervision only exacerbated the difficulties. It seems likely that had there been adequate supervision of the Egypt-Israel cease-fire of 18 July 1948, Israel could not later have been able to provoke Egypt into violating the cease-fire. The lack of adequate supervisory procedures allowed Israel to do just that, however, and resulted in Operation Ten Plagues, Israel's offensive taken in "self-defence." During the Suez crisis (1956), supervision of the cease-fire was entrusted to a group of observers (UNTSO) never numbering more than 600, and sometimes being as low as 50,[83] numbers which must be considered less than adequate. During the Indonesian crisis of 1948, only 68 observers were allocated to supervise the withdrawal of 30,000 men, a number the Security Council Committee of Good Offices saw as inadequate.[84] In Korea, too, there were concerns in the Unified Command that the Neutral Nations Supervisory Commission would be "unable to detect even the most blatant evasion of the armistice obligations by the Communist side."[85] Randle notes that the International Commission on Control and Supervision in Vietnam had insufficient numbers of supervisory personnel (it consisted of 1160 men), and were unable to prevent violations or clearly establish areas of control.[86] One student of the war estimates that in the first year of "peace," violations resulted in 80,000 deaths (including 14,000 civilians) from combat or crossfire.[87] One might also recall the failure to implement the cease-fire orders of 22 October during the October War. Israeli Major-General Adan commented that "it was only natural that the cease-fire [of 22 October] was not being observed, given the complicated state of affairs in the field, and of course we were permitted to open fire in self-defence."[88] UN personnel were not on the spot at the time of that first cease-fire, and as a result, Israel was able to claim Egyptian violations (which may or may not have been valid), and was able to continue the war. As a final example, consider the words of Margaret Anstee, leader of the UN monitoring team in Angola, and interviewed about her work there in October 1993. Having presided over six weeks of negotiations and made major advances in an agreement -- she was told there would be no UN troops available for at least six to nine months after a ceasefire: "What was I supposed to do? Was I supposed to say 'You are very good boys. Thank you very much. Now be very good, stay where you are and if you really behave in nine months we will provide a nanny for you.'? A big danger is that rebels everywhere are looking at Bosnia and seeing what they can get away with."[89]

As noted earlier, this whole question of adequate supervisory personnel is even more important where issues of military control are present. A large network of observers, monitors, or peacekeeping troops might be capable of isolating those units out of control, and they may be even be able to deter them from attacking forces which have ceased fire. (There is no guarantee, however, that they will be able to do this; uncontrolled units will fire on any unit they wish to.) In order to do this, however, those observers and peacekeeping troops must be emplaced before or as the cease-fire agreement comes into effect -- not after, when it is simply too late to deter, prevent, or monitor violations by either side during the ever fragile opening stages of the cease-fire.

All of this once again makes the point that if a third party is seriously considering attempting to force a cease-fire, it must realize that the attempt may include intervention in the form of observers, peacekeeping troops, or even more heavily armed troops.[90] This is necessary in order to deal with the domestic situation, units out of control, and disputes about the agreement. If the coercer is not prepared to do this, if it is not willing to guarantee the cease-fire in some way, the only thing it will be able to force is an agreement to cease-fire; an actual cease-fire will generally remain out of the question.

The Yugoslav Conflict

The Slovenian and Croatian phases of the Yugoslav conflict of 1991 illustrate almost all of the problems associated with an imposed cease-fire in the case where most or all belligerents want to continue the fight, where goals have not been achieved, and where the coercer is not in a patron/client relationship with the belligerents. In this case, the European effort to impose a cease-fire involved both direct threats (of sanctions and the revocation of economic aid), and direct action (the carrying out of the threats). While the tactics were effective, in that the parties agreed to cease-fire, and while many agreements to cease-fire were signed, the failure of the community properly to guarantee the cease-fire agreements which it forced allowed the conflict to continue virtually unabated. Control over federal forces and Republican and federal irregulars became an issue, as did the effectiveness of monitoring and the lack of a specific agreement. All parties were able to claim at various points that they could not cease fire because they were not in control of all their forces, and that the other belligerent had not ceased fire or had not complied with the agreement in some way. Whether or not the claims were true could never be fully ascertained due to ineffective monitoring and non-specific agreements, and the result was inevitably that the signed cease-fire agreements were never fully implemented.

There is no doubt that many of the cease-fire agreements in Yugoslavia came about through European coercion in some form. During negotiations for the first cease-fire in Slovenia (28 June), the EC "troika" mission, consisting of the foreign ministers of Italy, Luxembourg and the Netherlands, had laid down conditions for cease-fire including the withdrawal of Yugoslav Federal Army (YA) to barracks, a moratorium on implementation of independence, and the election of the president and vice-president of the Yugoslavian State Presidency.[91] When that cease-fire broke down, the troika returned (30 June) and when de Michelis, the Italian foreign minister, stepped off the plane it was clear that his objective was not to help the parties settle, but to dictate the settlement. "I don't want any more words," he said. "I want signatures."[92] It was at this point that the mission threatened to suspend the EC's US$ 1155 million 5-year aid program to Yugoslavia unless the cease-fire was implemented and the YA returned to barracks.[93]

A meeting between Ante Marković (the Yugoslav Prime Minister), Milan Kućan (the Slovenian president), and Lojže Peterle (the Slovenian Prime Minister) was held, and it was agreed that the YA would withdraw on 1 July. After that cease-fire failed as well, a third attempt at Brioni was made, and it, too, was made under pressure. After the agreement was signed on 7 July France Bučar, president of the Slovenian parliament, commented on the plan, saying that the EC insisted on dictating its own terms: "The troika decided by itself what to offer us. We found ourselves in a situation to accept or reject. It was said that no amendments were possible."[94] This agreement went the way of the first two, at least in Croatia[95] and subsequent attempts were all based on similar coercive methods. The agreement (the ninth) of 8 October, for example, came about as a result of the threat of EC sanctions.[96]

As we have seen in previous chapters, issues of control over military forces were present in Yugoslavia, as were difficulties posed by non-specific agreements. Europe, regardless of its intentions, was in large part to blame for the latter of these two problems, but solutions to both appeared to require the existence of effective monitoring or, even better, effective peacekeeping or peacemaking forces. By 1 July, for example, agreement had been reached to suspend operations, and all armed formations were to withdraw to their starting positions. Near Mokrice, on Croatia's border, YA units returning to barracks were attacked by the Slovenian Territorial Defence (STD). When Marković demanded an explanation, he was told by Peterle that the battle broke out because the Slovenian forces had not known where the YA units were headed.[97] Later, by 23 August, it was clear that the 7 August cease-fire was not going to hold. Irfan Ajanović, a member of the presidential committee assigned to monitor the cease-fire, noted that virtually none of the conditions of the cease-fire had been respected. Opposing sides had not been separated, settlements had not been unblocked, demobilizations and withdrawals had not taken place, and indeed new movements and regrouping had been occurring. The blame for this, Ajanović argued, lay in large part on delays in getting observers into conflict areas.[98]

The number of European Community cease-fire monitors originally considered for Yugoslavia was *ten*, and that was the number which did eventually constitute the advance group which went to Slovenia. Over two hundred were eventually in place, but even of that number, only 120 were actual monitors -- the remainder fulfilled support roles.[99] It was clear that this number was simply inadequate for the task at hand. The issues of control within the military and agreement misinterpretation required that observation of any given cease-fire agreement coming into effect assume a high priority, but this failed to occur. A journalist who travelled with the advance team on 18 July 1991, for example, highlighted some major failings. The advance mission was called "a comedy of errors";

among other incidents, one observer had been left behind in the drive from Zagreb to the Slovene border, three wrong turnings had been taken, and one observer mistook a truck transporting beef for a military vehicle. The Slovenian foreign office official who greeted them at the border said "I was surprised the EC wanted to visit this border crossing. I don't know what they have come here for," apparently because there had been no fighting going on in the area since the outbreak of war.[100] The journalist in this case was perhaps unduly critical in his attempts to write something satirical, but the article does raise serious issues. Not only could monitors not be everywhere at once, it appeared that they did not know where they ought to be at all. They were too few in number, and their purpose was unclear, even to them. In what possible way, after all, can ten, or even two hundred monitors do to adequately supervise a cease-fire over every battle area in the former Yugoslavia? Joop van der Valk, Dutch head of the later European observer force, in complaining of the insufficient numbers allotted to them, noted that "You cannot hope to control every man on the ground."[101] Given the issue of control over and within the military, however, and the numerous disputes over agreement implementation, if any agreement was to come into effect, being able to watch every man on the ground was exactly what was required.[102]

In his 45-page report to the Security Council on 25 October, de Cuellar noted that the situation on the ground was "very serious":

> successive cease-fire agreements have not been observed. On the contrary, hostilities continue to escalate, fuelled by high emotions and deep mutual distrust among the parties. Lines of military command are sometimes not clear among fighting forces, and even where lines are clear, these have come under great stress. Civilians have paid, and continue to pay a high price.

Over 300,000 refugees had been created (a number which would increase to 600,000 by 5 January), and as far as de Cuellar was concerned, there was a clear need for objective information and an independent party to help forge local cease-fires. The EC monitoring mission, while appreciated, was "faced with very great difficulties in terms of security, logistical backup, and manpower."[103] Unofficial UN comment on EC monitoring was even more critical. UN officials described the mission as "pathetic," criticizing both their training and their communications equipment.[104]

The solution therefore appeared to point to the need for a very large group of well-supplied and well-managed peacekeeping forces. Interestingly enough, the Dutch did in fact push for such forces in September, arguing that the monitors were unable to do their job, being largely ignored or brushed aside.[105] The force they had in mind was rather more than the scant two hundred then in place: they were speaking now of force levels ranging from a minimum of 5,000 to a maximum of 30,000. (It is noteworthy that the eventual UN peacekeeping force sent to Yugoslavia would consist of well over 12,000 men.) WEU governments, however, insisted that two conditions for such a force would have to be met: consent by the involved parties and a durable cease-fire.[106] These same conditions would apply when it later came to the question of UN peacekeeping troops.[107] The requirements are interesting. Consent had admittedly been an initial problem. Milošević, the Serbian president, for example, had ruled out any suggestion of Western or European peacekeeping troops,[108] but the problem was later resolved with the introduction of UN peacekeepers. Nevertheless, the WEU condition of consent may seem somewhat specious to some; no consent was required for the Europe to intervene and attempt to force the parties to sign cease-fire agreements, so why should consent be required to take steps to follow the initial intervention through to its logical conclusion?

Apart from the condition of consent, however, requiring a durable cease-fire before allotting peacekeeping troops does seem an illogical position to take. As argued earlier, observers, monitors and peacekeeping troops are essential in any imposed cease-fire to assure compliance and implementation. This was a Catch-22 for the Yugoslavian situation: no peacekeeping troops would be emplaced without a durable cease-fire, but a durable cease-fire was highly unlikely to occur without emplacement of peacekeeping troops, or at least a larger group observers with a clear mandate and better overall support. Given this, it should be evident that while Europe was willing to go so far as to bully the parties into various cease-fire agreements, it was not willing to go so far as to guarantee those agreements. Whether they should have gone so far as to guarantee the agreements is arguable, but the point, once again, is that those who force belligerents to sign a cease-fire agreement need to take responsibility for guaranteeing it. If they are not willing to do so, their intervention may only succeed in creating worthless agreements and increasing distrust.

It is more than significant that by 15 February 1992, and given the rapidly disintegrating cease-fire agreement of 2 January, the UN Secretary-General (Boutros Ghali) came to the conclusion that

> the danger that a United Nations peace-keeping operation will fail because of lack of cooperation from the parties is less grievous than the danger that delay in its dispatch will lead to a breakdown of the cease-fire and to a new conflagration in Yugoslavia.[109]

The agreement to which he referred was brokered by Cyrus Vance (the UN envoy as of 8 October) and had been holding remarkably well for over a month, but violations, primarily but not exclusively committed by irregulars, had been threatening to escalate once again into major conflict. Up to this point, the UN (like Europe) had consistently maintained that no peacekeeping force could be sent until a durable cease-fire had been implemented. By 15 February, however, it had finally become clear to the Secretary-General that a durable cease-fire simply was not going to exist without UN help, and he therefore recommended that the Security Council set up the UN Protection Force (UNPROFOR) "with immediate effect" and that it instruct him to "take the measures necessary to ensure the earliest possible deployment of the Force."[110] (The Security Council accepted the recommendation[111] but, and despite the Secretary-General's emphasis on rapid deployment, full troop deployment did not actually begin until 15 March.)

The Yugoslav case provides a clear example of what can happen when third parties attempt to impose a cease-fire under difficult circumstances. Here, unlike the October War, the party attempting to coerce the belligerents had less coercive power than could be expected under a patron/client relationship. Furthermore, while the political leadership was willing to agree to cease fire, military forces under their command were generally not willing to stop fighting, and few (if any) had accomplished any of their war aims when the cease-fires were agreed to. Many agreements were signed, but the failure to guarantee those agreements made the outcome predictable -- the agreements to cease fire were rarely implemented. In the Yugoslav case, the issue of control over the military was an important one, and made effective monitoring all the more essential. The monitoring, such as it was, was unable to deter or prevent military activity which should not have been taking place, and was even unable to note *what* activity was taking place. As we saw in a previous chapter, agreements failed to be specific enough, allowing the parties to declare that violations were taking place, and to therefore refuse to cease fire. Worse, in the absence of any procedure to monitor, punish, or otherwise deal with violations, hostile acts could be committed with impunity. Europe, while prepared to bully the parties into various cease-fire agreements, failed to guarantee those agreements and the result was essentially no result; until the point of UN involvement and a concomitant recognition of the issues to be dealt with, the conflict continued virtually unabated and interest in and optimism over any new initiative decreased with every new agreement.

It is noteworthy that despite UN successes maintaining the Croatian cease-fire, the problems encountered by Europe soon began to plague UN operations well into the Bosnian phase of the conflict. In the early months of 1994, when there seemed to be some progress being made towards a wide-ranging cease-fire, the British UN commander in Bosnia, General Michael Rose, made a number of comments to the effect that his staff was being overstretched and that he simply was not getting the support he needed. "We're in a very, very fragile and sensitive time," he said, "and the longer it goes on where we're having to fill gaps by taking troops from elsewhere, inevitably the thing will start to crumble."[112] In his report to the Security Council in May 1994, Secretary-General Boutros-Bourtros Ghali noted the following:

> From the outset, shortage of troops and the resultant inability to place United Nations troops in the area, coupled with the unwillingness of the parties to negotiate, made it impossible to achieve a specific safe-area agreement for Gorazde or to delineate the boundaries of the area. UNPROFOR's presence was limited to no more than eight observers. As a result, UNPROFOR was in a position only to observe when the Serb offensive on that area began in March 1994.[113]

Conclusions

For third parties attempting to impose a cease-fire, there are a number of questions which need to be answered. First, will the coercive tactic being considered aid in achieving a cease-fire, or will it only serve to increase the intransigence of the belligerents? If a tactic is only threatened, is the coercer really prepared to carry out the threat, and be subject to all the consequences that entails? Have all the potentially negative effects of using coercive tactics been considered, and is there any way to minimize those effects? Finally, and most importantly, the third party needs to consider whether or not it is prepared to guarantee a cease-fire agreement which it has forced upon belligerents. Is it prepared to detail a specific agreement (the need for which we have discussed in a previous chapter) which allows for little or no excuse for belligerents evading the cease-fire? In order to implement the agreement (to reach the point of cease-fire) is it prepared to intervene with the use of observers, peacekeeping troops, or even armed peacemaking troops if the domestic or military situation requires it? Even if the domestic or military situation does not require it, is it prepared to intervene with such forces in order to deter perceived or actual violations of the agreement should that become necessary? If the answer to any of these latter questions is "no," then the third party considering forcing a cease-fire should probably decide against the attempt. In the absence of third party willingness to guarantee a cease-fire which it has forced upon belligerents, the likelihood is that the only achievement will be a signed but worthless cease-fire agreement, and an increase in distrust between the belligerents and of the third party. An unwillingness to guarantee an imposed cease-fire agreement may therefore act as an obstacle to peace, prolonging instead of ending a war.

Notes

1. For the definition of negative intervention, see Chapter 2, p. 43.

2. Barry M. Blechman and Stephen S. Kaplan, "The Use of Armed Forces as a Political Instrument (Executive Summary)" (Brookings Institute, 1976), p. 3. The time period under study ran from 1 January 1946 to 31 October 1975.

3. Stephen S. Kaplan *et al.*, "Mailed Fist, Velvet Glove: Soviet Armed Forces as a Political Instrument" (Brookings Institute, September 1979), pp. 3-4. The period in question was from June 1944 to June 1979.

4. Before the Gulf War of 1991, the only exceptions included Southern Rhodesia (sanctions imposed under Article 41 in 1966 and 1968) and South Africa (arms embargo imposed in 1977). Even in Korea (1951), UN action was not action taken under Chapter VII. A cease-fire was ordered in the October War (1973), but not under Chapter VII.

5. Chapter VII (incl. arts. 39-51) was invoked in at least *nine* resolutions during the crisis (UN Resolutions 660, 661, 664, 666, 667, 670, 674, 677, and 678). It was also invoked in Resolution 686 (2 March 1991), and 689 (9 April 1991) after the war.

6. For some general comment on this, see D.W. Bowett, *The Search for Peace* (London: Routledge and Kegan Paul, 1972), p. 109; John Burton, *Conflict Resolution and Provention* (London: Macmillan, 1990), pp. 160-161; Thomas N. Hull, "The Organisation of African Unity and the Peaceful Resolution of Internal Warfare: The Nigerian Case," in David D. Smith (ed.) and Robert F. Randle (commentary), *From War to Peace: Essays in Peacemaking and War Termination* (New York: Columbia University Press, 1974), p. 95; Leo Kuper, *The Prevention of Genocide* (London: Yale University Press, 1985), p. 85; Young, pp. 34-35. More specifically, see Nick Lewer and Oliver Ramsbotham, "'Something must be done:' Towards an Ethical Framework for Humanitarian Intervention in International-Social Conflict," *Peace Research Report* 33 (Bradford: Dept. of Peace Studies, 1993).

7. Even if the means are ineffective -- if a threat is not believed, for example -- this is still classed as coercion as the intent was to compel, even if the action had no effect.

8. G.R. Berridge, "Diplomacy and the Angola/Namibia Accords," *International Affairs* 65 (1989), p. 476.

9. See Selig S. Harrison, "Inside the Afghan Talks," *Foreign Policy* 72 (1988), pp. 31, 35.

10. Berridge, "Diplomacy and the Angola/Namibia Accords," p. 466.

11. Ibid., p. 475.

12. Ibid., p. 475, and see Fred Charles Iklé, *How Nations Negotiate* (London: Harper and Row, 1976), pp. 71-72, and Roger Fisher, *Basic Negotiating Strategy* (New York: Harper and Row, 1969), p. 108. Iklé has also called this the "Sybilline Book tactic," after the myth of Sybil of Cumas (see Iklé, Ibid., pp. 210-211).

13. See Berridge, "Diplomacy and the Angola/Namibia Accords," p. 476, for a successful use of the technique.

14. Sydney Bailey, *How Wars End: The United Nations and the Termination of Armed Conflict, 1946-1964* (2 vols.) (Oxford: Clarendon Press, 1982), Vol. I, p. 283; and see Sydney Bailey, *Four Arab-Israeli Wars and the Peace Process* (London: Macmillan, 1990), p. 53.

15. See Brian Urquhart, *Hammarskjold* (London: Bodley Head, 1972), pp. 135-48, and Bailey, *Four Arab-Israeli Wars*, pp. 117-119.

16. *Independent*, 1 July and 9 November 1991.

17. Bertrand de Montluc, *Le Cessez-le-feu*, Ph.D. thesis (Univérsité de Droit et d'Economie et de Sciences Sociales de Paris, 1971), p. 32.

18. Klaus Knorr has also noted this problem (for a general discussion, see his *Power and Wealth: the Political Economy of International Relations* [New York: Basic Books, 1973], pp. 177-190, or see Yaacov Bar-Siman-Tov, *Israel, the Superpowers, and the War in the Middle East* [London: Praeger, 1987], p. 7).

19. T.W. Milburn, in C.R. Mitchell, *The Structure of International Conflict* (London: Macmillan, 1981), pp. 150-151.

20. Mitchell, *The Structure of International Conflict*, p. 230.

21. See Chapter 3.

22. F. Edmead, in Mitchell, *The Structure of International Conflict*, p. 152.

23. Mitchell, *The Structure of International Conflict*, p. 63.

24. See Bar-Siman-Tov, *Israel, the Superpowers, and the War in the Middle East*, pp. 233-34.

25. Blechman and Kaplan, "The Use of Armed Forces as a Political Instrument," concluding summary.

26. Donald Wittman, "How a War Ends: A Rational Model Approach," *Journal of Conflict Resolution* 23 (1979), p. 785.

27. Ibid., p. 752.

28. Lincoln P. Bloomfield, and Amelia C. Leiss, *Controlling Small Wars: A Strategy for the 1970s* (London: Penguin Press, 1970), pp. 239, 283.

29. Fred Charles Iklé, *Every War Must End* (London: Columbia University Press, 1971), p. 41.

30. Iklé, *Every War*, p. 55, and see also Janice Gross Stein, "The Termination of the October War: A Reappraisal," in Nissan Oren (ed.), *Termination of Wars* (Jerusalem: Magnes Press [The Hebrew University], 1982), p. 234.

31. Philip A.G. Sabin and Efraim Karsh,"Escalation in the Iran/Iraq War," *Survival* (May/June 1989), p. 250.

32. Ibid.

33. Paul Pillar, *Negotiating Peace: War Termination as a Bargaining Process* (New Jersey: Princeton University Press, 1983), p. 183.

34. Ibid., p. 183.

35. Kenneth Boulding, in Harry B. Hollins, Averill L. Powers, and Mark Sommer, *The Conquest of War* (Boulder: Westview, 1989), p. 93.

36. See Efraim Karsh, "The Iran-Iraq War: A Military Analysis," *International Institute of Strategic Studies Adelphi Paper* 220 (1987), p. 28.

37. In this chapter, intervention refers to negative, coercive intervention, *i.e.* the use of coercive methods -- such as military intervention or withdrawal of support -- by a third party intended to force belligerents to cease fire (see Chapter 2 for further).

38. Milton Leltenberg and Gabriel Sheffer, *Great Power Intervention in the Middle East* (New York: Pergamon, 1979), p. 32.

39. Kissinger, *Years of Upheaval* (London: Weidenfeld and Nicolson, 1983), p. 539.

40. Bar-Siman-Tov, *Israel, the Superpowers, and the War in the Middle East*, p. 215; Kissinger, *Years of Upheaval*, pp. 539, 545.

41. Chaim Herzog, *The War of Atonement* (London: Weidenfeld and Nicolson, 1975), p. 234.

42. Bar-Siman-Tov, *Israel, the Superpowers, and the War in the Middle East*, p. 215.

43. Ibid., p. 217; Kissinger, *Years of Upheaval*, p. 543.

44. Kissinger, *Years of Upheaval*, pp. 547-48.

45. UN Resolution 338 (S/11036), 22 October 1973; and see Kissinger, *Years of Upheaval*, p. 554; Bailey, *Four Arab-Israeli Wars*, p. 327; Bar-Siman-Tov, *Israel, the Superpowers, and the War in the Middle East*, pp. 219-221.

46. The text of the message can be found in Kissinger, *Years of Upheaval*, pp. 555-56.

47. Bar-Siman-Tov, *Israel, the Superpowers, and the War in the Middle East*, p. 221.

48. Ibid, p. 222; and see Donald Neff, *Warriors Against Israel* (Vermont: Amana and Battleboro, 1988), pp. 266-67.

49. See Howard M. Sachar, *A History of Israel* (Oxford: Basil Blackwell, 1977), pp. 780-81.

50. Hod, in Bar-Siman-Tov, *Israel, the Superpowers, and the War in the Middle East*, p. 225.

51. David Hirst and Irene Beeson, *Sadat* (London: Faber & Faber, 1981), p. 164.

52. Bailey, *Four Arab-Israeli Wars*, pp. 330-331.

53. Hirst and Beeson, *Sadat*, p. 164.

54. Marshall D. Shulman, "The Super-powers," *Survival (Strategic Forum: The Middle East Conflict, 1973)*, January-February 1974, p. 2.

55. Bar-Siman-Tov, *Israel, the Superpowers, and the War in the Middle East*, p. 227; Neff, *Warriors Against Israel*, pp. 176-77; Kissinger, *Years of Upheaval*, pp. 571-72.

56. Bailey, *Four Arab-Israeli Wars*, p. 330; Kissinger, *Years of Upheaval*, p. 573.

57. UN Resolution 339 (doc. S/11039, 23 October 1973).

58. Kissinger, *Years of Upheaval*, p. 576.

59. Ibid., p. 576.

60. Ibid., pp. 574-575.

61. See UN. doc. S/PV.1749, p. 2 (24 October 1973).

62. Galia Golan, *Yom Kippur and After* (Cambridge: Cambridge University Press, 1975), p. 123.

63. Hirst and Beeson, *Sadat*, p. 165.

64. Leltenberg and Sheffer, *Great Power Intervention in the Middle East*, p. 32.

65. Kissinger, *Years of Upheaval*, p. 590.

66. UN Resolution 340 (S/11046/Rev.1, 25 October 1973).

67. Bailey, *Four Arab-Israeli Wars*, p. 332; Bar-Siman-Tov, *Israel, the Superpowers, and the War in the Middle East*, p. 232.

68. Bailey, *Four Arab-Israeli Wars*, p. 333.

69. Kissinger, *Years of Upheaval*, pp. 608-09.

70. Bar-Siman-Tov, *Israel, the Superpowers, and the War in the Middle East*, p. 233-34.

71. In fact, this threat probably had little effect on Kissinger. While in Moscow, Nixon had personally assured him that he was prepared to "pressure the Israelis to the extent required, regardless of the domestic political consequences." The message was taken by Kissinger to refer specifically to the American Jewish lobby (see Kissinger, *Years of Upheaval*, pp. 550-51).

72. Bar-Siman-Tov, *Israel, the Superpowers, and the War in the Middle East*, p. 233-34.

73. Kissinger, *Years of Upheaval*, p. 610; Bar-Siman-Tov, Ibid., p. 235.

74. Sachar, *A History of Israel*, p. 784.

75. Bailey, *Four Arab-Israeli Wars*, p. 334.

76. Lord Carrington, in interview, *The Independent*, 14 August 1992; Lord Owen, in *The Independent*, 16 May 1993.

77. "Communications from the Mediator about the Maintenance of the Cease-fire," August, 1948, August 7, 1948, in Bailey, *How Wars End*, Vol. II, pp. 297-98.

78. Bailey, Ibid., Vol. II, pp. 224, 227, 229.

79. See Chapter 6.

80. Thus, we do not go so far as to state that effective war termination strategies and cease-fire effectuation *require* belligerent political control, as do James Foster and Gary Brewer, "And the Clocks Were Striking Thirteen. the Termination of War," *Policy Sciences* 7 (1976), p. 228.

81. This was the opinion, for example, of Bernadotte in Palestine (see Bernadotte, *To Jerusalem*, pp. 124-125).

82. Quoted in *The Independent* 23 July 1992.

83. Bailey, *How Wars End*, Vol. I, pp. 135-136; II, pp. 280-284, 543.

84. Paul Mohn, "Problems of Truce Supervision," *International Conciliation* 478 (1952), p. 70.

85. Bailey, *How Wars End*, Vol. I, pp. 277-84, 289.

86. Robert Randle in David S. Smith (ed.), and Robert F. Randle (comments), *From War to Peace: Essays in Peacemaking and War Termination* (New York: Columbia University Press, 1974), p. 52. One student of the war estimated that this failure clearly to delimit areas of control, and to follow that delimitation with adequate supervision, resulted in 8,000 deaths between September 1973 and April 1974 as forces manoeuvred for strategic position (see W.S. Turley, *The Second Indochina War: A Short Political and Military History 1954-1975* [Boulder: Westview Press, 1986]), pp. 151, 158-62).

87. Turley, Ibid.

88. Avraham Adan, *On the Banks of the Suez* (London: Arms and Armour Press, 1980), p. 401.

89. Margaret Anstee, interviewed in *The Financial Times*, 9 October 1993.

90. Such forces may come to be considered as occupying forces, or even as other belligerents -- yet another negative aspect to consider when attempting to impose a cease-fire.

91. FBIS-EEU-91-126 (1 July 1991).

92. *International Herald Tribune*, 1 July 1991.

93. Marković had actually warned this might happen on 12 June, when he begged Slovenia and Croatia not to secede. The sanctions were eventually imposed on Croatia and Serbia on 8 November, after the failure to implement numerous cease-fire agreements.

94.   *International Herald Tribune*, 9 July 1991.

95.   That the fighting more or less stopped in Slovenia after this agreement does not invalidate the point. Violations of the agreement were reported in many places in Slovenia, and complaints were common. It seems likely that the only reason the level of violence dropped was that it was in both parties' interests that the YA de-escalate the conflict in Slovenia (the YA preparing for the Croatian phase, and the Slovenes simply wanting an end to fighting). That the agreement was coerced is beyond dispute; the only question is whether it was coercion, or political will, which allowed it to hold in Slovenia; it was probably the latter (see James Gow and J.D.D. Smith, "Peacemaking, Peacekeeping: European Security and the Yugoslav Conflict," *London Defence Studies* 11 [London: Brassey's for the Centre for Defence Studies, 1992], p. *9ff.*) The agreement was not the best one Slovenia could have achieved, and it probably accepted it more because it seemed the best way to stop the YA at the time, and less because it was an agreement they liked.

96.   *Independent*, 9 October 1991.

97.   FBIS-EEU-91-128 (3 July 1991).

98.   FBIS-EEU-160-B-11 (25 August 1991).

99.   "Report of the Secretary-General Pursuant to Paragraph 3 of Security Council Resolution 713 (1991)," UN doc. S/23169 (25 October 1991).

100.   Christopher Bennet, "High Comedy in the Slovenian Alps for EC Cease-fire Team," in *The Daily Telegraph*, 18 July 1991.

101.   *The Times*, 13 September 1991.

102.   The lesson remains unlearned. When, in September of 1994, monitors were installed on the border between Serbia and the Serbian-controlled region of Bosnia, there were only 130 of them.

103.   "Report of the Secretary-General," 25 October 1991.

104.   *The Independent*, 7 January 1992.

105.   *The Financial Times*, 18 September 1991.

106.   *The Times*, 19 September 1991.

107.   See, for example, UN Resolution 721 (1991), operative paragraphs of which are reprinted in the "Report of the Secretary-General," 11 December 1991.

108.   *The Daily Telegraph*, 30 August 1991.

109.   "Further Report of the Secretary-General Pursuant to Security Council Resolution 721 (1991)," UN doc. S/23592 (15 February 1992).

110.   "Further Report of the Secretary-General," 15 February 1992.

111.   By UN Resolution 743 (adopted 21 February), UNPROFOR was established for an initial 12-month period.

112.   *The Independent* and *The Financial Times*, 4/5 March 1994.

113.   "Report of the Secretary-General Pursuant to Resolution 844 (1993)", UN doc. S/1994/555 (9 May 1994).

PART FOUR

Conclusions

10

The Road Ahead

When looking at how we get from war to peace, there is a tendency to make vague pronouncements about the inscrutability of the process. Comments are general, not specific, and most people will conclude that wars end when the belligerents want them to, or that "war weariness" sets in: wars stop because the warring parties no longer want to fight them. Conversely, wars do not end because belligerents want them to continue. These explanations, however attractive, are both deceptive and oversimplified. The existence of strong and effective political will to stop a war is the result of a complex process, and can be inhibited by a number of factors.

This book has attempted to show at least two main things. First, that the transitions from war to peace — and the cease-fires which inevitably accompany that shift -- are neither as inscrutable nor as vague as they may at first seem. There are identifiable obstacles and processes at work in the ending of any given war, most particularly in the process leading to cease-fire. Second, the obstacles involved in achieving a cease-fire appear not only to be common to the particular wars under study -- crossing the border between international in intrastate war -- but are themselves enmeshed in such a way that the presence of one may engender the presence of others. Thus, not only are cease-fires subject to analysis, but that analysis reveals an array of identifiable obstacles which appear to recur and may feed off one another in any given war. So what are these obstacles -- and what can be done about them?

The most obvious obstacle -- and perhaps the most common -- is a simple unwillingness to consider a cease-fire. One reason for this lack of interest is that there may be fear of what the enemy will gain under any proposed cease-fire, or fear of what it will gain if it is violated. A second explanation is that there is a simple belief in the ability to achieve given objectives, or prevail in the conflict (a conviction founded on expectations of victory or third party support in one form or another). Underlying these explanations, however, there is a basic disagreement between belligerents about the amount of power they wield with respect to each other, and until there is agreement about that power balance, the political will to cease-fire will be absent. In sum, the political will to cease fire requires the belligerents to agree about three things. First, it requires agreement that one side is winning by a decisive margin, or that there is a clear stalemate. Second, it requires mutual acceptance that the situation (stalemate or clear victory) will remain unchanged for the foreseeable future, or alternately that both sides believe that continued military action will yield more positive results for their enemy than for themselves. Third, both sides need to believe that a cease-fire (or its violation) will decrease the enemy's power, increase their own, or they must both agree that it would hold the military situation in stasis. Yet even a willingness to cease-fire is no guarantee that a cease-fire will occur: even without the presence of a third party who may be able to mediate or impose a cease-fire, at least five main obstacles stand in the way.

First, it is clear that belligerents have a marked tendency to avoid looking weak and to seek the appearance of strength. It is also clear that these behavioral patterns may be unavoidable, as they are based on practical considerations of the potential consequences of appearing weak. The war may be prosecuted with renewed vigor, more may be demanded in any peace settlement, or future enemies may attempt to take advantage of the perceived weakness. This obviously makes stopping wars that much harder, however, as the means of avoiding the appearance of weakness are often incompatible with those used to achieve cease-fire. Coercive tactics and threats, for example, while conveying strength, must be responded to in kind lest the recipient appear weak also.

Second, out of fear of looking weak, or for any number of other reasons, belligerent leaders will often make uncompromising public statements, usually concerning war aims or conditions for cease-fire, and usually in the form of "We will never ... " or "We will always ... " While such behavior is understandable, it once again poses an obstacle to cease-fire. It boxes the political leadership into a corner, as domestic populations, inner circles, or the military itself may reasonably come to expect the publicly-defended position to be upheld at all costs. Thus, if the war begins to go badly, and a reversal or change in position is required, that reversal may be impossible if the leadership desires to remain in a position of power. The desire to remain in power may simply prevent the required reversal of position, a reversal which may nevertheless be in the interests of the nation. The problem is both a psychological and a political one, and it is not a problem easily overcome.

Third, decision-making structures of belligerents are themselves a problem. Assuming the case where the ultimate leadership has no political will to cease fire, the determining factors affecting the likelihood of cease-fire are the amount of power the inner circle wields, and the willingness of the inner circle to go against the policies of the ultimate decision-maker. Inner circles with low power and high willingness to criticize will have little chance to bring about a cease-fire, unless their leader is a willing listener. More likely, the critics will tend to be ignored or punished, and in the latter case, critics become voiceless. Inner circles with high power and a high willingness to criticize obviously have the greater opportunities for affecting the possibilities of cease-fire, but they also have the greater possibilities of creating civil divisiveness. Moreover, where their power is insufficient to bring about a change, but sufficient to have their views heard by their enemies or third parties, they run the possibility of earning even greater distrust should they be forced to abandon those overtures in the face of an ultimately powerful leader.

Fourth, and even supposing all these obstacles are overcome, and both sides genuinely desire cease-fire, they may be unable to achieve it. They may still see themselves as unable to cease-fire, or actually may be unable to do so, in many cases because interests are irreconcilable (or are seen as such), or because of the existence of military forces beyond the control of the main belligerents.

Fifth, there will be problems associated with arriving at an acceptable formula for cease-fire, a process which will be hindered by a refusal to communicate with the enemy, or an unwillingness or inability to manoeuvre due to a failure to define one's own interests clearly, or to define those of the enemy accurately or at all. The most common form this situation will take is where one belligerent will demand negotiations before cease-fire, and the other will demand cease-fire before negotiations. It is also the case that demands for unconditional surrender or unconditional cease-fire are at the same time unacceptable and unrealistic. (Whatever belligerents may like to believe, there are *always* conditions to any agreement, and no matter what the situation, not all conditions will be unacceptable.) Finally, even when proposals are accepted, a failure to be clear about the contents of an agreement may prevent the agreement from coming into effect, or may result in its breakdown soon after implementation.

It is clear that the presence of a third party in the negotiation process may help to solve a great many of the obstacles we have discussed. Proposals may be made through third parties, thus avoiding looking weak, or third parties may be able to help belligerents explore ways of coming up with an acceptable proposal for cease-fire. In general, there are two kinds of third parties who can act as a mediating influence in any given war: the pure mediators and the power mediators. Both types have their advantages and disadvantages, but both can act as obstacles to peace where they fail in their very different responsibilities.

Pure mediators are by their nature non-coercive. They are invited by the parties to help them find an acceptable settlement, and they do their best to change perceptions and explore options which may be open to them. They are at base facilitators of settlement, and one of their main strengths lies in their ability to remain outside normal diplomatic process, which is usually public and which usually results in posturing of one kind or another. But because they have been invited, and because they have no coercive powers, pure mediators rely exclusively on building a relationship of trust with each of the belligerents; that trust will be stretched or broken entirely where a pure mediator is perceived as biased. Any time a pure mediator engages in judgemental behavior, or is perceived as having more than one role in the conflict, belligerents will view the mediator as biased, and that mediator's efforts to bring peace will end. A pure mediator, perceived as biased, will not be able to stop the fighting.

Power mediators, and third parties who have coercive power at their disposal, can act as obstacles of a different kind. This latter type of third party offers incentives for compliance, and punishment for non-compliance. Their strength lies in their ability to force belligerents to agree to cease fire where no other option seems preferable or possible. One of their main weaknesses, however, lies in their unwillingness to guarantee any cease-fire which they may coerce. If the coercing third party fails to guarantee the cease-fire agreement which it brought about, that agreement may simply fail to be implemented, or will be in danger of collapsing if it comes about. Where coercive power is the instigator of settlement, responsibility for the agreement is taken away from the belligerents, and there will therefore be cases where one or both of them will use any excuse available to avoid complying with the wishes of the coercing third party. The third party who coerces agreement but fails to guarantee it does not help in stopping the war if for no other reason that belligerent distrust will tend to increase -- and possibilities for future peace agreements will tend to decrease -- with every failed agreement.

It is clear, then, that there are identifiable obstacles to cease-fire; the process is subject to analysis. It is also clear that those obstacles occur frequently in both civil and international wars. The expectation of victory, for example, prevented consideration of cease-fire in the Nigerian Civil War, the October War, the Iran-Iraq war, and in the Algerian War of Independence. The fear of looking weak was a major obstacle to cease-fire in the Gulf War, the Nigerian Civil War, and in Algeria as well. Not all obstacles were present in all the wars. Most obstacles, however, were present in some form in most of the wars, and that itself is interesting.

More interesting, however, is the way in which those obstacles appeared to interact, or held out the potential for interaction. Thus, not only will one obstacle hold out the possibility for the creation of other obstacles, it may interact with others in such as way as to form an intricate circle of stumbling blocks, the possibilities for cease-fire ever-diminishing as barriers respond to the presence of other barriers, which in turn may create still more. The pattern is not always circular, and there may be a simple cause-effect relationship which ends with the creation of a second barrier. In the least complicated case, for example, a simple inability to cease-fire (due to forces out of control or for other reasons) may result in the intervention of a third party who attempts to force a cease-fire and may succeed in that attempt. At that point the path ends; a cease-fire has occurred. Success at any point in the cycle breaks the chain of potential causation -- but success comes neither easily nor often. Obstacles may be present in one form or another, may engender the existence of other obstacles, and if they cannot be overcome, the pattern may become more and more complex, and the possibilities for cease-fire may all but vanish. The most important point about all of this is of course that the outcomes are only *potential* outcomes. The existence of one obstacle does not necessarily *cause* the existence of others. The most that can be said is that the existence of one obstacle may increase the likelihood of others, and that the presence of one may lead directly to others. (See Appendix 2 for an illustration).

The possibilities for stopping wars are probably not as bleak as this portrayal may at first make them seem. Cease-fire agreements *are* concluded, and cease-fire agreements *do* last. Even better, belligerents do succeed in achieving political settlements; all wars end. But it is a question of discovering *why* this occurs on some occasions and not on others, and this book has been an attempt to answer that question, at least in part. Even more important than this question are those concerned with finding the solutions. As noted at the outset of this book, no solution will be forthcoming before a thorough understanding of the problem -- thus the focus of this book on the latter -- but if the obstacles detailed here are indeed the most common, what can be done to overcome them? If techniques can be found to surmount them, what then? Making agreements *last* once they are in force is of obvious importance, but what prevents this from happening? Are there common obstacles to the durability of a cease-fire agreement? What sorts of things are commonly thought of as violations of the agreement? Are there solutions to these problems? The questions are numerous, and remain to this point unanswered. This book has been an attempt to make a beginning. There is so much we do not know about stopping wars, yet so much we need to know if we are to find ways of both getting cease-fire agreements, and of making them last long enough to effect a political settlement.

What follows below, then, are some recommendations about possible courses of action which could be taken by the international community, individual states, the belligerents themselves, or sometimes even by individuals. They are all derived from the analysis of the obstacles we have discussed, are listed in approximately the order in which their corresponding problem occurred in the text, and are intended to be an aid in bringing about successful cease-fires in future. As mentioned in the introduction, these recommendations are not intended to be the ultimate answers to questions related to cease-fires. This book was about defining and understanding problems. Thus, these recommendations are meant to be vehicles for discussion; they are starting points for a journey down an entirely new road.

Perhaps the single most encouraging thing that comes from this study is the recognition that the information needed to deal with all the problems that have been mentioned -- and the information needed to implement most of the recommendations set out below -- already exists: there is no lack of case studies. Knowledge about cease-fires is available from almost every war ever fought in this century, and the data gets more detailed with every war fought. There is a tendency to ignore that kind of knowledge in favor of analyses of how the war began and was fought. That, too, is useful, but it is hardly sufficient. Even now, and even with the addition of this effort, it is still not unfair to say that we spend a great deal of time studying how wars begin and how they are conducted, but little or no time thinking about the best way to end them. Perhaps it is time for a change.

Recommendations

1. There must be international recognition of the principle of "no advantage" -- the idea that bargaining power of belligerents should remain stable under a cease-fire as far as that is practicable. Where belligerents believe that the whole situation will remain "in stasis" for the duration of the cease-fire, where they can see that their opponent will make no gains either under the cease-fire or through its violation, they may be more willing to accept a temporary end to the fighting. (Chapter 2)

2. Achieving "stasis" under a cease-fire will require, first and foremost, international agreement about what is and is not permissible under a cease-fire (not to mention defining what exactly a cease-fire is). (Chapter 2 and Appendix 1)

3. Where a stalemate exists, or where victories are overweighted, belligerents themselves often simply do not objectively understand their situation. In such cases, methods need to be found to persuade belligerents

that their situation is not as good as they may believe. Such persuasive methods could include providing something as simple as aerial photographs (as Kosygin used to persuade Sadat in the October War). Information should come from allies, or from sources who have no interest in the war itself, and have nothing to gain from providing false information. (Chapter 2)

4. Where countries use positive intervention, the intention of the intervention should be made clear, whether it is to achieve the goals of one or the other belligerent, or to bring the situation to balance point where both sides can negotiate without fear of looking weak by doing so. (Chapter 2)

5. With regard to the whole question of looking weak, it is clear that third parties may be invaluable, for belligerents may be able to approach their enemy indirectly, and thereby avoid appearing weak. Beyond this, however, it is clear that timing, approach, and rhetoric are everything. Since both sides are trying to avoid looking weak, threats and the rhetoric of strength should almost always be avoided in manoeuvres towards peaceful settlement. Instead, rhetoric should be used to advantage (Ridgeway's, "I am informed that you may wish to discuss an armistice ... " is a good example). Such approaches can be catalogued and analyzed. In the world of international negotiations, people continually come up with creative means of allowing people to back out gracefully -- we need a clear understanding about the alternatives open to people who want to do this.[1] Not allowing its opponent to save face may make a belligerent look strong, but it will not end the war. (Chapter 3)

6. The political and cognitive dissonance trap is one that can be avoided, and therefore should be avoided. One is always hesitant to use Saddam Hussein as any kind of positive example, but the lesson he provides in the Gulf War is a good one: propaganda and rhetoric can be skilful, strong, and can raise morale without committing the leader to anything. Leaders in war need to avoid using the language of firm and inflexible commitment whenever possible. This does not mean that promises should not be made, but leaders need to be more realistic about what they can promise, particularly if the outcome is uncertain. In sum, belligerents should be more careful with the rhetoric they use in prosecuting a war, as leaders need a way to back out of the political dissonance trap in a way that will allow them to save face. (Chapter 4)

7. Through some kind of institutional mechanism, and in order to come up with a wide variety of alternatives, leaders in wartime should actively encourage -- not penalize -- criticism of their policies within their inner circle. In order maintain sound relations with the military and with the general population, an appearance of consensus should still be the goal, but criticism within the group should nevertheless be a conscious goal. Leaders need to constantly question what they are doing. Have goals

changed? Is war still the best way to achieve them? Is military force still the best way to achieve them? The process of examination should be an ongoing one, with the focus on interests, not positions, and should additionally include a focus on the goals and interests of the enemy. (Chapters 5 and 6)

8. In the case where at least some military forces are out of control of central authorities, making a general cease-fire difficult, but where a cease-fire is still desired by those authorities, the idea of limited, local cease-fires should be considered. Cease-fire areas can be designated, monitored and their size can be increased as the military situation allows. Local cease-fires of this kind must include mechanisms to cope with violations by those outside political control. (Chapter 6)

9. Communications between the political centre and military forces at the "sharp end" must be improved, and reasonable amounts of time must be allowed after the signing of an agreement for the orders to filter down to front line troops. A cease-fire agreement may be signed by political authorities, but if military forces are either unaware of the agreement or cannot be contacted in time, that agreement may fail simply because of military action which took place after it was signed. (Chapter 6)

10. It should be accepted that in some cases, parties' goals and interests really are irreconcilable. In such cases, third parties can provide no answers save to either force or persuade the belligerents to stop fighting and continue their dispute at the negotiating table. Moreover, it must be accepted that things do not always run smoothly under a cease-fire, and that some degree of violence may be inevitable -- but this should not give an excuse to belligerents to end the cease-fire and continue the war. (Chapter 6)

11. Leaders need to communicate clearly and usually directly with each other, avoiding demands for unconditional surrender, or unconditional cease-fire. (Chapter 7)

12. Political authorities must learn that bargaining with those who have the power and the authority to stop the fighting can be done without necessarily giving them the advantage of political recognition. (One could argue that this was a major factor which led to the "cease-fire" between the PIRA and the British government in the summer of 1994, for example.) If necessary, conclude agreements between military commanders, leaving political decisions until later. Use semantic juggling to avoid political wrangling over agreements. (Chapter 7)

13. Realise that it is the *recipient* of a cease-fire proposal who, in the final account, is the last to decide whether or not there will be an end to the fighting; ensure that proposals fit the opponent's interests to a great an extent as is possible. Consider the use of third parties both to help formulate and communicate an agreement. (Chapter 7)

14. When considering the question of whether to demand a cease-fire prior to political negotiations, or whether to demand political negotiations before cease-fire, the cease-fire should almost always take priority. The major fear related to the demand for political negotiations prior to cease-fire rests on the proposition that if it is violated, or while it is in effect, parties will be worse off than they would have been had they kept fighting. Negotiate first about how to avoid this, and create a situation where the cease-fire simply fixes the situation in "stasis." Political negotiations could then take place after cease-fire (and this must be *ensured*: too often, cease-fires and peacekeeping troops take the place of political settlement). Stopping the killing should be of primary concern, and the idea of "stasis" can be used so that force is still an option should the political negotiations fail (perhaps a time limit to come to agreement can be included, to avoid misuse of the cease-fire). Negotiating while fighting has serious drawbacks -- even slight victories have negative effects on events at the negotiating table. (Chapter 7)

15. Cease-fire agreements must be absolutely clear with regard to at least the following questions:

When will it take place? Specify an exact time *after which* there is to be no firing -- but avoid the word "immediately," and allow enough time for the order to filter down to front lines.

Where will it take place? Define areas to be taken into consideration, and ensure maps of these areas are agreed and accurate. Ensure that procedures are included to deal with irregular units in or adjacent to these areas.[2]

Who is to take what actions, in what order, and who is to oversee the process? Where troops must withdraw, say by when, to where, and with what equipment. If certain equipment is to either be abandoned or removed, specify the procedures to deal with this. Avoid the word "should" and use the word "must." Even by September 1994, cease-fire agreements in Croatia continued to be unclear. A local Canadian commander reported that the cease-fire agreement "failed to specify anything about anti-tank systems, machine guns or APCs. Again the unit saw the results of a poorly conceived CFA, written with vague terminology."[3]

Will the cease-fire be monitored? Wherever possible, it should not be left up to either belligerent to determine who violated the cease-fire, or indeed if it has been violated. It is strongly recommended that authority to make these decisions be transferred to an objective third party, who will monitor the cease-fire. (With this in mind, there must be a corps of monitors available, trained in specific skills -- which could include at a minimum an understanding of the most common types of cease-fire violations -- and ready to move into conflict areas when required.) Ensure those monitoring arrangements are adequate in terms of personnel, equipment and geographic coverage. Where monitoring teams exist, either as observers or as investigators of violations, they should probably consist of at least one or more individuals with the following skills: 1) **military:** military personnel with combat experience are essential for a number of obvious reasons, including their ability to detect situations which have clearly been set up to look as if the other side has committed a violation; 2) **socio-cultural/linguistic:** someone who knows the language and culture of the area being monitored is essential to avoid misunder-standings; and 3) **conflict resolution:** individuals trained in conflict resolution skills and/or low level negotiations should be required on monitoring teams in order to help resolve disputes under the cease-fire, whether these disputes concern alleged or actual violations, or concern the way in which the conditions of the agreement are being carried out.[4]

What counts as a violation? To a great an extent as possible, define what will count as a violation. Decide which violations are minor, and which are considered to be more serious. (UN troops in Croatia, for example, rarely count small arms fire across the zone of separation, as a serious violation.)

What is to happen in the case of a violation? Violations of the cease-fire will probably be inevitable, and since it is impossible to think of all actions which could potentially be considered violations, there will be disputes. Agree on clear procedures to deal with violations, or alleged violations. If at all possible, use third parties for this function, and give them the authority to decide if a particular action should be considered a violation (arbitration), and to mediate other serious disputes. All of this includes taking into consideration what will happen if a particular deadline set in the agreement is not met. If parties do *not* do certain things by certain times set out in the agreement, what happens to them? (Chapter 7)

Who will take responsibility for uncontrolled forces? Independent or uncontrolled forces should *not* be allowed to operate freely, and someone -- either the belligerents themselves, or a third party -- must take responsibility for them. Parties who have ceased fire should not be expected to refrain from defending themselves if they are attacked by such forces. Conditions under which such attacks would be considered "violations," as well as what responsibilities and duties lie on the belligerent allied to such forces, would therefore have to be spelled out in the cease-fire agreement to a great an extent as is practicable under the circumstances.

Ensure that those signing the agreement have the *authority* to do so, that it does not need to be ratified by other parties, and that if it does require ratification or further discussion, that deadlines are included (and detail what the next step is should the deadlines not be met).

16. Provide adequate numbers of **trained** observers, monitors, and peacekeepers. There is not yet any readily-available source for individuals trained in these skills. Mediators and practitioners of conflict resolution generally work at the local or organizational level. Nevertheless, these individuals, as well as seasoned diplomats or civil servants, could form the core of trainees in a new organization specifically devoted to training international mediators and cease-fire monitors.

It is noteworthy that with regard to cease-fire monitoring, and even international mediation generally, current "mediators" only rarely have training in conflict resolution skills, and instead gain their position either because they have a name which people recognize, because they are acceptable to both sides, or because they happen to be available. (This was the case in the former Yugoslavia, for example.)[5]

The situation with regard to peacekeeping is only marginally better. Most UN contingents from most countries receive no training in peacekeeping, although some countries (including Canada) get some basic training on the technical side (including learning how to conduct searches of vehicles, for example). Peacekeeping -- not to mention monitoring -- must be considered a role different to normal military operations, and it requires different skills, including the ability to negotiate and mediate disputed situations.[6] No peacekeeping forces, to my knowledge, receive such training, but are instead thrown into difficult situations where they must do the best they can. (Chapters 7 and 8)

17. Since it is highly desirable to guarantee agreements, since peacekeeping and monitoring requires massive numbers to be effective, and given the financial difficulties faced by the UN, countries should be persuaded to fund UN peacekeeping out of their defence budgets. Current arrangements have countries funding peacekeeping out of their Foreign Office, External Affairs, or similar government departments. These departments have limited funds, and the lack of capital has caused financial hardship in the United Nations. Peacekeeping should be considered in the national defence, and money to maintain it should come from defence budgets. (Chapter 8)

18. As a rule, pure mediators in international situations must refrain from passing judgments on the disputants, and must ensure that they enter the conflict as a third party who has no more than one role. Failure to do

so will usually result in accusations of partiality and bias, and their efforts will be terminated. (Chapter 8)

19. Where third parties attempt to mediate the conflict, decide on which style is most appropriate to the situation -- pure or power -- and do not confuse them at any point. Pure mediators probably cannot come from the United Nations, but should instead come from other sources (Quakers, or independent mediation organizations). Consider using mediators whom the parties themselves would trust to promote a fair settlement, even if others think that party may be biased or has perceived interests in the conflict. (Chapter 9)

20. Third parties forcing people to stop fighting must guarantee any agreement they broker. This includes having standby peacekeeping forces, or other kinds of interventionary forces, where necessary. (Chapter 9)

21. If coercion is used to impose a cease-fire, decide on a strategy, whether indirect coercion (control over resources) or direct coercion (threats, use of force). Escalation from indirect to direct coercion can be considered, but the problems of using coercion must be taken into consideration, including an increase in intransigence, and the fact that the parties will look weak if they cease fire.[7] Be clear about any threats made, and ensure they are not just threats: be willing to carry them out.[8] (Chapter 9)

Notes

1. Face saving is of importance at even the lowest level of operations. In Croatia in the summer of 1994, part of the responsibilities of Canadian forces in the UN Zone of Separation included disarming Serbian or Croatian forces transgressing the zone. In at least one case, Canadian troops negotiated the surrender of transgressors by allowing the officer in charge to retain his personal sidearm, while his men were disarmed. This allowed the officer to save face in front of his men, and the cease-fire remained stable. (Interview with men of 1PPCLI, September 1994. Opinions expressed are those of the men alone, and should not be taken as the official position of the Department of National Defence, Canada.)

2. Another example of how important this can be comes from Canadian peacekeepers in Croatia, who found that the cease-fire lines had been drawn *around* a local Serb village, thus placing it inside the zone of separation (and giving local Serbian forces an excuse to enter the zone and ensure that it was "protected"). The local Canadian base, on the other hand, was not placed inside the zone, but in Serbian Krajina, where local forces were in a position to cut it off completely. Canadian logistic supply lines ran through a narrow Croatian corridor, again susceptible to local forces. (Interviews with men of 1PPCLI, Croatia, September 1994, Ibid.)

3. From "Operational Lessons Learned", Maj. D.J. Banks, 1 PPCLI in Operation Harmony, Roto 4, April to October 1994 - draft copy. The opinion expressed is taken from a draft report, and is the personal opinion of Major Banks. It should in no way be taken as the official opinion of the Department of National Defence, Canada.

4. This third element was noticeably missing from monitoring teams in the former Yugoslavia, and is generally not considered.

5. These observations come from speaking with former British monitors in Croatia, most of whom came from the Foreign Office.

6. As one Canadian commander has noted, "There is still a need for UN-specific training prior to a deployment. While training for mid-intensity operations provides the solid base for success, training in such skills as low-level negotiations, crowd confrontation, and documenting of incidents, provides the finishing touch which assures success." (Major D.J. Banks, report, Ibid.).

7. Imposing the cease-fire can indeed work. Canadian peacekeeping forces entered the "Medak pocket" of the UN zone of separation in 1993, and they physically forced a Croatian Police Brigade to stop their activities (evidence of mass murder was well-documented by the Canadian troops) and leave the area.

8. The entire history of the Yugoslav wars has been one of the international community making threats, and only rarely carrying them out; belligerents soon learned not to treat them seriously.

Appendix 1:
Notes on the Definition
of "Cease-fire"

Historically, there has been a great deal of confusion surrounding the definition of "cease-fire" or, rather, as to how it differed from other related terms such as "truce," "suspension of arms," "cessation of hostilities" and "armistice." The term "cease-fire" itself is a relatively recent one. It was used neither in the Hague Regulations (1907),[1] nor did it appear in major works on international law such as those by Oppenheim (1952), Greenspan (1959), and Schwarzenberger (1968). It has been called a "novel" term by authorities on international law even as late as 1956.[2] Madame Paul Bastid, one such authority, contends that the term's first appearance dates from the United Nations' use during the Indonesian conflict (1947),[3] and it seems likely that it was not until this time that any clear idea of the distinction between "cease-fire" and its related terms came to light.[4] Mohn maintains, and Bailey and de Montluc agree, that with the creation of the United Nations came a general consensus that the terms "cease-fire," "truce," and "armistice" represented a particular chronological sequence, each term used in succession to designate a general transition from war to peace.[5] Even if this is the case, however, this only points out that there are distinctions between the terms, not what those distinctions might be.

Regardless of where the term first appeared, however, attempts to define it, or to distinguish it from its relations, have been confused at best. At worst, theorists make no or only token efforts at making distinctions; several writers use the terms synonymously:[6]

1. Suspension of arms or "cease-fire" referred to an agreement by belligerents in a particular theatre of war to refrain from hostilities for a day or more to bury the dead, exchange prisoners, or negotiate a longer peace. "Armistice" or "truce" referred to such an agreement applicable to a larger area or to the entire war for a limited time or indefinitely ...
2. ... if the war could be stopped, it might be a simple cease-fire that would do it. Considering the difficulty ... of reaching a truce, simple arrangements would have the strongest appeal. ... The argument that, of all forms of armistice, the simple cease-fire is the most plausible and likely, is a strong one.
3. A peace settlement is usually achieved in two stages. The first ... includes the cessation of hostilities and the subsequent deployment of the armed forces of the belligerents during a period ... after the truce.
4. ... the study addresses the making of armistices -- i.e. agreements that end combat ("cease-fire" and "truce" will be used interchangeably with "armistice").[7]

This confusion of terms is not limited to political and military theorists, but extends also to the works of authorities on international law and, in the worst case, to international agreements themselves. "Cease-fire," the term with which we are most concerned, has at various points, and by various authorities on international law, been called a component of an armistice,[8] been equated with general and local armistices,[9] and has even been assumed to encompass general and local armistices within it.[10] Thus, depending on the writer, it has been assumed to be the case that

1. all cease-fires are armistices, but not all armistices are cease-fires;
2. cease-fires and armistices are one and the same; or that
3. all armistices are cease-fires, but not all cease-fires are armistices.

Examples of this kind of semantic befuddlement appear in international agreements as well. The Paris agreements on Vietnam (27 January 1973), for example, use the terms "cease-fire" and "cessation of hostilities" virtually interchangeably.[11] In the end, and as de Montluc points out, the problem comes down to this:

> Cease-fire, truce and armistice are not ... absolutely exclusive, one from the other; they can intersect or superimpose themselves [on one another] by so much that a certain terminological confusion dominates the matter.[12]

Perhaps little can be done to avoid this lexical chaos, but here, at least, the attempt can be made to formulate a definition of "cease-fire" which will be generally distinguishable from other related terms. *A cease-fire, then, is an implemented agreement between belligerents (either explicit or implicit), involving all or the greater part of their military forces to, at a minimum, abjure the use of violent force with regard to each other, for a period of time (not necessarily specified), regardless of the intention for doing so, and regardless of the eventual outcome of such agreement.*

The definition is cumbersome, but it is also extremely precise. To begin with, it distinguishes itself from a "truce," perhaps the broadest of all the related terms. Grotius defines "truce" as *any* agreement "by which war-like acts are for a time abstained from."[13] The definition of cease-fire would obviously be narrower than this, as it excludes a number of such agreements (such as those involving only local military forces, for example). Both de Montluc and Bailey see the term "truce" more narrowly than Grotius, but neither is so narrow as to approach the definition of cease-fire given above. Moreover, and regardless of either author's own definition of "cease-fire," both agree that, in the field of international relations, cease-fire is a narrower concept than that of "truce"; the definition given herein conforms to that practice. According to de Montluc, the truce involves supplementary strengthening and stabilisation of a cease-fire[14] and Bailey's conclusions concerning the United Nation's tacit acceptance of the three-stage sequence of cease-fire-truce-armistice,[15] all go to support the conclusion that "truce" must be considered the broader term.

The given definition of cease-fire is further distinguishable from the armistice. In most cases, the cease-fire cannot be considered an armistice as, firstly, it involves "all or the greater part" of belligerents' military forces (armistices may apparently be local in character[16]) and, secondly, the cease-fire does not require that belligerents have the intention to conclude a more permanent peace (as some authorities have implied be a necessary condition of an armistice).[17]

More specifically to armistices, the definition of cease-fire can not in all cases be equated with the "general armistice." Oppenheim states that general armistices are *always* "conventions of vital political importance affecting the whole of the war,"[18] but there may be occasions on which the cease-fire is not of "vital" political importance, and/or does not affect "the whole of the war." It may, for example, merely keep the military situation in a state of stasis. It is important, however, to be able to include such occasions under the definition of "cease-fire," as these situations may lead to more important agreements of "vital political importance"; that they may not do so will not be considered reason enough to exclude them from the category of "cease-fire."

Because the "partial" or "local" armistice is also "always of political importance," a cease-fire can be distinguished from this term also, although it should be noted that in most other respects, the "partial armistice" comes very close to what is herein called a cease-fire.[19]

The definition in nearly all cases can be distinguished from a mere "suspension of arms." Suspensions of arms may involve a cessation of violent force between "small" military forces;[20] cease-fires involve "all or the greater part" of belligerent forces. Suspensions of arms are entered into regarding "momentary and local military purposes only";[21] cease-fires may be entered into for other purposes, local or momentary military purposes being only two. Oppenheim further states that suspensions of arms have nothing to do with political purposes,[22] in which case they must be excluded from the category of cease-fire, as the latter allows for cases which may have political results, and which may be entered into for political purposes.

The definition, then, can occasionally (and unavoidably) be superimposed over those of "armistice," "general armistice," "partial armistice," and even "suspension of arms" -- the reason such terms are used later in this work with reference to "cease-fires" -- but it is nevertheless distinguishable from all these terms in most cases. In general, the cease-fire as here defined generally *includes* a suspension of hostilities, and *is included within* both a truce and an armistice, the general tendency being towards more and more political content (see Figure A-1). In any case, the intention of providing the given definition of "cease-fire" is not to make the term distinguishable from similar terms in every instance, nor to subsume within it every existing definition of "cease-fire"; it is to have a working definition which both conforms to international practice, and which allows for the inclusion of those cases which are of interest in the study at hand. A dissection of the definition illuminates this latter point, and should clarify any residual confusions.

A cease-fire shall be deemed ... :

1. *... an implemented agreement between belligerents (either explicit or implicit) ...*
   There is a difference between an agreement to cease fire, and an actual cease-fire. The former is a declaration of intention, and the latter the proof of that

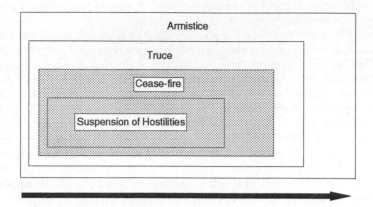

FIGURE A.1: Political Content of War Termination Terminology. The historical tendency appears to favour different terms depending on the how much political content the agreement contains.

commitment. The signing of an agreement to cease fire by no means leads to a situation where the fighting stops, and it is only in those cases where people stop shooting at one another that the term can be applied. Moreover, cease-fires, armistices, truces, and suspensions of arms are all *agreements*, in most cases having neither the force nor the effect of a treaty.[23] Treaties are concluded between states, and they must be written; cease-fires may be concluded between non-state armed forces, and may be oral or implicit (as in the case where belligerents simply cease fire without ever having communicated the intention to do so).

2. *... involving all or the greater part of their military forces ...* Such phrasing allows for the inclusion of those cases where not all of a belligerent's forces were able or willing to cease fire (due to communication difficulties and the like), and also the exclusion of those cases involving only local military forces (such as the local armistice or suspension of arms) where no wide-ranging political results were forthcoming. (Exactly what proportion of belligerents' armed forces must cease fire before the situation can be called "a cease-fire" can never be precisely defined. Suffice it to say that while that point may always be subjective, it is usually relatively clear).

3. *... to, at a minimum, abjure the use of violent force with regard to each other ...* Cease-fire agreements may contain more stipulations than this (and usually do); this phrasing allows for the inclusion of such cases, as well as those cases where the only agreement was to stop violent attacks against each other. (Belligerents who stop attacking each other, but continue to use violence on other parties [such as their own citizens, or internal paramilitary groups,

for example] have nevertheless "ceased fire" for the purposes of this study.)[24] Moreover, this phrasing again distinguishes the cease-fire from general and partial armistices, which require that the agreement be of political importance. It also obviates the confusion which may arise from using such phrasings as "cessation of hostilities" (or "hostilités"),[25] or "abstention from hostile military action,"[26] which could be taken to include such things as economic warfare or hostile propaganda. The phrasing, then, allows for both the "bare minimum" case, where belligerents stop violent attacks upon one another, as well as for those cases where other conditions may have been stipulated.

4. ... *for a period of time (not necessarily specified)* ... This again allows for the inclusion of those cases in which there was a de facto cease-fire in the absence of any specific written agreement. It also avoids the requirement that a cease-fire be of considerable duration; those cases in which the cease-fire broke down almost immediately are of as much interest for our purposes as those which did not.

5. ... *regardless of the intention for doing so* ... As opposed to those cases where the agreement was entered into with the intention of establishing a more permanent peace (the armistice agreement), such phrasing allows for the inclusion of those cases in which the cease-fire was entered into for other, less noble, purposes (such as to re-group or re-arm one's forces). Such cases are of interest because the very fact of the cease-fire may allow for a more permanent peace to be implemented even if that was not the intention of the belligerents at the outset. Third parties may more easily intervene, for example, or it may be that at such a time belligerent will be more receptive to suggestions that a more durable peace would be desirable.

6. ... *and regardless of the eventual outcome of such agreement* ... Cease-fires may have a number of different outcomes,[27] and the phrasing is intended to allow for this fact. Cease-fires (unlike armistices) do not always have wide-ranging political effects. This final clause once again avoids the requirement that a cease-fire be of considerable duration. Whether of not the cease-fire results in a more permanent or durable peace, it is of interest.

Notes

1. R.R. Baxter, "Armistices and Other Forms of Suspension of Hostilities," *Recueil des cours de l'Academie de Droit Internationale* 149 (1976), p. 357; Adam Roberts and Richard Guelff (eds.), *Documents on the Laws of War* (2nd. ed.) (Oxford: Clarendon Press, 1989), p. 55.

2. L. Oppenheim, in H. Lauterpacht (ed.), *Oppenheim's International Law, vol. 2: Disputes, War and Neutrality* (7th ed) (London: Longmans, Green & Co., 1952); Morris Greenspan, *The Modern Law of Land Warfare* (Los Angeles: University of California Press, 1959); Georg Schwarzenberger, *International Law, Vol. II: The Law of Armed Conflict* (London: Stevens & Sons, Ltd., 1968); Colonel Howard S. Levie, "The Nature and Scope of the Armistice Agreement," *American Journal of International Law* 53 (1956), p. 890.

3. Madame Paul Bastid, "Le Cessez-le-feu," *Société Internationale de Droit pénal militaire et de droit de la guerre [Actes du]*, 6ᵉ Congrès internationale, La Haye, 22-25 May 1973 (1974), p. 34.

4. Sydney D. Bailey, *How Wars End: The United Nations and the Termination of Armed Conflict, 1946-1964* (2 vols.) (Oxford: Clarendon Press, 1982), Vol. I, pp. 29-32.

5. Paul Mohn, "Problems of Truce Supervision," *International Conciliation* 478 (1952), p. 53; Bailey, *How Wars End*, Vol. I, p. 33; Bertrand de Montluc, *Le Cessez-le-feu*, Ph.D. thesis (Université de Droit et d'Economie et de Sciences Sociales de Paris, 1971), p. 252.

6. Bailey, *How Wars End*, Vol. I, p. 36; Bastid, "Le Cessez-le-feu," p. 31; Paul R. Pillar, *Negotiating Peace: War Termination as a Bargaining Process* (New Jersey: Princeton University Press, 1983), p. 4; Robert F. Randle, *The Origins of Peace: A Study of Peacemaking and the Structure of Peace Settlements* (New York: Free Press, 1973), p. 7.

7. (1) Quincy Wright, "How Hostilities Have Ended: Peace Treaties and Alternatives," in William T.R. Fox (ed.), *How Wars End -- Annals of the American Academy of Political and Social Science*, Vol. 392 (Philadelphia: Academy of Political and Social Science, 1970), p. 55; (2) Thomas Schelling, *Arms and Influence* (London: Yale University Press, 1966), p. 209; (3) Randle, *The Origins of Peace*, p. 7; (4) Pillar, *Negotiating Peace*, p. 4; see Paul Mohn, "Problems of Truce Supervision," *International Conciliation* 478 (1952), pp. 52-59, and Bailey, *How Wars End*, Vol. I, p. 36, for further examples.

8. Levie, "The Nature and Scope of the Armistice Agreement," p. 882; if Oppenheim is using "cessation of hostilities" to mean "cease-fire," then he agrees with this point (see Oppenheim, in Lauterpacht, *Oppenheim's International Law*, p. 547).

9. Baxter, "Armistices and Other Forms of Suspension of Hostilities," p. 358.

10. Ibid., pp. 364-65, and de Montluc, *Le Cessez-le-feu*, p. 5.

11. Bastid, "Le Cessez-le-feu," p. 31, and see Bailey, *How Wars End*, Vol. I, p. 36, for further examples.

12. de Montluc, *Le Cessez-le-feu*, p. 20 (my translation); (*"Cessez-le-feu, trêve, et armistice ne sont toutefois pas absolument exclusifs l'un de l'autre, ils peuvent se recouper ou se superposer, d'autant qu'une certaine confusion terminologique règne en la matière"*).

13. Hugo Grotius, in Bailey, *How Wars End*, Vol. I, p. 29.

14. de Montluc, *Le Cessez-le-feu*, p. 185 (*"un affermisement et un stabilisation supplémentaires"*).

15. Bailey, *How Wars End*, Vol. I, p. 33.

16. Hague Regulations (1907), in Baxter, "Armistices and Other Forms of Suspension of Hostilities," p. 357, and Roberts and Guelff, *Documents on the Laws of War*, p. 55.

17. See Baxter, "Armistices and Other Forms of Suspension of Hostilities," p. 374; Paul Mohn, in de Montluc, *Le Cessez-le-feu*, p. 35.

18. Oppenheim, in Lauterpacht, *Oppenheim's International Law*, p. 548.

19. See Ibid., p. 549.

20. Ibid., p. 547.

21. Ibid.

22. Ibid.

23. Baxter, "Armistices and Other Forms of Suspension of Hostilities," p. 370; Levie, "The Nature and Scope of the Armistice Agreement," p. 881; Oppenheim, in Lauterpacht, *Oppenheim's International Law*, p. 546.

24. My thanks to Dr. Trudy Govier of the University of Calgary for making this point clear to me.

25. Oppenheim, in Lauterpacht, *Oppenheim's International Law*, p. 546; de Montluc, *Le Cessez-le-feu*, p. 2.

26. United Nations Security Council, in Bailey, *How Wars End*, Vol. I, p. 35.

27. See Paul Seabury, "Provisionality and Finality," in William T.R. Fox (ed.), *How Wars End: Annals of the American Academy of Political and Social Science* (Philadelphia: Academy of Political and Social Science, Vol. 392, 1970), p. 102.

Appendix 2:
"Why can't they just stop fighting?"

"Why can't they just stop fighting?"

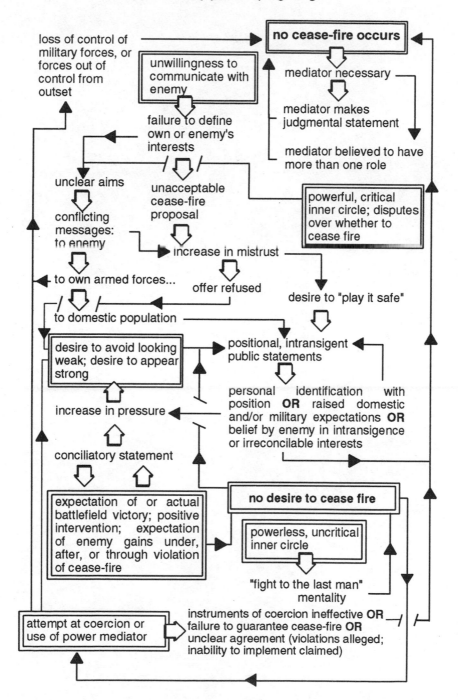

Appendix 3:
Case Study Chronologies

Appendix 3a: The Algerian War of Independence (1954-1962)

1	November	1954	FLN proclamation of independence
12	November		Mendès-France declares French position of "no compromise"
	February	1955	Mendès-France falls; Edgar Faure forms new government
30	June		de Gaulle privately sees Algerian independence as inevitable
	January	1956	Faure falls; Guy Mollet forms new left wing government
	April	1957	FLN meets French representatives for the first time
21	May		Mollet falls
12	June		Bourgès-Maunoury becomes Prime Minister
30	September		Bourgès-Maunoury falls
5	October		Félix Gaillard becomes Prime Minister; declares that France will never accept Algerian independence
15	April	1958	Gaillard government falls
12	May		Pierre Pfimlin forms government
24	May		French paratroops take over Corsican capital, and call for the return of de Gaulle
28	May		Pierre Pfimlin resigns
1	June		de Gaulle forms new French government as president
	October		Ferhat Abbas interviewed by West German journalist; declares that demand for independence before peace talks
23	October		de Gaulle offers the "Peace of the Brave"
25	October		de Gaulle invites FLN to go to Paris to negotiate a cease-fire. FLN counter with proposal for talks in neutral country. De Gaulle does not reply
	January	1959	Michel Debré, the French Prime Minister, re-offers de Gaulle's offer of 25 October 1958; FLN responds as before
16	September		de Gaulle re-offers the peace of the brave; gives Algerians three choices: secession, complete integration, or self-government to be achieved over four years
28	September		Provisional Govt. of Algeria is prepared to enter into negotiations with France for cease-fire and self-determination – conditions offer on withdrawal of French troops
10	November		de Gaulle appeals to FLN to cease-fire, offers to allow representatives to visit France to reply; no cease-fire, but negotiations acceptable, on condition FLN negotiators be FLN leaders held in French detention; de Gaulle rejects offer de Gaulle meets with Si Salah and others
19	June	1960	FLN agrees to send a delegation to France
20	June		Talks at Melun between France and the FLN
25	June		de Gaulle repeats offer to negotiate, this time without four-year period for transfer autonomy
5	September		
8	January	1961	referendum in Algeria for self-determination; 58% vote yes
20	April		army rebels take over Algeria
25	April		regular army back in control
	May-July		first talks at Evian
19	March	1962	1200 hrs, cease-fire comes into effect

Appendix 3b: The Nigerian Civil War (1968-1970)

15	January	1966	army coup; Prime minister, two premiers, and top army officers assassinated; power goes to Major-General Ironsi
18	January		Ojukwu appointed governor of Eastern Nigeria
24	May		Ironsi announces abolition of regions and civil service unification
29	July		mutiny by Northern troops; Ironsi killed
1	August		Gowon comes to power
31	August		Gowon restores federal system in Nigeria
4	January	1967	Ghana summit at Aburi; first and last time Gowon and Ojukwu meet face to face
27	May		Gowon replaces federal system with 12-states structure
6	July		war begins with Federal invasion at three points
9	August		Biafran counter-attack
2	September		Gowon announces "total war"
11	September		OAU summit meeting at Kinshasa
	September		Arnold Smith of Canada asked by Gowon to arrange talks
	October		Smith talks break down
	February	1968	Gowon offers cease-fire with third party to police lines
9	March		Ojukwu wants talks without preconditions
13	April		Tanzania recognizes Biafra
8	May		Gabon recognizes Biafra
14	May		Ivory Coast recognizes Biafra
20	May		Zambia recognizes Biafra
23	May		beginning of Kampala peace conference
31	July		France appears ready to recognize Biafra; French arms begin to arrive in Biafra
6	August		talks in Addis Ababa begin
14	August		Curle takes cease-fire proposal to Gowon, who refuses idea due to belief in victory
24	August		Gowon announces "final push"
7	September		Ojukwu's top men believe time has come to settle
9	September		Addis Ababa talks broken off; de Gaulle announces support for Biafra
14	October		French arms have effect on Biafran morale
	October '68 - October '69		military stalemate
24	January	1969	new federal offensive announced
24	March		Haiti recognizes Biafra
22	April		Umuahia captured by Federal troops
25	April		Owerri recaptured by Biafran troops
27	April		controversial AFSC advertisement nearly spoils private Quaker mediation effort
23	June		new federal offensive
6	September		OAU summit at Addis Ababa
10	October		slight softening of position of Gowon
17	October		publicity leak spoils talks
	December		military breakthrough by Federal troops
9	January	1970	Ojukwu has final cabinet meeting
12	January		war ends at 16:30

Appendix 3c: The October War (6-27 October 1973)

6	Oct.(Sat.)	Egypt-Syrian attack on Israel begins at 1400hrs (0800 Washington time); first days' fighting prompts superpowers to attempt acquiescence in cease-fire
7	Oct. (Sun.)	minor US airlift to Israel begins
8	Oct. (Mon.)	Security Council meets; Israeli counter-offensive begins; Syria begins retreat
9	Oct.(Tue.)	Golda Meir (Israeli PM) reportedly authorizes deployment of Israel's nuclear weapons; US promise to replace Israeli losses, freeing up Israeli reserves
10	Oct. (Wed.)	major Soviet airlift to Syria; Soviet sealift begins; Golan mostly recaptured by Israel; Egypt now entrenched on the Suez Canal
11	Oct. (Thu.)	Israel drives into Syria; Israeli forces reported heading for Damascus
12	Oct. (Fri.)	Israel willing to accept cease-fire "in place"
13	Oct. (Sat.)	primary US airlift to Israel begins
14	Oct. (Sun.)	US aid begins to arrive in large amounts; new Egyptian offensive
15	Oct. (Mon.)	defeat of Egyptian offensive; US airlift continues at rate of 1,000 tons per day; Hafiz Ismail, Egyptian Security Advisor to Sadat (Egyptian president), in letter to Kissinger (US Sec. of State), invites settlement
16	Oct. (Tue.)	Sadat offers cease-fire with conditions Israel would reject; first Israeli tanks cross Suez behind Egyptian forces; Alexei Kosygin, Soviet Premier, in Cairo
17	Oct. (Wed.)	Kissinger warns Simcha Dinitz, Israeli Ambassador to US, that US will support cease-fire linkage with Res. 242 and to complete operations within 48 hours
18	Oct. (Thu.)	Israel consolidating bridgehead across canal; Meir responds negatively to US cease-fire proposal based on linkage to Resolution 242
19	Oct. (Fri.)	Kosygin returns to Moscow; arrangements made for Kissinger to visit Moscow
20	Oct. (Sat.)	Sadat makes decision (?) to actively seek cease-fire; Kissinger leaves for Moscow
21	Oct. (Sun.)	Superpower agreement over cease-fire; Moshe Dayan, Israeli Defence Minister, makes cease-fire proposal; Nixon's message to Meir
22	Oct. (Mon.)	UN passes Resolution 338 0052 hrs (New York time); Kissinger arrives in Israel 1300 hrs; Egypt accepts Res. 338 effective 1700 hrs local time (two hours ahead of deadline); Israel follows suit; cease-fire breaks down
23	Oct. (Tue.)	Israel moving to complete encirclement of Egyptian Third Army; 1000hrs Brezhnev message to US warning breaking of cease-fire unacceptable; 1100hrs, Meir denies Israel broke cease-fire first; 1236hrs Brezhnev urging joint superpower action; Kissinger replies US will take responsibility for Israel to cease-fire; Meir rejects idea of new UN resolution; 1515hrs Sadat asks for US troops to intervene; UN Resolution 339 passed
24	Oct. (Wed.)	Egypt (in Security Council) calls for joint superpower troop intervention; Brezhnev warns Nixon that Soviet Union may act unilaterally; US forces go to DefCon III; Kissinger threatens Israel with disassociation; threatens to resupply Third Army; end to Soviet airlift
25	Oct. (Thu.)	Resolution 340 passed, calling for a "return" to the cease-fire line of 22 October; Israel allows single convoy of supplied to reach Third Army
26	Oct. (Fri.)	Third Army attempts to break encirclement; renewed fighting; US threatens that unless Israel complies with cease-fire by 0800 27 October, it will support enforcement action in the Security Council
27	Oct. (Sat.)	Cease-fire after Sadat accepts Israeli offer of direct talks

Appendix 3d: The Iran-Iraq War (1980-1988) -- Major Events and Third Party Intervention

(events are in **boldface type**)

Date	Third Party	Comment/Event
23 Sept. 1980		**Iraqi forces cross the border into Iraq**
"	UN Sec. Council	statement by President of Council
27 Sept. 1980	President Zia ul-Haq of Pakistan	"...to ascertain their views in regard to a settlement of the conflict in the spirit of Islamic solidarity"
28 Sept. 1980	UN Sec. Council	Resolution 479 (1980)
1 Oct. 1980	Edmund Muskie (U.S. Sec. of State)	"urges" the Iraqi foreign minister at the UN to stop fighting and negotiate
	Leonid Brezhnev	urges both sides to negotiate
2 Oct. 1980		**Iraq offers unilateral cease-fire; rejected by Iran**
17 Oct. 1980	Habib Chatti (Tunisian Diplomat)	announces a peace effort, which fails
28 Oct. 1980	NAM led by Cuba, and including PLO, Zambia, India, Pakistan, Yugoslavia, and Algeria	announcement that NAM will attempt to intervene
5 Nov. 1980	UN Sec. Council	statement by President of Council
11 Nov. 1980		**Olaf Palme appointed special UN representative**
28 Nov. 1980	Olaf Palme	preliminary visit unsuccessful
---	---	---
5-11 Jan.1981		**Iranian offensive (fails)**
15 Jan. 1981	Olaf Palme	second visit unsuccessful
6 Feb. 1981	NAM leaders	a "goodwill" mission
6 Mar. 1981	NAM leaders	proposal made; rejected 7 March
2 April 1981	NAM leaders	modified proposal; abandonment of high-level shuttling
4-5 Apr. 1981	Olaf Palme	unsuccessful third visit
13 Sept. 1981	NAM leaders	renewed effort
8 Oct. 1981	Habib Chatti, NAM chairman	announces formation of 3 commissions to examine various sticking points in negotiations
6 Nov. 1981		**Iraq offers temporary cease-fire for Moslem month of Muharram; rejected by Iran**
30 Dec. 1981	Asad (Syria)	announcement of peace effort
31 Dec. 1981	Kuwait	to join Syrian effort
---	---	---
2 March 1982	Olaf Palme	fourth failed visit ends
8 March 1982	Organisation of Islamic States	announcement of a new effort
21 March 1982		**beginning of successful Iranian counter-offensive**
14 April 1982		**Iraq offers full withdrawal if Iran agrees war over**
10 June 1982		**Iraq ready to accept cease-fire and arbitration**
20 June 1982		**Iraq announces "withdrawal" from Iran**
2 July 1982		**Iraq calls for cease-fire and peacekeeping force**
12 July 1982	UN Sec. Council	Resolution 514 (1982)
15 July 1982	UN Sec. Council	statement by President of Council

24 Aug. 1982	Islamic Conference	announcement of new effort
4 Oct. 1982	UN Sec. Council	Resolution 522 (1982)
6 Dec. 1982	Algeria and UAE	announcement of new mediation efforts
---	---	---
6-16 Feb.1983		**failed Iranian offensive**
21 Feb. 1983	UN Sec. Council	statement by President of Council
April 1983		**failed Iranian offensive**
16 May 1983	Algeria	renews efforts after setbacks
21 May 1983	Gulf states	beginning of new mediation effort
22 July 1983		**Iranian offensive (Operation *Dawn II*)**
30 July 1983		**Iranian offensive (Operation *Dawn III*); repulsed**
20 Oct. 1983		**Iranian offensive (Operation *Dawn IV*)**
31 Oct. 1983	UN Sec. Council	Resolution 540 (1983)
---	---	---
Feb. 1984		**beginning of "tanker war"; first "war of the cities"**
15-24 Feb.		**Iranian offensive**
24 Feb. -		**Iranian offensive**
19 March		
30 March 1984	UN Sec. Council	statement by President of Council
6 April 1984	Indira Gandhi	offers to mediate; rejected by Iran
10 April 1984	Egypt	announces it has plan to end the war
12 April 1984	Japanese For. Minister	attempts to convince Iran that its international reputation is being damaged by the war
29 April 1984	Egypt, Yugoslavia, India	present Iran with a plan to end the war
22 May 1984		**US now officially supporting Iraq**
24 May 1984	Syria	begins effort starting in Tehran
28 May 1984	Zayid (UAE)	offers to mediate
29 May 1984	Islamic Conference Organisation (ICO)	announcement that new plan by Arafat being considered
5 June 1984	Japan	"feeler" offer to mediate if both sides request it
11 June 1984		**de Cuellar secures agreement to avoid hitting civilian targets**
16 July 1984	ICO	"peace team" to be "re-activated"
6 Aug. 1984	Kuwait	seeks Syrian help to mediate
7 Aug. 1984	Egypt	talks to Yugoslavia about increasing NAM role
29 Sept. 1984	Japan	makes proposal; accepted by Iraq 8 Oct; Iran rejects 30 November
30 Nov. 1984	Gulf Coop. Council	draws up plans for a settlement
---	---	---
28 Jan. 1985		**Iraqi offensive**
5 March 1985	UN Sec. Council	statement by President of Council
15 March 1985		**second war of the cities**
"	UN Sec. Council	statement by President of Council
22 March 1985	Rajiv Gandhi	to send NAM peace mission to Gulf; urges 3-month unilateral cease-fire
30 March 1985	United States	appeals to Iran to recognize stalemate and accept negotiated settlement
25 April 1985	Rajiv Gandhi	asks both sides to halt civilian bombing as first step in de-escalation
6 June 1985	UN Sec. Council	statement by President of Council

25 June 1985	India, Egypt	talk over plans which include a cease-fire and a peacekeeping force
18 Nov. 1985	ICO	conferring; fails in absence of Iranian response
	Ronald Reagan	announces he will proposes joint US/USSR pressure
---	---	---
9 Feb. 1986		**Iranian offensive; Fao peninsula captured**
22 Feb. 1986	Egypt	launches fresh effort
24 Feb. 1986	UN Sec. Council	Resolution 582 (1986)
21 Mar. 1986	UN Sec. Council	statement by President of Council
27 June 1986	PLO	dismissed by Iran as "nothing new"
"	Sudanese PM	plans peace mission
30 June - 9 July		**Iranian offensive; capture of Mehran**
8 Oct. 1986	UN Sec. Council	Resolution 588 (1986)
22 Dec. 1986	UN Sec. Council	statement by President of Council
---	---	---
Jan. 1987		**third war of the cities**
16 Jan. 1987	UN Sec. Council	statement by President of Council
22 Jan. 1987	Ronald Reagan	calls on parties to negotiate
29 Jan. 1987	ICO	sends delegation to Iran with "new" initiative; Iran says it will ignore ICO resolutions
March 1987		**final Iranian offensive; tanker war prompts Kuwait to request reflagging of its tankers**
14 April 1987	Saudi Arabia	proposes that Saddam Hussein step down "temporarily" in order to pacify Iran
3 May 1987		**USSR announces joint superpower effort to end war**
5 May 1987	Japan	wants to try again
14 May 1987	UN Sec. Council	statement by President of Council
17 May 1987		**USS Stark attacked; 37 dead**
26 June 1987	M. Gaddhaffi	report that Gaddhaffi is to mediate
20 July 1987	UN Sec. Council	Resolution 598 (1987) demanding cease-fire
23 July 1987	West Germany	puts out mediation feelers; spoiled by West German foreign minister Genscher's branding of Iraq as the aggressor on 25 July
1 Sept. 1987		**Iraq renews tanker war (stopped after UN Res. 598)**
24 Dec. 1987	UN Sec. Council	statement by President of Council
8 Jan. 1988	Syria	attempts to mediate; reports some success
29 Feb. 1988		**"SCUD-B" missiles launched at Tehran**
16 March 1988	UN Sec. Council	statement by President of Council
2 April 1988	Turkish PM	visits parties in attempt to end war
18 April 1988		**Iraq retakes Fao**
9 May 1988	UN Sec. Council	Resolution 612 (1988)
3 July 1988		**US destroys Iranian airliner; 290 killed**
12 July 1988		**UN Security Council meets at Iran's request**
17 July 1988		**Iraq offers cease-fire**
19 July 1988		**Iran accepts UN Resolution (598) on cease-fire**
8 Aug. 1988	UN Sec. Council	statement by President of Council
20 Aug. 1988		**Cease-fire**

Appendix 3e: The Gulf Crisis and the Gulf War
(2 August 1990 - 29 February 1991)

2 Aug.	1990	Iraqi invasion of Kuwait; UN Resolution 660, condemning invasion, demanding withdrawal
6 August		UN Resolution 661, imposing embargo
9 Aug.		UN Resolution 662, rendering annexation of Kuwait invalid
18 Aug.		UN Resolution 664, demanding release of third party nationals
25 Aug.		UN Resolution 665, ensuring naval blockade
13 Sept.		UN Resolution 666, considering humanitarian needs of Iraq and Kuwait
16 Sept.		UN Resolution 667, demanding release of foreign nationals and protection of diplomatic staff
24 Sept.		UN Resolution 669, dealing with requests under art. 50 of the Charter
25 Sept.		UN Resolution 670, ensuring air and naval blockade
29 Oct.		UN Resolution 674, regarding treatment of nationals and compensation
28 Nov.		UN Resolution 677, regarding changes to demographic composition of Kuwait
29 Nov.		UN Resolution 678, outlining 15 Jan. 1991 deadline, and authorization of states to use "all necessary means" after that date
17 Jan.	1991	war begins
18 Jan.		five Iraqi missiles hit Israel
20 Jan.		allied POWs shown on Iraqi television, causing widespread international outrage
21 Jan.		de Cuellar transmits Algerian, Indian, and Soviet Peace plans
22 Jan.		Iraq sets fire to several oil installations in Kuwait
23 Jan.		Iran calls for "Islamic solution", with little response
28 Jan.		accusatory letter from Aziz to de Cuellar; new Iranian peace proposal first Iraqi ground attack at Khafji -- caused first US casualties
29 Jan.		new Soviet initiative announced
30 Jan.		joint Soviet-American cease-fire offer
31 Jan.		Jordanian convoy hit
5 Feb.		Iraq breaks diplomatic ties with US, UK and others
7 Feb.		New Indian peace plan; Hammadi's announcement concerning willingness
11 Feb.		to negotiate
12 Feb.		Primakov visit
13 Feb.		US bombers destroy air raid shelter in Amiriya, Baghdad, killing 300+; coalition insists shelter was military target, and civilian deaths unintentional; accusations that Saddam Hussein put civilians there deliberately; NAM missions announced Security Council meeting; first session
14 Feb.		SC meeting, 1st resumption, after Hussein announces his willingness to deal
15 Feb.		with Resolution 660
16 Feb.		SC meeting, 2nd resumption; adjourned to 23 February
19 Feb.		Gorbachov announces last ditch Soviet effort
22 Feb.		Hussein accepts Soviet proposal
23 Feb.		SC meeting, 3rd resumption; 2000 hrs Baghdad time, expiry of US deadline to begin withdrawal
24 Feb.		0400 hrs Baghdad time, coalition ground offensive begins
25 Feb.		SC meeting, 4th resumption
27 Feb.		Aziz cables president of Security Council
28 Feb.		Hussein agrees to comply with all SC resolutions; 0500 hrs Baghdad time, coalition forces cease fire

Appendix 3f: The Yugoslav Conflict (Slovenian and Croatian Phases)
25 June 1991 - 7 April 1992

CF -- refers to a cease-fire agreement; *CF refers to a cease-fire agreement made but not implemented, or an agreement made but only partially implemented.

Note: the chronology details only the first two phases of the conflict (Slovenian and Croatian), and the beginnings of the third (Bosnian) phase -- not the conflict in its entirety.

25 June 1991   Croatia and Slovenia declare independence; federal government orders federal police and army to take control of borders.
27 June   YA troop movement begins 0900; units head for borders with Austria and Hungary; Slovene forces resist; Croatia orders federal army to withdraw to barracks; EC Council of Ministers meets at Luxembourg summit -- decides to send "troika" to Yugoslavia ("Troika" -- Gianni de Michelis, Jacques Poos, Hans van den Broek, foreign ministers of Italy, Luxembourg and the Netherlands)
28 June   YA stops activity at 1500 having secured border posts; Slovenia refuses cease-fire, says YA should first return to barracks; troika arrives -- cease-fire negotiated (CF1); terms include federal troops to return to barracks, 3-month suspension in implementation of Slovene declaration of independence, Stipe Mesić (Croatian representative of the federal rotating presidency) to be elected to the office of President of the Collective Presidency; falls apart within 24 hours
30 June   EC mission returns; threatens to freeze economic aid if no cease-fire; meeting between Ante Marković (Federal PM), Milan Kučan (Slovene President), and Lojže Peterle (Slovene PM), agreement that YA should return to barracks on 1 July. Mesić takes office
---   ---
1 July   YA begins return to barracks; Slovenes blockade some units on basis that YA should leave equipment behind
2 July   Mesić and Kučan, supported by Kiro Gligorov, (Macedonian president), send joint statement to Marković and General Veljko Kadijević (Federal Defence Secretary) calling for cease-fire, return to barracks, and high-level talks
3 July   CSCE Committee of Senior Officials (CSO) meets in Prague, endorses EC mission return to barracks continues, but further disputes over control of border posts
4 July   Slovenia demobilizes 10,000 men; EC arms embargo imposed on Yugoslavia;
5 July   sporadic fighting across Croatian-Serbian border
               EC troika meets with Yugoslav parties at Brioni, cease-fire plan agreed (CF2),
7 July   calls for army return to barracks, 3-month freeze on implementation of independence declarations, unarmed European observer mission (OM) to monitor cease-fire for three months, YA to withdraw to barracks, blockades of barracks to be lifted, and Slovene police to control borders
               Federal presidency complains that blockades still not lifted
8 July   further accusations of violations
9 July   Slovene parliament ratifies peace plan; federal troops complaining of tank traps
11 July   and minefields outside army barracks; attempted YA incursion from Croatia - retires after "discussions" with Slovene police at border
15 July   major fighting near Croatian-Serbian border, YA attacking Croatian police station
17 July   Slovenia cuts power to five federal army bases in protest against federal refusal to re-open Slovene airspace
18 July   Federal announcement that all troops to be withdrawn from Slovenia over next three months; Kadijević assures Croatia that it will not be attacked; advance team of EC observers arrives

22 July	federal proposal that if Croatia demobilized all its "illegal" paramilitary forces, federal troops would return to barracks
23 July	meeting of Yugoslav leaders in Ohrid; Franjo Tudjman (Croatian President) walks out of talks; tells Croatia to prepare for all-out war; Hans Dietrich Genscher (German Foreign Minister) suggests extension of OM to Croatia
31 July	Croatia announces fresh forces to be thrown into conflict with Serbian guerrilla forces in Croatia; offers to talk to any democratically chosen representatives of Serbian minority; Federal presidency endorses cease-fire proposal, Croatia given 2 days to accept

---   ---

1 August	EC announces new cease-fire initiative
2 August	Tudjman calls for EC observers
3 August	Serbian veto blocks Yugoslav Presidency accepting extension of OM
6 August	EC Council of Ministers decides to extend OM
7 August	Federal presidency redrafts cease-fire proposal; rejected by Mesić
8 August	unilateral cease-fire declared by Serbian rump-federal presidency; accepted in part by Croatia (CF3); CSO endorses extension of OM and appeals for cease-fire
9 August	cease-fire apparently holding; minor violations alleged
14 August	Federal presidency says cease-fire holding; Croatia complains of serious violations
26 August	general increase in military action; Croatia accused by Federal cease-fire commission of launching "large-scale armed conflict"
27 August	Croatian-YA representatives meet; decision to attempt truce again
28 August	Federal presidency "insists" on cease-fire; Mesić says YA out of control; EC plan announced detailing cease-fire deadlines, agreement to an international peace conference, and Western arbitration; Slobodan Milošević (Serbian President) rejects suggestion of EC or Western peacekeeping troops; YA now openly supporting Serb rebels in Croatia

---   ---

2 September	first EC-sponsored cease-fire (*CF4) in Croatia comes into effect; federal authorities and all republics agree to EC convening Conference on Yugoslavia; fighting continues virtually unabated, though some signs that it might take effect
3 September	CSO meets in Prague, confirms extension of OM and backs EC Conference
5 September	Serb rebels and YA now control about one-quarter of Croatia
7 September	EC sponsored Conference on Yugoslavia under Lord Carrington, EC "Special Envoy", opens in the Hague, all sides commit themselves to truce (*CF5); EC announces it would grant formal EC association status to republics if Yugoslavia committed itself to long-term settlement; Dutch officials argue for emplacement of observers
8 September	OM extended to Croatia; Mesić warns that continued refusal to do so would result in his declaration that a coup had taken place
12 September	Mesić threatens to call for foreign intervention; Kadijević agrees to return to barracks on condition that Serb irregulars and Croatian forces do so simultaneously; complaints of violations on all sides; EC observers complain of insufficient numbers
13 September	EC concedes OM not successful
16 September	Croatia goes on offensive, taking federal barracks and fighting for ports
17 September	cease-fire agreed, to take effect at noon 18 September (CF6)
18 September	EC monitors call for instant and simultaneous withdrawal of YA, Serbian and Croatian forces from battle zones; cease-fire does not take effect as planned; Lord Carrington suggests both sides be allowed 24 hours to enforce the agree-

ment; WEU ministers discuss Dutch proposal for lightly-armed peacekeeping troops

20 September federal bases continue to be blockaded by Croatian troops; large YA armored column leaves Belgrade, heads for Croatian border; Dutch call for lightly armed peacekeeping troops, Helmut Kohl (German Chancellor) and François Mitterand (French President) agree that effective cease-fire monitoring and peacekeeping force needed; Croatian call not just for peacekeeping forces, but peace-making forces

21 September YA column moves into Croatia with 700 tanks, APCs and troop trucks cease-fire agreed (CF7), this time between YA and Croatia; takes effect at 1500;

23 September fighting decreases dramatically but many apparent "violations"; YA steps down blockade of Croatian ports; Croatia restores power and water to blockaded barracks

25 September parties meet in secret, agree to "maintain and fortify the truce"; heavy fighting reported at Vinkovci, site of surrounded and besieged federal unit; UN Resolution 713 passed, imposing arms embargo, considering question of peacekeeping force, and encouraging peaceful settlement

30 September WEU ministers discuss four proposals for peacekeeping force; further violations, observers note that both sides have problems of control

---   ---

1 October   400 YA tanks head for besieged barracks in eastern Croatia

3 October   Croatian ports re-blockaded; Dubrovnik under attack; fighting near Vukovar at blockaded barracks

4 October   Milošević, Tudjman and Kadijević meet with van den Broek (President of the Council of EC Ministers) in the Hague; meeting produces further agreement (*CF8): Milošević ostensibly forswears territorial ambitions in Croatia in exchange for special minority status for Serbs in Croatia; negotiations to continue on basis of right to independence of those republics wishing it, recognition to be granted in a 3-part framework resulting in loose association of sovereign republics; Tudjman agrees on steps to lift blockades of federal barracks; Kadijević promises to order regrouping of federal units in Croatia with assistance of EC monitors; EC discusses possibility of "diplomatic quarantine" for Yugoslavia

5 October   Tudjman refuses to lift blockade of barracks until federal troops cease fire; federal troops refuse to cease fire until the blockade lifted; Tudjman offers simultaneous lifting of blockade and cease-fire, offer rejected; Yugoslav forces continue to attack Dubrovnik

6 October   Tudjman calls Croatia to arms; EC threatens that unless parties cease fire by 2400 on 7 October, EC threatens to suspend trade and co-operation agree ment with Yugoslavia (in effect, imposes economic sanctions on Yugoslavia)

7 October   Presidential Palace in Zagreb attacked from air; YA appear poised for major offensive on Zagreb

8 October   Croatia-Slovenia implement declarations of independence (Brioni 3-month mora-torium now over); Croatia-YA agree to cease-fire 1800 (CF9), cease-fire agreement specifies army to leave all barracks in Croatia, with equipment, simultaneous lifting of land and sea blockades; Mesić asks for military buffer zone between Serbia and Croatia; EC decides not to impose sanctions because of agreement; Cyrus Vance appointed as UN Secretary-General's "Special Envoy"

9 October   YA begins to dismantle blockade; some violations, probably by Serb irregulars

10 October   EC talks with Yugoslav parties, van den Broek pressurizes Serbian camp; CSO meets in Prague, backs EC

11 October	base blockades in Zagreb lifted; federal naval blockade lifted; YA denies agreement to leave Croatia within one month was made; van den Broek says agreement was verbal; Vance begins first mission
15 October	Muslim and Croatian deputies in Bosnia-Hercegovina declare republic's sovereignty; Serb deputies declare move illegal; Milošević and Tudjman meet Mikhail Gorbachov (Soviet President) in Moscow, pledge themselves to peaceful settlement; CF9 continues to hold in general, some violations, especially at Vukovar
18 October	Republican leaders tentatively accept new EC draft constitutional plan; cease-fire deadline set for 1100, 19 October (CF10); local cease-fire agreed at Vukovar for humanitarian aid
22 October	CSO reaffirms support for EC
23 October	continued fighting at Vukovar; sporadic fighting elsewhere
24 October	Dubrovnik under heavy attack; Hague peace talks boycotted by Serbian rump-Federal Presidency
27 October	federal forces cease fire on Dubrovnik to allow evacuation of civilians
28 October	EC gives Serbia until 5 November to accept new peace plan, failure to accept will result in "escalating" sanctions; plenary sessions of EC Conference suspended; bombardment and siege of Vukovar continues

--- ---

3 November	Vance begins second mission (ends 9 November)
4 November	Serbian Socialist Party rejects EC plan for new Yugoslavia; Greece considers veto of sanctions
5 November	Carrington receives verbal agreement from Kadijević and Tudjman that they will make a cease-fire last
8 November	EC sanctions imposed - 1980 trade agreement suspended, but compensatory measures for those republics considered to be working for peace; Yugoslav Presidency approaches Security Council, requests UN presence in Yugoslavia; NATO summit supports efforts of EC, CSCE, and UN
11 November	Yugoslav participation in G24 blocked
12 November	Carrington returns to discuss possibility of peacekeeping troops after both sides make request; EC agrees to ask UN to send peacekeeping troops
13 November	EC relief ferry arrives in Dubrovnik; UN Security Council begins deliberations on possibility of peacekeeping troops
14 November	new YA offensive in Croatia
15 November	EC sanctions come into effect
16 November	Vance's third mission (to 24 November) to determine whether republics are prepared to respect a cease-fire, a basic precondition of decision to send peacekeeping troops; new cease-fire agreed (CF11) which reaffirms terms of CF10 -- to come into effect at 1800
17 November	fighting continues near Vukovar
18 November	Vukovar falls after 92-day siege; WEU agrees that members' naval vessels might be used for humanitarian aid
20 November	Osijek shelled
23 November	new cease-fire (CF12) agreed in Geneva
27 November	UN Security Council Resolution 721, gives full backing to peacekeeping force, provided cease-fire holds; continued shelling of Osijek
28 November	Italy, Germany, UK announce readiness to recognize Slovenia and Croatia
29 November	Croatian forces lift blockade of Marshal Tito barracks in Zagreb; YA begins withdrawal from Zagreb; cease-fire appears to be holding; CSO meets in Prague, confirms earlier CSCE positions, Yugoslavia does not attend

--- ---

1 December   some violations; cease-fire generally holding
2 December   EC restores trade benefits, financial co-operation and PHARE to Slovenia, Croatia,
             Bosnia-Hercegovina and Macedonia, back-dated to 15 November
4 December   Vance and Kadijević hold talks in attempt to make cease-fire hold; fighting
             at Osijek continues
6 December   YA assault on Dubrovnik; US imposes sanctions on all republics; general increase
             in fighting in all areas
10 December local cease-fire in Zagreb as troops withdraw and prisoners exchanged
14 December UN Security Council Resolution 724, agrees to send advance team of observers,
             probably 12 civilian, 6 military
27 December UN observers arrive; fighting continues
28 December Vance arrives for fifth visit (to 4 January); confirms that no peacekeeping force
             will go to "Yugoslavia" until cease-fire observed
---   ---
2 Jan.   1992 Croatia and Serbia agree to UN force deployment, which hinges on stable cease-
             fire; new cease-fire (negotiated by Vance) agreed (CF13), to come into effect
             on 3 January
3 January   CF13 comes into effect
6 January   UN prepares to send 50 military observers to "Yugoslavia"; some violations
             but cease-fire generally holding
7 January   YA air force shoots down EC helicopter; five OM members killed
8 January   UN Resolution 727, adopts plan to send 50 military liaison observers; Kadijević
             resigns, replaced temporarily by General Blagoje Adžić, YA Chief of Staff
9 January   EC peace conference reconvenes in Brussels
10 January   Milan Babić (Serbian leader of the self-proclaimed "Krajina Republic") opposes
             UN plan on basis that it provides insufficient guarantees for minority Serbs
             in Croatia
15 January   EC members recognize independence of Slovenia and Croatia, withholds
             recognition of Macedonia and Bosnia-Hercegovina; UN advance team of 45
             arrives as cease-fire holds generally
20 January   Babić again rules out deployment of UN observers in Krajina region
21 January   both sides accuse each other of violations; Serbian draft law to allow "nations
             wishing to remain in common state" to form new parliament and other institu-
             tions
23 January   "Helsinki Watch" reports that Serbian irregular forces responsible for executions
             of up to 200 civilians
31 January   Serbian regular and irregular leaders meet to "discuss" deployment of UN
             peacekeeping forces
---   ---
3 February   Babić claims his agreement with other Serbian leaders for UN deployment
             extracted by "police methods and torture"
4 February   Carrington arrives in Yugoslavia to "knock heads together in Zagreb and
             Belgrade"; advance UN force to be increased to 75 as cease-fire holds
6 February   Tudjman drops objections to UN force; Babić now only remaining opposition
             to UN plan; some Security Council members argue for partial deployment,
             Vance disagrees; Carrington announces talks on future of Bosnia-Hercegovina
             to be held within a week
7 February   UN Resolution 740, calls for hold-out leaders to accept UN plans for deployment
             and increases observers from 50 to 75; Babić announces plan for referendum
             on question of deployment
11 February Croatia renews opposition to UN plan after Boutros Boutros Ghali (new UN
             Secretary General) announces that Serb areas within Croatia will remain outside

	Croatian control under UN peacekeeping plan; Tudjman claims this is not what was agreed
16 February	Europe discusses merits of recognising Macedonia and Bosnia-Herc.
18 February	Babić postpones referendum on UN plan
19 February	UN announces that political settlement of Yugoslavia to be left in hands of Carrington; Ghali recommends immediate dispatch of peacekeeping forces (to be known as UNPROFOR: UN Protection Force)
21 February	UN Resolution 743 establishes UNPROFOR for 12 months; Babić agrees to peace plan and disarming of militia, explaining that basic objections had been satisfied (including explicit UN acknowledgement that Croatian authority would not apply in Serb enclaves); YA to be withdrawn from areas occupied by UN; Croatia announces Croatian law will apply in all areas; Genscher states that after his visit, Tudjman has no more objections; ethnic leaders in Bosnia-Hercegovina agree that republic's borders should remain unchanged
24 February	US, UK, France argue that UNPROFOR budget too high and needs to be reduced by half before approval
26 February	Serbian sources report Babić ousted, replaced by Goran Hadžić, "Prime Minister of the (self-proclaimed) Serbian Autonomous Region of Slavonia, Baranja and Western Srem", Hadžić supports UN plan; Serbia offers new commitment to EC peace conference
27 February	artillery attacks in Croatia; first major violation of 4 January cease-fire
---	---
1 March	Bosnia-Hercegovina independence referendum; 63 per cent (99 per cent of those who vote, mostly Muslims and Croats) vote "yes"; sporadic violence in republic in wake of vote; Montenegrin referendum vote in favor of continued union with Serbia
2 March	Serbs in Bosnia-Hercegovina raise barricades around Sarajevo
3 March	agreement reached to dismantle barricades; Vance in Belgrade to discuss UNPROFOR deployment
6 March	Vance visits Bosnia-Hercegovina; claims agreement between ethnic communities reached, promises to seek peaceful settlement; announcement that UNPROFOR to be fully deployed by 15 April -- headquarters to be in Sarajevo; Alija Izetbegović (President of Bosnia-Hercegovina) announces he will seek negotiations to allow YA withdrawal from Bosnia-Hercegovina if republic is recognized
10 March	General Satish Nambiar (Indian commander of UNPROFOR) arrives in Zagreb; fighting continues in east and south Croatia; UNPROFOR to be deployed in Serb-controlled regions of Eastern and Western Slavonia, and in Krajina
12 March	European Parliament calls for EC recognition of Bosnia-Hercegovina
16 March	UN troops begin full deployment; 350 advance troops head for war zones
17 March	UN advance troops now in forward positions
18 March	agreement between ethnic groups in Bosnia-Hercegovina signed; basic agreement to divide republic into ethnic "cantons"
23 March	fighting in Hercegovina between YA and Croatian forces
26 March	Slovenia urges CSCE to recognize Bosnia-Hercegovina and Macedonia; fighting continues in Bosnia-Hercegovina at Bosanski Brod and Derventa; western diplomats warning that slow pace of UN deployment allowing militants on all sides to prepare for Spring campaign
27 March	more violence in Bosanski Brod; leader of Serbian "assembly" in Bosnia-Hercegovina announces creation of "Serbian Republic of Bosnia-Hercegovina" which would join Yugoslavia
30 March	leaders of Bosnia-Hercegovina meet in Brussels
31 March	1300 French UN troops leave France

---   ---

1 April	4-point agreement in Brussels between presidents of all republics, undertaking to dismantle trade restrictions, restore transport and communication links, work to restore power and flow of oil
3 April	Bosnia-Hercegovina asks UN for military help to end fighting, which has now spread across northern Bosnia-Hercegovina (local ethnic militias attempt to gain territory before recognition and division)
5 April	severe escalation of fighting in Bosnia-Hercegovina; casualties now in the hundreds (massacres of Muslims by Serbs reported at Kupres and Bijeljina); leaders agree to new political talks and all call for cease-fire
6 April	Serbian forces in Bosnia-Hercegovina fight for control of Sarajevo; large demonstrations for peace there; UN headquarters attacked
7 April	EC recognizes Bosnia-Hercegovina; recognition of Macedonia withheld because of continuing Greek objections, despite Macedonia's meeting of conditions for recognition; fighting continues; US recognizes Slovenia, Croatia, and Bosnia-Hercegovina; Security Council authorizes earliest possible full deployment of peace-keeping troops; Ghali announces that violations of January cease-fire now total 100-200 per day; 800 French UN troops in Krajina region.

Bibliography

Books, Theses, Memoirs, and Journal Articles

Abbas, Ferhat. 1980. *Autopsie d'un Guerre*. Paris: Editions Garniers Frères.

Abt, Clark Claus. 1965. *The Termination of General War*. PhD Thesis. MIT. Supervisor: William Kaufmann.

Acland, Andrew. 1990. *A Sudden Outbreak of Common Sense*. London: Hutchinson.

Adan, Avraham. 1980. *On the Banks of the Suez*. London: Arms and Armour Press.

Agee, Philip. "Speech by Philip Agee" (available on CRTNET, or through Mike Cole, University of California, San Diego).

Akpan, Ntieyong U. 1971. *The Struggle for Secession 1966-1970*. London: Frank Cass.

Albert, Stuart, and Edward C. Luck, eds. 1980. *On the Endings of Wars*. London: Kennikat Press.

Bailey, Sydney D. 1974. "The Prospects for Real Peace." *Survival (Strategic Forum: The Middle East Conflict, 1973)*.

_____. 1982. *How Wars End: The United Nations and the Termination of Armed Conflict, 1946-1964* (2 vols.). Oxford: Clarendon Press.

_____. 1985. "Non-Official Mediation in Disputes: Reflections on Quaker Experience." *International Affairs* 61: 205-222.

_____. 1990. *Four Arab-Israeli Wars and the Peace Process*. London: Macmillan.

Bakhash, Shaul. 1985. *The Reign of the Ayatollahs: Iran and the Islamic Revolution*. London: I.B. Tauris & Co.

Bani-Sadr, Abol Hassan. 1991. *My Turn to Speak: Iran, the Revolution, and Secret Deals with the U.S.* Washington: Brassey's.

Bar-Siman-Tov, Yaacov. 1987. *Israel, the Superpowers, and the War in the Middle East*. London: Praeger.

Bastid, Madame Paul. 1974. "Le Cessez-le-feu." *Société Internationale de Droit pénal militaire et de droit de la guerre [Actes du]*, 6ᵉ Congrès internationale, La Haye, 22-25 Mai, 1973: 19-41.

Baxter, R.R. 1976. "Armistices and Other Forms of Suspension of Hostilities." *Recueil des cours de l'Académie de droit Internationale* 149: 353-399.

Behr, Edward. 1961. *The Algerian Problem*. London: Hodder and Stoughton.

Bella, Ben. 1967. *Ben Bella (transliterations of recordings made by Ben Bella by Robert Merle)* (translated by Camilla Sykes). London: Michael Joseph.

Beloff, Max. 1968. "Reflections on Intervention." *Journal of International Affairs* 22: 198-207.

Ben Khedda, Benyousef. 1986. *Les Accords d'Evian*. Publisud-OPU.

Bercovitch, Jacob. 1991. "International Mediation." *Journal of Peace Research* 28: 3-6.

Bercovitch, Jacob, J. Theodore Anagnosen, and Donnette L. Wille. 1991. "Some Conceptual Issues and Empirical Trends in the Study of Successful Mediation in International Relations." *Journal of Peace Research* 28: 7-17.

Berman, Maureen R. and Joseph E. Johnson. 1977. *Unofficial Diplomats*. New York: Colombia University Press.

Bernadotte, Count Folke. 1951. *To Jerusalem* (translated by Joan Bulman). London: Hodders and Stoughton.

Berridge, G.R. 1989. "Diplomacy and the Angola/Namibia Accords." *International Affairs* 65: 463-79.

Blainey, Geoffrey. 1973. *The Causes of War*. New York: Free Press.

Blechman, Barry M. and Stephen S. Kaplan. 1976. "The Use of Armed Forces as a Political Instrument (Executive Summary)." Brookings Institute.

Bloomfield, Lincoln P. and Amelia C. Leiss. 1970. *Controlling Small Wars: A Strategy for the 1970s*. London: Penguin Press.

Bowett, D.W. 1972. *The Search for Peace*. London: Routledge and Kegan Paul.

Brace, Richard and Joan Brace. 1960. *Ordeal in Algeria*. Princeton: D. van Nostrand Co.

Brown, Bert R. 1977. "Face-Saving and Face-Restoration in Negotiation," in Daniel Druckman, ed., *Negotiations: Social-Psychological Perspectives*. Pp. 275-299. London: Sage.

Brookmire, David A. and Sistrunk, Frank. 1980. "The Effects of Perceived Ability and Impartiality of Mediators on Time Pressure in Negotiation." *Journal of Conflict Resolution* 24: 311-327.

Bull, Hedley, ed. 1986. *Intervention in World Politics*. Oxford: Oxford University Press.

Burton, John. 1990. *Conflict Resolution and Prevention*. London: Macmillan.

Burton, John, and Frank Dukes. 1990. *Conflict: Practices, Settlement, and Resolution*. London: Macmillan.

_____. 1990. *Conflict: Readings in Management and Resolution*. London: Macmillan.

Carroll, Berenice A. 1969. "How Wars End: An Analysis of Some Current Hypotheses." *Journal of Peace Research* 6: 295-322.

_____. "War Termination and Conflict Theory: Value Premise, Theory and Policies," in William T.R. Fox, ed., *How Wars End: Annals of the American Academy of Political and Social Science*. Pp. 14-29. Philadelphia: Academy of Political and Social Science, Vol. 392.

Castel, J.G. 1965. *International Law (chiefly as interpreted and applied in Canada)*. Toronto: University of Toronto Press.

Cervenka, Zdenik. 1971. *The Nigerian War 1967-70 (History of the War and Selected Documents)*. Frankfurt am Mein: Bernard and Graefe.

Chubin, Shahram, and Charles Tripp. 1988. *Iran and Iraq at War*. London: I.B. Tauris and Co. Ltd.

Cimbala, Stephen. 1987. "The Endgame and War," in in Stephen J. Cimbala and Keith A. Dunn, eds., *Conflict Termination and Military Strategy: Coercion, Persuasion, and War*. Pp. 1-14. Boulder: Westview.

Cimbala, Stephen J. and Keith A. Dunn, eds. 1987. *Conflict Termination and Military Strategy: Coercion, Persuasion, and War*. Boulder: Westview.

Clark, Michael K. 1960. *Algeria in Turmoil: A History of the Rebellion*. London: Thames and Hudson.

Cook, Don. 1984. *Charles de Gaulle*. London: Secker and Warburg.

Coser, Lewis. 1961. "The Termination of Conflict." *Journal of Conflict Resolution* 5: 351-357.

Cronje, Suzanne. 1972. *The World and Nigeria: A Diplomatic History of the Biafran War 1967-70*. London: Sedgewick and Jackson.

Crozier, Brian. 1973. *De Gaulle: the Statesman*. London: Eyre Methuen.

Curle, Adam. 1986. *In the Middle: Non-Official Mediation in Violent Situations*. Bradford Peace Studies Papers (New Series No. 1). New York: Berg.

_____. 1990. *Tools for Transformation: A Personal Study*. Stroud: Hawthorne.

Dayan, Moshe. 1976. *Story of My Life*. London: Weidenfeld and Nicolson.

Dismukes, Bradford, and James M. McConnell, eds. 1979. *Soviet Naval Diplomacy*. New York: Pergamon.

Druckman, Daniel, ed. 1977. *Negotiations: Social-Psychological Perspectives*. London: Sage.

Dunnigan, James F., and William Martel. 1987. *How to Stop a War: The Lessons of Two Hundred Years of War and Peace*. London: Doubleday.

Eban, Abba. 1978. *An Autobiography*. London: Weidenfeld and Nicolson.

Festinger, Leon. 1957. *A Theory of Cognitive Dissonance*. London: Row, Peterson and Co.

Fisher, Roger. 1969. *Basic Negotiating Strategy*. New York: Harper and Row.

Fisher, Roger, and Ury, William. 1981. *Getting to Yes*. London: Hutchinson Business.

Fisher, Ronald J. 1972. "Third Party Consultation: A Method for the Study and Resolution of Conflict." *Journal of Conflict Resolution* 16: 67-94.

Fisher, Ronald J. and Loraleigh Keashly. 1991. "The Potential Complementarity of Mediation and Consultation Within a Contingency Model of Third Party Intervention." *Journal of Peace Research* 28: 29-42.

Foster, James L. and Gary D. Brewer. 1976. "And the Clocks Were Striking Thirteen: the Termination of War." *Policy Sciences* 7: 225-243.

Fox, William T.R. 1970. "The Causes of Peace and Conditions of War," in William T.R. Fox, ed., *How Wars End: Annals of the American Academy of Political and Social Science*. Pp. 1-13. Philadelphia: Academy of Political and Social Science, Vol. 392.

de Gaulle, General Charles. 1971. *Mémoires of Hope* (translated by Terence Kilmartin). London: Weidenfeld and Nicolson.

Golan, Galia. 1975. *Yom Kippur and After*. Cambridge: Cambridge University Press.

Gow, James, and J.D.D. Smith. 1992. "Peacemaking, Peacekeeping: European Security and the Yugoslav Conflict." *London Defence Studies* 11 (London: Brassey's for the Centre for Defence Studies).

Greenspan, Morris. 1959. *The Modern Law of Land Warfare*. Los Angeles: University of California Press.

Greffenius, Steven, and Jungil Gill. 1992. "Pure Coercion vs. Carrot-and-Stick Offers in Crisis Bargaining." *Journal of Peace Research* 29: 39-52.

Handel, Michael. 1978. "The Study of War Termination. *Journal of Strategic Studies* 1: 51-74.

_____. 1982. "War Termination -- A Critical Survey," in Nissan Oren, ed., *Termination of Wars*. Pp. 40-71. Jerusalem: Magnes Press (The Hebrew University).

Harbi, Mohammed. 1981. *Les archives de la révolution algérienne*. Paris: les éditions jeune afrique.

Harrison, Alexander. 1989. *Challenging de Gaulle: The OAS and the Counterrevolution in Algeria, 1954-1962*. New York: Praeger.

Harrison, Selig S. 1988. "Inside the Afghan Talks." *Foreign Policy* 72: 31-60.

Hastings, Max. 1987. *The Korean War*. London: Pan Books.

Hay, Robin. 1990. "Humanitarian Cease-fires: an Examination of their Potential Contribution to the Resolution of Conflict." Ottawa: Canadian Institute for International Peace and Security.

Herzog, Chaim. 1975. *The War of Atonement*. London: Weidenfeld and Nicolson.

_____. 1987. "A Military-Strategic Overview," in Efraim Karsh, ed., *The Iran-Iraq War: Impact and Implications*. Pp. 255-268. London: Macmillan.

Hirst, David, and Irene Beeson. 1981. *Sadat*. London: Faber & Faber.

Hollins, Harry B., Averill L. Powers, and Mark Sommer. 1989. *The Conquest of War*. Boulder: Westview.

Horne, Alistair. 1977. *A Savage War of Peace*. London: Macmillan.

Howard, Michael. 1983. *The Causes of Wars*. London: Temple Smith.

Hull, Thomas N. 1974. "The Organisation of African Unity and the Peaceful Resolution of Internal Warfare: The Nigerian Case," in David D. Smith (ed.) and Robert F. Randle (commentary), *From War to Peace: Essays in Peacemaking and War Termination*. Pp. 93-124. New York: Columbia University Press.

Hutchinson, Martha Crenshaw. 1978. *Revolutionary Terrorism: The FLN in Algeria, 1954-1962*. Stanford: Hoover Institution Press.

Iklé, Fred Charles. 1971. *Every War Must End*. London: Columbia University Press.

_____. 1976. *How Nations Negotiate*. London: Harper and Row.

Ikoku, S.G. "La Sécession Biafran: Mythes et Réalités." *Revue Français d'Etudes Politique Africaines* 49: 56-64.

Ilan, Amitzur. 1989. *Bernadotte in Palestine, 1948*. London: Macmillan.

Janis, Irving L. 1972. *Victims of Groupthink*. Boston: Houghton Mifflin.

Jervis, Robert. 1976. *Perception and Misperception in International Relations*. Princeton: Princeton University Press.

_____. 1989. *The Logic of Images in International Relations*. New York: Columbia University Press.

Jester, Robert S. 1990. "The 1988 Peace Accords and the Future of Southwest Africa." *International Institute of Strategic Studies Adelphi Paper* 253.

Joy, Vice Admiral C. Turner. 1978. *How Communists Negotiate*. California: Fidelis.

_____. 1978. *Negotiating While Fighting: The Diary of Admiral C. Turner Joy at the Korean Armistice Conference*. Stanford: Hoover Press.

Kaplan, Stephen S. *et al*. 1979. "Mailed Fist, Velvet Glove: Soviet Armed Forces as a Political Intrument." Brookings Institute.

Karsh, Efraim. 1987a. "From Ideological Zeal to Geopolitical Realism: The Islamic Republic and the Gulf War," in Efraim Karsh, ed., *The Iran-Iraq War: Impact and Implications*. Pp. 26-41. London: Macmillan.

_____. 1987b. "The Iran-Iraq War: A Military Analysis." *International Institute of Strategic Studies Adelphi Paper* 220.

_____. 1988. *Neutrality and Small States*. London: Routledge.

Karsh, Efraim, and Rautsi, Inari. 1991. *Saddam Hussein: A Political Biography*. New York: Macmillan Free Press.

Kimche, Jon and David Kimche. 1960. *Both Sides of the Hill: Britain and the Palestine War*. London: Secker and Warburg.

King, Ralph. 1987. "The Iran-Iraq War: The Political Implications." *International Institute of Strategic Studies Adelphi Paper* 219.

Kirk-Greene, A.H.M. 1971. *Crisis and Conflict in Nigeria: Volume II -- A Documentary Sourcebook 1966-1970*. London: Oxford University Press.

Kissinger, Henry. 1974. "Excerpts from the Press Conference of Secretary of State Henry Kissinger, 25 October 1973." *Survival (Strategic Forum: The Middle East Conflict, 1973)*. January-February 1974: 28-34.

_____. 1982. *Years of Upheaval*. London: Weidenfeld and Nicolson.

Knorr, Klaus. 1973. *Power and Wealth: the Political Economy of International Relations*. New York: Basic Books.

Kriesberg, Louis. 1991. "Formal and Quasi-Mediators in International Disputes: An Exploratory Analysis." *Journal of Peace Research* 28: 19-27.

Kuper, Leo. 1985. *The Prevention of Genocide*. London: Yale University Press.

Lacouture, Jean. 1984. *Pierre Mendès-France* (translation by George Holoch). New York: Holmes and Meier.

_____. 1991. *De Gaulle: the Ruler* (translation by Alan Sheridan). London: Harvill.

Lauterpacht, H., ed. 1952. *Oppenheim's International Law, vol. 2: Disputes, War and Neutrality* (7th ed). London: Longmans, Green & Co.

Leltenberg, Milton and Gabriel Sheffer. 1979. *Great Power Intervention in the Middle East*. New York: Pergamon.

Levie, Col. Howard S. 1956. "The Nature and Scope of the Armistice Agreement." *American Journal of International Law* 50: 880-906.

Lewer, Nick and Oliver Ramsbotham. 1993. "'Something must be done': Towards an Ethical Framework for Humanitarian Intervention in International-Social Conflict'. *Peace Research Report* 33 (Bradford: Dept. of Peace Studies).

Lewidge, Bernard. 1982. *De Gaulle*. London: Weidenfeld and Nicolson.

Lieurance, Peter R. 1974. "'Negotiation Now!': the National Committee for a Political Settlement in Vietnam," in David D. Smith (ed.) and Robert F. Randle (commentary), *From War to Peace: Essays in Peacemaking and War Termination*. Pp. 171-195. New York: Columbia University Press.

Luard, Evan. 1986. *War in International Society*. London: I.B. Tauris & Co. Ltd.

Macfarlane, Neil S. 1985. "Intervention and Regional Security." *International Institute of Strategic Studies Adelphi Paper* 196.

Marantz, Paul and Janice Gross Stein, eds. 1985. *Peacemaking in the Middle East*. London: Croom Helm.

Martin, Walter. 1984. "'Quaker Diplomacy' as Peace Witness." *The Friend* 142: 973-975.

Maull, Hanns, and Otto Pick. 1988. *The Gulf War: Regional and International Dimensions*. London: Pinter Publishers.

McNaugher, Thomas L. 1987. "Walking the Tightropes in the Gulf" in Efraim Karsh, ed., *The Iran-Iraq War: Impact and Implications*. Pp. 171-199. London: Macmillan.

Meir, Golda. 1975. *My Life*. London: Weidenfeld and Nicolson.

Mitchell, C.R. 1981. *The Structure of International Conflict*. London: Macmillan.

Mohn, Paul. 1952. "Problems of Truce Supervision." *International Conciliation* 478.

de Montluc, Bertrand. 1971. *Le Cessez-le-feu*. Ph.D. thesis, Univérsité de Droit et d'Economie et de Sciences Sociales de Paris. (Photocopy available from British Library Lending Service, ref. No. fF6 8526.)

Murphy, John F. 1983. *The United Nations and the Control of International Violence: A Legal and Political Analysis*. Manchester: Manchester University Press.

Neff, Donald. 1988. *Warriors Against Israel*. Vermont: Amana and Battleboro.

Nwanko, Arthur Agwuncha, and Samuel Udochukwo Ifejika. 1969. *The Making of a Nation: Biafra*. London: C. Hurst & Co.

O'Ballance, Edgar. 1967. *The Algerian Insurrection, 1954-1962*. London: Faber and Faber.

_____. 1979. *No Victor, No Vanquished: The Yom Kippur War*. London: Barrie and Jenkins.

Ojukwu, Chukwuemeka Odemegwu. 1969a. *Biafra*. New York: Harper and Row.

_____. 1969b. *Biafra: Selected Speeches of Ojukwu*. New York: Harper and Row.

_____. 1989. *Because I Am Involved*. Ibadan: Spectrum Books.

Oren, Nissan. 1982. "Prudence in Victory" in Nissan Oren, ed., *Termination of Wars*. Pp. 147-163. Jerusalem: Magnes Press (The Hebrew University).

Persson, Sune O. 1979. *Mediation and Assassination: Count Bernadotte's Mission in Palestine, 1948*. London: Ithaca Press.

Pillar, Paul R. 1983. *Negotiating Peace: War Termination as a Bargaining Process*. New Jersey: Princeton University Press.

Princen, Tom. 1991. "Camp David: Problem Solving or Power Politics as Usual?." *Journal of Peace Research* 28: 57-69.

Probst, Raymond R. 1989. *Good Offices in the Light of Swiss International Practice and Experience*. Dordrecht: Martinus Nijhoff.

Quandt, William B. 1969. *Revolution and Political Leadership: Algeria, 1954-68*. Massachusetts: MIT.

_____. 1986. *Camp David: Peacemaking and Politics*. Washington: Brookings Institute.

Randle, Robert F. 1970. "The Domestic Origins of Peace," in William T.R. Fox, ed., *How Wars End: Annals of the American Academy of Political and Social Science*. Pp. 76-85. Philadelphia: Academy of Political and Social Science, Vol. 392.

_____. 1973. *The Origins of Peace: A Study of Peacemaking and the Structure of Peace Settlements*. New York: Free Press.

Reich, Bernard, and Rosemary Hollis. 1985. "Peacemaking in the Reagan Administration," in Paul Marantz and Janice Gross Stein, eds., *Peacemaking in the Middle East*. London: Croom Helm.

de Reuck, Anthony. 1985. "The Foundation for International Conciliation; Theory and Practice of Conflict Resolution." 35th Pugwash Conference on Science and World Affairs, Campinas, Sao Paulo, Brazil, 3-8 July 1985.

Richardson, Lewis Frye. 1960. *Statistics of Deadly Quarrels*. Pittsburgh: Boxwood Press.

Roberts, Adam, and Richard Guelff, eds. 1989. *Documents on the Laws of War* (2nd. ed.). Oxford: Clarendon Press.

Rotberg, Robert I. and T.K. Rabb, eds. 1983. *The Origin and Prevention of Major Wars*. Cambridge: Cambridge University Press.

Sabin, Philip A.G. and Efraim Karsh. 1989. "Escalation in the Iran/Iraq War." *Survival* 31: 241-54.

Sachar, Howard M. 1977. *A History of Israel*. Oxford: Basil Blackwell.

Sadat, Anwar el. 1978. *In Search of Identity*. London: Collins.

de St. Jorre, John. 1977. *The Nigerian Civil War*. London: Hodder and Stoughton.

Schelling, Thomas C. 1966. *Arms and Influence*. London: Yale University Press.

_____. 1982. "Internal Decision-Making" in Nissan Oren, ed., *Termination of Wars*. Pp. 9-16. Jerusalem: Magnes Press (The Hebrew University).

Schneider, Barry. 1987. "Terminating Strategic Exchanges: Requirements and Prerequisites" in Stephen J. Cimbala and Keith A. Dunn, eds., *Conflict Termination and Military Strategy: Coercion, Persuasion, and War*. Pp. 109-122. Boulder: Westview.

Schwarzenberger, Georg. 1968. *International Law, vol. II: The Law of Armed Conflict*. London: Stevens & Sons, Ltd.

Seabury, Paul. 1970. "Provisionality and Finality," in William T.R. Fox, ed., *How Wars End: Annals of the American Academy of Political and Social Science*. Pp. 96-104. Philadelphia: Academy of Political and Social Science, Vol. 392.

el-Shazly, General Saad. 1980. *The Crossing of Suez: The October War (1973)*. London: Third World Centre for Research and Publishing.

Shulman, Marshall D. 1974. "The Super-powers." *Survival (Strategic Forum: The Middle East Conflict, 1973)* January-February 1974: 2-3.

Sigal, Leon V. 1988. *Fighting to a Finish: The Politics of War Termination in the United States and Japan, 1945*. London: Cornell University Press.

Singer, J. David, and Melvin Small. 1972. *The Wages of War, 1816-1965*. New York: John Wiley and Sons.

Skjelsbæk, Kjell. 1991. "The UN Secretary-General and the Mediation of International Disputes." *Journal of Peace Research* 28: 99-115.

Smith, David S., ed., and Robert F. Randle (comments). 1974. *From War to Peace: Essays in Peacemaking and War Termination*. New York: Columbia University Press.

Stein, Janice Gross. 1975. "War Termination and Conflict Reduction or, How Wars Should End." *Jerusalem Journal of International Relations* 1: 1-27.

_____. 1982. "The Termination of the October War: A Reappraisal," in Nissan Oren ed., *Termination of Wars*. Pp. 226-245. Jerusalem: Magnes Press (The Hebrew University).

Staudenmaier, William O. 1987. "Conflict Termination in the Nuclear Era," in Stephen J. Cimbala and Keith A. Dunn, eds., *Conflict Termination and Military Strategy: Coercion, Persuasion, and War*. Pp. 15-32. Boulder: Westview.

Stremlau, John J. 1977. *The International Politics of the Nigerian Civil War (1967-70)*. Princeton: Princeton University Press.

Talbott, John. 1980. *The War Without a Name: France in Algeria, 1954-62*. New York: Alfred A. Knopf.

Tedeschi, James T. and Thomas V. Bonoma. 1977. "Measures of Last Resort: Coercion and Aggression in Bargaining," in Daniel Druckman, ed., *Negotiations: Social-Psychological Perspectives*. Pp. 213-241. London: Sage.

Thomas, Roy. 1994. "Sarajevo UNMOs," *Esprits de Corps* 4(1): 9.

Touval, Saadia. 1975. "Biased Intermediaries: Theoretical and Historical Considerations," *Jerusalem Journal of International Relations* 1: 51-69.

_____. 1982a. "Managing the Risks of Accommodation," in Nissan Oren, ed., *Termination of Wars*. Pp. 17-39. Jerusalem: Magnes Press (The Hebrew University).

_____. 1982b. *The Peace Brokers: Mediators in the Arab-Israeli Conflict*. New Jersey: Princeton University Press.

Turley, W.S. 1986. *The Second Indochina War: A Short Political and Military History 1954-1975*. Boulder: Westview.

Urquhart, Brian. 1972. *Hammarskjold*. London: Bodley Head.

Uwechue, Raph. 1970. "Des concessions réciproque pour une paix juste et durable." *Revue Français d'Etudes Politique Africaines* 49: 24-39.

_____. 1971. *Reflections on the Nigerian Civil War*. New York: Africana Publishing Co.

Viorst, Milton. 1987. *Sands of Sorrow: Israel's Journey from Independence*. London: I.B. Tauris & Co.

Wedge, Bryant. 1990. "The Individual, the Group and War," in John Burton, *Conflict: Readings in Management and Resolution*. Pp. 101-116. London: Macmillan.

Wehr, Paul and John Paul Lederach. 1991. "Mediating Conflict in Central America." *Journal of Peace Research* 28: 85-98.

Winham, Gilbert R., ed. 1988. *New Issues in International Crisis Management*. Boulder: Westview.

Wittman, Donald. 1979. "How a War Ends: A Rational Model Approach." *Journal of Conflict Resolution* 23: 743-755.

Woodward, Bob. 1991. *The Commanders*. New York: Simon and Schuster.

Wright, Quincy. 1970. "How Hostilities Have Ended: Peace Treaties and Alternatives," in William T.R. Fox, ed., *How Wars End: Annals of the American Academy of Political and Social Science*. Pp. 51-61. Philadelphia: Academy of Political and Social Science, Vol. 392.

Yarrow, C.H. Mike. 1978. *Quaker Experiences in International Conciliation*. London: Yale University Press.

Young, Oran. 1967. *The Intermediaries: Third Parties in International Crises*. Princeton: Princeton University Press.

Zartman, I. William, and Maureen Berman, Maureen. 1982. *The Practical Negotiator*. London: Yale University Press.

Newspapers and Periodicals (selected)[*]

The Christian Science Monitor (World Edition).
The Daily Telegraph.
Egyptian Gazette.
Egyptian Mail.
Foreign Broadcast Information Service.
Frankfurt Allgemeine Zeitung.
The Financial Times.
The Guardian.

---

[*] **Not all papers were scanned for all periods under study.**

Guardian Weekly.
Hindu International Edition.
The Independent.
The International Herald Tribune.
Japan Times.
Le Monde.
The Los Angeles Times.
Mid-East Economic Digest.
*The New York Herald Tribune (International
  Edition).*
The New York Times.
The Observer.
Pravda.
Strategic Survey 1973 (International Institute of Strategic Studies).
Summary of World Broadcasts (BBC World Service).
The Sunday Times.
Time.
The Times.
The UN Chronicle.

UN Documents (selected**)

United Nations Security Council Resolutions

46 (S/723, 17 April 1948); 48 (S/727, 23 April 1948); 50 (S/801, 29 May 1948); 56 (S/983, 19 August 1948); 338 (S/11036, 22 October 1973); 339 (S/11039, 23 October 1973); 340 (S/11046/Rev.1, 25 October 1973); 479 (28 September 1980); 514 (12 July 1982); 522 (4 October 1982); 540 (31 October 1983); 582 (24 February 1986); 588 (8 October 1986); 598 (20 July 1987); 612 (9 May 1988); 619 (9 August 1988); 660 (2 August 1990); 661 (6 August 1990); 662 (9 August 1990); 664 (18 August 1990); 665 (25 August 1990); 666 (13 Sept. 1990); 667 (16 Sept. 1990); 669 (24 Sept. 1990); 670 (25 Sept. 1990); 674 (29 Oct. 1990); 677 (28 November 1990); 678 (29 November 1990); 686 (2 March 1991); 689 (9 April 1991); 713 (25 September 1991); 721 (27 November 1991); 724 (15 December 1991); 727 (8 January 1992); 740 (7 February 1992); 743 (21 February 1992).

United Nations Security Council Official Record (SCOR)

2nd yr., Special Supplement No. 4; 35th yr., docs. S/14199 (26 Sept. 1980), S/14203 (29 Sept. 1980), S/14210 (6 October 1980); 37th yr, doc. S/15196 (10 June 1982); 37th yr (2nd Su) docs. S/15292 (14 July 1982), S/15448 (2 October 1982); 39th yr, docs. S/16384 (2 March 1984), S/16604 (6 June 1984); 40th yr, docs. S/17084 (4 April 1985), S/17097 (12 April 1985); 41st yr, docs. S/17864 (25 Feb. 1986), S/17932

** All Security Council documents for the period under study were scanned. Listed here are those finally selected for inclusion.

docs. S/16384 (2 March 1984), S/16604 (6 June 1984); 40th yr, docs. S/17084 (4 April 1985), S/17097 (12 April 1985); 41st yr, docs. S/17864 (25 Feb. 1986), S/17932 (21 March 1986), S/17934 (23 March 1986); 42nd yr, doc. S/19031 (11 August 1987), 46th yr., docs. S/22188 (1 February 1991), S/22273 (27 February 1991), S/22274 (27 February 1991), S/22275 (28 February 1991).

United Nations Security Council Provisional Verbatim Record (SCPV)

S/PV.1749, (24 October 1973); S/PV.2977 (14 Feb. 1991); S/PV.2977 (resumption 3) (23 February 1991); S/PV.2977 (resumption 4) (25 February 1991).

Other UN documents

1. "Report of the UN Mediator on Palestine to the Security Council." UN doc. S/888 (12 July 1948).
2. UN Yearbook, vol. 27 (1973). Office of Public Information. United Nations (New York, 1973).
3. de Cuellar, Javier Perez. 1991. *Report of the Secretary-General on the Work of the Organization.* New York: United Nations.
4. "Report of the Secretary General Pursuant to Paragraph 3 of Security Council Resolution 713 (1991)." UN doc. S/23169 (25 October 1991).
5. "Report of the Secretary General Pursuant to Security Council Resolution 721 (1991)." UN doc. S/23280 (11 December 1991).
6. "Further Report of the Secretary-General Pursuant to Security Council Resolution 721 (1991)." UN doc. S/23363 (5 January 1992).
7. "Further Report of the Secretary-General Pursuant to Security Council Resolution 721 (1991)." UN doc. S/23513 (4 February 1992).
8. "Further Report of the Secretary-General Pursuant to Security Council Resolution 721 (1991)." UN doc. S/23592 (15 February 1992).
9. "Report of the Secretary-General Pursuant to Paragraph 4 of Security Council Resolution 752 (1992)." UN doc. S/24049 (30 May 1992).
10. "Report of the Secretary-General Pursuant to Resolution 844 (1993)." UN doc. S/1994/555 (9 May 1994).

Selected Cease-Fire Agreements

1. Text of Brioni Declaration (reprinted in FBIS-EEU-91-130 (8 July 1991), 22-23).
2. "Agreement on Cease-fire," Belgrade, 1 September 1991, in 10 copies (available through United Kingdom Foreign and Commonwealth Office).
3. Statement by Lord Carrington, the Presidents of Croatia and Serbia, and the Minister of National Defence at Igalo, Yugoslavia, on 17 September 1991 (available through United Kingdom Foreign and Commonwealth Office).
4. "Cease-fire memorandum of agreement," 8 October 1991, reprinted in FBIS-EEU-91-196 (9 October 1991).

Other Documents and Official Texts

Nigeria

Lagos: Nigerian Ministry of Information. Gowon, Yakubu. *Official Speeches: Faith in Unity.*

Norway

Norwegian Royal Ministry of Defence Press and Information Department. *Norwegian Defence Facts and Figures 1990.*

Miscellaneous

Editorial (anon.). 1968. "Biafra: Les Contradictions de l'Afrique," *Revue Français d'Etudes Politique Africaines* 1968: 12-14.
US Deputy Secretary of State Warren Christopher, Speech to Boston Newpaper Editors, 8 October 1980.

Interviews and Letters

Interview with Adam Curle, 19 September 1991.
Letter from Andrew Acland to the author, 30 April 1992.
Interviews with officers and enlisted men of Canadian Peacekeeping Forces in Croatia, 1 Princess Patricia's Canadian Light Infantry, 20-24 September 1994, including a draft report, by Major D.J. Banks, "Operational Lessons Learned: 1 PPCLI in Operation Harmony, Roto 4, April to October 1994."

Index

About the Book and Author

The road from war to peace is a puzzling and uncertain one. To those who fight and die on it, it is seldom clear where the journey will end—and those responsible for finding the path are rarely more perceptive. Of the few signposts that exist, perhaps the most visible is the cease-fire. No war ends without one. *Stopping Wars* is the first attempt to catalog the reasons why some wars are so difficult to stop—even when both sides want the fighting to end.

James Smith examines the problems encountered by protagonists as well as third parties attempting to achieve a cease-fire. Each chapter is devoted to a specific obstacle that Smith analyzes and then illustrates via in-depth case studies, drawing on such conflicts as the Iran/Iraq War, the Gulf War, and the Yugoslav wars. Smith assesses the role of third parties in trying to persuade or force people to stop fighting and examines what happens when obstacles to a cease-fire cannot be overcome.

James D.D. Smith received his Ph.D. in war studies from the University of London, where he was a Commonwealth Scholar. He has published with the *Journal for Peace Research* and the Centre for Defense Studies (London), and he currently lectures in the Department of Peace Studies at the University of Bradford.